SO MUCH THINGS TO SAY

ALSO BY ROGER STEFFENS

AS AUTHOR

The World of Reggae featuring Bob Marley:
Treasures from Roger Steffens' Reggae Archives

The Family Acid

The Family Acid Jamaica

AS COAUTHOR

Bob Marley: Spirit Dancer

One Love: Life with Bob Marley and the Wailers

Bob Marley and the Wailers: The Definitive Discography

Roger Steffens and Peter Simon's Reggae Scrapbook

Bob Marley and the Golden Age of Reggae:
The Photographs of Kim Gottlieb-Walker

AS CONTRIBUTING WRITER AND/OR PHOTOGRAPHER

Reggae International

Rebel Music: Bob Marley & Roots Reggae (UK)

Every Little Thing Gonna Be Alright: The Bob Marley Reader

Chanting Down Babylon

The New Grove Dictionary of Music and Musicians

All Music Guide: Reggae

A Magia Do Reggae (Brazil)

We Gotta Get Out of This Place: The Soundtrack of the Vietnam War

The Rolling Stone Illustrated History of Rock & Roll

Rolling Stone: The '70s

Jimi Hendrix: The Ultimate Experience

Hollywood Shack Job

Smokestack El Ropo's Bedside Reader

Reggae Vinyls (France)

Turn Up the Radio! Rock, Pop, and Roll in L.A. 1956–1972

This Is Rebel Music

Rastafarian Children of Solomon

Bob Marley Songs of Freedom

The Greatest Album Covers That Never Were

Remembering Peter Tosh (Jamaica)

Bob Marley (Taschen Music Icons)

Global Reggae (Jamaica)

Sur la Route Avec Bob Marley (France)

Bob Marley: Le Reggae et Les Rastas (France)

Couleur Reggae (France)

Lonely Planet: Jamaica

Itations of Jamaica and I Rastafari: The Third Itation

Stay Up! Los Angeles Street Art

Bob Marley de Voetballer (Netherlands)

It Was 50 Years Ago Today: The Beatles Invade America and Hollywood

1967: A Complete Rock Music History of the Summer of Love

POETRY ANTHOLOGIES (AS EDITOR)

Podium

My Favorite Poets

Light Benders

Life as a Werewolf Is Never Easy

SO MUCH THINGS TO SAY

THE ORAL HISTORY OF BOB MARLEY

TEXT AND PHOTOGRAPHS BY

ROGER STEFFENS

INTRODUCTION BY LINTON KWESI JOHNSON

W. W. NORTON & COMPANY

Independent Publishers Since 1923

New York • London

For information about permission to reproduce selections from this book,
write to Permissions, W. W. Norton & Company, Inc.,
500 Fifth Avenue, New York, NY 10110

For information about special discounts for bulk purchases, please contact
W. W. Norton Special Sales at specialsales@wwnorton.com or 800-233-4830

Manufacturing by Quad Graphics, Fairfield, VA
Book design by Chris Welch
Production manager: Anna Oler

ISBN 978-0-393-05845-1

W. W. Norton & Company, Inc.
500 Fifth Avenue, New York, N.Y. 10110
www.wwnorton.com

W. W. Norton & Company Ltd.
15 Carlisle Street, London W1D 3BS

1 2 3 4 5 6 7 8 9 0

LIVICATION

To the ineffable CC Smith, cofounder of The Beat *magazine, devoted friend and partner, without whose efforts on my behalf this book would never have existed.*

And to my beloved wife, Mary, and our children Kate, and Devon, whose constant support and tolerant overstanding are a gift from Jah.

There are no facts in Jamaica, only versions.

—*Old folk saying*

CONTENTS

INTRODUCTION: THE PEOPLE SPEAK
            BY LINTON KWESI JOHNSON   xiii

PREFACE   xix

CHAPTER 1.   **Where Is My Mother?**   1

CHAPTER 2.   **Trench Town Rocks**   8

CHAPTER 3.   **The Wailers at Studio One**   22

CHAPTER 4.   **Good Good Rudies**   40

CHAPTER 5.   **Love and Affection**   59

CHAPTER 6.   **Rasta Shook Them Up**   71

CHAPTER 7.   **Wailers A Go Wail**   80

CHAPTER 8.   **Nine Mile Exile**   87

CHAPTER 9.   **The JAD Years**   94

CHAPTER 10.   **Leslie Kong Meets the Tuff Gang**   107

CHAPTER 11.   **Lee Perry and Jamaican Politricks**   117

CHAPTER 12.   **Cold Cold Winters in Sweden and London**   133

CHAPTER 13.   **Island's Kinky Reggae**   149

CHAPTER 14.   **Burnin' Out in London**   158

CHAPTER 15.   **The End of the Beginning**   169

CHAPTER 16.   Natty Dread   179

CHAPTER 17.   Hope Road Runnings   189

CHAPTER 18.   Cindy Breakspeare and the 1975 Tour   198

CHAPTER 19.   Rastaman Vibration and the Fatal Reissue   207

CHAPTER 20.   Ambush in the Night   216

CHAPTER 21.   The CIA and the Assassination Attempt   227

CHAPTER 22.   Smile, You're in Jamaica   235

CHAPTER 23.   Who Shot Bob Marley?   255

CHAPTER 24.   Exodus to London   264

CHAPTER 25.   Blackwell, Bob and Business   274

CHAPTER 26.   The Bloody Toe in the Paris Match   282

CHAPTER 27.   The One Love Peace Concert   288

CHAPTER 28.   Babylon by Bus from the U.N. to Ethiopia   305

CHAPTER 29.   Charity and Survival   315

CHAPTER 30.   From the Apollo to Gabon   330

CHAPTER 31.   Natty Mash It inna Zimbabwe   346

CHAPTER 32.   Uprising   363

CHAPTER 33.   Madison Square Garden Then Everything Crash   370

CHAPTER 34.   Dr. Issels and the Final Days   386

CHAPTER 35.   Marley's Legacy and the Wailers' Favorite Songs   399

EPILOGUE   407

ACKNOWLEDGMENTS   409

LIST OF INTERVIEWEES   415

INDEX   417

The People Speak

Linton Kwesi Johnson

In an essay I wrote on the lyrics of Bob Marley's *Exodus*, voted album of the twentieth century by *Time* magazine, I said of his lyrical genius that it was based on his "ability to translate the personal into the political, the private into the public, the particular into the universal."* Genius, it can be argued, is not merely an exceptional personal attribute; it is historical in the sense that it becomes manifest when there is a conjunction of the biographical and the historical. The second half of the 1970s, the period when Bob Marley began to reap the rewards of his long apprenticeship as a musician, was a time of turbulence not only in Jamaica but around the globe. The Cold War was at its most intense; proxy wars were being waged between East and West in developing-world countries; anticolonial wars were still being fought in Africa; there were anti-imperialist struggles taking place in South America. Jamaica was on the brink of all-out civil war as the opposition, aided and abetted by the CIA, sought to wrest power from Michael Manley's democratic socialist government. Bob Marley almost lost his life during that conflict. His music is resonant of that period; it reflects the zeitgeist. At the apotheosis of his career he had become a kind of Che Guevara of popular culture.

I have the dubious distinction of having written a critique of Mar-

---

* Richard Williams, ed., *The Poetry of Exile* (London: Weidenfeld and Nicolson, 2007).

Linton Kwesi Johnson at Herne Hill, London, May 27, 2003.

ley's rise to fame at a pivotal time in his career. As a fan of the Wailers triumvirate of Bob Marley, Peter Tosh and Bunny Wailer, I was deeply disappointed when they went their separate ways. Then, on top of that, Marley was being hailed in the rock music press as the new "king of rock" following the release of his first solo album, *Natty Dread*. As far as I was concerned that was a travesty—and I was not alone in harboring such sentiments. Bob Marley was, after all, a top-ranking Jamaican reggae artist who belonged to the world of black music and was being appropriated by the white rock world. In the article I wrote, titled "Roots and Rock: The Marley Enigma," published in *Race Today* in October 1975, I not only criticized the way Marley was being marketed, I laid the blame at the doorstep of Chris Blackwell, founder of Island Records.* Back then I was a twenty-three-year-old sociology undergraduate and I had just published my second book of poems, *Dread Beat an Blood*. Three years later I was signed to Island Records by Blackwell and, a year after that, by Marley to Tuff Gong. With the benefit of hindsight I can say that my analysis of the marketing strategy was more or less correct, even though the sentiments were misplaced.

When it became clear that Bob Marley would not recover from the cancer he was battling, the newly elected Jamaican government, led by Edward Seaga, awarded him the Order of Merit, the nation's highest civilian award. It was in recognition not only of Marley's enormous popularity in Jamaica but also of the kudos he had brought to the nation by his achievements abroad. No other Jamaican has done more to boost the brand name Jamaica. As reggae music's greatest ambassador, Marley made an enormous contribution to its globalization and its impact on popular culture around the world. Since his demise he has grown in stature from superstar to legend to iconic status, a remarkable achievement for someone from such a humble background. The astute and at times obscene marketing of Marley as a brand cannot detract from the fact that no other recording artist in the late twentieth century, in any genre, has had the global reach and influence that Marley has, continuing into this millennium.

The Rastafarian soul rebel, armed with his distinctive voice, a guitar, a great backing band and fine backing vocals, was a man on a mission to challenge the "isms and schisms" of principalities and powers as he fought against "spiritual wickedness in high and low places." His legacy of catchy danceable songs of defiance, resistance, rebellion, love

---

* Republished in Theo Cateforis, ed., *The Rock History Reader 2007* (New York and Abingdon: Routledge, 2012).

and hope continues to reverberate around the world; his lyrical and melodic genius guarantees the contemporaneity of his music. What kind of man and musician was Nesta Robert Marley? Many books have been written about him, including a Marley reader for the academy. He has appeared in fiction too. What makes Roger Steffens's *So Much Things to Say: The Oral History of Bob Marley* unique is that the author does not present a portrait of the artist through his own lens but instead presents us with a collage of impressions seen through the eyes of others. For many years Steffens has traveled the world telling Marley's story with his illustrated "Life of Bob Marley" lecture. Here he allows those who knew Marley to give their versions. Roger Steffens, writer, broadcaster and photographer, a respected scholar of reggae and renowned archivist specializing in Bob Marley recordings and ephemera, has put together seventy-five interviews with people close to Marley who speak candidly about what they witnessed of the singer's life and times. The respondents range from people who knew Marley intimately to those who crossed paths with him, including family, friends, musicians, record company personnel, journalists, photographers and filmmakers. The evidential nature of this book, with at times conflicting narratives, guarantees a riveting read. Some of the testimonies confirm what was already known, some offer different versions, some contest myths about Marley; others say more about the witness than the man.

There are some startling revelations and contentious claims. We hear from Clement "Coxson" Dodd about the young Marley's time at Studio One; the reputedly mafia-connected Danny Sims on his dealings with Marley and Johnny Nash; Bunny Wailer on his friend's composition technique; Beverley Kelso, an original Wailer, on the relationship between Rita Marley and Bob; Joe Higgs on his schooling of the original Wailers and Marley's character; Dermot Hussey, Jamaican broadcaster and musicologist, on the interview about the breakup of the Wailers that Marley wanted destroyed. There are interviews with all of the original

Wailers. Other voices include Cedella Booker, Marley's mother; Cindy Breakspeare, former beauty queen and mother of Damian "Junior Gong" Marley; Allan "Skill" Cole, Marley's close friend; Third World's Cat Coore; and Rastafarian guru Mortimo Planno.

Steffens sometimes makes editorial interventions, introducing a speaker or providing context for what is being said. He rarely opines, allowing his witnesses to tell their stories in their own words, structured chronologically from Marley's childhood to his demise. The overall impression we get of Marley is that of a man of some complexity: taciturn and jovial by turns, worldly and spiritual, a sleeping lion capable of violent rage, a peacemaker, a ladies' man and a man of prodigious generosity. The most striking observation that emerges from several witnesses is how serious Marley was about his art: his single-mindedness and his consummate professionalism. Marley's story is a poignant one of humble origins, privation, struggle, survival, trials and tribulations, triumph and tragedy.

PREFACE

There are, it is reported, over five hundred books written in many languages and published all over the world about the Reggae King. So, why this book, and why now? What is left to say?

To provide the proper answer, allow me to explain how this music lover became so deeply involved in researching Bob Marley's unprecedented life and impact on the world. I have been a fan of the Wailers' works since discovering them through a revelatory 1973 *Rolling Stone* article by Michael Thomas, who said that reggae music crawls through your bloodstream like some vampire amoeba from the psychic rapids of Upper Niger consciousness. That unforgettable sentence sent me rushing out the door of my Berkeley apartment to find *Catch A Fire*, the Wailers' first international album on Island Records. The following evening I saw *The Harder They Come*, Jamaican director Perry Henzell's exuberant film, which brought the imagery of reggae and Rastafari to the outside world. My life has never been the same since.

As a fan, I sought out others who had caught what Peter Tosh called "reggae mylitis." Among the first teacher-mentors I discovered was a man from Kingston named Ruel Mills who had a small record shop on Fillmore Street in San Francisco called Trench Town Records. There he introduced me to the likes of Count Ossie and the Mystic Revelation of Rastafari, Ras Michael and the Sons of Negus, Alton Ellis, the Techniques, Slim Smith and a host of obscure singers and musicians whose ethereal works moved my heart and elevated my consciousness.

In 1976, after moving to Los Angeles, my wife Mary and I traveled to Jamaica hoping to find records I had only read about, mainly in British magazines such as *Black Music* and in occasional Jamaican publications such as *Swing* magazine. We arrived the week that prime minister Michael Manley declared a national state of emergency, throwing the opposition into prison with no charges and placing tanks on all the island's crossroads. I felt like I was back in Saigon during the Tet Offensive. We spent most of our time in the bucolic area around Lucea on the northwest coast of the island, but we just had to go to Kingston to check out the Wailers' record shop as well as Randy's and Joe Gibbs's emporiums on the main square of Parade. Our first stop was on a deserted back street where Marley had a tiny shack. There, within two minutes on the ground, one of the biggest reggae stars at the time tried to pick my pocket. A half hour later we found ourselves in Jimmy Cliff's house, with some of the most important musicians of the era revealing the best and worst of life in Yard, as the locals referred to their island home.

Two years later I met Hank Holmes, an avid collector of omnivorous tastes, who had amassed over eight thousand ska, rocksteady and reggae records without leaving Los Angeles. We became instant friends. I thought with his vast collection and knowledge we could do a great radio show together, as there was no reggae on the air in L.A. at the time. We fought for a year, unsuccessfully, to find a station willing to let us reveal the great wealth of music being created just south of the U.S. Finally, we found a spot on a tiny NPR station in Santa Monica, an L.A. beach city, called KCRW. It had only 110 watts at the time, but there were great plans afoot for it to grow. The station itself was in a tiny converted classroom in a junior high school, across the street from the license holder, Santa Monica College. KCRW was always desperate for monetary support. During the first fundraising drive while we were there, they gave us an extra hour to beg for money—three hours on a Sunday afternoon. That day we made history, amassing in those few hours what the station's previous fundraising drive had made in ten days. Immediately our airtime was doubled to four hours a week, and our *Reggae Beat* show became, according to the *L.A. Weekly*, "the most popular non-commercial radio show in the city." Hank decided not to do any of the fascinating storytelling he did in private, preferring to "let the music speak for itself." So it fell on me to do the interviews and study up on things I could add to make our broadcasts stronger. Hank had such a stupendously deep collection that there was hardly an artist who came through our gates who didn't discover records of their music that they had never seen before—primarily Peter Tosh, who became one of our biggest early supporters.

The program was the first in a series of events, each building on the one before, that caused me to interact with virtually all of the major players in the Wailers' careers. Our first musical guest was Bob Marley. We had been on the air for only six weeks when Island Records called and asked if we'd "mind going on the road for a couple of weeks" on his *Survival* tour. It was one of the most important events in my life, as we shared a wide variety of experiences, both public and private, with Marley and his band. We told Bob about our show and he urged us to remember that reggae music was for "head-ucation, not just jol-lification." Ironically, the happiest person on the road with us was the bus driver. He got to sweep up all the roaches at the end of each evening and some nights, he told us, he'd go home with several ounces of discarded herb.

During this period, Bob asked me to arrange for showings of the two most important films of his life at that point: Jeff Walker's documentary and film of the Smile Jamaica concert and the assassination attempt on Bob's life that preceded it, and the One Love Peace Concert film, *Heartland Reggae*. He had seen neither of them before. During both screenings, it was instructive to watch Bob watching Bob, and some of his reactions, described in this book, are sure to be provocative. His final show in L.A. was a benefit concert at the Roxy, and Hank

and I were among the very few allowed into the show's sound check
that afternoon. Bob spent close to an hour singing something over and
over again that we'd never heard before, about redemption. It would
be the last time we would see him before he passed a year and a half
later from melanoma.

Peter Tosh came through a few months later, saying grudgingly that
at least Bob's death would make room for other artists to be noticed—a
belligerent stance that cost him the support of many of his fans. But
he had a very warm and humorous side to him too, and over the next
seven years we grew close and I interviewed him several times for
Reggae Beat and also for a cable TV show that producer-director Chili
Charles had started called *L.A. Reggae.* I would get several calls a year
from Peter in various far-flung locations, asking for copies of this or
that record. He didn't have any of his own history, he explained sadly; it
had all been stolen or begged off. Just before his murder in September
1987, he called asking for a copy of "Here Comes the Judge," to remake
for a sequel to his then-new album, *No Nuclear War.*

Bunny Wailer came into my life later. A recluse since his departure
from the group in 1973, I first met him at the Sunsplash Festival in
Montego Bay in 1985, and gave him eleven ninety-minute tapes of old
Wailers singles. The following year he called me and asked me to be
the publicist for what would be his first foreign show after thirteen on-
island years of exile from overseas stages. That show was held in L.A.,
and he came on the *Reggae Beat* the next day for a four-hour special.
In 1990 Bunny again called, asking this time if I would be willing to
cowrite his autobiography. I readily accepted, and requested that I bring
along my dear friend Leroy Jodie Pierson, a brilliant blues guitarist
and historian and founder of the Nighthawk record label, which had
already released some of Bunny's music. He agreed, and Leroy and I
went on to spend three weeks locked in a hotel room in Kingston in
October 1990, compiling sixty-four hours of interviews about the entire
history of his relationship with Bob and Peter. Sadly, Bunny has never

allowed that book to be published; ten years of work, and 1,800 pages of transcripts of the history that every Wailers fan is yearning to read, remains in limbo. (Nonetheless, Leroy and I combined over thirty years of research to complete our 2005 book, *Bob Marley and the Wailers: The Definitive Discography*, to date the only true discography ever compiled for any Jamaican artist.)

In 1984, NARAS, the National Academy of Recording Arts and Sciences, asked me to organize and chair a reggae Grammy committee, which I did for the next twenty-seven years. That same year, I was invited to do a presentation of unreleased Marley films and videos as part of the National Video Festival at the American Film Institute. This drew positive reviews in local press and led to invitations from colleges—and then clubs—to do it again. My multimedia program, "The Life of Bob Marley," has been presented over 500 times all over the world since then, from the Outback of Australia to the bottom of the Grand Canyon, bringing the words and works of reggae's prophet to the far reaches of the globe. This has led to hundreds of encounters with those who interacted with Bob personally, each of whose stories I taped or filmed for posterity. Many of these appeared in *The Beat* magazine, which was cofounded by me and CC Smith in 1981 and lasted for twenty-eight years. Each May I edited a Bob Marley Collectors Edition, which included writing by some of reggae's finest observers, all working for free for the love of the music.

The Wailers Band and I have remained good friends for almost four decades now. In 2013, the Family Man Barrett–led Wailers invited me to go on the road with them for two months as their opening act as they played the entire *Survival* album live. I slept on the floor of their bus throughout January and February, working in some of the coldest cities in North America, showing pictures I took on the original tour and telling of the crucial importance of the album and explaining its lyrics. It left me with a lasting and enormous respect for the road life that these intrepid warriors have committed themselves to, at great personal cost, carrying Bob's timeless creations to a hungry younger generation.

Back in 2002, I approached Norton's Jim Mairs with an idea for an oral history of Bob Marley. My original conception was for the complete transcripts of some eighty crucial interviews to be published in full, so that readers would know each person's whole story in their own words and see the context in which each question was answered. I wanted to present the raw material of history for writers in the future to have full access to.

I had nearly completed the book by 2005 when disaster struck. Having been born in 1942, I'm definitely part of the techno-igno generation, and when my computer suffered an unfixable crash, I lost everything: the manuscript, the interview transcripts and all my notes. I went into a two-year funk and couldn't face starting from scratch again. When Jim came looking for the book in 2007, I had to confess what had happened. I am eternally grateful for his patience and understanding, and he urged me to get started again. A few years later I sent him about 80 percent of the book. He wrote back that the folks at Norton had decided it would be far more readable if I broke up the voices into topics, in the manner of the superb biography *Bill Graham Presents* by Robert Greenfield. With a heavy heart, realizing how much more work still lay before me, I agreed. Now I see that Jim's decision was the right one in so many ways, and I am grateful for him standing by me with infinite patience and belief in the project. In 2015, Jim passed the project over to Norton's meticulous senior editor Tom Mayer, himself a former reggae broadcaster in California and at Columbia.

So, to answer the questions posed at the beginning, I have compiled this book with the knowledge that there are several superb books that deal with various portions of Bob's life, and I do not feel the urge to repeat previous works. Cedella Booker tells *A Mother's Story* about his childhood. Her ghostwriter, Tony Winkler, who told me once that he never listens to reggae and only likes classical music, helmed a tome that is curiously devoid of music but does give valuable information about Bob's youth. For his years in Delaware, Christopher John Farley's *Before the Legend* fills in many blanks of that pre-Island period. One of my very favorite books ever is John Masouri's brilliant *Wailing Blues: The Story of Bob Marley's Wailers*, which is basically the autobiography of Family Man Barrett and his drummer brother, Carlton, the very heart of the Wailers sound since 1970. Every song done by Bob since then is deconstructed in this invaluable book. My friend Stephen Davis was one of the first out of the gate with *Bob Marley*, which gives a fine overview of Bob's life and remains justifiably in print after more than thirty years. Photographer Kate Simon covers the mid-seventies years in her massive *Rebel Music,* which is filled with extraordinary intimate photographs and reminiscences by several of those with whom she toured. Likewise, Chris Salewicz's instructive fiftieth-birthday coffee-table book, *Songs of Freedom,* gives much detail on Bob's childhood and European touring. Vivien Goldman's exhaustive eyewitness account of the making of Marley's "album of the century," *The Book of Exodus,* is a major work of scholarship.

With all of these already on the shelves, what's left to add? With *So Much Things to Say,* named after one of Bob's most evocative compositions, I have set out to illuminate with first-person depth the parts of his life that have been only partially explored. My main topics include his pre-recording years in Kingston; the backstage reality of Coxson Dodd's Studio One; his exile from Kingston in 1966 and 1967; the Danny Sims–Johnny Nash maneuverings of the late sixties and early seventies; the perilous history of the group's relationship with Lee Perry and the disquieting reasons for their split; the breakup of the group in 1973; the assassination attempt in 1976; an inquiry into whether the CIA was complicit in the attempt on his life; the controversial events leading to the One Love Peace Concert; his trips to Africa, including shocking behind-the-scenes stories of Gabon and Zimbabwe; and the history of his fatal cancer and its treatment.

Over the past thirty-seven years, scores of his friends, associates and family members have shared with me intimate details of their interactions with the Reggae King. Now you can read their revelations too. There are many contradictory accounts, among them the controversy surrounding the recording of the Wailers' first record, "Simmer Down," and the circumstances surrounding the wedding of Bob Marley and Rita Anderson. Let history decide. This is its raw material.

There are some important omissions in this book, which can't be helped. My biggest regret is never having had the chance to speak to Johnny Nash, whose influence on the Wailers from 1968 to 1972 is crucial to understanding the artist that Bob became. Bunny Wailer makes some astounding charges in these pages, and I tried over the decades to get Mr. Nash to respond. His people replied as this book was about to go to press: "Over the many years that there have been numerous accounts of that time frame, John's posture has and continues to be that of not dignifying them with any sort of response; it would not serve a meaningful purpose other than giving a false platform to get attention. Those events are a part of history, they cannot be relived and those who were a part of creating the historical events of that era know the truth. Debating on any level, for John, would be counter-productive to serve a purpose for whoever's views are not on point. With all that being said, John sends his appreciation for your concerns of misgivings and wanting to give him a voice, but it's really not his style, he prefers to remain silent and let the records speak for themselves." Regardless, Johnny Nash has my utmost respect and admiration for his incredibly important work in exposing reggae to the masses and making vital contributions that molded Bob and the Wailers into finest quality international entertainers.

There has never been an artist like Bob Marley, "the artist of the century." His works are more popular than ever, with *Forbes* magazine listing him at number five among the highest-earning dead celebrities for 2014. Bob was psychic, and he declared that his work would last forever. It was just one of his many prophecies, some of which have yet to manifest. His abilities were recognized in 1976 by the Jamaican poet and author Geoffrey Philp, who wrote about meeting Bob for the first time at the Mona Heights Community Center in Kingston and reconfirmed them to me at a Marley seminar in Florida in 2015: "When I got there Bob was sitting under an acacia tree. I walked up to him, introduced myself and he told me to sit down. This was the first time I had experienced Bob's so-called psychic ability because he began to tell me things about my life that no one else—not even my mother—knew about me. I still don't remember the details because I was in a state of shock. I just couldn't believe that anyone upon meeting me within the space of five minutes could have told me so much about my life."

Here, now, his closest friends and associates tell you about the life of the Bob they encountered. As one of the early readers of this manuscript observed, "After reading this I feel like I really know the man." My hope is that you will too.

—Echo Park, L.A.,
July 2016

SO MUCH THINGS TO SAY

CHAPTER 1

Where Is My Mother?

ROGER STEFFENS: Cedella Malcolm Marley Booker, Bob Marley's mother, was eighteen at the time of his birth. Her white husband, born in Clarendon, Jamaica, was named Norval Marley. He was around sixty-four when Nesta Robert Marley was born on February 6, 1945, in a tiny rural village called Nine Mile, which had no electricity or running water. Christopher Marley, a member of the white Marley family, has spent years tracing Bob's bloodline and has been sharing his research with me as new discoveries come to light, debunking many of the false claims that continue to this day, including the idea that Norval was born in England and was an army officer.

CHRISTOPHER MARLEY: Bob's father was Norval Sinclair Marley, born to a British father and a "colored" mother. Norval was not a "sea captain," nor was he a "quartermaster" or "captain" or "officer in the British Army." He was a "ferro-cement engineer." His British Army discharge papers show that he worked in various "labour corps" in the UK during the First World War and was discharged as a private. He did not see active service on the battlefield. Norval Marley's family was not Syrian, as has been suggested. He was a restless, wandering man. He traveled and worked all over the world at a time when travel was not the simple thing it is today—to Cuba, the UK, Nigeria and South Africa.

He was supervising the subdivision of some rural land in Saint Ann Parish for war veteran housing when he married eighteen-year-old Cedella Malcolm, whom he had got pregnant. He provided little financial support and seldom saw her and their son. He died of a heart attack in 1955, stone broke and living off an eight-shilling-a-week army pension (about US$1.20).

Norval was seriously unstable, to put it mildly. The rejection of Bob by the Marley family was a rejection of Norval.

CEDELLA BOOKER: Norval was living in Nine Mile at the time, watching the lands that the government gave people—certain amount of land to work on during the war. He was like an overseer.

ROGER STEFFENS: If there was any true direction in Bob's earliest years, it would come from his grandfather Omariah, who was known locally as a myalman—a benevolent practitioner of healing arts—as opposed to an obeahman, whose darker intentions cast fear into the hearts of superstitious country folk. Omariah was reported to have fathered as many as thirty children.

CEDELLA BOOKER: My father Omariah was a very spiritual person, he's like the Blackheart Man [a practitioner of traditional healing methods]. He's a man like, when people sick he can help them and give them medicine and things like that. He had his own medicine that him fix and mix, and just cure people. Omariah taught Bob not to steal, to tell the truth, to obey. He owned enough land, here there and everywhere. Not no big great properties, but good parcels, like thirty acres, twenty acres, ten acres, five acres all over the place. Bob moved donkeys, goats, carry food from up in the field to the home. Then him ride the donkey and pick up corn, cut corn bush to go feed the other animals. Them have to do manual work. We have to go to spring to get water.

ROGER STEFFENS: Bob's cousin Sledger, who was raised alongside him in Nine Mile, recalls that Bob was a fearless rider of his favorite donkey, Nimble, and could jump bareback over a five-foot wall with ease, sometimes even doing it backward! He and Sledger loved music and would listen especially on Sundays, when Omariah would plug his radio into a generator and play it for the locals, tuning in to a Miami station. Elvis Presley, Fats Domino and Ricky Nelson were early favor-

Bob Marley's mother, Cedella Booker, atop Mount Wilson above
Los Angeles on Mother's Day, May 1988.

ites of the boys. Bob's nascent musical instruction came directly from Cedella's dad.

CEDELLA BOOKER: My father played organ, guitar, a little violin. Everyone in the family played music. My cousin Marcenine, he make a little banjo guitar and they put the string on it. That would be Bob's first instrument. And when he got bigger he would start holding guitar. Sometimes he hum along with me on songs like "Precious Lord Take My Hand."

ROGER STEFFENS: At the age of three, Bob began to evince intuitive powers of surprising accuracy.

CEDELLA BOOKER: I remember when a woman we called Aunt Zen used to love to play with Bob as a little boy. So she came to the shop where I worked and he start to read her hand and tell her some things. And she said, "Everything that the child tell me is right."

Another man, Solomon Black, a district constable, he came to the shop and stopped by and as a little boy, Bob take his hand and start to look at it, start to tell him some things. And whatever he told him, the man say, "You might be taking it for a joke, but everything the child tell me is right."

Bob knew he wasn't going to be here for long, so he have to do what he have to do. I have this friend, Ibis Pitts. He was Bob's first friend that he made in Delaware in 1966. Ibis said that one day he and his friend Dion Wilson went over to the park where I used to live and Bob climbed into a tree and that Bob said, "When I am thirty-six I am going to die." This was in 1969.

ROGER STEFFENS: Cedella Booker, affectionately known as Mother B, has visited my Reggae Archives several times over the years. Many of our conversations went unrecorded, although I made notes of each one afterward. In one she recalled Norval showing up at Nine Mile when Bob was five, asking that she allow Bob to come with him to Kingston so he could educate him and give him a shot at a better life. Cedella agreed, but when Norval and Bob arrived in Kingston—one of the only times they were together—instead of taking him home and enrolling him in school, Norval sent him to live with an elderly woman friend of his named Miss Gray. During the next couple of years Bob was essentially an abandoned child on the streets of Kingston. Cedella would write Norval and ask when she could visit, but he discouraged her every attempt and told her the boy was in a boarding school in St. Thomas. Eventually someone from Nine Mile recognized Bob on a Kingston street and told Cedella where he was and she came and got him.

CEDELLA BOOKER: Bob was about five when he went to Kingston, not quite two years when he came back, and Mrs. Simpson asked him to read her hand and he said, "No I'm not reading no more hand, I'm singing now."

ROGER STEFFENS: Neville O'Reilly Livingston, later to be known as Bunny Wailer, cofounded the Wailers. He first met Bob when they were both youngsters.

BUNNY WAILER: I was about nine [in 1957] when my father took me up to live in Nine Mile, where I first met Bob. We moved, migrated. My father bought some land there, about twenty-five acres, built a house, built a shop. We stayed there about nine, ten months. I didn't live there too long though. The place was too cold. Very cold area. I wasn't prepared for that kind of cold. I used to get cramps in my stomach, so they had to ship me back to the city. And then, a short time after that, Bob came to the city to live with his mother.

ROGER STEFFENS: As a youngster, Bob would explore the area around Nine Mile, and sometimes went places he was forbidden to go. During one of these excursions he cut open his right foot after stepping on a broken glass bottle. He was afraid to show the wound to his mother for fear of being punished. But it became infected and he was in great pain for months. Eventually his cousin Nathan made a plaster of warm orange pulp and a yellow powder called iodoform, and within a couple of weeks the wound completely healed. This was the first of numerous wounds to the foot in which his fatal cancer would eventually take hold.

Bunny Wailer in Aspen, Colorado, September 1994.

BUNNY WAILER: Bob was a wild child. He was like the ugly duckling. He had to find his own little brush to pick, and his own little cornmeal. Nobody wanted him around their corn, so he get what's left. He just had to survive. His most serious endeavor was just to eat and drink. There were many nights of cold ground for his bed and rock stone for his pillow. Countless nights. Bob was not a child who get anything that he sought. He didn't get what any other child got.

ROGER STEFFENS: Bob's earliest years were filled with neglect and rejection by both races. Whites thought of him as a black child; blacks, critical of mixed-race children, taunted him as "the little yellow boy." Even his revered great-grandmother, known as Ya Ya, referred to him as "the German boy." Racism was rampant in those days, and the light-skinned leaders of the country were deeply influenced by four hundred years of British colonial rule. For Bob, his color seemed to be an impediment wherever he turned, causing him to turn inward, a solitary soul relying on his own inner strengths. Even more significantly, the rejection by his father weighed heavily on him throughout his life.

His early sojourn in the city of Kingston, where he went weeks without a proper meal, steeled him for his return there when his mother left Nine Mile to join Bunny's father in 1957. Kingston would force the young Marley outward into a world of crowded slums and stimulating companions, in a nation on the brink of overthrowing the yoke of imperialism.

CHAPTER 2

Trench Town Rocks

ROGER STEFFENS: Once established in Kingston, Bob's mother entered into an on-again, off-again relationship with Bunny's father, Thaddeus "Toddy" Livingston. Their affair produced a daughter named Pearl, sister to Bunny and Bob, born in 1964.

The music swirling in Bob's head was developed with the help of neighbors in Trench Town, a crowded enclave near the edge of the port area, where so-called government yards ["yard" is a common Jamaica term for a house] had been erected to give poor people housing and running water.

One of the first friends Bob made as a young teenager was a prize-winning singer named Segree Wesley. He and I met in the studios of WBAI in New York City in May 2003, where we spoke for several riveting hours about the early days of Bob's training, and his own short career.

SEGREE WESLEY: I was raised in Trench Town in the government yards. They had what were called L-shaped houses, which were one single room. But on every street there was six double-decker houses, what you called upstairs houses, more than one floor. So my parents and the whole family, we lived in one of those on 16 Row First Street, Trench Town.

Bob Marley entered in my awareness in the early sixties, and when he came I know for a fact he was at Third Street, same street as Joe Higgs and the rest. That's where I met him on Pipe's [Winston "Pipe"

Marley's childhood friend Segree Wesley in New York City, May 2003.

Matthews of the Wailing Souls] side. I heard the guys crooning in the back 'cause in Trench Town everywhere you go there's always a little group. Groups that made it and groups that didn't make it. But I went over and I heard him singing. But they all knew me and knew who I was. And then after he was living on Second Street, which was behind the yard I was living on First.

And then I know when he was living with Bunny Wailer and Bunny's father Toddy. And we were friends—and he would say, Segree, come let's go rehearse. So we'd go and rehearse in the kitchen. But even then my mom used to say, "Segree, I don't want you hanging with those boys," because of course they weren't working people. They weren't even going to school.

ROGER STEFFENS: Trench Town was known as a ghetto and it was difficult for people from there to find jobs once potential employers discovered their address. Among the only ways that law-abiding people were able to escape were through sports or music, and the area was known as an incubator of great talents in both fields. One of the most important was Joe Higgs, among the earliest of Jamaica's recording artists, who became Bob Marley's most significant mentor. Higgs not only coached Bob; he was a musical teacher and guide to a host of other Jamaican artists, including superstars from the earliest days of ska and rocksteady, the predecessors of reggae. Today he is widely regarded as "the father of reggae." For almost twenty years, before his passing in 1999, he lived in Los Angeles. I worked with him throughout the late nineties on his never-completed autobiography, from which his quotes in this book are taken.

JOE HIGGS: I first encountered Bob Marley when he was on Second Street and I was on Third Street. Bob was known as a very light-skinned chap living in the ghetto. People called him the little red boy, and he would be beaten up by a lot of guys. This is when Bob and Bunny were living in Toddy's house with Cedella.

A guy by the name of Errol Williams, whose father was a man who had a scrap iron yard on Spanish Town Road and Bread Lane near Back O' Wall, used to tell me he'd like me to teach Bob Marley to sing and play music. Errol was like Bob's father and mother, he'd give him daily ten shillings or a pound. A half Indian guy, from a family of the owners of Queen's Theatre, King's Theatre and a Vineyard Town theatre. Errol was always a father figure to Bob, older.

Errol was a very nice guy, wasn't doing anything to get anything back. He liked us both. It was as a favor, no money changed hands. He called him Robbie. "I want you to help Robbie," he said to me.

We would meet early in the mornings, and whatever I did, soccer, go to the sea, he would be among us. I was always giving him insight into the music. How to use his breath control—talking a lot of times is part of the whole thing. Teach him craft, technique—like I taught a lot of people. When I started with Bob there was hardly any voice there.

ROGER STEFFENS: Intriguingly, Joe Higgs says Bob Marley lived next to Delroy Wilson, a famous child star of the ska and rocksteady era.

Neville Garrick, Marley's art director, and Joe Higgs, the Wailers' first teacher,
Long Beach, California, February 1996.

JOE HIGGS: When Bunny and Bob were growing up together, Bob was not treated as one of the family. He was like an outcast in the house. His mother today comes with this legacy, as if she were there. Bob was sent to learn welding, while Bunny was sent to school. Toddy didn't put any money into Bob's corner. The mother, Cedella, wouldn't allow anybody to know he was her son. One day he was holding tightly to her, and she box him away. He slept beneath the bottom of the house.

SEGREE WESLEY: In Joe Higgs's yard, we used to go like in the evenings, you'd come from school. I remember it wasn't actually where Joe Higgs lived. A lot of people say it's where Joe lived, but Joe is from Third Street, [but the gatherings] used to be on Second Street. And there was a guy, Skipper Lako, we used to go on his little veranda. And that's where we used to rehearse. Bob was really the least among the group but he had more love for it than I've seen anybody have love for singing. He had the time and he would get there and like, he would be the first one. He didn't even know how to play guitar then 'cause the only guitarist in that little group that was formed (we didn't even know the name of the group, they didn't even name it yet), it was Peter. But Peter Tosh wasn't there at the start. There was Bob and the girls. When you went there you'd hear other people singing with them. So I don't know if other people want to proclaim and say they were part of the group. Cardo Scott was among them, Junior Braithwaite, Bunny and Bob. Every day together. Joe helped them. He used to mentor and like sort of tell them what to do and what not to do. Joe was helping him because Bob never really was a person who had any kind of excellent voice per se. Because even when the group became famous and started doing recordings, in my opinion Bob had the worst voice of all. I think Bunny had the best voice of all of them.

ROGER STEFFENS: Ricardo Scott, also known as Ras Cardo, was raised in Trench Town in that early time. He has written not only that he was an original Wailers member but also that it was he who came up with the group's name. He has also claimed publicly that he invented the word "reggae" in 1962 by combining the patois word for a woman of the street, "streggae," with the Latin *rex, regis*, meaning "king," so reggae was of the people but also of King Selassie I. It is questionable that this is true, particularly when one realizes how quickly new words are adopted in Jamaica, so a gap of six years or so between the creation of the word and its first use on the Maytals' "Do the Reggay" in 1968 seems to put the lie to Ras Cardo's claim.

JOE HIGGS: I would not oppose Cardo's belief that he was an early person around the Wailers. Today you have a set of kids, and tomorrow two or three more. But to say he was an original member of Wailers, I contest that statement very, very strongly—I don't know of it. The lead singer was Junior Braithwaite ('cause it was not Bob Marley who was leading), but Bob was the one who really put the group together. 'Cause through me Bob did what he wanted to do, and I spearheaded his thought. I believe this group belonged to Bob Marley, not Cardo or anyone—not Errol the Indian guy who brought Bob to me. Cardo neither founded the group nor came up with the name. The Wailers came because I was teaching the kids, especially the boys, how to be accountable as individuals, while we maintain a musical basis. It's not jazz they were learning, I was teaching them to wail. There were songs the Wailers did without Bob Marley. I have never heard that Cardo came up with the idea for the group to be called Wailers.

ROGER STEFFENS: Many other people have claimed credit for the Wailers' name, and suggested various titles for the group. Bunny's memory of their adoption of the name Wailers is quite mystical.

BUNNY WAILER: That's another mystery now. This is how it went. We always had in mind to call ourselves like maybe the Teenagers or Roosters. One specific day me can remember Joe Higgs cook a nice pot of cow cod soup [soup made with a bull's penis] when we were rehearsing inna him kitchen there. And the spirit was high. We were closer to going into the studio now. Everybody say Wailers ready, ready, but we never have the name yet. So everybody did call names, you, you, and suggest names, and it's like a man was there next door or in a bathroom or something, and we just hear a voice that say, "The Wailers." And every man say: "The Wailers. The Wailers? The Wailers. The Wailers?" No one know which voice or which man say "The Wailers" 'cause him don't show his face. Him just say "The Wailers" in a big, strong voice, say "The Wailers." Everybody hear that and them start to say "The Wailers." The Wailers. Everybody heard that. That sound good, weeping and wailing, 'cause we a weep, 'cause we are in Trench

Town there and we a feel the pain. So, "the Wailers" fit. Do you think that a joke thing?! Think that the name Wailers a joke?! Look here, that what the name Wailers mean. Wailing means to suffer, to cry, to bawl, to you name it—and who go through the dark like the Wailers, who go through the sufferation. So the name Wailers wasn't a name that was given to the Wailers by an individual who would come now and get credit—who is he that can say that? Who is he that can say he was responsible for giving the name—not even a Wailer. We hear a voice bawl out, "The Wailers." Every man remember that. And we did our first session right after that—like about the next week.

ROGER STEFFENS: To wail, in Jamaican terms, meant to cry out for justice, to beseech the Almighty and the powers that be for a better life. It was not just crying; it was imploring from the depth of your soul, stripped of all pretense and inhibition. As Joe Higgs says, "Everyone is capable of wailing, like a gospel concept."

One of those who recognized early on the potential power of the group was the movie-star handsome Allan "Skill" Cole, a soccer star in Jamaica who became Bob's closest friend and sometime business associate. He was a frequent guest at the Trench Town home of a charismatic Rastafarian named Mortimo Planno, who kept a library of Black Power books and Rasta tracts in his house. Planno would become deeply involved in Marley's career following his return from America in late 1966.

ALLAN "SKILL" COLE: I first met Bob probably about twelve years of age over at Mortimo Planno's house in 1962. In those days at that time I was going to Kingston College [a high school]. I had schoolmates that lived in that area, Trench Town. So we sometimes, like on a weekend, would pass through and look for them guys. Mortimo Planno was a very famous man in Trench Town, Rasta man, Rasta leader in the area. And we as youth seeking to know certain things pass through, so we get to know Planno.

The Bob I knew and I met in the very early sixties was a very, very

Allan "Skill" Cole, soccer star and Marley's best friend,
at the Reggae Archives, Los Angeles, November 1988.

shy young man. He was the type of person that when you look at him
you think you were seeing someone who was afraid of even speaking
with people, very, very timid. He was so quiet, well reserved, but a very
warm young man. Very, very artistic. Very creative.

ROGER STEFFENS: The Wailers group began to coalesce through informal rehearsals in the early sixties.

JOE HIGGS: I started to teach the Wailers to sing harmony, structur-
ing, and all those different things, basic principles of singing, how to
try to preserve as much energy as you can. And I had the Wailers on

a certain level at that time, sometimes they would be doing good, but every now and again someone would make a slip in my presence.

ROGER STEFFENS: Higgs believed they weren't ready to record yet, but Bob felt the desire to sing so strongly that he auditioned as a solo artist for the Beverley's label, owned by a sharply dressed, well-groomed producer named Leslie Kong. Bunny tells the story of the roundabout way Bob came to meet Kong.

BUNNY WAILER: When he left school Bob began working at a big welding shop. He was learning a trade same time, welding, getting maybe fifteen shillings or a pound a week, depending on how Millard the boss felt. One time Bob had a flash when the spark flies from the welding iron, got him in the eye. And he cried day and night. And when he went into the sun, he had to wear glasses. Then he had to have a cap on his nose, to take even the glare of the sun off the glass, because his eyes would just run. A lot of pain, like gravel in your eye, when you squint it's like gravel's sticking you under the eyelid and down the ball. Both eyes! We treated it with an herb we call bissy [a popular panacean Jamaican herb that is rubbed on or preferably made into a tea]. But that event kind of made him want to stop working in the welding.

Desmond Dekker [a preeminent rocksteady singer] had been working at the same welder's place, and encouraged Bob into going into the studios. He introduced Bob to Beverley's Leslie Kong. Dekker had recorded "Honor Your Mother And Your Father," then Bob went in and cut "Judge Not," his first record, with "Do You Still Love Me" on the B-side.

I was there when "Terror" was cut, the second [unreleased] session. I was to have been on the session to do "Pass It On," but I was late. Bob got twenty pounds, and he bought some good clothes.

ROGER STEFFENS: Unfortunately "Judge Not" and its follow-up, "One Cup Of Coffee," a cover of a country and western song by Claude Gray, failed to capture the public's attention. "Pass It On" would not appear until more than a decade later.

RAS MICHAEL: In 1963 when Bob do his first record, "Judge Not," Bob was like a little youth in him own style. The vision within Bob was a fullness already. And it led to his most important works like "One Love" and "Them Belly Full."

ROGER STEFFENS: Ras Michael was another early supporter. Considered by many to be the most important Rastafarian musician in Jamaica, Ras Michael is the natural inheritor and defender of Rasta dogma, which suffuses the tradition of Nyabinghi music, a style first popularized by the foundational group Count Ossie and the Mystic Revelation of Rastafari. He was a lifelong friend of the Wailers and played the penultimate set of 1978's historic One Love Peace Concert, between Peter Tosh and Bob Marley. We spoke at the Reggae Archives in December 2011.

RAS MICHAEL: Joe Higgs was the maestro of a lot of things, not just only Bob alone, but most man! Because Joe comes like he was a very stern teacher in nuff things. Many a time he say, "Man, you not hitting that note right." He coached most of the trios. From you there and sing, him going to get involved in the perfection of certain things what will make you be elevated. Show you how to hit a note and all of that. Him not going to get paid for that.

Me older than Bob is, yes, but not much years older than him. The whole of us grow in a certain place. Because Bob Marley's mother and my mother were higglers. Higglers are people who sell in the market—Ewart Street, Princess Street.

Bob was a loving spirit brother. When them come everybody just irie [joyful] in them own vibration, we had that communical spirit of love within our own self. Because I remember Peter Tosh, Bunny Wailer, Bob Wailer, Junior Braithwaite, the originals. Man and man were just like brothers. When we see each other, you see a man's thirty-two teeth, 'cause is pure smiles, happiness. "Wha'ppen, mon, wha'ppen?" And Bob say, "Yeah, mon, everything all right." We did have that love that money can't buy. Priceless. We share things. Our togetherness was our

Singers Alton Ellis and Ras Michael, childhood friends of Bob Marley,
in Los Angeles, June 1997.

richness. It never took money to make we rich. The togetherness alone
bring that richness among we. Oxford Street and Salt Lane, Back O'
Wall, were like playgrounds.

I remember one of the time, Bob did have a little record shop on
Beeston Street near King Street corner, just a little teeny thing. We
laugh, me and Peter and him sit down 'pon a step in front of the shop
and record blast. Not even one record sell in them days! But we orga-

nized. It's like we achieved the message at the time that we want to see come out. And people step and snap their fingers, and we feel the vibes. So we're happy for the things that the Almighty allow us to put to the people. Although at that time no great dividends. But we know we score a goal already. Because from the people start listen, them guy start react. Because it is the truth, it is the roots of the people, it is the heartbeat for the people.

ROGER STEFFENS: Peter Tosh was one of the final additions to the group. Raised on the remote western end of the island in Westmoreland, he arrived in Kingston at the age of fifteen with great optimism about the musical path he wished his life would take. The Wailers were impressed because he had his own guitar, which none of them had as yet, and because of his militant attitude.

PETER TOSH: I was born in the country, Westmoreland. I didn't live with my mother, but I am my mother's only child, and I didn't grow with her, I was grown with my mother's aunt, my grand-aunt, when I was three years old until I was fifteen. But she never had a lot of influence in my life. I was three years in size, but fifty years old in the mind, seen? Because I was born with a matured mind, and born with a concept of creativity, and any time there's a controversy within me, it create an inner conflict, seen? And any time that inner conflict is created, something is wrong, so you must internally investigate it. I grew up with that mind. I was born, raised in righteousness, not to say that my parents was righteous, because they did not know what was righteousness. They were being led away to a shitstem [his word for "system"], or being deceived by deceivers, you see, because they wanted to know what was righteousness.

I left Westmoreland at fifteen to learn. Music was playing me from such time. I was born in music, from ever since I could talk and exchange verbal thoughts I could sing. The first instrument I ever played was a guitar. I made it out of a piece of board, sardine can, and

Wailers co-founder Peter Tosh at the Sunset Marquis Hotel, Hollywood,
wearing a crown with all the words to "Legalize It" on it,
made for him by Mary Steffens, September 1979.

some plastic line, the plastic you use for fishing. Get good sound too. When I left for Kingston all I took was my little grip, and some food to eat on the way, and meself, and Jah in my heart.

JOE HIGGS: Peter came from the country when we were living in Trench Town. He had some family that were cabinetmakers and they used to sell syrup, that's how I first saw him. He used to sleep in the cabinet shop sometimes. But he was introduced to me by Bob Marley.

BUNNY WAILER: Peter was a revolutionary, Peter was a man arrogant, outspoken, no really worry about if him head a go cut off if him make certain statements. He wasn't an actor. Everything that he stood for from the early stage, he was really serious about. He was very conscious of Africa from an early stage.

Peter make you laugh for a million different reasons. Peter loves to touch girls [pinching and squeezing them]. You know that's a serious kind of joke still. You see Peter touch a girl going down the road with her husband and gazes in her eyes in a split second that she almost broke her toe, because this tall, dark and handsome man touches her and gazes, that she almost slips.

ROGER STEFFENS: His habit brought him the nickname Peter Touch, a name that even appeared as a credit on several of his recordings.

BUNNY WAILER: Peter just love to fool around. And we just laugh pure laugh. Anytime Peter come, there is something fe laugh about, 'cause him always have a story to tell you 'bout something what just happen weh him see happen, or something he just hear. He always have a drama. Always! A laugh, a laugh, a pure laugh!

SEGREE WESLEY: I know Peter when he used to come from West Road. Peter was always the type who always portray a sort of rough image. We always used to say, "Peter, you're resolute." Peter's not the type to listen to reasoning. He'll tell you whatever he wants to tell you but he ain't listening to what you have to say. Which was the opposite of Bob. If you say something to Bob he'll listen and he'll talk back to you and you'll converse with him for hours. But Peter is not one like that with the kind of patience, you know? As a matter of fact, one day I look at him, I says, "I think Bunny is more Rastaman than all of you guys."

ROGER STEFFENS: By early 1964, Bunny, Bob and Peter would join with Junior Braithwaite and a pair of female singers to form the nucleus of a group that would change Jamaican music and bring the Wailers and reggae to worldwide attention.

CHAPTER 3

The Wailers at Studio One

ROGER STEFFENS: After the failure of Marley's two solo singles on Leslie Kong's Beverley's label, Joe Higgs helped shape the group of eager but raw vocalists into a quintet ready to enter the ranks of professional recording artists. Together they were drawn to Kong's biggest rival, Studio One, owned by producer and sound system proprietor Clement "Coxson" Dodd.

At the time, June 1964, Coxson was one of the most powerful dons of the music business. Though his reputation was mixed, with some artists questioning his fairness, he was respected as a consistent hitmaker. His studio band was the Skatalites, the inventors of ska, and they would play behind the Wailers from their very first session onward, an incredible break for these inexperienced teenagers. Their first release, "Simmer Down," skyrocketed to number one and a reported eighty thousand sales, marking the group's initial flowering as professional musicians. But despite recording scores of songs over the next two years, they would end up parting with the producer in frustration over a lack of proper recompense for their efforts.

Dodd's name is often spelled "Coxsone," but I have used "Coxson" in this book. In his studio on Brentford Road in Kingston in 2003, he explained the difference to me.

COXSON DODD: Well, when it's me, it's Coxson. When it's the label or the sound system, it's Coxsone.

ROGER STEFFENS: He then proceeded to autograph an early Wailers seven-inch record "Coxsone Dodd."

COXSON DODD: Somebody gave me that name. There was a cricket side in England, it was popular. One of its stars was a man called Coxson. So they just label me that way, like making some wonderful catches.

ROGER STEFFENS: In 1983 I visited Coxson's mother, Mrs. Darlington, at her shop in Spanish Town, just west of Kingston. She recalled her son working in the fields of Florida in the early fifties picking crops, and buying records for her to play on one of Jamaica's first sound systems. At the time Mrs. Darlington was the girlfriend of another early Jamaican producer, Duke Reid, who had already begun to supply records to her. It was extremely rare to find a woman behind the turntables at that time, so she is considered a groundbreaker. As the fifties drew to a close, Coxson also began to produce records by local artists for use at his dances. Mrs. Darlington had fond memories of those pioneering days, referring to her son respectfully as "Mr. Dodd."

MRS. DARLINGTON: Mr. Dodd play the radio in the night until three o'clock in the morning, listening to various singers. His favorite was Billy Eckstine. When he start the company, he generally travel and I was in charge of the whole operation, supervising the studio and the factory and the office. At times even a talent scout.

Bob Marley started in the early sixties and he was a young chap at that time, sixteen, seventeen, and he came to the studio and Mr. Dodd interview him. He found that his sound was okay and he started to record him. And he brought his wife in. And they got Marley right in there. Mr. Dodd marry the both of them.

COXSON DODD: My mother has been of great help to me. She was the first person to operate my sound system. A woman DJ! When I worked in the States in the early fifties, I used to send a lot of records to Jamaica, and that's how my mother started operating the sound, called Coxson's Downbeat. I had a Bogen amplifier, about 35 watts. Had some English-made speaker, Celestion twelve-inch. They could take a lot of beating and things like that. Along with some University horns to carry the sounds. My mother, Mrs. Darlington, would spin the records.

ROGER STEFFENS: Jamaican radio in the fifties was limited to a kind of cable radio system called RJR Rediffusion, or more properly Radio Jamaica and Rediffusion Network, which played mostly foreign music. Local tunes in a nascent recording industry were limited to cover songs and calypsos, music identified with Trinidad, which originated the form. It was left to mobile discos known as sound systems to give exposure to ambitious young Jamaican creators.

JOE HIGGS: Before Bob Marley, the sound systems kings of those days were Count Nick the Champ, Tom the Great Sebastian, Roderick's, Dean's, Sky Rocket and V-Rocket. All of these were before Duke Reid and Coxson.

ROGER STEFFENS: Sound system "clashes" were held between competing systems. The ones with the better records drew the bigger crowds. They often battled sonically at different ends of a field, as the crowd drifted between them searching for the hottest shots of the moment. The bigger the crowd, the more drinks you could sell and the more money you could make. Sometimes, particularly in the early sixties, the clashes would end up in violence, as thugs associated with one or another of the entrepreneurs would "mash up" (destroy) their opponent's equipment or terrorize their audiences.

JOE HIGGS: The first "Eleven Sound" contest that Reid and Coxson entered into, Duke was third, and Coxson fourth, to Nick the Champ first, and Tom the Great Sebastian second. The contest was at Charles Street and Spanish Town Road. It's a yard on a corner with a fence around it.

When I was about fifteen, Coxson, we used to call him Downbeat, had a little sound and he always come to a family whose name was Tucker: Harold, Keithy, Leslie, Eddie, Gladstone, Desmond, all these are brothers, and the most famous one, Jimmy. Coxson used to come by and serenade, play in that yard, gospel music like "Be There When I Come." You could stand outside and listen, but almost all of the sounds had their speakers in a tree up in the air or on a light post, big speaker horn, sound draw people. I could hear Coxson from miles away, you follow the sound. Duke Reid had a better sound, but Coxson had better selections. During that time, Bob, Seeco Patterson and me used to hang together most of the time, from Trench Town to Back O' Wall and different ghettos.

ROGER STEFFENS: Working under the stern tutoring of Higgs, the early nucleus of the Wailers included Junior Braithwaite, Cherry Green, Bunny Livingston, Peter Tosh and Bob Marley, with several others from the neighborhood sitting in at various times.

JOE HIGGS: Junior did have the best voice in the group, I'm positive. Definitely. Bob had no voice. In those days, Junior was withdrawn. He stuttered, but he had a very nice voice. He was a very good singer, there from the start of the group's training. He had a voice like Frankie Lymon, appealing. "It Was Your Love," "It Hurts To Be Alone," were his leads. That [latter] one had Ernest Ranglin on lead guitar and it was one of the Wailers' biggest songs. Junior was related to my partner, Roy Wilson, cousins perhaps. Junior's father was a politician, Zebedee Braithwaite, who supported the elder Manley.

ROGER STEFFENS: Junior's parents migrated to the U.S., so he left with them shortly after the group began recording for the Studio One label in 1964. I spoke with him in Chicago in 1985, one of the only interviews he ever granted.

JUNIOR BRAITHWAITE: I was born in Kingston, Jamaica, on April 4, 1949, on Third Street and West Road. That is in the heart of the ghetto. People now know it as Rema, the Jungle. I was living on Third Street and Bob Marley was living on Second Street. Joe Higgs was also on Third Street. My grandmother raised a youth named Roy Wilson, we were like brothers. Roy Wilson and Joe Higgs were the number one best harmonizing group in Jamaica at that time, and they used to rehearse in the back of our yard. So we as kids hang out around them, 'cause we had something in common, because we loved singing. Singing was a natural gift, I know that I was ordained to be a musician.

Bob, Bunny, Peter and myself, along with a sister, Beverley Kelso, as an early Wailer. The five people in the original Wailers are really Bunny, Bob, Peter, Beverley and myself. And the Wailers was like just a singing group, a harmonizing group. We had nothing to do with instruments. So the commercial Wailers that you had touring later with Bob was like a group of musicians that he needed to back him up and he called the Wailers. But they aren't the original Wailers.

We grew up in roots and culture, we was born in it, and we as a people then were closely knitted in a social atmosphere. To do anything, whatever projects at any time that we would undertake, would be easy, because it was just a vibe of oneness. We weren't so clinging to material things, we were like, everything seemed so easily done, so natural to us, in that spiritually we were at our highest level, and we could so easily do anything.

ROGER STEFFENS: In addition to Junior there were two women who sang with the Wailers in their early stages of recording. I tried for over twenty years to get Cherry Green (real name Ermine Bramwell) and Beverley Kelso to speak on the record with me. Although the material on which they appear has never been out of print since the mid-sixties, they never made a penny for their work and were angry because of that. Finally, in May 2003, my friends the Midnight Ravers, broadcasters on WBAI in New York City, arranged for Cherry to fly up from her home in Florida, and for Beverley to come in from her home in the Bronx, to speak with me privately and, in Cherry's case, live on the air.

CHERRY GREEN: I was born in Upper Trench Town, August 22, 1943. Ermine Bramwell was my original name, my father's name. My father was a dentist who died in the late fifties. Cherry was just my little nickname 'cause my skin was red, so they called me Cherry. I guess my mother called me that. My brother's last name is Green. I guess

Early Wailer Cherry Green, a.k.a. Ermine Bramwell, on the
Midnight Ravers radio program, WBAI-FM, New York City, May 2003.

the boys know that, so that's why they call me Cherry Green. I went
to Trench Town School. And I went to a private school, too. My father
lived in Jones Town off Oxford Street, we lived there, he do his work
there. So after he died we moved down to Trench Town. My mother get
one of the rooms and we lived there. We was poor but we was happy. I
mean, never dirt poor that we couldn't go to eat, you know? We always
have something to eat and always have something clean to wear. We
had bicycle. My father used to take me to school in his car or on his
motorcycle. He had two motorcycle when he die and a car.

We used to have a big radio, you played a record on top. So every
Saturday evening when Duke Reid come over the radio, I would turn
that up so the neighborhood could hear. He play all the hit songs.

I used to be in school play and we always sing. I always try to stay
on the back burner, kinda shy. But I be doing something and I be singing, just like when I sing with the Wailers. I used to listen to Harry

Belafonte, Nat King Cole, Duke Ellington and those kind of big band people. Joe Higgs was the one who discover me. He used to sing. And we used to listen to him and he would tell us little things.

One day I was washing clothes and [I was singing] an American song, I can't tell you what it was. But my voice was way up there and he stopped immediately. He said, "Cherry, that's you?" So I said yeah. So then I guess when Bob need somebody, when Braithwaite left, they get me.

Trench Town, you know, we had nice people live there, but people just sometimes drift away. They migrate to England or to the U.S. We had good people from out of that little area. They make it look so bad now, when I see the houses. It wasn't like that when we was growing up. It wasn't like that at all. Most people come from the country. They don't have running water, they don't have electric light. There you come, you have nice bathroom, toilet, kitchen. And we keep it clean 'cause, I tell my boss, in my country as poor as we are, people have one room and when you look underneath the bed you can see your face. It's clean.

The Wailers always rehearse and we were always there. You know, sit around with them rehearsing and we would try to butt in and try to sing. Sometime you go up too high and Joe Higgs would say—he was like a teacher. He tell us what to do to bring the notes out and that kind of thing, technique. He was like that 'cause he know all of that. We just sing, you know. Joe was a boasty kind of guy, 'cause he always dress nice. See, Joe went to Mico Teachers College, so I guess he probably learned all of that from there, you know?

When Bob first come, we used to call him "little white boy" 'cause his hair was curly. He was teenager. Him and Bunny, they used to dress nice in the Fifth Avenue shoes and nice shirt. Bunny, Bob and Peter, when they started, they started down Third Street and West Road. They used to sit on the sidewalk and sing by the branch yard run by the JLP [the right wing Jamaica Labour Party] where they have meetings. So they just sit down there, singing with Cardo and the boys. But, like, we was girls, I mean, we pass and hear them singing, but when they start coming in the yard that's when we would go, and then Peter come with his guitar.

My earliest memory of Bob, the little girls—like before Rita—come and used to like him. 'Cause he used to come over by me, so then Rita get to come over by me so she could see him. We didn't call him Bob. We called him Lester [a variation of his birth name Nesta]. That's what we know him as. Nice boy, he was funny, cracking jokes, teasing. Oh, yes. He used to be shy, though. You know, kinda shy. But I don't remember Bob being picked on.

ROGER STEFFENS: By now, all the supporting cast was in place. Under the direction of Coxson Dodd, they would have their first release, beginning a steady string of hits, joining the ranks of the most important vocal groups on the island.

One of the biggest puzzles over the years has been to ascertain the circumstances of the first Wailers recording. Most observers credit "Simmer Down" as the first recording and release, but there is wide disagreement among its participants as to the exact details. Percussionist Alvin "Seeco" Patterson, who was close to Bob throughout his life, from his early Trench Town days forward, spoke to me in the summer of 2012 and was precise in his recounting of the momentous day. In his telling the Wailers went to Coxson Dodd for a Sunday afternoon audition, sent there at his urging.

ALVIN "SEECO" PATTERSON: The Wailers come back to me from audition and tell me say, Mr. Dodd turn them down. So me take them back there right away and ask the man, "Why you turn away them, mon?" Him say him couldn't hear nothin'. So me say, "Simmer Down." And Mr. Dodd get a smile on him face and say, "I like that. Play that." And when him hear it he sent me to find Roland Alphonso, the saxophone player. And when we come back, him take us right into the studio and we record the song that night. Next day, dem play it on soft wax on a sound system in Jones Town.

Percussionist Seeco Patterson at Sunsplash '81, the annual reggae festival
which that year celebrated the life of Bob Marley, Montego Bay, August 1981.

ROGER STEFFENS: In a prior interview backstage at the Universal
Amphitheater in Los Angeles in 1991, Seeco gave a longer version.

ALVIN "SEECO" PATTERSON: Bob and me was close. Very close. It
was a spiritual thing, from he was very young he was planning to
sing to people. And then he find me musically and so him say bwoi,
he figure I was the best person to take him to Coxson. So we plan for
that, you know.

At that time there was a little friction between Bob and Joe Higgs.
And between Coxson and Joe, some whole heap a things. So Joe prefer
me to take him. But that day, it wasn't so nice. Because when he went
down there Coxson put him off for a next while. But I wasn't there, I
never went. I was cooking. I send him and the boys. And he come back
and say Coxson put him off for a couple of more weeks. And he come
and say, oh, Coxson is fuckery. You understand? He can't deal with
Coxson. So I say no sir and I ask him what is the tracks he do? So him

name the songs what him do. So I say, no you don't do the right songs. Right? You should do certain songs like "Simmer Down," 'cause we had just finished "Simmer Down" you know. So him say boy me never think of that you know. So I say come. We go back up there same day, man. And me say, "Coxson you know, you don't listen to the man good, the man didn't do all the songs." Him say, "Then him have any more songs?" I say, "Yes, man, a lot of songs him can do." So I say "Simmer Down." And him say "Simmer Down, what is that?" I say, "One of the track dem." Him say, "Make I hear that one." And him do "Simmer Down." And that was it. [Claps his hands.]

ROGER STEFFENS: Bunny Wailer tells a different version of the story.

BUNNY WAILER: We sang about four songs before we actually went to "Simmer Down." Coxson wasn't as turned on, so I said, "Why don't we sing 'Simmer Down'?" And Peter started playing "Simmer Down" even before Bob even answered. Peter started play the riddim, I started singing. We didn't even sing the song through, we didn't even sing a verse before Coxson said, "OK, that one. You come tomorrow and we'll record that one first."

COXSON DODD: Bunny Wailer claims they recorded "Simmer Down" the day after the audition. I say, no, no. You know why it couldn't be the next day? They had songs that was all do-over material, so I instructed them to try and do some writing. So that evening we started and we found a topic. And we set up "It Hurts To Be Alone." They came in for a rehearsal after that. Then me sent for guitarist Ernest Ranglin, got them together. But it took some time for them because all they had was like their early doo-wop stuff. But I was very impressed with them the first time, because I was hoping to really get a kind of group with that teen feel, young voices and thing like that. People say that Junior had the best voice. Well, that was definitely so. It's after he left that I demand that Bob do the lead.

ROGER STEFFENS: Cherry concurs with Coxson, recalling that although "Simmer Down" was the group's first hit, there were a couple

Clement "Coxson" Dodd, founder of Studio One, the Wailers' first label,
at his headquarters in Brooklyn, February 1993.

of songs before that. Joe Higgs appears to support Seeco's version.
Coxson gave an expanded explanation in an interview at his studio in
Brooklyn in 1993.

COXSON DODD: When the Wailers came for audition, all they had was
songs done earlier by groups, American groups. If they were covering
a song, they come with a style of their own. I then told them I love the
sound of the group, but they need to come with their own material.
Well, I played a couple of American recordings, so as to give them the
theme, or lyrics, Garnett Mimms and the Enchanters, "Cry Baby," stuff
like that. I'm the one who selected all this stuff for Bob.

ROGER STEFFENS: Throughout this period, Coxson was experiment-
ing with a wide variety of sounds, from deep soul covers to gospel and
novelty songs, and he urged the Wailers to cover artists as varied as Bob
Dylan and Dion and the Belmonts. The Skatalites' flexibility and the

fact that he owned his own studio allowed him to expose the Wailers to an enormous range of influences.

COXSON DODD: It's because having my own studio I was able to get it done. "What's New Pussycat?"—that was done just around the time when stereo recorders started coming out. Because we start through them early from mono.

JOE HIGGS: The Wailers started to lean on the Impressions 'cause of Coxson's suggestion. Songs like "It Hurts To Be Alone" and all those tunes, they got a lot of Impressions songs to do.

COXSON DODD: I gave them the idea how to approach "It Hurts To Be Alone," because they had to come up with some title or a couple of lines. They went home. They didn't sing "Simmer Down" for me and they didn't come back a second time that day to sing it. That is after. The reason why I'm saying this, now I can remember, because when they did "Simmer Down," it's just around the time when "Little Did You Know" by the Techniques came out. "Simmer Down" was not their first release. "Habits" came early, along with "Hurts To Be Alone," and then after that came "Simmer Down."

JUNIOR BRAITHWAITE: The first session [he makes a distinction between the audition and the group's initial recording session] . . . we did "Lonesome Feeling," we did a lot of tunes like "Straight and Narrow Way," we did so many tunes, man. I sing background on "Simmer Down" and "Lonesome Feeling."

JOE HIGGS: The first song, "Simmer Down," it have more people than what is there. [He means that more people were singing than were credited for the track.] About seven or more—more girls doing that song. It was more. It was a gossiping kind of song, really a more folkish thing, "Simmer Down." Someone in the ghetto trying to get too big, telling him to simmer down 'cause the battle will be harder, trying to caution the guy who is too hot. Bob was good at showing words. "Old time people used to say"—all those things are phrases from folk singers or slaves, whatever. Almost every song he sang had at least one of those things in it.

ROGER STEFFENS: Beverley Kelso was one of those many voices on the "Simmer Down" recording. She was a last-minute addition, having joined the Wailers hours before the session. She spoke to me in New York City in 2003.

BEVERLEY KELSO: I was born in Jones Town, April 14, 1948. I got to meet Bob because of a friend, two brothers, Pete and Calvin Richards. We'd go to school together. We were like family; Trench Town people on the whole was like family. Everybody was equal then because in those days, looking back now, I would say there wasn't no poor people in Trench Town because majority of Trench Town people go to high school.

ROGER STEFFENS: Beverley was an accomplished singer who often performed in church.

BEVERLEY KELSO: Once I sang for the Queen. That day was more

Beverley Kelso, founding member of the Wailers, in New York City, May 2003.

than a day. I wasn't shy because I knew that I was the lead singer to sing that day and all of these official people were going to be there. And when I started to sing the whole church, their back turned to me—and the whole church it was just like *twinkling*. Everybody was taking pictures when I started singing and I didn't get scared, I didn't. I just sing out the tune.

ROGER STEFFENS: How Beverley became an "instant Wailer" is a fascinating tale and contradicts other accounts.

BEVERLEY KELSO: They used to have meeting, like PNP [the left-wing People's National Party] meeting, Labour meeting, political meeting. They have it for the grown people and they have it for the young kids. The young kids would go out and they would teach them to sing, sew, whatever they want to do. And at that time Edward Seaga [a local right-wing politician who would go on to become prime minister in the 1980s] was the one who give them—because it was a Labour meeting and they used to keep this meeting at Chocomo Lawn.

So, at that time my friends used to bother me and say come to Chocomo and sing, come. I was urged to come on stage and sing "Down the Aisle." You know, Patti LaBelle? The minute when I said, "Down the aisle I'll walk with you," the fence tear down, everybody coming out. I get all frightened. The fence tear down because the people, they couldn't wait to come inside. The gate was too small so they couldn't come in. I don't know where they come from, but a lot of people just burst through and the fence teared down, everybody coming in to see who was singing. They probably think it was Patti LaBelle. And I get scared and frightened. I get so nervous, I start the song all over again. It's my spirit break and I couldn't continue singing. And that was it.

The following evening after school going home, I was doing my little work and things and I hear somebody knocking at the door. And I come out and I see Bob. And I asked him, you want somebody? He said yes, you. I said, me? And he said, yeah. He said I'd like it if you'd do a song with me and I'd like it if you'd sing with me. And I said no, you'll have to ask my mother if you want me to sing with you, but she's not here now.

Later he came back and he asked her and she said yes, but you'll have to take care of her. He asked me if I could come and rehearse the same evening. So, I said all right. It was the fourth yard on Second Street. That's where Bunny used to live.

My first impression of Bob was ordinary. Ordinary. I didn't think of him as nobody special, you know? We were just ordinary, to me, just ordinary young man at that time. Very polite. Never sad. Even that evening he was just smiling. He was just looking at me, like, oh, pretty girl. That's what I have in my mind. Because he was, like, just staring at me, you know, when he was talking to me.

That evening after he said meet him at the place, I said, "OK, go ahead and I will come meet you there." I went up and when I went there Peter was there, Bunny and Junior, all sitting on a tree. Bob wasn't there. So I asked for Bob and they said Bob went to get the guitar or something. And Bob came and introduced me to Peter, Bunny and Junior. But I didn't call him Bob. Nobody in Trench Town called him Bob. He introduced himself to me as Lester. And after they introduced me to Peter, Bunny and Junior I tell them my name is Beverley and then they started to play.

So we rehearsed "Simmer Down" the same evening he met my mother. I didn't go to school the next morning because Bob said we're going to the studio.

ROGER STEFFENS: That morning Beverley, Junior, Bunny, Bob and Peter walked to 13 Brentford Road, Kingston 5, and entered history.

BEVERLEY KELSO: The "Simmer Down" session was in the morning because we went to the studio after I finished tidying up my mother's house. We walked to Brentford Road. We used to walk on the road where they used to call it Almshouse burying ground. That walk was quick quick, because we lived at the bottom of the road.

That first day when we went to record "Simmer Down," when we go there we didn't have no problem. Bunny and Bob probably set up the arrangement with Coxson before because when I go I just go straight into the studio with them. The Skatalites was there, everybody. Siddy Bucknor was the engineer at the time. We never leave there that day. It was just "Simmer Down." One track. But that day, you know something? I think we had a better cut than the release, because if you notice [on the recording] Peter come in and says "Simmer." And Coxson say that's it. Peter wasn't supposed to say "Simmer," he was supposed—we was singing when the musician should come in, Peter come in and say "Simmer." Coxson said that's it—that was the one that he wanted. It was a mistake, but it wasn't a mistake.

ROGER STEFFENS: Controversy remains about the precise recording date. Bob, Bunny, Peter, Junior and Beverley have all identified "Simmer Down" as their first recording. The session date was gleaned from the original Studio One tape box containing "Straight and Narrow Way," dated 6 July 1964. This may be the date a copy was made or it may be the original recording date. Bunny clearly recalls that the Skatalites backed the Wailers on their first session, and he places the session in June or July 1964 because the record got heavy play during independence celebrations in early August of that year.

Some accounts put that final rehearsal on a Sunday evening. Beverley remembers differently.

BEVERLEY KELSO: I don't remember that we rehearsed on a Sunday night. I know it's during the week because my mother went to work that day and then when she came home from work that's when Bob talked to her. Saturday morning "Simmer Down" was on the air.

ROGER STEFFENS: The song was an instant hit.

BEVERLEY KELSO: It was like Trench Town light up when "Simmer Down" come on the air. I was cleaning the house and—"Simmer Down"! Everybody radio turn up blast high: "Simmer Down." And they played it, they played "Simmer Down" like about six times. RJR. It was like, just constant. They put it on the air and they said it's brand-new from the Wailers. They played it about six times. I remember that clearly. And Trench Town was like light up like it was Christmas.

SEGREE WESLEY: Oh, man, when we guys heard it first, I mean, we had been hearing the rehearsal on a daily basis, or a nightly basis as we used to say, because we used to do more of the rehearsal in the nights. And when they went to record and we started hearing them on the radio we all felt good. Like it was one of us got out there; I mean, that record took off. It was a big hit, number one.

BEVERLEY KELSO: And then it was like, oh, the Wailers!

SEGREE WESLEY: "Simmer Down" was at that time one of the biggest sales of any records done by a Jamaican.

COXSON DODD: When "Simmer Down" come out, in those days, anything from five thousand was a hit. I would say twenty thousand would be a strong hit.

ROGER STEFFENS: At the height of the success of "Simmer Down" it kept four pressing plants going and sold a reported eighty thousand copies on an island with only about two million inhabitants.

JOE HIGGS: Toots and the Maytals and I were on tour with other artists in Jamaica, [places] like Manchester or Clarendon, hanging out together. We had lots in common; we like to smoke. So we went into some deep bush with some Rastas smoking some herb, when on the radio "Simmer Down" came on, new. Toots turned to his partner, listen to this, this is the group that's going to give us a hard time, and they can't even find their key, some are out of key. It was true and I said, Toots, give them six more months now. Six more months you're going to have to run away. Like a joke I was making. And in no time, the Wailers were kicking ass.

BEVERLEY KELSO: The happiest memory of being in the Wailers was being with them when they're talking about going to the studio and laughing and talking. They were making fun of everyone they would see and they was just nice. They were just having fun. But I didn't crack no jokes. I couldn't keep up with them, really. I didn't know what to say.

Nobody did bow down to us. I understand and I read it in the paper, that people used to run around the Wailers, coming to the Wailers. Nobody didn't care who we was because Higgs and Wilson was there singing. Hortense Ellis was there singing. Bunny and Scully was singing. Toots and the Maytals, Delroy Wilson, everybody was right there singing. Bob was just another person to everybody. But they loved the music and people gathered to hear us sing but nobody would really— it's not like you would have Michael Jackson. But they were proud of us and when we would go to the studio people would just wave. And the Wailers, it was just like ordinary people, you know?

JUNIOR BRAITHWAITE: Who would expect that Bob would become the great King of Reggae and all this? To us, it was just fun. At the time, to the people in society it was like a shame if you didn't have a trade. If you was a singer, you couldn't make no money, man. And the people would discourage us, telling us to go learn a trade. Plus I wanted to be a doctor or something, too. I think singing was just something that everybody needed to do, had to do. And it so happened that we were in a situation, we got a chance of recording. Because around us everybody sang, in churches everyone sang, and dance and sing, it's just a part of the culture. It wasn't like something special that no one else couldn't have done.

What it proved was that we were more rootically based, like we were stronger. When you're living in a deeply rooted cultural environment, then everything flow so easily. We were stronger then, because we didn't have any problem, we hadn't journeyed out and had to counteract and encounter racism or anything. I didn't know anything about the color barrier until I journeyed out of Jamaica. We didn't know anything about that, man. So it goes to show them that we were like a people firm, stable, we had stability, and at our best at all times.

CHAPTER 4

Good Good Rudies

ROGER STEFFENS: At the time the Wailers' recording career commenced, Jamaica had recently achieved its independence from Great Britain and there was a tremendous surge of nationalistic pride. Politics were divided between the ruling right-wing Jamaica Labour Party (JLP) and the left-wing People's National Party (PNP). One of the first things the JLP did upon assuming the power of government was to bulldoze an impoverished PNP area called Back O' Wall, claiming that it was full of criminal elements—including followers of the Rastafari faith. Dr. Clinton Hutton of the University of the West Indies has identified this act as the beginning of "garrison politics," tribalizing the population, especially the young, and hamstringing the development of a democratic culture. Each party was buoyed by its affiliations with gangs, which ultimately would devolve into drug "dons" controlling the entire political process.

The Wailers were keenly aware of what was taking place. "Simmer Down" was a reaction to the turmoil in the ghetto, calling on the youth to "control your temper." The group was aware of the controversies surrounding their producer, Coxson Dodd, and his parsimonious reputation. As their popularity grew, people would gather around them as they made their way to the studio.

JUNIOR BRAITHWAITE: Peter used to walk with his guitar. Peter and Bob knew a few chords on the guitar at the time. And we used to walk together, we used to just hang together, man, and people would ask us to do a tune. And we would stop and sing on a street corner or at the tailor shop, or anywhere for that matter.

BUNNY WAILER: Wailers was almost the first group that went over three people, even over two people. It was always duos in those times. Blues Busters were a duo, Higgs and Wilson, Alton and Eddie, Bunny and Skully. But the Maytals trio came about two years before us.

ROGER STEFFENS: There has been some confusion about the band's name in this period, with people referring to them variously as "the Wailers," "Bob Marley and the Wailers," "the Wailing Wailers" and "the Wailing Rude Boys."

JOE HIGGS: Our first understanding is "Wailing Wailers" 'cause Coxson was trying to use that name, even though they were the Wailers.

BEVERLEY KELSO: We never have no other name than the Wailers.

JUNIOR BRAITHWAITE: It was the Wailing Wailers, not Bob and the Wailers. We were never called the Wailing Rude Boys.

BUNNY WAILER: Wailers didn't have to sing no dirty things. Wailers bring down the house without that. See songs like "Rude Boy." We used to sing "ska quadrille," but the rude boys [thought we] were saying "cyan go a jail, cyan go a jail, cyan go a jail." That relate to his happening, 'cause that's the only thing he fears—jail—until he gets used to it. But until then jail is his only enemy, where he's locked away from the freedom that he's had. It was like a bet between rude boys and rude boys [about which lyric was right]. So they would meet us, wait for us, to stop the Wailers to find out, because man already bet a pound, ten shillings. One man say it's "ska quadrille." One man who was close to Wailers, hearing Wailers rehearse, might be at the studio, those people would actually know what was said. So the people who was like on the streets now, the song just come to them on the jukebox, on the radio, on the sound system—them hang on to "cyan go a jail." So there was always a controversy about what the Wailers really said, so we had to be clarifying these things too all the time.

ROGER STEFFENS: The group's first ballad to make a big impression was composed by the teenaged Junior Braithwaite and recorded on August 28, 1964, the day before he left the island for Chicago.

JUNIOR BRAITHWAITE: I was only thirteen at the time, and my parents were already in the States, so I had to just move along with my family. I only sung lead on "It Hurts To Be Alone." And that was the day just before I flew out of Jamaica. Because they had to have me do a solo just before I left, and so it only took a few hours to learn this new tune, and one take. We didn't have no problem in recording, it was the one cut, and it was only two-track studio too. I mean, everything playing on one track, one cut, just like that. It's not like it is today, sophisticated, and more studio techniques. We were that tough, man.

You know, we did a few stage shows just before I left home, and they used to pick us up off the stage, man. I mean, I remember them picking me up over their heads, the people, and it was a thrill! We played at the Ward, we did about three shows together.

BUNNY WAILER: Junior Braithwaite led "It Hurts To Be Alone" originally, and that was really a smash. In that song, what happened is that when we started listening to the Impressions in those times, we were just acquainted with Curtis Mayfield's writing and arrangements, and we were fascinated by the way he did this song, "I'm So Proud." And out of that song came "It Hurts To Be Alone."

We never met Curtis Mayfield, however. When he came to Jamaica in the early sixties we went to see him. We were in the first row of the Carib Theatre and we took in the Impressions. They were our loved ones, we fought our way to get in the front row. But that's as close as we got to the Impressions in real life. We never met them. I don't know if Bob did, maybe Bob did, I don't know.

SEGREE WESLEY: Junior left, I say, when they became famous. Junior had the better voice. You know, that childish, child voice. But Bunny could always hold a note and sing in the more melodic setting, you see? While to me Peter was a person, well, if you have a song, you give him a song that would be like a protest song per se, Peter would deliver that better. But Bob had a chanting thing about him where it was unique, you know? He would make some funny sounds and it still a part of what is, you know? So Bob had the versatility to flow from here to there but Bob didn't really have the voice to carry, you know? But from where he was he came a long way and it was through practice that put him where he is.

ROGER STEFFENS: In this period, the Wailers began to work on their musicianship.

SEGREE WESLEY: One thing I'll give Peter credit for teaching Bob was the early starting of playing the guitar. Bob and Bunny would come without Peter to my home and say, "Come, Segree, we're going to work." That's how he said it. And then we'd go in this kitchen, we used to call it the kitchen, Metty's kitchen.

BUNNY WAILER: Wailers playing guitar was a self-taught thing. The man have no time to sit down and teach man nothin'. Every man has his season to develop having the guitar. Sometimes Pete plays the guitar so much that he is tired of it. So I have it for a couple of days, maybe a week, like a football; sometimes, every man has a time to keep the ball. So within their time of keeping the guitar, you learn, you teach yourself, by just looking at people holding different chords.

CHERRY GREEN: Most of the time Bob led the group. When we rehearsed, Bob would just pick his guitar and he come out with something and then sometimes we'd add words to it. We all wrote. We didn't even have a tape recorder. We were out there in the dark with our kerosene tin lamp or the fire or the stars.

I agree that Junior had the best voice in the group. Oh, yes. He carried. I sing "Lonesome Feeling." The voice up there is me. And "There She Goes." And then "Maga Dog," you can hear me and Peter.

BEVERLEY KELSO: Going to the studio they would walk and sing. They would walk and carry on with a lot of clowning. Bob would be pushing Bunny, Bunny would be pushing Bob and Peter and they laugh and they clown and they tease each other. They would laugh at people. They used to do a lot of funny things, the little things that they talk you just sit down and just crack up. At that time they didn't used to smoke, nobody never smoked. And Junior, me and Junior was two little short ones, so me and Junior would stay in the back hold each other's hand and walking and start talking our little talk and Bunny and Peter would be there and Bob carrying. They were fun to be around, I'm telling you. I used to love just to hear them talk and carry on with their antics. I want to be in the midst of them. Whatever they're talking about I wanna be around them, you know?

ROGER STEFFENS: Studio One was a large, high-ceilinged room on Brentford Road in a rough area of downtown Kingston. A typical session for the Wailers would find them backed by the cream of Jamaica's most hard-core Rasta musicians, known collectively as the Skatalites. The Skatalites recorded for other producers too, under a wide range of different names. Among the chief members were Lloyd Knibb on drums, Lloyd Brevett on bass, "Jah Jerry" Haynes on guitar, Jackie Mittoo on piano, Don Drummond on trombone, Roland Alphonso and Tommy McCook on tenor sax, "Dizzy Johnny" Moore on trumpet, and Dennis "Ska" Campbell on baritone sax. Mr. Dodd served as both engineer and producer of the earliest sessions. Cherry Green and Beverley Kelso spoke to me in New York City in 2003 about their initial experiences at Studio One.

CHERRY GREEN: My first recording session we rehearse all the night until we know the song. And they said tomorrow we going over to the studio. I'd never been in a studio before. It was scary. It's nervous. I mean, a lot of people there.

BEVERLEY KELSO: I wasn't nervous. They said I was shy still, you know. But I don't think I was shy to sing, but after singing I wouldn't say a word. If you say something to me I would answer you, but other than that being in the limelight, I would sing and Bob and Peter and Bunny would be one place with all the rest of the guys and I would be just by myself. I was an observer.

They used to say I'm sneaky and I'm this and that. But that didn't bother me because I know they respect me. I used to look up on them and they look up on me. With respect. They treat me like a sister and they treat me good. They talk to me good and everything. I enjoyed being with them.

ROGER STEFFENS: For Beverley, it was clear from the start that Bob was head Wailer.

BEVERLEY KELSO: Bob always taught me the part that he wanted me to sing. Bob was the acknowledged leader of the group. After the first session, it was like every day or every other day we would be in the studio actually recording. Doing something. If we're not recording for ourselves, we were backing up other people because we have other people coming and singing and we'll be singing backing up, you know? We're not a part of their group but if anybody were recording we would be there backing up, singing with, for instance, Tony Gregory. Anybody else in the studio singing and want backup we would just come in and harmonize. Everybody would just backup sing, clap, whatever you wanna do over there to back up everybody. And everybody would have the different part harmony to hold.

I know sometimes that you don't hear me and I just couldn't hold the harmony and Bob would say what? I used to walk off and Bob said, she wouldn't even try, she won't try, she just walk away and just leave people alone. She wouldn't even try. You know, that's how he used to talk. I just walk away and leave them.

So we was in the studio most of the time.

JOE HIGGS: Every day they would go to the studio after a while, and whatever they wanted, Coxson would give them five shillings or ten shillings.

BEVERLEY KELSO: We were like Mr. Dodd's family. And there were times when we didn't go home. We would be in the studio like two, three days. When Junior was leaving to come to America they were doing an album and for like, two, three days we would be in the studio. We didn't have place to sleep. We didn't even have no time to sleep. It was just fun in the studio. We would eat and we would sit down and get a little nap, you know. Sometimes I would run home and come right back.

ROGER STEFFENS: Over the years, Coxson has given several different variations on how long the Wailers were involved with him. Their recordings for him began in June 1964 and continued through late 1966, when they began their own label, Wail'n Soul'm, angered by what they alleged was Coxson's financial mistreatment of the group.

COXSON DODD: I signed the Wailers as both performers and songwriters. The first contract was for five years. The second was for five, but they did about two of the second. We had a guardian sign the agreement for each of the three.

Bob boarded by me for at least four years. He stayed, I find boarding for him. Also, the others, the rest, when they came in and see what he had there, I had to open up the three-bedroom there and let them live there for a period of time. On Brentford Road. We had a three-bedroom at the back of the premises. They lived on Brentford Road for a number of years.

ROGER STEFFENS: Their tutor, Joe Higgs, began to feel slighted by his students, saying that they had used him and not properly acknowledged his crucial work in helping form the group.

JOE HIGGS: I think the first person who taught them to use people was Seeco Patterson. Why? I had had experiences with Coxson before, and I already excluded him from any association musically. Higgs and Wilson had done a chart-topper called "How Can I Be Sure" for Coxson. Years after that I come to do a song for Coxson again, called "There's A Reward." That riddim, that beat, was done by me in the same session the Wailers did "Lonesome Feeling." Same people did the voicing on both songs, including one of my baby mothers, Sylvia Richards, along with Bunny, Bob and Peter and Cherry Green and Beverley Kelso and me.

The Wailers originally went to Coxson without me, because I was not going to tell them to go to Coxson—I didn't want to go back somewhere I didn't like. Seeco thought that whatever my problem was with a producer was not their problem, so he decided to take them to Coxson. When they made "Simmer Down" for Coxson, they must have got 120–130 pounds in that time.

[Calypso singer] Lord Tanamo taught me to protect your rights as a writer. I taught Bob Marley and Bob Andy, Derrick Harriott and all them guys. I'm angry because a lot of people didn't know they could make money from that kind of angle, there was no knowledge among them about performing rights, and I was hearing this from Lord Tanamo and teaching it years after to other people.

ROGER STEFFENS: Despite the later disagreements and acrimony, Coxson Dodd was a crucial figure in the Wailers' early breakthrough and successes. He backed them with his very best musicians, picked interesting songs for them to cover and actively promoted their records through his sound systems and on the radio.

COXSON DODD: I'm the one who selected all these foreign pop hits for Bob, the more meaningful ones. [These include covers of Tom Jones's "What's New Pussycat," Dion and the Belmonts' "Teenager in Love" and the Beatles' "And I Love Her."] There are no unreleased dubplates [single-disc pressings of unreleased material on soft vinyl, good for only a few plays] of the Wailers with me. But they did mime the records at yard dances. That's how we got them launched.

ROGER STEFFENS: Engineer Dennis Thompson, who would tour with Bob during the final five years of his career, was an early supporter of the Wailers, playing their Studio One hits on his local sound system.

DENNIS THOMPSON: Me used to just fool around in the studio, mainly for the sound system, mixing dubplates. I had a sound system at that time but it had no name. You could never advertise the name. We knew enough people that we could get a crowd together. No need no name. And Bob would give me dubplates to play to check out the crowd's reaction. I remember we previewed "Burial." He played at a place called

VIP. I used to run a system called Merritone. Every time we played at VIP, it crowded up. And "Dreamland," we just played it and watched the crowd's reaction. We used to program stuff. We played four records you know and stick one in between, brand-new, and watch you react to it without telling them it was the Wailers. We had a club called Lotus. [A merchant named] KG had just bought this big place in Halfway Tree, and didn't know what to do with it. All they want is a record store, and we turned the back of it into this big discotheque. First discotheque Jamaica had ever seen. Coxson used to come down every Saturday night, 11:30. You see Coxson walk in with armload of dubplates. Duke Reid would send down all the stuff he recorded for a week, put on a reel-to-reel, riddim one side, vocals one side, and we dub it. Some people dance, used to turn off the riddim and they sing along. All them effects King Tubby do, I used to do long before that in '66, '67.

ROGER STEFFENS: Although Bunny Wailer would claim writer's credit, "Dreamland" was a record by a group called El Tempos titled "My Dream Island," given to them by Coxson to do over, composed by a man named Al Johnson. But the Wailers were doing more than covering songs; they were also writing original music. Junior remembers a collaborative writing environment; however, not everyone got the credit they deserved.

JUNIOR BRAITHWAITE: I wrote "It Hurts To Be Alone," and for the main part we all assisted in the recordings, in all the other tunes, too. We had to do what we felt, we worked together. But then, surprisingly, most of the tunes didn't come out written by the Wailin' Wailers, but like Bob and the Wailers, even though we all participated in that as a group. But, at the time we really hadn't expected no fortune and fame either. But I personally haven't seen a dime of royalties after all these years. I consider all of them songs a blessing or gifts from the Most High, Jah Rastafari.

SEGREE WESLEY: In the beginning, I thought Bunny was the best writer. And the only reason why I would say I thought Bunny was—

maybe now I'd say that—because Bunny was the only one I know that went to somewhat of a junior secondary school, more so than an elementary school. So, I know Bunny as a worker, he was the hardest worker musically and even though all of us always had a little pad that we write on, but, it was his dedication. Yeah. In the beginning I thought Bunny was the best.

BEVERLEY KELSO: We just go in the studio and you know the thing about it, I never see Bob sit down with pencil and paper and write. I don't know how we used to sing because he would just start singing the music, playing the guitar, Bob and Peter, just start playing the guitar. And they would come out there and say sing, sometimes I don't even know the song, but we just start to sing. I never see Bob sit down. And, no really rehearsal—rehearsal, nothing. They just come up with a song and that's it. Bob, Peter and Junior all contributed to the songs, they were all cowriters, they all shared. We'd just go in the studio and whatever have to be done we just sing right there for the band, right there and then, and they pick up and start to play the music. Bob would tell the instrumentalists what he wanted them to play. Or he would say do it in A this [A minor, A major, etc.]. We would, yes, rehearse some of the time. But just shortly before a recording. They would say, well, we're gonna do this song, and you would sing this and you would sing that.

I don't know if Bob get paid. I don't know if Bob get money every week, but I know I didn't get any. I know Peter didn't get any because Peter—it seems to me when money hand out, if Bunny did hand out, Peter know about it and Peter would get upset and say Bunny and Bob is brothers, so, they're keeping it in the family. I think this is one of the reasons why Peter leave the group. I never asked about money and I never made any money as a Wailer. We was having fun and whatever. The first stage show, at the Palace, my mother had to make my clothes.

ROGER STEFFENS: Coxson recalls the show taking place at the Ward Theatre, although Bunny backs up Beverley's memory that it was at the Palace.

COXSON DODD: How we got the Wailers launched with the crowd, it was with our sound systems. We had sessions at Success Club with several of my artists, and we used to tour the country parts, taking them also. And the first big show they did for me was at the Ward Theatre, I think it was Christmas. In the beginning they need a lot of polishing but Bob had a gift, you know, he was willing just to get his steps together. He had the makings. Their chief competitors at the time were the Techniques. When the Techniques came out with "Little Did You Know," man, it was really, really a big struggle for [the Wailers], because [their lead singer] Slim Smith was really a better vocalist than Bob, you know.

BUNNY WAILER: Our first appearance was at the Palace, Wailers were hot. When we hit the stage it was just fire. The place was packed till people was dripping off the walls. When we came on, half the people left their seats and were down almost to the edge of the stage, 'cause Wailers were like gymnastics. Flickings and splits and snap falls. All Wailers split. We did stuff where Bob would take me and throw me in the air and we'd split. Bob would kneel down, I would go over his back—splits. Peter would come there and bounce us like rubber balls, just comin' up and goin' down like that. I would run to him, he catches me, and as my belly cross his arm he just flicks and split.

The people never seen nothing like that in Jamaica before, a group hit the stage and people just dancin' and doing all kind of stuff and singin', 'cause we were really fit, fit. Fit.

ROGER STEFFENS: In the midst of their performance there was a massive power outage. Thugs descended upon the audience, stealing everything they could and mashing the show. The riot led to the Wailers recording what many consider to be the first "rude boy" song ever, "Hooligans." The song was written by someone who had entered it in a competition. The track somehow landed on Coxson's lap and he had the Wailers cover it. Veteran hornsman Bobby Ellis was an eyewitness to the mayhem at the Palace.

BOBBY ELLIS: When the power cut, nobody could leave. The man say nobody leave because power will come back. Anybody try come out is just a lot of bottle crash crash crash. You haffe get back into your seat. Must have been around one o'clock before they eventually realize it no come back.

BUNNY WAILER: Me say me never see bottle fling so, and all Palace screen mash up. Certain man instrument mash up. And the chair dem mash up. It comes like the promoter, Coxson, lose back all the money what him make, to fix back up Palace Theatre. Him rue!

ROGER STEFFENS: Third World's Cat Coore witnessed another early onstage mishap.

CAT COORE: [Bob] fell at Ward Theatre one time at Nuggets for the Needy show. I'll never forget that. He fell onstage, on his back. It was a live televised concert. Must have tapes of that. A telethon.

SEGREE WESLEY: At Ward Theatre, I remember Downbeat Coxson put on shows and also at Regal Theatre. And the audience acceptance of the group was good because you must remember that when Jamaica first heard about the Wailers they didn't hear about them as the Wailers entertaining. They heard about them as the Wailers, as a recording artist. So they came [to the live shows] with [hit songs] like "Simmer Down" and music like that. So they were accepted right away. I know they didn't have to go through the competitive setting where they'll boo you or whatever because they would just appear on shows, which you appear and you entertain and you go. But they were good. And they worked on their wares.

PETER TOSH: You see, when you go up on stage them love you mon, cho! Them stone you with the herb, money. One time I was performing at the Ward Theatre, Wailers. Well now, me start sing, bwoi! Is just all kind of money come up on stage. Poof! Drop beside me some, poof! Blood-claat! [Jamaica's worst curse, literally "blood cloth."] Me look at some two-and-six-pence piece lick me head, and all them things. By the hundreds! Why, me say, me couldn't do that, so I stop sing and just go on and pick them up. You know what me pick up man, pick up me two pocket *full!* And before I come off the stage, it was begged out! Every man in the audience come beg it out back. Just beg out everything! Man just beg it out, and me look and me have about two-and-six left in me hand, with the two pocket full of money, yeah mon! But those amusing still, 'cause me just laugh.

Me have some very fantastic experience on stage, mon. One time me was performing at the Palace Theatre and the people was waiting to see the Wailers, and them can't see the Wailers, and a band named the Vikings was playing and the people were, "We want the Wailers! Wailers!" And them can't see no Wailers. The time, we was in the dressing room waiting, but we had to wait until that band finish. Well the people was impatient and some blood-claat back like this—WOOF! [Furious pitching motion.] Man haffe run off stage, mon. Yes, mon. Every instrument mash up. 'Cause the people want to see the Wailers.

BEVERLEY KELSO: My first show with them, the audience react by stoning us. The show started and the next thing we had a blackout. After the blackout, we started like about half an hour later, light came back on. And then when the show started again, Bob coming from one side like he was flying. Peter coming from one side like they were flying, flapping their arms. And when they started to sing, right there, the light went out again. And the place was stormed with bottles, whatever they could throw on the stage. And Bob, they have to run backstage and we were in the backstage for a long time. We couldn't come out until everything, everybody come out of the theater. But that night the theater was ram-packed, jam-packed. They get a good turnout that night, but we just didn't sing.

The second show was actually the same thing in Montego Bay. We drive actually one whole day for the stage show. When we went there they didn't have no music box. They didn't have no light. Something was going on. Bob tried to calm down that crowd. He said we would sing without certain things. And I think that was a setup. I was saying I wonder if Coxson want to get the money and then not going to come up and then it just break up like that because we didn't get to sing. That was the second show we didn't get to do nothing again. It was a disaster right there again. The next thing, the best show we did was the one at Sombrero. That was a club so they had their own sound system in place and everything else, right? And the audience response was great. Great.

So I only did three live shows. The first was the Palace. The second was a dance hall thing in Montego Bay. And the third was at the Sombrero.

CHERRY GREEN: I only played on one live show. Coxson give us five pound to buy a dress. We were going to play at the Sombrero, me and Beverley, we had the same dress. But when they went and take the picture for the album they didn't carry me, they just sneak away. Maybe I was working that day. I used to work at Caribbean Preserving. They do grapefruit. It was like a season job. So when the season come you got to work. So I can buy my clothes and my shoes. And I had a child to take care of. I used to make seven to eight pounds. That was big money in them days.

ROGER STEFFENS: As the Wailers started to perform and record more, Cherry had to step away from the group sometimes.

CHERRY GREEN: You feel good to hear your voice on the radio. I can remember my daughter, she probably was three, and every time she hear "Lonesome Feeling" she say, hear my mother. Hear my mother! When I leave there she probably was four. She was born in '61 and I was gone. I leave her with my mother and I just go rent a room somewhere in Jones Town, me and a friend, Doreen. So by 1965 I had stopped singing with them because sometimes they go and record and I'm not there. And they didn't say to me Cherry, we going to the session tomorrow, next week or when. Cherry gone to work and they just gone. They just leave me. So, I got to go where I make money. So I go and do my thing and they do their own thing. And they was like, they didn't have any responsibility. I had a responsibility.

BEVERLEY KELSO: We didn't do too much show because during that time was like the group was kinda drifting away from Mr. Dodd. Everything started happening so fast.

ROGER STEFFENS: As the Wailers began to be seen more and more by the public at dances, clubs and theaters, their records continued to dominate the charts. Bob Marley was beginning to be recognized as an important new artist who didn't just cover foreign music but was capable of composing his own classics.

BEVERLEY KELSO: After I was in the group, I used to go see them, but I never see anyone carrying them on their shoulders, standing ovations. They were just another group. They could have been the Heptones. They could have been the Gaylads. They could have been the Maytals. But the Wailers really did stand out as *the* group on the island. They stand out because of the music, hits.

ROGER STEFFENS: Among the dozens of artists at Studio One during this period was a brilliant stylist named Alton Ellis. He had started his career in a hit-making duo with Eddie Parkins. Alton became the king of rocksteady, and, early on, tried to give Marley advice about working with Coxson "Downbeat" Dodd. We spoke on the *Reggae Beat* show in 1983, two years after Bob's passing.

ALTON ELLIS: Bob is just something else, you know. It's going to take up a long time fe I tell you what I know about Bob. Bob is not an easy person to get along with. Bob is strong, very strong. Bob is sure of himself and need no help from when he was a youth. I'll tell you the first conversation I had with Bob. He came to Downbeat studio and did a couple of records. He was living up Third Street and I was living at Fifth Street. Joe Higgs live at Third Street and Joe Higgs help tutor him, 'cause Joe was out there before even me. I was passing Bob's house and saw them rehearsing under a tree, and I say to him, "My bredren, I want to tell you something. I love the song you do, but you see that producer what name Downbeat? Watch him." And to my surprise, Bob stop and say to me, nicely, "Don't need any advice. I can manage when I get to Downbeat." And I left there that day spinning,

The author with Alton Ellis, the king of rocksteady, holding a stack
of his singles in the Reggae Archives, Los Angeles, June 1997.

how him just answer me so abrupt. Is years after I realize it was the
positiveness within the man, the strength within the man. So all my
little advice wasn't necessary, 'cause him did pass that.

Bob is a man, you go in the studio one morning and say, "Hail
Dread," and pass him, and you come out in the evening and don't talk

to him, he's angry as if you is the most enemy for months. And big tall guys afraid of Bob, everybody afraid of Bob, and him never fight yet. Him don't fight. He was so powerful spiritually that even big guys stand back. The right word at the right time every time make even the big mountain guys step back. That's the man I'm telling you about, not the music. Bob can put a story into words so easy! Things that are around you every day and you would step past it, and Bob would see it as a big story when him put the lyrics together. He can tie the lyrics with the music so the music embrace the lyric so close that it form a melodious flow. This is a problem I find with a lot of singers, their lyrics is so strong and without the combination of it and the music together it sound as if—it doesn't come over. Something missing, you know. Bob have that combination of embracing lyrics with melody. It's only the Beatles I put in front of Bob as recording artists.

ROGER STEFFENS: King Sporty, real name Noel Williams, was an early colleague of Bob's at Studio One. He moved to Miami in the 1970s and opened a studio there. Bob heard Sporty sing a song he wrote called "Buffalo Soldier," and made his own version which remained in the vault until after he passed, becoming his biggest posthumous hit.

KING SPORTY: I recognized Bob as a messenger early on. We grew up together. We know who could take it further. I saw what happened on stage. We saw who got outsung, we saw where the dimension was. I was with the game from it started. I was there in the back room, there was a room that Clement Dodd had at Studio One, and we were the only ones who could go in the back room, me, Bunny Wailer, Peter Tosh, Bob Marley, the Gaylads, B. B. Seaton, Leroy Sibbles. We went in the back room 'cause there was a piano back there. Other than that, the guys had to stay out. I used to audition the singers before they even could come through the door. I did that for Dodd, I did it for Duke Reid. At that time I didn't know that I had one of the most important jobs that is up for grabs in the United States.

ROGER STEFFENS: In 1965, the Wailers had the number one, two, three, five and seven songs in the Top Ten at once: "Simmer Down," "It Hurts To Be Alone," "Rude Boy," "Jailhouse," and "Put It On." During this time they became friends with Bob Andy, a prolific singer and songwriter. On his website, he shared an intimate interlude with the Wailers.

BOB ANDY: There was a room at Studio One where we used to listen to records. Coxson would give artists music to listen to on this turntable and speakers, but there was another room between Coxson's inner office and the music room where you could go and lock yourself in and

Bob Andy, composer and singer, in Kingston, Jamaica, displaying his page in the catalog of the author's Reggae Archives exhibition at the *Queen Mary*, July 2001.

no one else could enter. The Wailers had access to that, and I did too. One particular day, I was the witness to a very special performance. It was like being let into a secret. I was very high from smoking, and they were always high too. It was the first time I had seen each of the Wailers with a guitar, and each time I remember this, it's like remembering a dream. I sat there, and they were just messing around with various songs for a while, but finally it climaxed with a song called "Ten To One," which I later found out was a Curtis Mayfield song.

Bob sang the first line, then Bunny came in on the second, and all three came in on the next line. Peter sang a line, and then all three sang in harmony, then Bob and Bunny sang solo again. When they started that song, I saw a side of the Wailers I felt no one else had seen. It was like my own personal revelation. I've never heard music so beautiful, and I've never seen such love and camaraderie in all my life. I knew then that the Wailers were special people, but they were special by being the Wailers, as a unit. When I reflect on that occasion, it was divine. It was like being on a spaceship, listening to the music of the spheres. I was spellbound, and that memory will stay with me forever.

CHAPTER 5

Love and Affection

ROGER STEFFENS: The young woman who would become Bob Marley's wife, Rita Anderson, was raised alongside a cemetery on the edge of Trench Town. When she became pregnant out of wedlock, the baby's father was sent to England. After she gave birth to her daughter, Sharon, she went on to sing in the Soulettes, a Studio One group mentored by Marley. She would give birth to three of Bob's children, eventually becoming something of a protector to him and suffering his many extramarital liaisons.

According to her autobiography, *No Woman, No Cry,* Rita's relationship with the Wailers came about because they would pass by her house en route to work. When one day the trio she had put together sang for them, Peter suggested they come along to Coxson's studio and audition. The producer liked what he heard and asked Bob to help coach them. At first it was all business, but the more time they spent together, the closer she became to Bob, although Peter had been the first to make some shockingly bold advances toward her.

Rita's cousin, Constantine "Dream" "Vision" Walker, is one of the unheralded "original" Wailers whose voice can be heard on some of the most moving of the group's works. Beginning with Rita Marley and another young woman in the Soulettes, Vision stepped in for Bob Marley for several months in 1966 when Bob left to work in Delaware. His distinctive tenor is featured on such Wailers classics as "Sunday Morning," "Let Him Go," "I'm The Toughest," "Rock Sweet Rock,"

"Dancing Shoes," "I Stand Predominate," "Dreamland," and "I Need You." I caught up with Vision at the One World Music Festival in Aspen, Colorado, in September 1994, where he was performing as part of Bunny's backing band.

VISION WALKER: The way my nicknames come about, when my mother went to the doctor and he told her she was pregnant, she said, "Oh, doctor, that's a dream." Because she didn't believe that she could get pregnant, she was in her thirties. So when I went to Trench Town and started to sing with the Wailers, a brother named Fowlie one day said, "Not a dream, man, a vision." Because old men dream and young men see visions. That's how the name Vision came into play.

I was born the 19th of October, 1950—the same date as Peter Tosh. I started singing at thirteen. My whole family was musicians. One day Rita had a song named "Blood Stain" and she said, "Come and

Rita Marley's cousin Vision Walker sang with the Wailers during Bob Marley's
absence from Jamaica in 1966, and is a co-founder of the Soulettes,
Rita Marley's trio. Aspen, Colorado, September 1994.

help me sing harmony on this." And we started singing. It sounded like something that had been done before, professional. Marlene "Precious" Gifford went to the same school as Rita, Dunrobin. Rita came up with the name the Soulettes. The first time we did something with people listening on the airwaves was with Vere Johns [a radio amateur hour program]. We sang "What's Your Name" [a cover of the American R & B classic by Don and Juan]. When we harmonized that, it used to just knock people out, that sound just like the record! Our inspirations included Glenn Miller, the Impressions, Curtis Mayfield. He's a good writer. I respect him.

We met the Wailers through a friend named Andy who used to hear me and Rita sing. One day he decided to take us to Coxson, he knew Coxson, Coxson liked the group. He said, "We could have a little something in there." And that's how we met the Wailers, because they were signed to Coxson too at the time. We used to see them pass our yard in Trench Town going to Coxson. But we hardly knew them. But it was always an event to watch them, because it was like a gang going up the road! Like pied pipers, because they would walk and Peter would have his guitar in his hand, and kids and people start to follow them, because of the vibes the men moved with. We used to go through Kingston from east to west, me and Bunny, and sing for people. Not for money but for the grounation, because it was a Rastafari [thing], that unity we had, and we touched everybody with it. I can't really remember making any money, because it never really came into my hand, it came through Rita and then to me and there was nothing left.

ROGER STEFFENS: The "grounation" that Vision refers to means an expression of Rastfarian beliefs. However, Rita's oft-repeated account of their first meeting is challenged by Beverley Kelso, who was there throughout the initial encounters between the Wailers and Rita.

BEVERLEY KELSO: Rita tell a lot of story because she said that she meet us through she see a lot of people used to run behind us saying the Wailers, the Wailers, the Wailers. And that's how she meet us. It's

a lie. We weren't being followed through the streets. Because nobody
didn't, there was so many different singers in Trench Town, nobody
didn't bow to none of us. Nobody didn't follow us around and calling
the Wailers, the Wailers. We were just normal people. We were just
walking, going to the studio like normal people.

During that time, going back and forth to the studio, that's when
we used to pass by Rita's house. And during that time, Rita used to
stand by her gate with her baby in her hand and she used to wave to
us and Bob. Bob, Peter and Bunny they would bust out laughing when
they see Rita wave to us and you'd hear Bob say, "What a ugly black
girl." Bob would say, "What a ugly black girl! Who she call to?" And
Peter and Bunny would just join up busting a big laugh and you hear
one say, "What a monkey." Yeah, they used to call her a monkey, they
used to call her names. And that used to upset me so bad, you know?

When we were going, most of the time when we used to see Rita
is in the afternoon. So, she would stay there, standing there with her
baby in her hand, like she's standing waiting to see us, most of the
time when we were going, and I used to wave back to her. So until I
start to stop, you know, it looks so bad that she wave to us and I start
to stop and play with the baby and things like that. And then I would
run and catch them up. And when I'd run and catch them they would
say, "You want baby? Stop stopping at black girl-—you can't get no
baby as long as you're coming to the studio. Stop, stop with the black
girl, a pickney [child] you want?" And they would carry on. Carry on
and carry on until one evening now, I stop and I tell them, and then
I didn't run and catch them up that evening and Rita said to me she
want to sing a song. And I said, "What's the name of the song?" And
she said, "Opportunity." So, I tell her to sing a little part of it for me
and she sing a little part of it. And then I run and catch them and I
tell them that she want to sing a song. And when I went to Coxson I
tell him that I have a friend and she want to sing a song. And he said,
"What's the name of the song?" I said, "I don't know, but she sing a

little part for me." And I sing a little part for him and he say to me bring her, bring her come next day.

So the morning we was going to the studio, we had a session that morning and I stopped by and tell her and she said that she couldn't come in the morning, but she would come in the afternoon when Dream and Precious [Marlene Gifford, Rita's schoolmate] come home from school, because it was three of them, the Soulettes. So, he said, bring them. So she said they go there after they come from school. I asked her if she know where Coxson is and I told her 13 Brentford Road and that evening I was looking out for them. So she come and I take her in to Mr. Dodd. And that was it. Rita, the Soulettes, they did record the song and it was another family joined the group with us now. Rita wasn't no black girl anymore. Rita was Rita now, you know?

ROGER STEFFENS: Rita and the Soulettes joined the entourage of people involved with the Wailers at Studio One.

BEVERLEY KELSO: Rita joining with us, wasn't singing with us, but we'd all be in the studio together. Then the next person come and join in with us was Marcia Griffiths. Marcia come and that level off when Marcia started to sing with Bob Andy and Tony Gregory.

ROGER STEFFENS: Coxson Dodd has his own version of the story.

COXSON DODD: The Soulettes came to me separately and after working with them, they were all youths, I said get together, they would work together well. Bob was my main man somehow, so it's possible I could've asked him to help them along the way. Because some of their recordings I hear Bob's voice in the background also.

ROGER STEFFENS: Rita Marley told a British journalist that after her group, the Soulettes, signed with Coxson Dodd, Bob was "sort of the boss for us then, and he was like a father to me from a protective point of view. Like seeing to it that I wasn't attacked by any of the males around and keeping the producers away, which was a great help for me, which made me enter into the business in a respectful manner."

BEVERLEY KELSO: Some people say that Peter and Rita hook up. Well, to be honest about that, Peter and Rita didn't hook up. No. I know at one point it's like Peter watching Rita, Bob watching Rita, it's like the two of them in tug-of-war, which one was gonna get Rita? She wasn't the black ugly girl no more, so, which one of them was gonna get Rita? This tug-of-war thing. I was watching, I didn't say anything, but there was a tug-of-war thing going along.

SEGREE WESLEY: Rita's interest at the early stages, I know, was more a love interest. She wanted to be part of Bob's life. I mean, that's what I know. I mean, it's not that the Wailers were that famous per se at that time. They were doing recordings, they was just another little group, you know? There were times when she'd come down and we guys, like, doing a little singing in the corner or in the kitchen or whatever. She would be there lingering, it's like, waiting for Bob, you know? She didn't want to go, you understand, because she had to walk up to maybe from First Street to Seventh Street—that's seven blocks and then maybe another ten blocks. So she had to wait in the wee hours of the night. And when we're working he doesn't let anything come in front of whatever he's doing, rehearsal. Even when we're gone, I would go to Boys Town to play, he'd still be there strumming the guitar and you'd come back you'd see him in the same place. You'd swear it was madness. Yes, he was obsessed with it. The group wasn't there and he would sit there. He wouldn't wait for the group to do any kind of work.

ROGER STEFFENS: When I interviewed Bunny Wailer in 1990 he insisted many times that Rita's intention from the very start of their relationship was "to break up the Wailers." Segree Wesley demurs.

SEGREE WESLEY: To say Rita wanted to break it up, I think maybe Bunny or the rest, maybe it's difference of opinion. Okay, she may be in love with an individual at the time and that would take away from a group's rehearsal sessions. So, then it's gonna automatically affect the other guys and they'd say what is she doing, you know? Why is she waiting? Or whatever.

I know there was no question about [Bob] loving women. He's a girl's man, I know that. As a kid, you know, you run around, you play with different girls or whatever. But, when I knew Bob I think his first love was his music and soccer. I mean, we all had our little girlfriends and whatever, but I never see him romp with him and a lot of different girls, because he'll go anywhere to do a little rehearsal, you know? It's not like going to a stage show or a contest because he never appeared in any major contests. It was just straight into the recording studio. And from there he grew.

ROGER STEFFENS: Beverley witnessed a frightening encounter between Peter Tosh and Rita at this time.

BEVERLEY KELSO: With Peter being with Rita, it wasn't of Rita's will. How the studio make up, there was a little room on the side. We all would go into that side room and rehearse, relax, do anything in that side room. Well, at this day Peter was in there. I see when Rita went in; as I said, anybody, everybody could go in there. Once we didn't have any session going on, I feel like I want to sit down. So, I went in. When I was going inside I meet up on something. Rita's back turned to me, Peter could see me face, face on. So, Peter was forcing his self on her, it was like hold down, take way thing. It's like something, well, because Peter and Rita wasn't together. They was friends. It was like hold down like he wanted to have sex or whatever and she was pushing him off, So, when Peter see me now, I come in on them sudden, I just take my time and back out and I come out smiling. Bunny over on the other side was looking at me and see me smiling, I'm taking my time coming out. Bunny come around wanted to go inside and I wouldn't let him. You know, because I didn't want him to see what I see. So, I wouldn't let him. So, I was like backing him up, backing him back up. So Bunny realized something was going on. Until this day [2003] I never tell Peter, I never tell Bunny, I never tell nobody. I'm saying it on the tape now because—because they're giving Rita a play for that [i.e., she was being accused of coming on to Peter], which is not fair.

You could see that Peter was pushing his self on her. But I think what come out of that, after Bunny didn't get to go in—it's like Peter didn't get to do anything, so Rita came out after that. So I think what happened, Bunny realized what was happening and maybe he said it to Peter during the time we were still there going back and forth singing and all of that. Until, I don't think they say that Bob hear because if Bob hear about it I don't think Bob would get close to Rita.

But Bob get Rita during the same time. As I said, Peter was after Rita and Bob was after Rita so Peter probably was showing, trying to see which one of them could get her first by probably forcing his self on her, you know? But as far as I see nothing didn't come out of it because Bob, she automatically play into Bob and everybody know that the both of them was going together. Because as I said, Bunny said he liked me. But at the same time Bunny liked me, Precious come along with Rita so Bunny was going with Precious and Bob was going with Rita. So in the evening now, I would go home by myself and they would hang out with Rita and Precious because they were boyfriend and girlfriend.

ROGER STEFFENS: During this time, Rita was still in active correspondence with Sharon's father in England. When Bob caught Vision with a letter from Rita to her baby father, he grabbed it away from him and that ended their relationship. Bob now considered Rita *his* girl, and acted as a father to Sharon. Meanwhile, the Soulettes began to record, scoring their first hit with a song called "I Love You, Baby," featuring another precocious young singer, Delroy Wilson, on backing vocals. The Wailers at the same time were trimming down, leaving the women in the group behind. But Bob maintained contact with Beverley and often confided in her about the troubles he was having with Rita.

BEVERLEY KELSO: One thing I know and I would tell the world, Bob have a confidence in me. I don't know what Bob see in me but when he feel hurt about any little thing, after we grow up and I stopped going to the studio he would come to me. I didn't know that he wasn't talking to Peter, he wasn't talking to Bunny, he wasn't telling them anything. Like when he get in fight with Rita and any little thing wrong go down between him and Rita he would come to me. When Rita get pregnant and he didn't know what to do, he come to me. I was the one who tell him, when Rita get pregnant, to go to Dodd. So when Bob went to Mr. Dodd with that, he come back to me saying they're getting married. And the date was gonna be such and such and I am invited. Bunny and Peter didn't know. That Saturday afternoon Peter come with, "Oh, you couldn't tell me that Bob and Rita get married? I don't know why you didn't tell me anything." I said, "I didn't go to the wedding. I was invited but I was sick." Bob never talk to me about why he didn't invite them.

SEGREE WESLEY: I didn't hear about the marriage. When I first heard, these are all rumors, hearsay: "'Cause he was going away Bob asked to marry Rita 'cause she was pregnant" and stuff like that. But Bob never mentioned it. I don't know if in later years they made something legal where they were married. I figure Bob getting married to little Rita, he would have involved his friends unless they just went and did a quiet thing on the side.

It's weird, man, 'cause I really can't see Bob getting married without telling some of us at that point in time. Bunny didn't hear about it, Peter didn't hear about it. Beverley was close to Rita and it was probably Rita who told her about the wedding. But I still can't see Bobby going through a wedding and not where you invite your friends or you tell your friends. People you share a lot with. This is why I'm from that connotation, it must have been true that Coxson Downbeat arranged a wedding. But we didn't hear about it. As a matter of fact, I didn't even think he was married. Even at the point in time when we heard, I said I didn't think he was married. I said it's just a sham or something.

BUNNY WAILER: Every Wailer had made a pledge not to get married until he could afford to or never, so when Bob got married, he broke a rule of the Wailers. His mother didn't have knowledge of it neither. Me and Peter were at Tata's [Vincent "Tata" Ford] smoking some herb, rehearsing. A man come say, "Bob gettin' married up a church. Me say

the little black girl, Rita." Make me know Bob trimmed and look different like a man coming out of the army. Everybody marvel, everybody a
wonder what is. Me never see Bob until about three day later he come
with this apology. Say him sorry, no feel no way, but there are certain
things that man haffe do that he can't even tell his friends—and we
just accept that.

We wouldn't have agreed with Bob and we show him reasons why
him couldn't do that. That embarrass the whole of us. 'Cause Bob
married in his stage suit, not a suit what him could afford. But he
was tricked into a goddamn situation. How that marriage made was
not clean.

ROGER STEFFENS: In 1962 Bob's mother, Cedella Marley, moved to
Wilmington, Delaware, to marry a man named Edward Booker. For
the next few years she tried to arrange paperwork for Bob to join her
there. It finally came through in February 1966. Rita says that he was
afraid if he didn't marry her she'd find another boyfriend. Others claim
Coxson told Bob if he decided to stay in the States, he wouldn't be able
to bring Rita there unless they were married. An alleged "farewell
show" was arranged before Bob emigrated, the date of which is the
cause of much confusion.

RITA MARLEY: It wasn't a send-off. It was really a concert they had
the Wailers on at the Stadium. It was the same day we got married
on February 11, and he left on the 12th. I *know* that! [Although in her
book she maintains they were married on February 10 and Bob left
two days after that.]

BEVERLEY KELSO: But he didn't leave Jamaica the day after the wedding. He was in Jamaica for a long while. He did a show. But he didn't
leave the day after, because Rita was pregnant.

BUNNY WAILER: Bob's last show before he left for Delaware was the
Battle of the Giants show. It was the first time a show was held at the
National Stadium. There was an echo in the stadium that night, that

Rita Marley with editor/publisher CC Smith at the office of *The Beat*
magazine in Eagle Rock, Los Angeles, November 1996.

when you sang on the mic it fed back. So it confuse most of the artists
that went on stage, you could hear it. Well, we started to study, rehearsing it off mic. So we come on stage and we stood about two yards from
the mic and the band rolled off and we started singing and it was pure
beauty. There was a reverb on the voice because of that echo. We start
with "One Love," "Love And Affection," "Simmer Down," "Put It On."
Then we did a couple of slow songs, "It Hurts To Be Alone," "I'm Still
Waiting." We had a little plan for "I'm Still Waiting" where when Bob
said, "My feet," his feet just fell from under him and we caught him
before him hit the ground and just bring him back on mic. Me say
half of the stadium come down—all police barriers move. Then we go
right into "Rude Boy," and the police disappear. Police have to take off
them hat and duck, because is pure bottle to all who have a police hat.
And the barrier mash up, so everybody was now down near the stage
and on the stage, all the roughneck and the ragamuffin and the rude

boy—like a storm. There was no riot, no fight. But police get a beatin' still when we sang "Jailhouse keep empty, rude boy get plenty, baton stick get shorter, rude boy get taller." Police have to take off him hat and don't be police at that moment.

Is somewhere 'bout in December '65 Bob leave here, early or middle part Bob left.

CHAPTER 6

Rasta Shook Them Up

ROGER STEFFENS: During Marley's absence in 1966, Jamaica was abuzz about the imminent visit of Ethiopian Emperor Haile Selassie I. The belief in his godhead was a result of Jamaicans interpreting Bible passages that foretold the second coming of Jesus, this time in his regal character of King of Kings, Lord of Lords and Conquering Lion of the Tribe of Judah. When an Ethiopian nobleman known as Ras Tafari (Amharic for "Head Creator") was crowned emperor in 1930, he took as his title King of Kings, Lord of Lords and Conquering Lion of the Tribe of Judah. His new name, Haile Selassie, translated as "Power of the Trinity."

When Italy invaded Ethiopia, pictures appeared in the Jamaican papers of dreadlocked warriors known as "Nyabinghi men"—a name that meant "death to black and white oppressors"—hurling spears at Italian tanks. In emulation of them, the newly named Rastafarian adherents began to grow their locks too, as a covenant urged by the Bible. They kept an "ital livity," or natural way of life, eschewing meat and shellfish, and giving thanks and praise to the Almighty through their use of marijuana (ganja) as a sacramental way of unifying with the universal spirit. Composed mainly of the poor and dispossessed, these early Rasta lived primarily in the bush, and when they came into the city they were roundly despised and feared, accused of being "blackheart men," who reputedly ate little children and flouted all the colonial laws.

They had their own language, too, based on the holy trinity of word, sound and power. One conceives the word and when it is sounded from a pure heart it is the very power of creation itself. "Weakheart conception haffe drop," goes one of their favorite expressions. That is, if you have an impure motive, whatever you are saying is doomed to death and destruction. Everything in the Rasta lingua must therefore be positive and constructive. And there must be no separation among mankind—thus the locution "I and I," meaning you and I, God and I, God in I, because we are all one manifestation of the true and living God. "Yes I," say the Rasta, because they are really talking to themselves. Thus there are no plurals in Rasta-speak, underlining the "I"-nity of all. They don't go to a university but to an i-niversity; nor would they visit a library, rather a true-brary, because lies lie buried in a lie-brary.

In addition, Zion is meant to be achieved here on earth. No dying to see Jesus. "We know and we understand Almighty God is a living man," the Wailers would sing in their anthem "Get Up Stand Up." Selassie's visit led to a single recorded by Peter just a few days after His Majesty left the island, called "Rasta Shook Them Up," the Wailers' first record specifically mentioning Selassie.

Among the first people to introduce Bob to Rasta was a relative of Rita's.

BEVERLEY KELSO: This Rasta business started with Rita's brother. I think Rita's brother used to go to University of the West Indies. He didn't comb his hair. I remember it's like he used to preach to them, telling them things like Babylon, whatever he used to preach to them. That preaching start and they start to smoke more frequently now.

SEGREE WESLEY: I wouldn't say that ganja affected Bob. I know he was an adherent smoker so to speak, I know like in the mornings you'd see him, he take a smoke and he says, gotta have a slug. But I never see where it affected him in any way.

BEVERLEY KELSO: The smoking start coming in more and more and more and more. And then they start saying Rastafari and talking, you know, wild talk now about this Rasta business until Bob start to grow his hair, Peter start, Bunny, they're not combing their hair anymore. And I start to pull away 'cause they passing the spliff to me and I back away from it. I didn't want no part of that.

ROGER STEFFENS: Bob's eight months in Delaware saw the remaining Wailers record occasionally with the Soulettes, whose early recordings were distributed throughout Kingston by Rita, riding her bicycle.

VISION WALKER: Wailers and Soulettes had a sound that was building up from the first time we meet. We rehearsed together, so it was a buildup to that. When Bob went to America I replaced him. Bob didn't know when he left that I would be singing in the group. But it was a unity. It is a family. It wasn't just music.

ROGER STEFFENS: It was a politically restive time in the ghettos as they were being transformed in "garrisons" aligned with the two main political parties. The CIA was funneling guns to the right-wing government and the opposition PNP was beginning to arm themselves for protection. Economic opportunities were limited, and many Jamaicans were moving to the U.S. or to England, which actively recruited them for menial jobs there. A new underclass of disaffected youth came to be known as "rude boys." Vision Walker sang on two of the fiercest rude boy songs of the era, "Let Him Go" and "I Stand Predominate."

VISION WALKER: The definition of a rude boy in those times—a bad man was measured by the way he protected his community, he didn't need a gang. I stand alone. "I Stand Predominant." Whatever come, it comes, but you have to face it yourself. That's a bad man. He doesn't need a gang. And that's where the Wailers were, they were into their individual thing.

When we cut our songs we did three takes at the most. First take is always the best take. Because one-track recording days is what we come from, everybody playing and singing at the same time, or else every man got vexed. And you don't want to get the whole studio, the

Skatalites, angry at you; you have to do your part. They were getting paid by the side.

When I did "Don't Look Back," the version of the Temptations song, in 1966 with Peter, that was the time that I remember that Peter first used to play his guitar in the actual sessions. He had a kind of country-folk style, real sweet. Then there was an unreleased song called "Little Boy Blue." It was like a theme song for I and I [me and my bandmates] because of the lyrics. "You're crying little boy blue, you've lost your mommy." Because we are all like motherless children as boys coming up. Most of those guys don't have parents. That song was a very touching song, but it never came out. Politics.

RITA MARLEY: "Little Boy Blue." Whoosh! That's a Wailers song! They took it from the Impressions. Oooh! That was one of the things that they would always rehearse in the evening. And it was the harmony just like the Impressions. [It] has an Impressions sound. Because during that time all the Wailers listened to was the Impressions. And the Soulettes would listen to the Supremes. "Little Boy Blue" came from an Impressions song, just like "Keep On Moving."

VISION WALKER: It was doing everything for the love of the music. We didn't really know what it would be like. We were just doing our work. It's the Rasta vibes, you know, not political. The forces of evil in Jamaica tried to distort Rasta and make us look bad, and we can't get work, and they say things like "dirty boy from Trench Town." But it didn't take form until the man took his covenant [grew his locks].

ROGER STEFFENS: The imposingly dreadlocked Mortimo Planno was a major Rasta influence in Trench Town at this time. His yard at 35 Fifth Street contained a library of books about Ethiopian history and the Black Power movement, and became a magnet for sufferers and uptown youth as well, often including students from the University of the West Indies. Peter and Bunny were frequent visitors during Bob's absence and he avidly joined them at Planno's upon his return, yearning to learn more about the Emperor's life.

Marley's Rasta mentor Mortimo Planno and Vincent "Tata" Ford, alleged composer of "No Woman No Cry," at the University of Technology in Kingston, July 2001.

Peter, Bunny, Rita and Vision were present for the most momentous occasion in the troubled history of Rasta's quest for acceptance, when His Majesty, Haile Selassie I, the Rasta God, came to visit Jamaica during a tour of the Caribbean on April 21, 1966. There was widespread hope among the Jamaican establishment that Selassie would publicly deny the divinity ascribed to him by members of the Rastafarian faith. Rasta elders who met with him claimed that he told them, "I am who you say I am."

The reception given Selassie was unprecedented. Rasta camped out for days in advance at the Kingston airport, and the air was ripe with the smoke from thousands of chalices burning the holy herb. When the plane landed, the throng surged past the barriers and struck such fear into Selassie that he remained on board for nearly an hour before Mortimo Planno himself came aboard and urged him to show himself to the crowd. Pictures show Planno in a white robe preceding the Emperor down the gangplank to his ecstatic worshippers.

Rita Marley's eyewitness account of this life-changing event came in a private discussion with me in 1991 backstage at a nightclub in Ventura, California.

RITA MARLEY: Well, it was just a revelation, I see it as a revelation that came forth toward a doubtful mind. I was on my way to the airport, right by the cement company, when we heard that the motorcade was on its way, that it had left the airport and was coming, so everybody stood where they were. It was raining, and the sun was shining, and everything was happening. I went to the hairdresser the day before, and my hair was all permed and got wet and I said, "What the hell, why am I wetting up my hair and looking like this, just to see this little man? Who the hell is this man! What's important about this man, now? I feel stupid." But then again, another voice say, "No, if you feel that you are out here for being stupid, you are not, you are here for a purpose." And I say, "Well, the only thing can make me really believe this man symbolize himself with God or could be the returned Messiah or the Jesus Christ who should come in a new name, the only thing is if I see the nail print in his hands." I was so stubborn because I'd been reading. After we got married and Bob left, all I end up doing was reading and looking forward to either going up to Delaware or Bob coming back.

When His Majesty's car reach me it reach a slowdown and the man look right at me and went like this [waves, palm outward]. And then I look, reading eyes, he was talking to me. And I felt a surge of *zoom!* come through me and I look again, and he went like this [waves] and when I look, in the middle of the man's hand was the mark of the nail print that I said to myself was the only thing would convince me that this man is what they profess him to be. 'Cause he has not said anything about himself so far but they profess him to be. And I was convinced that this man was the Christ that I'm looking for. And when he waved and I see it, I was like a lamb, I was changed instantly. I mean all my power went somewhere else. The Rita that I knew, by the time I went home, she was gone somewhere else. She was nowhere to be found again.

Same time I go home and write Bob a long letter, say Bob, some-thing is happening here. Bunny and Peter were quite conscious before, in terms of being black, but there wasn't any dominant Rasta system in there. They were still pretty young boys, and the thing about not eating pork—Bob would insist, "Rita, don't eat pork, don't eat this, you mustn't eat that." But he didn't want me to stop pressing my hair because he figured that it fit me so well, and I must keep doing my hair, but just realize that God is black. But after I see this thing that day, I went back home and I started to read the Bible now, Isaiah, where it tell about the false beauty and the daughters of Zion who walk with a crisp tinkling of the feet, and what's abomination from. And I said, "Cho! This is a reality." 'Cause I look back and I said, "I'm gonna have to tell Bob about this." So I wrote to him, and he wrote back to me to say I'm getting crazy! He said, "You must be getting crazy, Rita!"

VISION WALKER: We all went to see Selassie, me and Rita and Pre-cious were together, we walk from Trench Town from west to east, Palisadoes Road, the main road, we caught the procession coming around from the ocean. It was like the man turn to us and go so [waves his hand back and forth once, slowly, with great dignity]. That rain got us wet coming in, and it was like we were just walking through the streets with flags waving. This was a special day for us, nobody really believed it. And then, "Look! His Majesty that!" He turned and go so [waves]. I saw the stigmata in his hand too. It was something! Boy, so much things I see. Everyone see something else. I just feel a power, like I see the power in this man. How he turned, like, to us, and just wave like that! That was the mystical thing. They were going by kind of fast, so that's why it touched us. That week was something to look forward to that Rasta prophesied about all these years, so there was a buildup for it. Men say, "Oh, Rasta God is coming!"

BUNNY WAILER: I remember it was Friday, April 21, going up to Coxson that morning to get some food money. He had us sitting down for about four hours waiting. Came in. Went away. Came in.

Went Away. Me, Peter and Dream, we were waiting on him. I think he gave us three pounds that morning. And we went down to the ghetto, because everybody was getting ready to go and see His Imperial Majesty—all the church people with waving palm leaves, and it was a hell of a thing. It was a great, great occasion for Jamaica. I never seen nothing like that since I heard about when Christ was passing through Palestine and people wave palms. Well, that's the way it was when King Selassie came in. One look on his face and I was changed. He was the Almighty. You look at the Creator of all things. And everything inside of you changes. It's like a switch switches on, and one switch is off. Everybody felt that way.

ROGER STEFFENS: The arrival of Selassie would have a profound effect on Jamaica, on the Rasta faith, and of course on the Wailers. Songs composed in Bob's absence started to have a much stronger political component. In particular, a song called "Rescue Me," which wouldn't surface until later, was inspired by Selassie's visit.

BUNNY WAILER: "Rescue Me" was also one of those songs we would be doing in the backyard. Peter did it also on one of his albums in a different way still, but it was that kind of song also, when all those guns were firing in West Kingston, about '67 when the politics really steamed up, when guns were just introduced, guns were just firing all over the place, anybody could get shot. It wasn't really aimed at anyone physically, just guns firing. Political motivations. Guys just want to get everybody involved, so it doesn't matter who you shoot, just shoot somebody and then that somebody would start shooting back at somebody and that was how it really ignited. And when we saw that we decided to sit down and compose a song, that was the Wailers' job to do, we were like newspapers. That was when His Imperial Majesty had just left [April 1966], that was when the politics started. So you was to notice, we were dealing with His Imperial Majesty to rescue us from these guns, these little youth who were given automatic weapons for reasons we couldn't even tell.

ROGER STEFFENS: The explosion of political violence was growing daily, fueled by fears of a Communist takeover of the island. The successful revolution in neighboring Cuba led the U.S. to try to undermine any similar activity in Jamaica. It was in this perilous climate that Bob would return to his homeland, with visions of the Black Power struggle fresh in his mind.

CHAPTER 7

Wailers A Go Wail

ROGER STEFFENS: Marley spent about nine months in Delaware, during which time he swept floors in the Hotel du Pont in Wilmington and drove a forklift in the parts department of a Chrysler plant, trying to earn enough money for the Wailers to start their own label and gain control of their careers. His frustration was great after charting hit after hit for the previous two years and reaping no financial rewards. He knew that he and his partners had all the tools necessary for a successful music career: interesting voices, composing chops, a loosely choreographed (and often amusing) stage act and, more and more, lyrics that meant something to their people, enabling them to stir the masses.

BUNNY WAILER: When Bob returned he went looking for Coxson by himself, without Peter or me, because I was at war with Coxson. Bob and Coxson reasoned, and then Bob came to us and told us that Coxson had asked, "Are you still going to use them?" Bob answered, "What do you mean 'use them'? You mean them fall off, them not improve? What do you mean?"

Coxson replied, "Sure, them improve, them improve a lot, but in those two years there, you were in charge, and I want to know if you are still." So he was trying to influence Bob, saying why bother with them, just come sing now, you, Bob Marley. He didn't come round straight and say it, but Bob didn't have any intention of doing that. So Bob just shake him off and said, "I don't know what you're talking about, them still good." Coxson knew that Bob was aware that there was a war between us, so that if he got sensitive with me, Bob would get turned off. So he went along with it and said, "Yeah, Bob, you can use them, them all right, them improving."

When Bob came out and told us that, I said, "Listen, if you a go sing fe Coxson, go on, because this is one time me naw join you. Me naw sing for Coxson no more!" But Bob wanted to do our first session, "Bend Down Low" and "Freedom Time," at Studio One. The money for the session came from the little that Bob brought back from America, combined with money that Coxson told us Chris Blackwell had sent him for our record sales in England. Now Blackwell might have given him a hundred thousand pounds but all Coxson gave us was ninety-five pounds, like crumbs falling off a table. And the Wailers took crumbs and turned it into a bread. Simple as that. We just take out some nickels to eat some food and put the rest aside for the record.

Now that we had our own label, we began to call ourselves the Wailing Wailers. We understood the meaning of the word Wailers some more. We had carried that name as a group of youth who were just searching. But now we found what we were searching for. It's the people who wail, the wailing ones. For we a wail for the people. We a wail for the oppressed. We a wail for all the people who wail. So we were now the Wailing Wailers.

We designed a label with our three hands holding one another and called it Wail'n Soul'm. The name came about because Bob married a Soulettes—so the Wailers and the Soulettes were now intertwined, mixed, gone in a blood. And we decided to call the label Wail and Soul Them, but we just shortened it and said Wail'n Soul'm, like Wail dem Soul dem.

So we go in, record the tracks, leave with the tapes, went away and pressed about a thousand copies of blank white-label seven-inch singles. "Freedom Time" was our cry of liberation from Coxson. The other side, though, became the hit. "Row fisherman row, you reap what you sow." So now we could be reaping the rewards for our own work. And even then Coxson took a cut of "Bend Down Low" and released it himself, though he didn't have the rights to it. We spent our own money and paid Coxson studio time and whatever it took to record that tune on our own label, and he put it out as his own. So it's a whole heap of tricks Coxson go on with. He's the father of the vampires.

"Bend Down Low" sold something like fifty thousand copies. It was number one in about two, three weeks. Initially the blanks would sell for twenty-one shillings, then we would drop it down to twelve-and-six and eventually to seven-and-six. When we recorded for Coxson, all we got was nine pounds a record, no matter what it sold. Now we were getting 100 percent. Coxson charged twenty-one shillings for a pre-released twelve-inch, and the musicians we being paid ten shillings a side total. Imagine how the musicians felt when they got ten shillings a side, and a single copy of that tune would sell for twenty-one shillings to the public. It fucked them up, like it fucked up Don Drummond. He used to sit down and think and his head couldn't take that kind of treatment, it just spun. [In 1966 the British pound was worth $2.80, so Don Drummond was being paid less than a dollar and a half per song.]

ROGER STEFFENS: It wasn't only money that was causing strife for the newly returned Marley. Conflicts continued to fester within the group and domestically as well. By 1966, even before Selassie's arrival, Beverley Kelso had left the group and become increasingly concerned about Bob's actions toward Rita.

BEVERLEY KELSO: After Bob and Rita get married, Bob didn't leave for a while. Before he leave for America, he build that record shop right in Rita's yard. Right in front of Rita's house, they build a little board record shop. 18A Greenwich Park Road, Kingston 5. And that record store was selling and doing a good little business. I did not used to go there regularly because I didn't like what I was seeing after the record shop in term of how Bob started, the lifestyle of how they start to live now.

SEGREE WESLEY: I know in the beginning Bob would rough her up. 'Cause there's one trait in him, he's a very stern person. If he say red he means red. That's the way he operates. If you say something that's what he's gonna do. He's not violent, but if you say something he says, "What do you mean?" It's like seeing the ball, you see he's going after that ball and he don't care what's up, he's gonna go get it. He was a real aggressive player.

BEVERLEY KELSO: And then when Bob married to Rita and he more getting more family [i.e. more kids], Bob starts straying. Other woman coming in, other woman seeing Bob now. They moved the shop from Greenwich Park Road to Orange Street. Then Beeston Street. But when the shop was on Orange Street it was like, Bob start to get popular, the group getting more popular. Woman coming around now, different, different woman. Precious was going with Bunny as I said. Then Bunny coming down back in Trench Town get involved with this other girl from First Street, her name was Dulcie. Her sister used to go by the shop also with Dulcie and Bob get her sister pregnant. Her sister name was Pat. Robert Marley Jr.—that would be his second child. So, in between that, I didn't like the whole setup because his [Robbie's] mother and his mother's sister was my friend. I was pissed over the whole situation to see that he didn't want Rita. He used to treat Rita so bad. I feel like she didn't deserve that treatment.

ROGER STEFFENS: A violent encounter would bring an end to Beverley's friendship with Rita and her final break from the group.

BEVERLEY KELSO: One evening me and Rita were walking in the area. Pat saw us coming down the street and she come down the stairs to fight Rita. Rita didn't know her. Rita didn't know anything. And I get involved. I almost lose my eye because the girl push her finger right into my eye. Bob hear about it and he didn't talk to me after it because I almost kill her. With a belly she could push her finger in my eye and I grab a stone and her family, her brother and everybody was there, they didn't say anything. So, because of that now I didn't go back up there.

I just stayed and pull away from the group. I leave the group because of she, the advantage that I see Bob was taking of her.

ROGER STEFFENS: Beverley left Jamaica before long, after learning that Rita was seeking to end her marriage to Bob.

BEVERLEY KELSO: The last time I saw Rita before I come to the States she was about to divorce Bob. I had a lawyer friend, Mr. Churchill Neita, and she wanted a divorce, right? So, I tell her that Mr. Neita wasn't a divorce lawyer, he was a criminal lawyer, but it's my friend so I could take her to him and probably he would get a lawyer for her. On our way to Mr. Neita that Saturday morning I turned to her and I said, "You know something Rita? You better not divorce Bob now because suppose anything should happen to him? You have the children and what you gonna get?" And Rita turned to me that Saturday morning, I never will forget, right at the corner of Orange Street and Spanish Town Road, she turned to me and she started to curse me out. And I just walked away from her and then she come back to me and she said, "No, no Beverley, don't." And she said, "All right." I said, "I'm going home." I said, "I'm not taking you to Mr. Neita anymore. I am going home, so go wherever you wanna go." So she turned up Orange Street and said she going by the record shop. This is in the sixties.

ALLAN "SKILL" COLE: What happened in that period, I think it was frustration. Because even some people thought that Bob Marley was getting mad one time in that era. You had some people said, "Bwoi, look like him a get mad," but it wasn't that, it was just the pressure. And they were looking at his features, and he's a man with a feature if, when things are not right you can just see it in his features. In those days he had a permanent, what they call "screw" on his face. Permanent, permanent screw on his face, even more than ever in those days, because things was rough. The screw came off a little bit after a while, that face that people was afraid of in the early days. Because I remember once when we just started touring we came to New York one day and these guys who knew him from Boys Town school, we used to play ball with them in Boys Town, they were like in America for about two years, and when I see them they wanted to go look for Bob and when they got in touch with me in my room I call him, and tell him we coming down. When they went in the room and saw Bob face they come back and say, "Oh my God man I can't take the face, I don't understand what happened." So I said, "Is the same man, no problem, him is a little bit tight up because a gig" and things like that. They said bwoi, they couldn't take Bob's face because of his features. But as I said, that type of feature that he had early on, that screw came down a little bit after that. It was more relaxed. It was nothing that he was making up, you know, it was just the pressure. It was nothing like you think a man was acting, nothing like that. It was just Bob. It was just a man who was looking at the earth and looking at what was happening and he saw things and when things didn't please him, sometimes he'd keep it inside and he'd show it outside.

ROGER STEFFENS: Finally, the pressure became so great that Marley abandoned the chaos of Kingston and returned to Nine Mile. He brought Rita, Bunny, Vision and Peter to help him farm and try to break through what was now a full-scale writer's block. It was a radical retreat for the always engaged Wailers.

SEGREE WESLEY: It was frustration. Bob went back to the country, he went back to do farming. I think he was frustrated, singing all these songs, doing what he was doing which was very good, all his production was first-class. And he was making no money! He had little kids just born, those days it was tough.

ROGER STEFFENS: It was almost biblical, this figurative exodus into the wilderness, mounting the favorite donkey of his youth on which he was sometimes seen to ride backward, He would experience terrible injury, find a new focus for his art and return with renewed confidence.

SEGREE WESLEY: Being a man from the woods, man went back to the country start doing some planting. But he used to come through Trench Town sometime. The thing was in him, he had to come back to the city and get back into the music business. Because the music was in him and it had to come out. It's like Jonah went into the belly of the whale! He had to come back.

CHAPTER 8

Nine Mile Exile

VISION WALKER: It wasn't long after Bob returned that we went up to Nine Mile. Bob wanted to go back to nature. Find himself. Plant food, dig up yams that had been planted from his father's days. I was there, Bob, Rita; Bunny was back and forth. We never used to stay in just one place; we used to stay, then leave and go back to town. But that's where he did plan to go for a certain time to get his head together. And there was still music. In the nights up at the same hut where he was born, that's where we used to do most of the rehearsals. But it would be cold at night! Chilly up there, the fog and the clouds would be passing at your doorstep. Bob wrote "Sun Is Shining" there and later in Delaware Bob wrote "Misty Morning." We were playing "Eleanor Rigby" by the Beatles and that's what gave him the inspiration to write that song. "Misty Morning" too, but we lost that tape! I wish I could find that.

SEGREE WESLEY: I remember what Bob's words were. He says, "Segree, when we go up to these places, like, in the country, it's quiet; we can concentrate. And you know, we're able to do a lot more than we can do down here." But he used to come back into the city, occasionally he would visit, but he says up there you ride your donkey and you do this and it's closer to nature. He didn't say he was away from the maddening crowd but that was what he meant.

BUNNY WAILER: There was a period where the Wailers dropped out. Bob was having a problem writing songs. So we decided to leave for

Nine Mile, where Bob came from and where I had lived for a while with my father. It was just after we recorded "Nice Time" [ca. June 1967], and was brought on by many things. We got frustrated with Planno because of his whole heap of whorehouse things. That cat started to carry us Friday nights downtown to the dancehalls. And we had stopped that kind of life. And we studied and accepted the Nazarene's vow that you should not cut your hair or drink any alcohol. Also, because we were from Trench Town and connected to musicians like the Skatalites, we were forced out of the limelight. And that was good for the Wailers. That gave us time to go and be strong writers and strong singers.

ROGER STEFFENS: Even as the Jamaican music business was becoming a firmly entrenched part of the island's economy, those who made the most popular music were often from the most impoverished communities. Great as they were, the members of the Skatalites were considered second-class citizens, as were the perceived rude-boy Wailers.

Nine Mile was a chance for them to regroup and think about what they really wanted to achieve and how to go about it. Tensions were always just under the surface among the trio. Though Bob was raised for some time in Bunny's father's home, he was never treated as an equal. This complicated their brotherly relationship.

BUNNY WAILER: All of the Wailers went—me and my girlfriend at the time, sister Jean Watt, Rita, Vision, Bob, Peter. And when we went, the people in the country really loved us, people that we have been used to, people we grew up with at the age of nine and eleven. So everybody was happy and joyful. The people really welcomed us, saying that because we were coming to farm, it made them feel even better, feel important. The Wailers came to farm, showing them what they were doing is good to be doing.

Bob's grandfather had this piece of land called Smiff [Smith], but we just called it Smit' or Simit. We used to say, "We a go a Simit, go farm." It was a beautiful piece of land between two mountains, along a short valley road. Sweet piece of land, not a slope, no way water can damage anything [i.e., flooding couldn't wipe out a crop]. We planted yams, cocoa, beans, corn, cabbage, chocho, some pumpkin—everything. The place was about three and a half miles walking from where we lived, seven miles round trip each day.

We had this donkey that was Bob's favorite when he was growing up, a long-living animal named Nimble. So when we went to farm, we had him ride with us. He carried all our heavy stuff in two hampers, our material, flour, whatever. Well, there was one evening now when the period of work was peak. We were cleaning the field with a hoe. We sharpened the hoe so finely that when we weed the bush, the spot was so clean that you could almost eat on the spot. Bob had sharpened the hoe, and must have left it turned up. The blade of the hoe is supposed to be turned down when it's sharp. Well, he put it back on the ground with the hoe facing up, and accidentally stepped back, forgetting that he left the hoe cocked up, and he cut his right foot bottom in half, from one side of the foot to the next side, right up till it was all white, maybe about half an inch up, opening the whole foot bottom.

He fell and we grabbed him, and tried to look after him. Everybody almost fainted, and Rita started hollering all kinds of things. It was like, what are we going to do? And all Bob did was just say, "Cool," and just scrape away at the dirt. Scrape the dirt, scrape the dirt, scraping away all the topsoil until there was that pure earth. And he scraped up some of that and just opened the foot, threw the dirt in and locked it up—tore off part of his shirt, and tied it up. And Bob worked on that foot every day until it got better. That's the kind of person, that's the kind of leader Bob Marley is. He would never weaken us by wanting us to sympathize with the position that he was in. But we let Nimble carry him, so he didn't have to walk while he was healing. It took about a month.

Peter didn't last too long with us at all. He never wanted to be in the country doing any farming, and after about a week he got town-sick. He told us, "Bwoi, me can't live this life. All dem peenie wallies [fireflies] and t'ings. Cho, me can't deal with it."

Finally Bob began to write songs again. He started to pick up again, the vibes came back again, because something really serious was happening to him at the time. And even when he started to write, you could still hear it in the songs he wrote there, like "Trouble On The Road Again." When we weren't working we were rehearsing. Many of our songs were born there: "Burial," "Wisdom," "Comma Comma." It was just pure harmony. We used to rehearse at the house on top of the hill that was Bob's first home. Neville Willoughby came up from Kingston and filmed Bob singing some songs with the big guitar we called Betsy, and riding Nimble over the hills.

ROGER STEFFENS: Neville Willoughby was one of the grand old men of Jamaican broadcasting. A graduate of Kingston College and the University of Toronto, he first worked for RJR and then for the Jamaican Broadcasting Company on radio and in the earliest stages of its TV operations. He would witness Marley's auspicious meeting with American soul-pop star Johnny Nash at a Kingston Rasta gathering known as a grounation, be an emcee at the historic 1978 One Love Peace Concert, and would go on to conduct two of the most famous interviews with Bob Marley, in 1973 and 1979.

NEVILLE WILLOUGHBY: Around 1967, '68, I was actually doing both radio and TV. It was the early days of television in Jamaica. I had a TV program and I was working at JBC radio, we jump from the TV to the radio for just about anything. On television one of my first shows was *See't Yah*, see it here. It was a talk–music program.

What really first caught my attention to Bob Marley was "Nice Time." It was so sweet. I loved that record so much and I used to play it a lot. And then one day I was in one of the studios at JBC and in walks this man. I was in the control room, so he went through the door, he went down the passage, and then when you saw him going inside—for some reason there was something about him that I found quite fascinating,

Veteran Jamaican broadcaster Neville Willoughby at his home
in the hills above Kingston, January 2003.

something about him in the way he walked. He had a full khaki outfit
and desert boots, I remember that distinctly. And he had a guitar in
his hand. He was growing locks. This is the first time seeing this guy
personally. I actually got up and went outside and asked the telephone
operator, "Who's that man that went into the studio?" He's nobody in
fancy clothes or anything, and he has the guitar case, almost battered
one would say. But he walked like he was somebody, regally, that's the
way to put it, I think. And so I asked, "Who is that man?" And she
said, "Bob Marley." Say, "You mean the one who sings 'Nice Time'?"
And from that moment I decided hey, I'm going to try to talk to this
man. Oh, it took a little while! Because he didn't want to talk to anybody. The airplay did interest him, but the talking to him had to be
approved by two people: either Rita, his wife, or Mortimo Planno. They
had to say that the person gonna talk to him was all right and didn't
want to do something. For apparently he had some bad experiences

with producers, interviewers, or whatever. I have no idea if anybody'd interviewed him before. In retrospect maybe it was because he was a shy person, I think.

But all I know is when I decided to go and try to interview him and I went to Trench Town (I found out where he lived), Rita opened the gate, and she was smiling, was very nice. You know, she is a very pleasant person, and I told her I wanted to speak with Bob, who I could see sitting down with Planno inside. I don't remember whose yard it was, but I remember he was sitting inside on a bench with Planno. And I said I would love to do an interview, and she said she was going to have to check with Bob, and eventually she said to come back another day and check whether he said it was all right, because she said she'd tell him that I'm an all-right person. I'm OK, you know! I think I'd met her once in the studio down at Federal, and so when I went back the next time she said, "OK, he'll talk with you." I said, "OK!" So actually what I decided to do was do a television interview with him on the same program, *See't Yah*. And I decided what we'd do is go to the country and make a film, a little short film: [in portentous voice] "The Legendary Film of Bob Marley on the Donkey." Bob coming out of the fog on a donkey in Prickly Pole, right up there near to Nine Mile. He actually suggested it there that night, because they had a bit of land, he told me, and they would just take the opportunity to go there and see how the yams that they had planted were coming on. Because before we actually went into Prickly Pole, we stopped at the land and Rita and himself went down and dug up some yams and things. And we decided to take some pictures of them digging up the yams, so we incorporated that in the film. It was the days of telecine, where you got negative film and it was transferred to positive on air. At the time I didn't realize that I should have kept the film.

This is when Bob had kind of retired from the business for a while, he was getting out of the business and going back to Nine Mile to live. In a way he was retired in Nine Mile. There was something that had bothered him, I don't know what it was. I don't know why he was so suspicious of people. But once Bob went to Prickly Pole, himself, Peter and Rita, and we shot that film, then I [was able to bring them] in the studio and we talked live. They showed a five- or six-minute film and then we talked in the studio. That was back there when you didn't have any tape business, everything was live, even the commercials are live. You had to learn them by heart. I have hunted that film down at the Institute of Jamaica, nobody seems to know what happened. Because JBC destroyed quite a lot of stuff in their libraries one time.

ROGER STEFFENS: Time passed slowly in the rolling hills as a visibly pregnant Rita toiled in the fields planting yams, potatoes and cabbages. Then, a sundering in the group caused a major realignment of the Wailers' sound. Bunny was busted for herb.

CHAPTER 9

The JAD Years

ROGER STEFFENS: From July 1967 until September 1968, Bunny was sent to prison on trumped-up ganja charges. He spent the first portion in General Penitentiary. Then he endured a year of hard labor at a work farm in Richmond. There, on the radio on Friday nights, when the prisoners would listen to the program *Wail'n Soul'm Time*, featuring songs from the Wailers' label, he heard tracks recorded in his absence: "Pound Get A Blow," "Hurting Inside," "Don't Rock My Boat," "Hammer," and "Play Play Play." Not one of the songs, Bunny insists, became a hit.

BUNNY WAILER: The Wailers came like they were dead now. In fact, at one stage Bob got in a frustration, just fling down his guitar and said, "Awhoah, Wailers there in prison to blood-claat. The Wailers aren't there anymore, we can't get it right."

NEVILLE WILLOUGHBY: After that was when Johnny Nash and Danny Sims came in, probably '67.

ROGER STEFFENS: Danny Sims was a controversial publisher and label owner. He would play a pivotal role in Bob Marley's emergence as a professional recording artist and songwriter. Danny and I last spoke in April 2012 at the home of his sister Donnice in Los Angeles, while he was visiting from his base in the Dominican Republic. He died a few months later.

DANNY SIMS: Cayman Music is a publishing company that I started in the mid-sixties. A lawyer friend of mine took me to the Cayman

Islands to set up my company, and I named the company after the Cayman Islands. I started working with Johnny Nash around 1962, and we formed a company, Cayman Music, JAD Records, about 1965–66. We signed Bob Marley and Peter Tosh as writers and recording artists, Rita Marley with a recording and publishing contract. Bunny was signed as a writer when he got out of prison [Bunny denies this].

ROGER STEFFENS: For years Sims maintained that he met Marley on Ethiopian Christmas in early January 1967. I now believe that to be incorrect. Because Bunny was in prison at the time Sims claims he met Bob, Peter and Rita, it had to be January 1968. In later years Sims moved the date back one or two more years. Here is Sims's version of the night he encountered the young singer.

DANNY SIMS: I had a very good friend in Jamaica named Neville Willoughby. [Willoughby's father was the lawyer who helped set up JAD Records.] I was good friends with his family, and when he came back to Jamaica from England from school he started to work at the radio station. And one day he came up and asked us to come down to a Rastafarian festival in Trench Town. Johnny Nash went, and that night Johnny came home raving about this guy he had met named Bob Marley. He said every song he heard him sing was an absolute smash and that we should sign him immediately to our label.

NEVILLE WILLOUGHBY: Danny was a good businessman. And Danny was a family friend. He's my niece's godfather, so he was always at the house. He had his own label, JAD. And the third person on the label—Johnny, Arthur and Danny—was the producer Arthur Jenkins. He was so good, a fabulous musician!

Danny's very smart, he signed just about everybody you could think of in Jamaica, just in case anybody made a record and then broke! I was signed by JAD too. And Derrick Harriott, Byron Lee, you name it. Danny signed everybody. Because Danny told everybody they're going to make a big hit. Now he was waiting for somebody to make a hit, and then he happened to hear about Bob Marley.

The night they met I took them to a grounation. Oh, it's like a dream now. It was like a solemn Rastafarian service. It wasn't Planno's yard. We ended up in this place, which was way, way down in Kingston and when we went inside we saw all these Rastafarians; the elders were there. It was like a church service. It was quite fascinating. It smelled of herb. I imagine forty to fifty people were there, most all of them Rastas of all ages, even including children. And Rita was there with Peter and Bob. They were singing as a trio. Everything had the *akete* drum and the sort of hypnotic sound of Rasta drumming.

DANNY SIMS: The following morning Bob came to our house with his wife Rita and Peter Tosh, along with Mortimo Planno. Bob played guitar and sang about thirty songs for us. I [had] invited Bob to my house for breakfast. But my servants refused to serve him and walked out: they would not serve a Rastafarian. The servants I had after that also refused to serve him, and they quit too. So Mortimo put a Rasta dreadlock named Jeff in our house to cook and work for us. He was a hit man [in a Mafia sense].

NEVILLE WILLOUGHBY: Did Danny bring him up to his house in Russell Heights the next day? I don't know if that's exactly what happened. But I know that after that, Bob, Peter and Rita and John and Danny, Arthur, myself and quite a number of other people were constantly at that house, rehearsing things, every day, and then we'd go down to the studio. The main thing, though, Bob was recording his songs upstairs at [producer] Randy Chin's Studio 17.

DANNY SIMS: Mortimo was his manager and Bob said he wanted Mortimo to work out a deal with us to handle his records. And we started talking; we started to hang around in Trench Town. Bob came up and stayed at our house and took over our house when we were away. Some nights I stayed so late that I slept there, so did Johnny Nash. We became friends. It was at 43 Russell Heights. He was there about two or three years. This is in the middle sixties, this is when being a Rastafarian in Jamaica was considered a cardinal sin. But coming out of the ghetto in America [it didn't bother me]. I hung around in Trench Town, I stayed down there.

ROGER STEFFENS: Jamaica's right-wing government's fear of American-style radicalism at the time led to the acute repression of Rasta, and even extended to those from abroad whose militancy was deemed a threat.

DANNY SIMS: We were looked on in Jamaica as Americans who came there to cause trouble, working with Rastas, going to Trench Town. Once Muhammad Ali came down to visit us and the Jamaican government turned him away at the airport, they wouldn't let him in the country!

NEVILLE WILLOUGHBY: I must confess at the time, certainly in '67 when I had Ras Daniel Hartman [the dreadlocked star of the groundbreaking Jamaican film *The Harder They Come*] on television, and I held up my hand and said, "Tell me something. How do you get your hair like this?" and touched it, everybody in the studio looked in horror because at the time nobody had ever touched a Rastafarian hair on television. As a matter of fact a policeman came from Halfway Tree police station and said, "The man say him smoke herb. Why you didn't hold him for us?" Can you imagine! That is the sort of ridiculous situation that obtained then, but by the time '70 came, it was a different matter, because Bob was getting famous and lots of Rastas were becoming famous and people start to sit back and say, "Hey, wait a minute. They're not all bad."

ROGER STEFFENS: Soon the Wailers began to work for Danny Sims, writing songs for Johnny Nash and other artists.

DANNY SIMS: I put Peter and Bob and Rita on a regular salary of a hundred dollars a week. Bunny was in jail. My contract with Bob Marley said that anything that Bob Marley records during his contract with me would be owned by Johnny Nash and Danny Sims. There is a verbal contract and letter agreement between Mortimo Planno, Bob Marley and Johnny Nash and Danny Sims, made up by Neville Willoughby's father, stating that any songs that Bob Marley recorded would eventually be put into a broader contract later on, which we wanted to sign in the U.S., because we doubted the validity of a contract signed in Jamaica which was primarily a bootleg market at the time, because they didn't have copyright laws. So we wanted a signed contract in the jurisdiction where we were from.

In the original contract, Mortimo Planno was to receive 1 percent of all the product we put out, then and in the future. Rita was to receive a royalty in place of Bunny Wailer while he was in jail. Rita was due a royalty on all of the product that we did on her and Bob in those days, either as background singer or lead. Bunny Wailer came out of jail and threw her out of the group, didn't want her to get a percentage. Bunny did not agree with the agreement to give her a piece.

ROGER STEFFENS: At the time of this book's writing, Bunny Wailer's attitude toward Sims has hardened to the point of contempt and fury. Sims maintains that their relationship was not always so contentious.

DANNY SIMS: I'm very fond of Bunny, we always got along good. I always understood his point of view. Peter Tosh was working with me when he died, on a daily basis. Both those artists came back with me later on in their lives. Because Jamaicans are very suspicious people, and they think all foreigners are thieves. They first start to work with you as a thief. The word was "He t'ief me." So I got accustomed to that. But I had so much respect for Bob and Bunny and Johnny, I worked mainly with Bob and Peter at the start. They were at my house every day. That's where he met Cindy Breakspeare, at my house.

NEVILLE WILLOUGHBY: One of the first songs of theirs that Johnny recorded was Peter Tosh's song "Love." I was actually in the room when Peter Tosh was writing that song. We were sitting down in one of the rooms in Russell Heights, waiting on Danny. And Peter was there, and it was sort of late in the evening, and Peter started strumming this thing, and strumming, strumming, and he started singing one line and do another thing, and do with love, and more strumming,

strumming. Then he started adding something, and adding something else. And I actually said to him, I said, "Hey, wait a minute. Are you writing a song?" And he said yes. So I just sat there and listened while this man wrote this song. And when I tell people about it, they say, "What Peter Tosh that, 'do every little thing you do with love?' That don't sound like Peter Tosh." You know, they think of Peter Tosh as Stepping Razor, the rebel all the time. But he had a spot in him that could write beautiful love songs. 'Cause that's a beautiful song, "every little thing you do with love."

ROGER STEFFENS: Unsatisfied with the poorly equipped Kingston studios and lack of formal training among Jamaica's musicians, the JAD team experimented in North America with some of the finest players of the 1960s, adapting the island's rhythms for a more sophisticated audience.

DANNY SIMS: Let me explain to you our formula for recording in those days. We went to Jamaica in a time when Jamaican musicians wouldn't get to the studios really on time and they really didn't play in key. So dealing with Arthur Jenkins and Johnny Nash, it was at a time that we just didn't feel the vibe. So what we did, we did [Johnny Nash's] *Hold Me Tight* album with Lynn Taitt out of Toronto [a major hit for Nash]. We did a lot of these sessions with [keyboardist–arranger] Jackie Mittoo. We found that the Jamaicans that lived in Toronto were equal musicians with anybody in America or Canada. So we did a lot of work with the Jackie Mittoos and those guys. We brought Eric Gale there, he played guitar. We brought Hugh Masekela there, he played trumpet on a lot of the sessions we had. Bernard Purdie, Chuck Rainey, Richard Tee, guys who played for Aretha Franklin.

We wanted to get the authentic rhythm instruments, but for the sweeteners we always went to America or England to finish the product. We never had the facilities or the additional tracks, we only had three tracks or two tracks in Jamaica. Three tracks was the biggest thing on the island at that time and we brought that in to Randy Chin.

The next step from two tracks was three tracks and Randy Chin had a three-track. We financed it for him and we recorded there every day. But when we transferred in America, the next step would be eight-track, and then next step would be twelve-track. So we developed the record a lot different than the average person would because we cut our record in stages and we finished it in stages. But we cut a lot of tracks.

ROGER STEFFENS: One of JAD's favorite engineers to work with was a New York native named Joe Venneri, who refined tracks there by Nash and the Wailers.

JOE VENNERI: After the tracks were laid in Jamaica they were brought to me here in New York to a studio I had called Incredible Sounds. Richard Alderson, who was the chief engineer at Harry Belafonte's studio, also worked here and in Jamaica, back and forth, for months at a time. They'd bring the tapes up from Jamaica and we'd fix them up. Our musicians were the main guys in the Atlantic Records stable, they were absolutely the best people of the time. We were like a clique, we did all the same sessions.

DANNY SIMS: Our intention was to fit the U.S. and British radio formats. We weren't at all concerned about selling records in the Caribbean. We wouldn't get paid anyway! Johnny was the creative guy. If he wanted it to happen, I made it happen. If it weren't for Johnny Nash, reggae would never have been a worldwide, international music.

ROGER STEFFENS: Johnny Nash would go on to record a number of Wailers songs like "Comma Comma," "Stir It Up," "Guava Jelly," "Nice Time," "Mellow Mood," "Reggae On Broadway" and "Rock It Baby." These songs were often Americans' first exposure to rocksteady and reggae sounds, albeit "cleansed" for foreign ears with much fuller arrangements. Of course ska had had its biggest hit around the world a few years earlier with Little Millie Small's "My Boy Lollipop," although it was treated as a novelty record. "Israelites" by Desmond Dekker and the Aces hit hugely in 1968–69, but it was not publicly identified as reggae.

Against this background, JAD has great hopes for mainstreaming the Wailers, and Marley in particular, as the group's principal song-writer. The company wanted to groom them to international standards.

DANNY SIMS: I was thinking about recording Bob. I saw him as a big record-selling artist. With Arthur Jenkins and Johnny Nash and Jimmy Norman we put the Wailers into the studio.

NEVILLE WILLOUGHBY: Arthur Jenkins was a very good arranger, he was a real pro. I admire him a great deal, what a good musician he was. He could jump on any instrument and show you what to do.

DANNY SIMS: Neville was around those sessions because he was a big radio personality. His family and me were like household friends. So he knew everything that was being recorded. We used Randy Chin's studios and sometimes we used Byron Lee's studios, but Randy Chin's most of the time. A lot of our stuff was done at Federal. Byron Lee distributed "Mellow Mood" for us. The label read Bob Marley plus two. At that time Bunny was in jail, so it's Rita and Peter.

ROGER STEFFENS: This first exposure to international pop music professionals necessitated new training for Marley and his partners.

DANNY SIMS: We brought Jimmy Norman down to coach Bob. He's the guy who wrote most of the Coasters' biggest hits. We got about twenty-three songs that Jimmy wrote that Bob sang. Those are surprises. And Johnny Nash wrote some songs for Bob like "You Got Soul." Jimmy Norman worked so hard with us in that time that I gave him two songs on the first album.

JIMMY NORMAN: My first meeting with Marley, I was impressed by how spiritual he was. He didn't have dreadlocks at the time, but he was all about music, just singing all the time. That's what drew me to him, because I couldn't understand anything that he and Peter said for the first three or four months, it was all patois. We'd sit on the lawn and write, then we'd go into Danny's guesthouse that we had converted into a rehearsal studio and record it right away. We had a little Nagra tape recorder set up in there. I remember Bob always saying music would teach them a lesson. I was impressed by how they could stagger their

JAD Records posse Danny Sims, Joe Venneri, Jimmy Norman and Arthur Jenkins
celebrating the launch of the *Complete Bob Marley and the Wailers 1967–1972*
boxed set series at S.O.B.'s, New York City, April 1996.

harmonies each time, like the Impressions, just a little bit behind. It
gave them something special. If it was about his music, he slept it, he
lived it, very serious. I seldom saw him without his guitar. I remember
taking him home. Shearer was prime minister at the time. Bob saw his
residence and said, "Bwoi, I'd like to live in a place like that someday."

DANNY SIMS: When I met Johnny Nash he was young, but he was
well trained with mic technique and all those things. And we wanted
Bob to sing so you could see his face, 'cause he had a very nice face. But
if you hold a mic in front of your face, you can't see his face. So we had
him hold his mic under his chin, and get the same volume. And that
took a long time. When he got into a song, he was animated. As soon
as the song started and he got in the groove, he was gone.

JIMMY NORMAN: One of the first things I remember is that we had to hold Bob still in front of the mic, he was just jumping all over the place. I had to teach him how to record properly.

ROGER STEFFENS: Marley learned a great deal from the American studio musicians he met through JAD's connections. And they would, in turn, be affected by him. Among these new guides was Bernard Purdie, an Atlantic Records master drummer and studio musician, who played on many of the 1960s Wailers' sessions for Johnny and Danny. Italian reggae fans have created a website which contains the following brief but fascinating interview.

BERNARD PURDIE: I played and recorded with Bob in Jamaica. I cherish the memory of the very relaxed mode of approaching the music and being allowed our time to set it right. His music was always entertaining, with great rhythm and exceptional melody. When thinking of Bob, here is a picture that always comes to mind. We would leave the studio for a break. Bob would always climb up the hill, find a large rock, lie down upon it, light up, commune with nature and be at peace. The musicians there taught me the real authentic reggae music, which usually has percussion played by five different people. Because of what I had learned with Bob Marley's musicians, I incorporated so much of the reggae feel into my music over the years. For example, listen to Aretha Franklin's "Day Dreaming" and "Rock Steady," Cat Stevens's "Foreigner," Donny Hathaway and Roberta Flack's "Where Is The Love?" to name a few.

ROGER STEFFENS: Joe Venneri, Purdie's colleague, formed a similar impression of Bob.

JOE VENNERI: The only time I met Bob Marley was in New York. It was in the late sixties, we were all together in his lawyer's office. I had no idea how huge he would become, but he had this charisma, this spiritual thing that's in his voice—it's still there in every song I hear him sing. It's not musically perfect; it just seems to be an association with the earth. He's got this honest thing that just comes across.

Whether he's sharp or flat or sideways, there's something to every-thing he sings.

DANNY SIMS: I did at least eight albums on Marley. But at that time I was recording a lot anyway. We did maybe sixteen albums on Johnny Nash. And Lloyd Price. We did an album with Byron Lee and an album on Neville Willoughby at the same time. I mean we were there; we recorded every day.

JIMMY NORMAN: "Soon Come" was my song, Peter put some other lyrics to it, same arrangement, same melody, same music. We did thirty or forty of my songs in about eight months in 1968. I sang bass on "Chances Are" and "Soul Rebel," and lots of others too. We were constantly working.

DANNY SIMS: A lot of the songs we did with Bob were just fooling around in the studio, seeing what we could come up with. Bob was totally flexible, and we did lots of different kinds of experiments trying to come up with a hit single. We published the Cowsills, and we've got tracks of Bob covering their songs. We were the ones who encour-aged the Wailers to cover the Box Tops song "The Letter." We did a lot of Curtis Mayfield stuff with Bob that's all there in the can; we even thought Bob wrote those songs by himself at first.

ROGER STEFFENS: Bunny was finally released from prison after serv-ing fourteen months.

BUNNY WAILER: When I returned from prison in September of 1968, as soon as me come it was pure hard work in the studios, harder hours of singing. Sing all dem "Milkshake and Potato Chips," and we sing a tune we have to learn in all two days and three days. 'Cause Jimmy Norman write them fast. And they chose who to lead this and who to lead that. They force down songs for you to lead, but the project is on and these guys know what they are doing. And they feel like your voice would fit that form, and so they give you that shit. Johnny Nash had a lot of money that time and I know a lot of money spent. They didn't come to Jamaica to do business, they came for fun. Sun island, sunbathing and a lot of girls, clean skin African girls. So that's what they came for and then ran into the Wailers and found this music and this group. And then he saw the opportunity of signing Bob's publishing. So he did all of that and it worked out for him.

DANNY SIMS: Bunny was probably, of the artists, I'd say strongest of the singers, so far as his singing straight contemporary American music. Bob had a style, a charisma, and was the obvious superstar. But you could tell in that setup, all three of those guys were superstars. They were brought together as kids, but they were all superstars. And they all wrote songs, and they all had singles out in those days. We did close to ninety tracks on them.

ROGER STEFFENS: Bunny's return changed the dynamic in the group once again, as he was immediately swept into the systematic working arrangements that JAD required of them, recording songs written by Jimmy Norman that seemed to be directed at a white teenage market. Meantime, Peter was accepting session work to supplement his meager income from Wail'n Soul'm sales, and released several instrumental singles for other producers. But he was a major contributor to the everevolving Wailers sound, even being brought to America to record in New York studios for other artists.

DANNY SIMS: Peter had his own agenda, but he was with us 90 percent of the time. We used his guitar on practically every track we did. He held us together; he held our rhythm together. Peter was the teacher, along with Paul Khouri, for that rocksteady sound. Peter directed us; we spun off Peter Tosh. I never worked with a guy I liked working with more than Peter. He was always with us, always! I saw him as the Rock of Gibraltar with the rhythm.

And we can't downplay the role of Rita Marley, either. I remember Johnny Nash calling her an "African Madonna with a voice like silk and honey." She was with Bob every single day, and she sang all the harmonies under him. I thought she had one of the most commercial voices I'd ever heard.

I was just so excited about them all, especially Bob. I remember calling Bob's mother, Cedella Booker, at her home in Delaware and telling her that Marley was going to be one of the biggest acts on earth. Every time I see her, she reminds me about that.

CHAPTER 10

Leslie Kong Meets the Tuff Gang

ROGER STEFFENS: The so-called JAD period (1968–72) ushered in parallel careers for the Wailers, in which they made and released recordings for the domestic Caribbean market on their own labels—Wail'n Soul'm and the renamed Tuff Gong imprint—and JAD productions for the international market. They still experienced difficulty in getting local airplay from a system that ran almost exclusively on payola, and never sold enough to enable them to fulfill their dream of building their own home and studio.

Marley would spend time in the winter of 1970–71 in Sweden working with Johnny Nash on a movie he was making there, helping him write the soundtrack. New opportunities, both ending in extreme frustration, came from Jamaican producers Leslie Kong and Lee "Scratch" Perry. Bob suggested that the Wailers use his football hero pal Allan "Skill" Cole as their manager; he was not unwilling to use unorthodox methods to get airplay for the Wailers newest compositions.

Meanwhile, legal affairs occupied much of their time as they tried to untangle themselves from Studio One.

DANNY SIMS: When Johnny Nash finished *Hold Me Tight* we had been working with Bob Marley for nearly a year before he signed the formal contract. We didn't officially sign the contract—although we were working together and recording every day—until we got Bob Marley into America, into Walter Hofler's office, the guy who was our lawyer. We went back to Delaware, and he and Rita and his mother came up, and we did the first contracts on him there, and we brought the contracts down and we signed everybody in Jamaica.

ROGER STEFFENS: This formalized the agreement under which Bob would write songs for Johnny Nash and other international artists under the JAD label.

MORTIMO PLANNO: It was a difficult time for the group. Me and Danny and Johnny decided that we didn't want the same situation that was happening to Bob—sitting down inna yard in Trench Town experiencing police brutality and harassment—to prevent our production. We wanted to produce the best of Bob Marley, and the best of Bob Marley was to get him in himself.

DANNY SIMS: Bob got in touch with us and said he wanted to have the right to release his records in the Caribbean and we gave him that right. He had to make a living. We had an exclusive right to release his records worldwide. That product then was illegally picked up by international pirates, and it's been pirated ever since, starting with [Leslie Kong's] Beverley's and Lee Perry.

ROGER STEFFENS: The agreement between Marley and JAD, as well as the piracy Danny mentions, would become a major source of tension later and lead to much conflict, but for now Danny was an outspoken advocate for Marley and his talents, and provided him with financial and professional support at a key moment in his career.

DANNY SIMS: My first duty with Mortimo Planno was to attack Coxson for royalties. Bob and Mortimo told me Coxson owed him hundreds of thousands of dollars of royalties, and wanted me to collect his money. So I went to Neville Willoughby's father who said, "Danny, you'll never beat Coxson in a Jamaican court." What about the power of the white Marleys? I went to Norval Marley's brother, who was a lawyer. The Marleys were very wealthy people. I told them I thought Bob Marley could be as big as Elvis, and they immediately became interested and said they would defend him to collect the money from Coxson, but they didn't believe they would be able to collect it. They said they'd take the case, but with the provision that Bob Marley would denounce Rastafarianism. [It should be noted that Rastafarians despise the term "Rastafarianism," insisting that their faith rejects all "isms" everywhere.]

So in 1967 I took Coxson to court and found that he did have a contract, and didn't owe Bob any money. If anything, he didn't sell enough records in the Caribbean to recoup his recording costs. So I apologized and walked away from it.

ROGER STEFFENS: Coxson's initial contract with the Wailers as performers and songwriters was indeed upheld in court, though it wasn't challenged until several years later.

COXSON DODD: It's been upheld in court in Jamaica, because [Island Records head] Chris Blackwell had issued a cease of pressing and it went to the High Court and the High Court was satisfied with the contracts that I had, also was their lawyer. And at that time I requested three million to go in bond if they want me to stop from pressing. Well, their lawyer was convinced with the contract shown by the High Court judge that it was legal. I think in '72.

ROGER STEFFENS: Mortimo Planno had acted as an adviser to the Wailers, but did not always have their best interests at heart. After Bunny was released from prison, Bob told him a story of Planno's treachery.

BUNNY WAILER: The Wailers wanted to do a free show for the people. Bob was at home preparing for the show when he got a message that Mortimo Planno was at the theater collecting money. Bob decided not to show. Bob took his little VW and go down to Nine Mile. So when people heard that Bob Marley wasn't coming, Planno had to give back every dime, which pissed Planno so much off that him drive all the way to Nine Mile to say he's going to kill Bob, with one little weak pipsqueak guy named Jeff Folks, a little batty bwoi, one of Planno's little girls.

ROGER STEFFENS: Tipped off in advance, as the car reached the edge of Nine Mile, a member of the feared Vikings gang stopped them and grabbed one of Planno's men and beat him, while the country people stoned the car with rocks. Bob had to beg them to stop and let Planno and Folks return to the city. Bob was angry that Planno was using his free show to con money from the audience, making Bob look like a hypocrite if he had come to perform, as if he were in cahoots with Planno. According to Bunny, Planno was always trying to set a trap for Bob.

Later, a friend of Bob's named Frankie Dark heard Planno's people planning to burn down the shack where Bob and Rita were living in her aunt's yard in Kingston. Bob alerted the Vikings, which were like his neighborhood protectors. They sprung an ambush on Planno's men as they approached their target. Led by Frankie Dark himself, they were willing to kill them all. Planno's thugs fled in terror. Nevertheless, Marley and Planno would come together again at various times in the future.

ALLAN "SKILL" COLE: In June of 1968 Bob cut "Selassie Is The Chapel," written for him by Mortimo Planno. I wasn't at that session, I was in school, but I knew about it. In the groove of the record it says "FVR." I think it was something like "For the Victory of Rasta."

ROGER STEFFENS: "Selassie Is The Chapel" is considered one of the rarest and most sought-after of all Bob's songs, with only twenty-six copies pressed. It is a solo version of "Crying In The Chapel" (a recent pop hit at the time for Elvis Presley) with altered Rasta lyrics written by Planno and, according to him, recorded at the JBC studios on June 8, 1968. Shortly after, the Wailers would move on from Planno as the group began to gain more control over their own affairs in Jamaica, working a parallel track to their JAD commitments.

ALLAN "SKILL" COLE: I'll tell you how my acquaintance with Bob turned into friendship. During 1968–69 I used to meet and buck up Bob when I passed through Trench Town. I pass through, hail him up, see him with Planno. Most of the time I meet him over at Planno's house. But what happened was, there was a period when I got involved playing for a [soccer] team with a fellow by the name of Gary Hall.

And he was into the music business. Gary was probably one of the first Jamaicans that was working at the BBC in London. At the time Gary was working at Dynamic Sounds as the general manager. So I was playing for his team, Real Mona, for a season. During that period of time now, Bob and myself and a couple of guys start playing ball against them. From Trench Town we bring a team and they come from the east and play us. So Gary Hall got us together. Bob at that time [and the Wailers] had gone independent after a while. They were having problems, so Gary got me together, started teaching me the business, and then I took Bob to meet him.

Back in '67, '68 going down in that period, they were going through a lot of hard times. Bob got so frustrated one time that he left and went to country. He wasn't making no money and getting no airplay. Everything changed though when I came into the scene, we start working together and we revolutionize everything. We made a way for a lot of independent promoters to come along and survive at that time. Because in those days it was very, very hard. The top companies controlled everything and independent producers in those times—oh my God, it was unbelievable. If you didn't go to the big Jamaican companies in those days there was no hope for you as a producer or even as an artist. It was the big companies that run the station, the big companies that control, the big companies that run the payola and everything. There was no space at all for you as an artist unless you went through those companies. And in those days the artists in the country didn't have no knowledge of the music business so they suffered. They were going there, they were doing all these hits for these top producers, didn't have no knowledge of the business, no contracts, so you end up at the end of the day getting no money. It was raw talent being exploited by some producers who didn't have no heart. So if you as an artist went and try to do a thing for yourself, you wouldn't get no play on the radio station. And that was the thing that was happening to the Wailers. They were no different from any other artist—no play. As I said, after that now we revolutionize everything. We came inside the industry and we sort of change up everything.

ROGER STEFFENS: The changes they wrought sometimes led to threats and physical altercations.

ALLAN "SKILL" COLE: The manufacturing companies in those days were the producers, so they controlled everything, they controlled the radio stations, the payola, the charts, everything. It wasn't until we came inside that we start to get a piece of it but we had to do it through force. Because nobody going to take our money in those days, nobody going to take the Rastaman money. We had to get the street forces and we did our things. If a guy didn't play our music we had to go up there, talk to him, threaten him, sometime we had to puncture them car tires and things like that. Those were the kind of things we had to do, put your hand in a man face, and jook him in the nose and box him. That's what we had to do, send the guys who do all those thing. That's the thing we had to do. We never kill nobody, you know!

BUNNY WAILER: Anything that Skill do to promote Wailers on the radio, him did fe him own personal reason. No do that on behalf of the Wailers, because we no support that. We never tell him at no time to beat nobody, hit no one! Intimidation, yes, because that was how the game was being played.

But as for beating people, Skill never beat nobody. Skill just walk with a couple of guys that were muscle guys, guys that you don't talk to, guys that you don't reason with, and when you see that, you don't want Skill to send these kind of guys on you. So you just make sure records are played and everybody's happy. And Skill would still give these guys a cut, give them some money. But it's just to make sure that the records was played! 'Cause most of the time when he took these records to the radio stations, I was there. Nobody beat up on anybody. But was just intimidation.

ROGER STEFFENS: As Skill began to achieve more public exposure for the Wailers, Bob took up once more with Leslie Kong, who had produced his first two solo records in 1962. Since then Kong had great local success with the ska hit "My Boy Lollipop" and the equally popular first international reggae smash, "Israelites," by Desmond Dekker and the Aces. The Wailers decided they would do something no one in Jamaica had done before: a thematic album like the Beatles' *Sergeant Pepper* and the Stones' *Satanic Majesties*, whose subtext would be a pep talk by the group to itself to get back in the game, with "Soul Captives," "Caution," "Go Tell It On The Mountain," "Cheer Up," "Do It Twice" and "Soul Shakedown Party" among its uplifting tracks, cut in May 1970.

BUNNY WAILER: We shot the cover for the album on Leslie Kong's Beverley's label called *Best of the Wailers*, in front of a rock at Race Course in downtown Kingston. They had this big thing there that they thought they were going to carve something out of it, so we were standing there before they actually did the carving. We conceived it as an album project, not a bunch of singles. No one had ever done that before.

ROGER STEFFENS: The album was a way for the Wailers to leave behind the dashed hopes of their unions with Coxson, Planno, Sims and Nash and find a new start with Kong.

BUNNY WAILER: We were always ready to start again. Every time we go to sleep, the Wailers come fresh with new ideas, new harmony technique, and sounding stronger every time. So these things were like challenges to the Wailers, all these experiences, because we had no intention of stopping until we made our mark.

ALLAN "SKILL" COLE: Bob would rehearse in advance with the Wailers on Second Street in Trench Town. The word would get around, like close confidants would know and one or two people would be allowed.

BUNNY WAILER: When we were rehearsing and Bob a write, him no tolerate people around him. He no like people watch him sing. He only wanted the three of we work together.

ALLAN "SKILL" COLE: The scene outside was something, a lot of herb, and getting the vibes and the buildup thing like that together. [But] we didn't crowd the studio much. Bob is alone in that recording studio. In the seventies when we were recording you'd find probably a little more brothers around the studio. But [at Kong's] the discipline was there in the studio. It wasn't a free-for-all thing. Bob was probably the most disciplined musician you'll ever meet.

BUNNY WAILER: We did "Caution" about our own settings, so is like "Caution" definitely point to the Wailers 'cause "when it wet it slippery, when it damp it crampy." The changes we did go through—Bob go through Coxson, go through Planno, is Beverley's we try now, we go in another existence. "Crampy" means it's frozen, slide, so he must have been experiencing winter, wet winter means you're sliding, you step on your car brake when it's wet, and it's crampy too, because the earth is very cold with the water settled on it, and it's slippery.

ROGER STEFFENS: For the Wailers, it was a time to reconnoiter and create a new sound with Leslie Kong, a proven hit-maker. They found a very different man from those with whom they had worked in the past.

BUNNY WAILER: He was a very feminine guy, I never seen him with a woman. His attitude, the way he talked, the way he moved, everything about him was really ladylike. Skinny Minnie, Skinny Ginny guy. Flat. Tall guy, maybe about six foot one.

ROGER STEFFENS: Kong's keen attunement to the international pop scene helped to channel the Wailers toward new discoveries.

BUNNY WAILER: Even "Soul Captives"—"now's the time when man must be free, no more burden and pain"—you can hear the rebirth even in our singing. We treated everything like part of the growth. That's why we redid all those tracks that we had done with Coxson, because we wanted to see if we could better all those tracks with quality. It was only that we didn't have the Skatalites. The Skatalites made a great, great difference to those music in those times. So with other people playing them, it didn't outdo the original. Never, ever, can't even come nearer. So that's vintage, that's forever, that's done. They say what don't break, don't mend. Well, the Skatalites were unbroken. When we were doing over these tracks to get them better, we were trying to mend something that wasn't broken, because they still outlive anything else we did afterwards.

ROGER STEFFENS: The breakup of the Skatalites following Don Drummond's murder of his partner, dancer–singer Marguerite, allowed the Wailers to eventually link with musicians who would become a crucial foundation to their sound as members of Lee Perry's studio band, the Upsetters. But for the moment they worked with Kong's house band, brilliant studio stalwarts Mikey "Boo" Richards on drums, Jackie Jackson on bass, Hux Brown on guitar, Gladstone Anderson and Winston Wright on keyboards, all helmed by engineer Carlton Lee at Dynamic Sounds Studio. However, dissension rushed in when the subject of the album's title came up. The resulting dustup has been elevated to myth because of a prophecy made by Bunny.

BUNNY WAILER: "Cheer Up" would have been a better title for the album, based on what the Wailers were going through at the time. So I told Kong, "Listen, I know that because you are not going to get another album, you might tend to want to use *The Best of the Wailers*. But don't do that because *The Best of the Wailers* would only mean that this is the best we'll ever sing—or you are finished, because you won't be releasing another album. This would be your last album, and it would have been the best you would have heard of the Wailers, because you won't be around to hear any more. So, you don't use that title, none at all. Let's find a title from the album and use that."

The album came out. I was very vexed when I saw the album called *The Best of the Wailers,* everybody was very vexed, Bob, everyone, because everyone was present when the conversation took place. And then Leslie Kong died around Christmas about a week after the album release in England. The album went right back into limbo, went right back into sleep. We just wanted to get some money, to go ahead with our business, and we decided to go and do this album for him. We told him everything, we told him that's what the whole aim was about. That's why we didn't want to do more than one album. It was just looking money for the Wailers to move on our own independent program. We got about five thousand dollars in advance.

ROGER STEFFENS: Kong's sudden death was a devastating shock to the group, leaving their collaboration stillborn.

BUNNY WAILER: We learned he died from a guy when we went to pick up a stamper and he said to us, "Did you hear what happened to Leslie Kong? Kong die this morning. He just come into the studios to work on some records, felt bad, felt sick, went home and died at home."

ROGER STEFFENS: In the summer of 1970 the Wailers changed their label's name from Wail'n Soul'm to Tuff Gong. They were no longer involved with the Soulettes and wanted a logo that was strictly their own.

BUNNY WAILER: Our original title was Tuff Gang. We realized that it was a little too gangish, like is bad boy business too much, in the sense of presumptuous. We no want that. So we just say Tuff Gong. Gong is a cymbal that sends a sound as far as the ears can hear. A big cymbal. So we say Tuff Gong, 'cause it sounds to deal with sound.

CHAPTER 11

Lee Perry and Jamaican Politricks

ROGER STEFFENS: From August 1970 through April 1971, the Wailers recorded around forty tracks for Lee "Scratch" Perry, the zany diminutive producer whose goal was "to hijack the world." They had originally encountered him at Coxson's studio. In late 1969 Scratch had just had a major hit in England with "Return of Django," featuring the Upsetters band: guitarist Alva "Reggie" Lewis; keyboardist Glen Adams; drummer Carlton "Carly" Barrett; and his brother, bass player Aston "Family Man" Barrett.

The eight months spent under Lee Perry's direction would be pivotal for the Wailers' development, as it introduced them to their main musical collaborators, the rhythm section of the Barrett brothers, who would stay with Marley to the end of his life, writing and arranging the backing tracks for his hugely successful international albums.

Their cousin George Barrett recalled how long it took for the Wailers to break through to a more mainstream audience.

GEORGE BARRETT: In the seventies, now, people just get to know the Wailers. Before that, when Family Man and his brother Carlton were in a band called the Hippy Boys, they used to play on a place they call Langston Road, East Kingston.

ROGER STEFFENS: Family Man and Carly's first band was named the Drive-In Cracker Boys, although other sources claim they were called the Jiving Crackerballs. Jon Masouri, in his exhaustively brilliant biography of the Barrett brothers, *Wailin' Blues: The Story of Bob Marley's*

DJ George Barrett, cousin of the Wailers rhythm section's Aston "Family Man" Barrett and Carlton Barrett, in Vancouver, Canada, February 1997.

Wailers, reports that Fams built his first primitive upright bass out of a couple of pieces of wood and used a curtain rod for the one string it contained, while his younger brother Carlton created his initial drum set out of empty paint and kerosene cans.

When Carly and Fams heard "Simmer Down" on a jukebox as teenagers, they felt they were hearing their future—that if the Wailers could play music like that they could too. Family Man, who worked as a welder, made his debut backing singer Max Romeo at a Christmas gig, and formed his first band with Romeo shortly thereafter, in early 1968, calling themselves the Hippy Boys. Glen Adams and Reggie Lewis soon joined them. Around this time, the still childless Aston gave himself the nickname Family Man, boasting of his talent in organizing things for the band as a kind of family unit.

Producer Bunny Lee helmed the first recording session that involved the rhythm team of Carly and Fams on a song that marked the transition from rocksteady to reggae, "Bangarang" by Stranger Cole. Soon they were among the island's most in-demand session musicians. Among their most successful producers was Lee Perry, who had begun as a singer and A & R man at Studio One years earlier, and had gone on to record novelty songs of his own, borrowing Bunny Lee's studio band and calling them the Upsetters. Fams became a hugely sought-after hit-making musician, playing guitar, piano and organ as well as his irresistibly propulsive bass for producers like Duke Reid, Sonia Pottinger, Lloyd "Matador" Daley and many others.

Organ great Glen Adams, inspired by a visit to New York in 1969 where he saw New Orleans's the Meters playing funk-style, brought this new inspiration to Perry, using it on a series of medically titled singles. The band's instrumental smash, "Return of Django," spent fifteen weeks on the British charts, climbing to number five in October 1969.

Jamaican politics were getting hot, too. The iron grip that the right-wing Jamaica Labor Party held on the island was being tested by the socialist-oriented People's National Party, and gunfire was heard nightly in the ghettos of West Kingston.

Dennis Thompson is a live sound mixer, one of the best in the world. Dennis was the man chosen by Bob to mix the Wailers' sound for their live performances from 1976 to the last show in Pittsburgh in September 1980. He remembered working with the Wailers in the early 1970s at Randy's Studio, where Lee Perry did the recordings for the band's seminal albums, considered by many critics to be the trio's finest work.

DENNIS THOMPSON: I met Bob when he used to come to Randy's Studio in Kingston, where I was doing mastering. One Saturday we had a Wailers and Count Ossie. Those tapes, don't ask me about, I've never heard them again. They were done for Bob at Randy's around '70, '71. "Mellow Mood," the greatest "Mellow Mood" in the world! We start three o'clock on the Saturday and finish Sunday morning. The air conditioning unit never worked again from that day. [Perhaps because of the monumental amount of ganja being smoked continuously in the narrow confines of the room.]

ROGER STEFFENS: Thompson often mastered tunes for Perry. The Wailers and Scratch had a fifty-fifty verbal agreement outlining the ownership of their collaborations. They would both invest their money, and from day one all proceeds from their works would be split, half to the band and half to Perry. This verbal arrangement would lead to great disputes in the following years about who actually wrote what. Perry claims authorship of songs like "Small Axe" and others, which is strongly denied by Bunny who was there during the entire process.

BUNNY WAILER: Nobody no write songs with Bob. Scratch would come up with certain little talk and would say him want a song go so or him want song named so or him want a song what deal with an issue there and then Bob would write a song. But him never really sit down and write with we. All Scratch would do in the studio would beat his foot if the song suits him, and he would say, "Yes!" But him can't tell you how to make it work. He didn't write anything on those albums. Maybe one song, "Soul Almighty." It have no substance to that.

ROGER STEFFENS: The song "Small Axe" is one of the disputed songs. Scratch came to visit the Reggae Archives in 2001 and signed my copy of "Small Axe": "I Upsetter write this song. I am the small axe. Bob was not even there when I wrote this song."

BUNNY WAILER: Bob Marley wrote "Small Axe." It was Peter's idea and Bob write the song. Coxson, Duke Reid and Federal had intended on forming an organization called the Big Three to manipulate, keep all the business with them, where all the artists would have to come to them. Well, the conversation was now, "We'll make a song, deal with this t'ree." Peter said, "All right, if them are the big t'ree, we are the small axe." And Bob now go ahead and wrote the song.

ROGER STEFFENS: Third World's Cat Coore witnessed a contemporary performance of the song.

CAT COORE: In the early seventies I first saw Bob at a high school concert, sixth-formers would put them on. I must have been about twelve or thirteen, and St. Andrew's High School, one of the best girls schools in Jamaica, had a concert, and they had Bob on. Incidentally, my older brother who had turned Rasta before me, was playing akete drums in a group from Jamaica College, and they won the competition that year as a band, and they had to back Bob. So the first time I really saw him, my brother was playing with him, which was a real trip. Made big, big impression. It was Bunny, Bob and Peter, and two others. They were great, mon, great! Bob had a patch over his eye at the time. He did "Small Axe," which was the big tune for him then.

ROGER STEFFENS: At the same time they were recording for Scratch, they also recorded songs to be released concurrently on their own Tuff Gong label.

BUNNY WAILER: In deciding which songs to keep for ourselves and which ones to give to Scratch, well, the thing about it is, we just choose songs. Scratch deals with things for the moment, and we a deal with songs what are eternal. If it's gimmick and Scratch a look gimmick, we can always rough up some gimmick, we flexible. It's just that Scratch got good songs that maybe should have been on Tuff Gong—and it go the other way round.

We always try and make the Wailers sound original every time. New, fresh. We always come creative every time, for is a challenge. And Bob write round the clock. The way how Bob write, is not that Bob haffe write out a song, like sit down and complete, start a song from top— Bob no do that. Bob write bits of songs, as the inspiration come him write, and then him just put them bits there together. That's how Bob do most of his songs. He played by ear, and sometimes you're playing and your finger licks a note accidentally, that note says a lot and you go with that. It's hard work because you have to be always in the position to hear that phrase, to hear that melody, you have to be playing your guitar a lot, every day, so that those things can come out of it. And then there are certain overtones and harmonics that come off, and accidents—because you're in tune and listening, you hear every thing that's happening within the sound. And Bob is a man what store them, little bits and pieces of melody and lyrics, and then later on which one did match with which, and put them together, as well as he wrote songs completely. He didn't wait for one song to be finished to start writing the next one. He would have ten, fifteen different songs writing, start different ways, different chords, different progression. And then he puts bits, and fit progression with progression that can fit, and lyrics with lyrics that can fit, or move lyrics and change whatever along the way, he gets lyrics to complete some of them and he just keeps going. Like writing machine! The inspiration that comes today might come back next month, so what you gonna do? Might never come back.

ROGER STEFFENS: Hits began to flow from the raw, bass-heavy productions helmed by Scratch, songs like "Duppy Conqueror," "Kaya," and the novelty "Who Is Mr. Brown." Now it was time to start dividing up the money. Scratch had gone to England and sold enough tracks to Trojan Records for them to release two albums, *Soul Rebels* and *Soul Revolution*. It would be the beginning of the end of their work together.

BUNNY WAILER: Everything was happening for the Wailers at that time. The radio stations was playing the Wailers, the records was selling. We were playing on stage shows, we were doing all kinds of stuff at that time. But one thing was left to be done and that's money. So we meet Scratch at the Sombrero club one night and say, "Scratch, we think it's about time we get ready now to get money. Because every-thing's looking good and we have been holding out long enough. We're excited. We want to see what the money's like now." So Scratch said to Bob, "What kind of money you talking about?" Bob say, " The money, record sales." Scratch say, "Oh that. Record sales and thing. How you see we a go do this money thing here now?" So Bob say, "What you mean, the basic agreement what we did have previously, about fifty-fifty split." Scratch said, "No that can't work. Fifty-fifty business can't work." So Bob said to him, "What you mean, fifty-fifty business can't work? So what will work?" Him say, "I can only pay a royalty."

So Bob weak, but I still stay to one side and I listen to the conversa-tion biting my lip, control myself. Because this look like is death now and murder, because this no sound good. I mean, me don't even want to believe what me a hear. Say it's another trick. Again!! Another trick! Another trip! Me didn't want to contend with it, believe me. Me did all just go hide. Go in a corner and get some herb and burn it and just go hide and know say, well, boy, this must be Wailers' tribulation. This must be our road. So there's no use even crying 'cause nobody want hear that. Because we never had a written agreement with Scratch first, people would a say we deserve this shit. All them things that me a go through just go through phase by phase by phase by phase, just now flash, everything a flash through my head! And Bob weak, him ask, "How much is the royalty, 'cause something have to happen now?" And him say, "Ten cents off of every record. Ten cents." So that make me really mad now. So me go up to him and say, "Scratch, how you mean ten cents after every record? After all of this, after everything that has been said and done, you a come now and say this?" Hear the guy say to me now, "Bunny Wailer I wasn't speaking to you, now, I was talking to Bob." Well, me lash out, me couldn't hold that now. Me just lash out and one lick me lick. He becomes nothing now in front of me, where me don't even see him. Me no respect him no more, me no see him no more. Got mad at the guy and me just go crush him. Me lick him, lick him, lick where the whole place, like about three-quarters of the chairs and everything—for the club floor smooth, well-shined and polished and it's very slippery. So when I lick him he fell on some chairs and hit some tables and lick all them chairs, the chairs a lick chairs go down the line, the whole of that section of the place clean out with chairs, everything tumble down, all people's drinks and people and everything turn over. This is humiliation now 'pon everybody's part. Place a go mash-up now. [Ghetto dons like] Claudie Massop and all the rebels them in there. And them man is Wailers people. So they say to we, "Play it cool and see if you can work out a thing."

Bob couldn't deal with it, because Bob come like him shock out of him wits. Him couldn't even understand it. We were at war now, because everybody feel bad about what Scratch was keeping up, Bob, Peter, we weren't as much into Scratch as we used to be. But we still had to deal with the guy because he had our rights. So I set up a meeting by his office around the back of his place on Charles Street. Myself, him, Peter. All receipts piled high there on the table. We were going to check what was happening with Wailers and what was happening with distribution and all that record stuff.

Before discussion he called to his girl Pauline, "Pauline, bring that bottle you see in my car with the yellow-looking liquid in the car there." She brings it. He takes it and he puts it down on the table where all the papers are. We don't know what the fuck that is anyway, but he sends for it, so it must have something to do with whatever is going to be done. So we were there discussing the business, he's checking up how many records have been sold and Peter takes up the bottle as Mr. Touch [he has to touch something]. Takes up the bottle curiously, looking on the bottle. So Scratch gets uptight immediately and says, "Put down the bottle there, man!" So we just say, "So what's so much about this bottle? Why you send for this bottle anyway? What is in this bottle? Is paste? Gum? What is it? What it have to do with what we do here?" So Scratch say, "Put down the bottle, put down the bottle!" So Peter say, "What about this bottle?" and start to pull the cork out of the bottle. Scratch say to him, "Is acid in the bottle!" So Peter say, "Acid in the bottle! What kind of acid?" The guy say, "The acid what them use to cut the metal stampers down at Dynamic Sounds." Hear the kind of acid the guy have—the acid that cut stampers, it cuts metal, they just pour it on the stamper and it cuts the metal, that silver-tough steel-like stuff.

So Peter said, "What you send this for?" Scratch can't talk. So me realize through me and him already in conflict twice, that could only be meant for me, because Peter and him never have nothing, Bob never have nothing in the context of what me and him have. I know that bottle was for me. But Peter took it up and pulled it, got mad and was hanging onto Scratch to pour it on him, because Peter wanted to know what the fuck Scratch meant to do. But Peter wasn't going to pour it on him, he just wanted to make sure that what he said was in the bottle was really in the bottle. Shit! The guy tumbled over about four times trying to run out of the place and can't move because there's not enough space for him to move and he's panicked now and he's mad. So Peter allowed this guy to run out and make nothing happen to him now, because this guy turn idiot. Is really acid in the bottle. So Peter just take a lick, smash it on the board, ras-claat! It smoke that! Smoke! Smoke!! Smoke!!! Like it a welding torch, it psssshhh on the wood, it drop on the wood. It smoke.

The meeting broke up.

ROGER STEFFENS: Scratch told historian David Katz, author of the Perry biography *People Funny Boy*, "There was no acid there, that come out of his thoughts. They always think me have something to do them something, but it was only in their thoughts because they know I wasn't a chicken."

BUNNY WAILER: Somehow later him and Bob sit down and he show

Bob some statements and figures where Rita take records from him without our knowledge that would be due us based on record sales. We consign records from him which we sold in our shops which we pay him the money. Rita at that time was taking records—thousands of records!—which she was distributing equally with Scratch in a whole-sale market without myself, Bob and Peter knowing, selling them even cheaper than Scratch was. And he knew all this and he didn't say any-thing to us until we were actually going to check money. He showed us all these bills that came from Rita taking records from him and by the time we deducted 10 percent or whatever percentage he had decided to give us from the sales of the records, the amount of money that she had owed him for records that she took and sold covered the amount of royalties that we would have got.

Bob just turn fool. Bob just turn idiot. Bob just walk out dazed. Dazed. And me talk to him and him say, "Rasta, just forget that. Because this is madness, believe me. Disregard that. Please! Don't bother go follow up that. At least she take it and spend it upon the youth them." Me personally feel no way. 'Cause them time there me no have no children and me understand what a reach Bob right there so, and me see the position where he's in, he might get himself in pure trouble now, this could be murder. Peter just went away, didn't talk, didn't say nothing. Just went away frustrated. Peter blamed the problem on Bob. That caused us to let go of Scratch. We just left him with everything and he just started to sell and sell and we got no money, no nothing.

ROGER STEFFENS: Scratch denies the charges. In a 1984 interview, he claimed that he and the Wailers "worked like brothers 'til Chris Black-well saw it was something great and came like a big hawk and grab Bob Marley up."* Rita Marley has never said anything on the subject in our conversations, but based on her own published version of her life with Marley, it seems likely that she would deny these allegations now.

* http://www.uncarved.org/dub/scratch.html.

Following this period Glen Adams moved to the U.S. and Reggie Lewis was superseded by Tyrone Downie who, along with Earl "Wya" Lindo, became one of Bob Marley's two keyboardists for much of his phenomenal solo career. He was also the youngest Wailer, deeply intimidated by the other members of the group at first.

TYRONE DOWNIE: I was born in the heart of Kingston on King Street, close to the intersection of North Street, on May 20th, 1956, at home. Peter Tosh used to live behind me. Everyone was into Black Power, like soul power, James Brown, Malcolm X, those things. Peter used to make these Afro combs, carve it out of wood and stick bicycle spokes in it. I used to be so amazed by that, fascinated. And I started to copy him and tried to make them too, with little fists at the bottom. I was good too! But I didn't realize who this guy was because I was in school, I was in the choir and I wasn't really much into popular music. My older brother, Donald, used to always bring the popular records home and be playing them. But not until I started messing with the record player did I really get interested in popular music. And then I didn't know this guy was a member of the Wailers! I mean, I grew up with this guy, living right there! He was always walking up and down with this guitar, and I always thought that was just a guy who loves to sing. 'Cause there were a lot of people like that in that area.

In school is when I really started to turn on to music itself, in the choir. Augustus Pablo was going to the same school, Kingston College, and he started to talk about me to people which I didn't even know. But apparently Pablo knew all the musicians. He knew the music scene downtown: he would be hanging out. He was Augustus Pablo! He was doing "Java" and all that stuff. And he told Family Man Barrett about me. Family Man was forming this little band, he wanted a keyboard player. And apparently Pablo didn't really want to go and play in any club on the weekends. His folks would probably kill him. But anyway, I said, "Why not?" Family Man sent this guy to school for me one day, Charlie Bass, who is a singer and DJ-type cat too. And Charlie said,

"We want you to come and play in this band! Follow me up to this club and meet the musicians." So I was excited! And he says, "And you're gonna have an organ." Jesus Christ! It was a Farfisa FAST 5 or something like that. With a Leslie command! Anyway, I went and there was Family Man. The first time in my life I actually laid eyes on him. Short guy—didn't have no beard, no locks then. But he looked like a guerrilla from Zimbabwe still, you know? The first session we did together was "Black Cinderella" by Errol Dunkley.

ROGER STEFFENS: After the Wailers split from Lee Perry they continued to perform with the Barrett brothers, taking them away from Perry's control. Some of their first live shows appeared to be political in nature. At that time, the two main parties in Jamaica were the JLP and the PNP. In a 1975 interview Marley said that self-proclaimed Democratic Socialist PNP leader Michael Manley was the best prime minister Jamaica ever had. Five years later he claimed that he had never supported Michael Manley. Yet the Wailers toured in support of Manley's election in late 1971 and early 1972.

STEPHEN DAVIS: It was called the PNP Musical Bandwagon and they went around playing on the back of a flatbed truck for two months.

ROGER STEFFENS: Stephen Davis is the author of a fine 1983 biography titled *Bob Marley*. I interviewed him in February 1985 on the *Reggae Beat* show on L.A.'s KCRW.

STEPHEN DAVIS: The funny thing is, the area that Bob comes from, Nine Mile, and that whole part of Saint Ann, has always been a JLP area. In fact, I got to know the minister from that area, Neville Gallimore, and it's always been a sort of JLP hotbed, and I think that Bob's support for the PNP just reflected this incredible trend towards socialism in the early seventies. Manley was seen as a savior and a reaction to all the stultifying years of colonial rule. We have to remember that Britain's rule of Jamaica was the longest colonial rule in history, almost four hundred years of straight colonial rule, from the middle of the 1500s to 1962.

GEORGE BARRETT: I saw one of the PNP Bandwagon shows. Michael Manley always wanted Bob Marley to come to play some of the sounds that he heard. But the reason why: the JLP politician, Edward Seaga, was in the business. He was partner with Byron Lee at Dynamic Sounds. [Manley wanted musicians] because Seaga was the opposition thing in the Labour Party that's coming on strong. He was not running for prime minister, he was just running for office. [Seaga would go on to become the island's prime minister in the 1980s.]

ROGER STEFFENS: Manley ran for office at the end of 1971 with the PNP Bandwagon and the Rod of Correction. This was an imperial staff that Haile Selassie had given him during his state visit in 1966, and it became known as "Joshua's stick," based on the name that Manley was being called by the Rastafarian community, who saw in his candidacy a hope that herb would be legalized and that their oppression would be ended. Manley held island-wide rallies to which several artists—Judy Mowatt, Third World, the Wailers—drew large crowds, after which he would come onstage.

GEORGE BARRETT: Seaga was representing Western Kingston. Bob lived in those areas. So Bob didn't want any conflict. He didn't enter the politics thing. 'Cause his music was beatin' down this politics that was breaking up the community. [The other] reason why Bob didn't do anything for the politician in those days, he would rather [not] get killed. For you to go on stage and sing in the sixties coming into the early seventies about any politics thing, bwoi, you have to have guards.

ROGER STEFFENS: And yet, Bob and the Wailers played the Bandwagon shows. Cat Coore, a classically trained cellist and mainstay of the band Third World, was a longtime friend of Bob Marley's. His father was a minister in Michael Manley's government, and he remembers the Wailers from the Bandwagon tour.

CAT COORE: First time I picked up the guitar was about 1968, and Bob first heard me play in 1971, going into '72, with Inner Circle, 'cause we were doing the Bandwagon for the PNP then. We had all these artists that we had to back every night: Dennis Brown, Alton Ellis, the Chosen Few, Scotty, Tinga Stewart, Judy Mowatt—nuff artists.

The Bandwagon started campaign time, late '71. The election was February '72. So the Bandwagon started about October, 'cause I remember I was doing exams and I had to stop. We'd play two, three times during the week and once on the weekend probably.

ROGER STEFFENS: I talked with Bunny Wailer about this and he seemed quite disingenuous, claiming that they "never supported Michael Manley." I said, "You put on a performance that drew thousands of people and you were part of the draw to get them there so that they would eventually listen to a speech by Manley. Now how do you think the public thought about you? They *must* have thought you were supporting him." And he said, "No, it was just because they paid the Wailers more money than we'd ever been paid before, $150 a performance, so we did it."

GEORGE BARRETT: I'd say the same thing to back up Bunny Wailer. They weren't there for the politician. To me they were there to expose themselves and getting paid. The more people you can play before the better. The Jamaican attitude toward those things sometime is the gathering of people to see them. They want exposure. All over the island! Just like that.

Some people might think that they were supporting Manley so. And some people just go there not to hear Michael Manley speech at all, just to hear the music. The musician is like independents to them. These things were kept up at the crossroad, so it was a public thing. The one I saw was in Brownstown, Windward Road; that is his constituency. Right in front of Club 21. East Kingston, Dunkirk. It's still a PNP stronghold same way. That night me and a guy name Ricky Valentine went. They no say it's politics thing. They say they have a street dance and Michael Manley going to appear. But we all know lots of gunmen and lots of violence go on around these meetings. So we went and we keep far. There was a bridge, and we sit on the rail of the bridge. So we can make a quick getaway!

When they say "Wailers," it wasn't like Bob Marley and the Wailers, it was just Wailers, all three of them. Wailers gonna be there, whoa! Everybody come out. Just the music take over. I don't think they come to see Michael Manley per se. Is a gathering of musicians and people hungry for the music too. And it's free. And it's place to sell little peanuts, sell little chewing gum, it's a hustling ground for all these things. Gunmen, everybody come, and you don't say nothing against that party for the whole night. You just keep your opinion to yourself, 'cause you don't know who you're standing next to.

CAT COORE: The Wailers were supporting Manley in a very subtle kind of way. I think that they probably felt that of any politician that had come to Jamaica for the time that Jamaica had been free and independent, Michael was the one who showed the most, during the early seventies, directive that he would be dealing with poor people. And it did really end up that way, because in the seventies Michael really did do a lot for poor people, no question about it. All poor people. See, when a politician in Jamaica becomes prime minister he gets pressure to think about the other side too. So most of the things that he does are done in the name of Eddie [Seaga] or Michael, and you know whose people they're looking out for. But it has to transcend that boundary too.

GEORGE BARRETT: How it go in Kingston back in the olden days, if I'm a PNP and you're a Labour, if your Labourite Party's in power and they build a community for you with your house, the house is not yours. It's for the politicians and the politics people. So if you lose, the PNP come and take the house from you. So this is why you have a fight; always have that fight with West Kingston against East Kingston. So if your party's out, pack up your baggage, man, this house is ours now.

At that time the bell [symbol] was the Labourites and the fist was the PNP. When they ring the bell we used to say the bell ringing is slavery business. It's like flashing gang signs. You can't ring a bell and you can't wear red!

When Michael Manley won the election in 1972 there was a procession from Dunkirk to Tivoli Garden. They give us three or four bus full and ride a coffin, to come bury Seaga! We make the coffin and a doll of Seaga. And we made a procession straight down Spanish Town Road; we're going to Maypen Cemetery. So that's where the war always started because you're entering into their turf. And we never reach Maypen, because it's like a test! If any of you can penetrate them, then we conquer. But we never reach there, man, because rock haffe drop and man haffe run and fight and stick and stone and bottle—bus mash up!

ROGER STEFFENS: While Jamaica was revamping its political stance, worrying the Nixon administration, which feared that the island would go the way of Cuba, the Wailers were refocusing their outlook internationally, hoping that under Danny Sims's direction, JAD would help them become big sellers in the U.S. and Britain. A contract with CBS in the UK seemed to be the big break they had been hoping for, but like all the promises that had been made to them by Coxson, Kong and Perry, it would prove to be another false hope.

CHAPTER 12

Cold Cold Winters in Sweden and London

ROGER STEFFENS: As the seventies dawned, Marley was being promoted in several directions by the Sims-Nash team. He would be brought to Sweden and England for several months at a time, scoring a film, touring with Nash and ultimately eclipsing him, signing with not one but two major labels and making the link that would bring him to world fame and cause the breakup of the Wailers, with much attendant tribulation along the way.

ALLAN "SKILL" COLE: The relationship of Bob with Johnny Nash and Danny Sims was interesting. I remember when Bob used to talk about them, he would refer to Danny as his manager and publisher and Johnny was his good bredren. The first time we went to meet with Danny and Johnny in New York was in 1969. Bob was always telling me how Johnny Nash's voice was like a bird, but I don't think Bob ever talk it and let Johnny Nash hear. Bob said, "I want you to meet this big baldhead don, my manager." He used to tell me, "Allan, when Danny Sims take me anywhere and he's finished talking about me, my head grow. He is something else when he is carrying me out." So it was interesting when I met Johnny Nash, very quiet guy, lotta smile. And when I met Danny, Danny was the talker, every time Danny was talking Bob was always looking at me and giving me the signal and saying, "See what I was telling you." They went to the health food store near Cayman Music. We ended up there that day, in the health food store.

Danny Sims was a health freak and we were strictly vegetarian at that time and he was introducing us to all these new meals. We were there enjoying and listening to him and Johnny and the type of things they start talking and teasing us, we didn't do as Rasta, you know, so it was interesting the first day, things that I won't talk about!

NEVILLE WILLOUGHBY: See, Bob was never a person who was chatty. When he came to do work, he came to do work. It was for Bob to write the hit for John. He definitely thought reggae was the next thing. When you were with them they were always working at music.

ALLAN "SKILL" COLE: With Johnny and Bob now, there was always a deep respect, from both sides. I know Bob had a lot of respect for him and the same thing, knowing Johnny and hearing how he talked and how he felt for Bob, I know that he loved Bob very much.

ROGER STEFFENS: During this period Bob was called to Sweden to help Johnny Nash write songs for a movie he was starring in. Lars Fyledal, a Swedish reggae writer and collector, did extensive research about Bob's experience in Scandinavia for *The Beat* magazine. The following is an edited version.

LARS FYLEDAL: Johnny Nash and his associates came to Sweden in November 1970 to begin filming a movie called *Vill Sa Garna Tro (Want So Much to Believe)*. Nash had had some acting success in Hollywood in the early sixties with *Take a Giant Step*.

Now Nash was set to costar with Christina Schollin, a Swedish actress who later became world-famous for her part in Ingmar Bergman's *Fanny and Alexander* in the eighties. The movie's storyline had a Swedish stewardess (Schollin) falling in love with her jazz-ballet teacher, a black American played by Nash. The relationship was filled with various complications, mostly due to the black–white situation and Nash's character's problem with the U.S. military.

Nash rented a house on Sigurdsvagen Street in Nockeby, which was located about ten kilometers from the center of Stockholm. The writer–producer had decided to let Nash make the film's music, in order to take advantage of the singer's name in the export of the movie and therefore add some extra interest.

Accompanying Nash were Fred Jordan, who was his manager and arranger, and a young white Texan keyboard player named Johnny "Rabbit" Bundrick, whose main function was to supply the songs but also to play the keyboards and arrange the music. They were joined by African percussionists and local Swedish musicians, including a young guitarist named Jan Schaffer.

Late in March 1971, Nash asked Schaffer to come to the house in Nockeby. He took him into a room and turned on a tape player. "I want you to listen to this," Nash said. The sound of roughly recorded music filled the room. "The singer and writer of these songs is called Bob Marley and he's very big in Jamaica and has had many hits there. What do you think? Isn't he great? Well, this man is coming to Sweden in a couple of days to start work with you."

Marley arrived, dressed in a suit, and was shown a small room to live in at the Nockeby house. Bundrick remembers: "This was the first time I met Bob Marley and I thought, 'Oh my God, this will never work! He can't even tune his guitar and I can't understand a word he says.'"

"Bob Marley was very shy and silent and strictly dedicated to his music," recalls Schaffer. "He talked only to Rabbit and seemed to communicate through his music. I especially remember one time when one of the Swedish musicians tried to loosen him up a bit and said, 'Say something Jamaican,' but Marley went even more sour and withdrawn."

Lars Rossin, who was the engineer at Studio 3 of Europafilm, where the soundtrack recording took place, says: "Bob Marley was silent and quiet and didn't like the style of living. And there was a special incident at the house in Nockeby. It really was an open collective typical of its time, and there were lots of persons that simply hung out around the place. It happened at a time when Bob was in the shower and was joined by a girl and he went really mad and started yelling and shouting at her. He was absolutely furious. Someone asked him why he became that terribly upset but Bob didn't give an answer."

Bundrick met a Swedish girl named Marlene Lingard during that stay and they lived together for nine years after that. She was hanging around the house and the studio. "I remember Bob well in Stockholm," she recalls. "He was sort of pushed away and wasn't taking much part in the work. He was, for example, living in the basement in the house for some time, just to be alone and stay away from the others. He was sulking a lot and playing his guitar, but it didn't sound like anything special. When he was in his better moods, he cooked for us and introduced us to fish tea and other exotic foods. He was very fascinated by the snow and Stockholm. Also, there were two girls living in the house that took care of him, taking him into Stockholm and buying him some new clothes, as neither Rabbit nor Bob got any payment."

"Bob taught us all how to play reggae," said Bundrick. "He would show us how the different instrumental parts should feel and be played and give examples. He was wonderful. At the house in Nockeby, I had a room, Bob had one and Nash had one. It was like a factory of music. If you walked through the house, you would hear reggae from Bob, ballads from Nash and rock ballads from me, all at the same time. Then we would huddle together and see what we all had that would fit together and then go into the studio."

Marley's main contributions to the soundtrack were in two instrumental tracks. The first, "Fifteen Minutes," is a relatively fast reggae shuffle dominated by Bundrick's organ; the sound is fairly loose. The second song, "Masquerade Dance," is more interesting. Bob's reggae guitar cuts much more effectively against another guitar, jazz drums and bass, and it weaves and plays against Rabbit's almost pastoral piano. The sound is very unusual and creates a rather surrealistic feeling.

The movie was eventually released on September 4, 1971, and was a flop, rejected by both the critics and the public.

DANNY SIMS: We had put a record out of Bob Marley called "Bend

Down Low" and "Mellow Mood," and we just couldn't get play on it. I guess that was a little disappointing for Bob. The problem we had with Johnny Nash and Bob Marley was that Johnny was a pop act and because he was on the Arthur Godfrey show the white people knew him. He did all the big shows that the white artists did. So when we broke Johnny's "Hold Me Tight," the producer out of Sweden was doing a movie and he wanted Johnny to star in the movie and do the soundtrack. We brought Bob Marley with us 'cause we wanted to keep him close to us to work on him and get his songs down and keep recording him. Bob played on the soundtrack and worked on the film from start to finish.

So after we got there in September there was a snowstorm. Even coming out of Chicago I never saw that much snow in all of my life. So we couldn't work on the movie and the filming had to stop. So we waited three months. And we were on a per diem. Everybody there was getting paid and we had a mansion in the city called Nockeby right outside of Stockholm. And it gave us plenty of time. Now we got a little demo studio setup, we're recording, we're doing the soundtrack. The film company paid for it. So the film took a year instead of three months.

ROGER STEFFENS: Meanwhile, back home in Jamaica, the Wailers' new Tuff Gong records were making significant inroads on the Jamaican charts.

BUNNY WAILER: "Lively Up Yourself," " Screw Face," "Redder Than Red," we had a nice little history in there. Nice run of songs. All these records were selling then. This Wailers business was making money at the time. We had thousands of dollars in the bank! Thousands! The first time we ever really had thousands of dollars. It was the first time where we ever saw we were going to have this house that we had been dreaming about. And Skill Cole fucked it up. Right after this we left Skill Cole in charge and went to Britain to deal with Johnny Nash and Danny Sims.

I knew Skill Cole as Allan from maybe the age of eleven because of football. He's just a bit younger than us. Before we go to England now we sit down with him and discuss the possibility of him managing the Wailers' business. Not managing the Wailers, but the Wailers' business. We were going to split it four ways. So Alan was now like one of the Wailers because we had to be trusting him with all our money, so we knew that he would be totally involved. And he had ideas of getting records played, and he had his methods of getting records played. We didn't want to deal with the radio station people, we just couldn't deal with them. They took our money, they took whatever we gave them, we tried to be nice to them, but they just didn't want to play Wailers records. I don't know if it was some plot or whatever. But Allan knew how to get to them and made them play the record.

We had this banking system where three people had to sign for any kind of moneys to come out of the bank. But Allan had some kind of power of attorney that we gave him when we were leaving to go to England the first time with Carly and Family Man, when Johnny Nash was doing his King of Reggae tour, and we were to have been opening act for him. So we left Allan in charge. We left Allan with about fourteen thousand dollars in the bank and we took a couple of thousand dollars in our pockets too, maybe three thousand to make sure we wouldn't get stranded with no airfare back.

When we come home Allan tell us we only have four thousand dollars in our account. He can't explain, he can't say nothing, he's dumb, dumb. Nothing not coming out of his mouth. Later we found out it was gambling that was where the money went, poker and horse racing. 'Cause he's addicting to gambling. So I had to talk to Bob and show him, well, don't get involved with Allan. For some reason Bob kind of fancied Allan. But at least we had some money to go in the studios, eight thousand pounds [as we'll see, this was the advance from Chris Blackwell for the *Catch A Fire* album]. Allan was now becoming a dreadlock and we didn't want nobody to hear us as Rasta quarreling over money, so we just dismissed it.

ALLAN "SKILL" COLE: You know why this couldn't be true? I was in Brazil the whole of 1972. The Wailers were in England with Chris Blackwell. When I got back in '73, the money I had made for the Wailers, Bob shared it all with Bunny and Peter. I never took a cent from them, ever! One signature on the account withdrawals was not enough. We never had an argument about the money on the face of this earth.

ROGER STEFFENS: Lee "Scratch" Perry added to the Wailers' woes. He had gone to England where he sold many of the tracks he had made with the Wailers to Trojan Records. Bunny claims it wasn't until Sims released the multi-album series *The Complete Bob Marley and the Wailers 1967–1972*, beginning in 1996, that he saw the first money from those sessions cut twenty-five years earlier. Sims also paid regular royalties to the estates of Bob and Peter from then on.

DANNY SIMS: Once Bob started to record for us, when we put that original product out, Bob came to us and asked that he could record product so that he could make a living and to release it in the Caribbean. That's how Trojan and all these companies got hold of that product. You see once that product was released in the Caribbean they bootlegged that product, those other places. As Don Taylor [Bob's manager from the mid-seventies forward] said when they went to England, they were pissed. They weren't happy that Trojan had their product, they were pissed that it happened. And I think that the guy who sold it to them or made the deal with them was Lee "Scratch" Perry. And I think they nearly beat him to death.

ALLAN "SKILL" COLE: The problem was that all the records that we release in those era, Trojan one month after they release in Jamaica they release in London.

DANNY SIMS: And Trojan never to this day pay the royalties. In those days it was this guy, Lee Gopthal, who was head of Trojan. We learn after that he was a figurehead.

ROGER STEFFENS: Eventually Trojan and all its holdings were broken up, after discovering that their various subsidiary labels were bidding for the same artists and forcing unnecessary price wars. All this piracy that Marley was experiencing caused him and Sims to be more careful about his publishing rights from then on. Bob reunited with Bunny and Peter in London.

DANNY SIMS: In Sweden after we got done with the soundtrack for Johnny Nash's film, I had a boy working with Bob, putting all of his songs down for publishing by Cayman Music. He worked every day 'cause Bob had so many songs. We did lots of tracks for the publishing company's lead sheets.

After the film I went to London [1972] and I brought everybody from Stockholm to London, the guy doing the lead sheets, everybody. And Sony rented a huge house for the band, so we had a group out of Texas. Johnny brought some boys, Rabbit Bundrick and that crew. So they lived in one house and Johnny Nash and I lived in another house.

BUNNY WAILER: We were sharing a house with Danny and Johnny. There was a lot of girls and that prostitution kind of living that we couldn't deal with, so we tell them to rent a place for us, we want a place for ourselves. We were in Neasden off the North Circular, I think it was called the D Circular. We stayed there and we rehearsed in a place called Kingston that was in North London. Johnny rehearsed at the same place.

DANNY SIMS: In 1972 Dick Asher was president of Sony UK [known as both Columbia and CBS Records in America, names that Sims uses interchageably]. Dick Asher happened to have been Johnny Nash's lawyer when I met him in the sixties, so he was a Johnny Nash fan. And being that Johnny was popular he went right into CBS and they signed him. I tried to get Bob Marley signed at that time but they weren't interested because they didn't know Bob. So Johnny got signed and the album was *I Can See Clearly Now.*

When Bob came to London then in '72 Dick Asher signed him and we put out "Reggae On Broadway" backed with "I'm Gonna Get You." Bob's record flopped, Johnny's took straight off. That year he had three or four hits when we were independent, and now we're with a major. *I Can See Clearly* took off like a flash. Bob then was a little bit unhappy that his record didn't hit. But then he was trying to do rhythm and blues type reggae. "Reggae On Broadway" wasn't the best song we had, but it was more soul. We still didn't know how to record him, but that was just a single that we thought was more commercial. And the A & R people thought the same thing. But they were following Johnny and me because we were record people and Dick Asher let us have our way.

Sony was very generous with money and per diem, because we had probably twelve people on per diems, and the house, at Sony. And then we recorded at Sony Studios with Bob. So when *I Can See Clearly Now* came out we had to tour to support the record. We did over a hundred concerts, mostly for free and at Sony's expense.

ROGER STEFFENS: On this tour, in support of his hit record, Nash was billed as "The King of Reggae."

DANNY SIMS: Johnny would do an hour and Bob would do forty-five, fifty minutes with Johnny Nash's band. And in the beginning, nobody knew Bob, just a few Jamaican people knew his records from Coxson and his early records that were hits. Few of them would come and see Bob backstage.

Bob in the very beginning got very little reaction. But as we toured Bob started getting as much reaction as Johnny. Then you could see the little bit of jealousy on Johnny's part and a little bit of jealousy of Bob on Johnny, because Johnny's record took off like an airplane.

BUNNY WAILER: Johnny Nash was very nervous about the Wailers. He didn't want the Wailers ever to be on the same stage as him. He could tolerate Bob coming to sing two tracks, which were his new stuff that they were trying to break Bob into that kind of a market. New guy you're trying to introduce, opening for Johnny Nash, the King of Reggae. Bob played without us, singing "Reggae On Broadway" and "Oh Lord I Got To Get There." He would just sing those two tracks, run off, steamed up the place!

ROGER STEFFENS: Danny Sims downplays the rivalry.

DANNY SIMS: I think Bob was content because he was our friend, he believed in us. And Johnny, he owned the company with me. Although all artists are jealous of other artists, especially if they start taking a little bit of the highlight. And we were the hottest tour on the road.

ROGER STEFFENS: Bunny's memory is more precise and upsetting.

BUNNY WAILER: Finally [Johnny Nash] lightened up a little, said maybe he would give us a chance to be onstage. We went way up in the country part of England, a place called Becks Hill, where no black folks are. You walk the whole place and you see not one black face because all windows were opening because this was a bunch of niggas. And we were dread. And we had all red, gold and green, colors were bright. You could see us a mile away!

That night they put a band on first, they played kind of Osibisa stuff, an African fusion band, little young group coming up with that kind of direction. They brought the house down. They came off, it was our turn next and we went on, because we were going to play the same instruments that the first guys played. When we went on we opened with this song called "Ringo," an old Skatalites record. But when we started playing we found out that Family Man's bass was out of tune—the people tuned out the bass. The fucking guitars were out of tune. People's mouths were open, staring to wonder what the fuck was wrong. And we just say, "Okay, Family Man, you drop out. All the guitars drop out. Just let me and Carly alone hold riddim. Carly playing drums and I playing drums, bongos, percussions. Doing things! Getting the groove, playing things, improvising. Bob had his guitar backstage but they fucked up the strap. When he put it on it fell off. He had to play without his guitar that night. We did "Small Axe," "Duppy Conqueror," "Put It On," "Rude Boy," "Nice Time," "Bend Down Low," "Keep On Moving," "Stir It Up." And we had this track we used to do, "Slipping Into Darkness." That was a foreign song that we did real good, we rehearsed it a lot. By now all the people were standing up dancing. There was a spirit in the place that was our first experience of feeling how the white folks reacted when they heard us. When we did "Keep On Moving" the people formed a line, they got up and put their hands on each other's shoulders and they formed like a big snake going through this little theater. Everybody got up and joined the line—old, young, everybody! The line went right through the theater, right through the seats, round the theater like a goddamn snake. Big snake! We were doing "Keep On Moving," we sang for maybe twenty minutes. And the people was just marching, just doing that, arms on shoulders.

After we mashed down the show flat, leaving the stage, we couldn't leave. When we went backstage, the promoter begged us, pleaded with us, if we don't come back we ain't gonna have no theater left because the people start breaking off the arms of the chairs and start smashing up the goddamn place outside. So we went out and we did "Reggae On Broadway" and two other tracks. We closed with "One Love" or maybe "Love And Affection." When we left the people were *worse* than before. But we couldn't go back. We didn't have any more songs to sing. So whatever mash was going to be mashed down—Johnny Nash didn't come yet—the show seemed to be ended.

So the promoter had to find something to tell people so he shouted, "OK, calm down, calm down! The King is coming," 'cause Johnny Nash really the people came to see. So they kicked off and before the first track ended 25 percent of the people got up and walked out. In the middle of the second track another 25 percent of what was left got up and walked out. Because they wanted to meet the Wailers now, they wanted autographs to be signed. And if they stuck around, Wailers might be gone by that time. Johnny's band got confused, the guy on the Mellotron started to play wrong notes and the band panicked, started playing foolishness. By this time there was maybe about ten people were sitting in the goddamn theater. Johnny panicked and went into his ballads thing. He was supposed to be King of Reggae and he started to sing "Mary's Boy Child." That ended it. The rest of the people that was there got up. The place was empty. The band had to stop playing prematurely in the middle of the track.

By this time Danny Sims had to leave this fucking scene altogether. Nobody could find him, because Johnny Nash was looking for Danny Sims to kill him dead. Then we found Johnny all by himself around the corner, kicking his boots in the walls, pounding his fist in the walls. We couldn't even stop him, or let him know we saw him in that kind of way, and we walked away and left him. And that was the end of Johnny Nash totally. We didn't hear about Johnny Nash up to this day. Just disappeared out of the business. Never talked to him again. But he don't hate the Wailers. He hates Danny Sims, him and Danny broke up, mashed up as partners. They were all at war.

ROGER STEFFENS: In fact, strictly in terms of sales and exposure Nash was a superstar compared to Marley's "bubbling under" career, and had succeeded in reaching an overwhelmingly white audience. He is still well known to this day, especially for his single "I Can See Clearly Now," which appears regularly in commercials and films. Sims does acknowledge, however, the difficulties Nash had in reaching the African-American audience.

DANNY SIMS: It was like a pop tour, it wasn't like an electric tour. Johnny was a pop act. Even today, we never got black play on Johnny Nash. He was strictly a white artist.

ROGER STEFFENS: After a decade of recording, all marked by dashed hopes, Marley was growing increasingly frustrated. He showed up one day at the record company's offices to register his displeasure.

DANNY SIMS: Bob was disgruntled. He went into CBS one day, I was told, and the A & R guy—I don't know why he went there, but they snobbed [snubbed] him. And I went in to CBS and tried to get to the bottom of it. But he shouldn't have gone there without me anyway. Because we put out two or three records right in a row and nothing happened. So I don't know whether he figured I was working too much on Johnny Nash and not enough on him. But whatever it was, he was in London now with all these Jamaican people in a big house. They had a car for that crowd. And Sony was spending a lot of money on him. And we started to rehearse for the Sony yearly convention. And Bob was getting very popular and Clive Davis, the head of Columbia Records, was a good friend of mine, and Dick Asher was his guy. And then, the night when Bob was going to do a full show—they had brought over Carly, Family Man, Peter, Bunny and another musician—Sony had them doing a full rehearsal for the show, and Bob's show was so hot at rehearsal that people started coming to the rehearsals. Bob was so bloody hot and just ready for the show. And Bob came to me and said he wasn't going to do the show. Clive Davis, everybody, was very disappointed. But Bob was despondent. He thought he got snobbed at CBS, and he thought they were more interested in Johnny than in him.

ROGER STEFFENS: Enter Chris Blackwell, a white Jamaican from a wealthy family who had been educated in England where, in the early sixties, he began importing and re-pressing Jamaican records. He was a cofounder and silent partner in the UK's controversial Trojan Records label. Don Taylor, the man who would become Bob Marley's manager, described the label's operations.

DON TAYLOR: Trojan in my opinion, what Trojan was: When Chris Blackwell first went to England, pirating of Jamaican records got big and serious. Because most of the records he put out were records he had no deals on. They were all pirate records. He'd get them and press them but he had no deal with them. Once Chris Blackwell had a chance to become legit after he had Jimmy Cliff and Millie Small hits on Island [his own label] he had to share that piracy, illegitimate underground stuff he was doing. So that's where Trojan came in with Lee Gopthal as the front.

ROGER STEFFENS: Contacted by phone in Jamaica in November 2016, Chris Blackwell denied Taylor's claim about piracy.

CHRIS BLACKWELL: I didn't pirate any records. I had deals with Duke Reid, Mr. Pottinger, and almost all the Jamaican producers except

Prince Buster. Trojan started in 1967 and I got immersed in rock. [The group] Traffic was taking off in England. It was a very exciting time with Traffic, and with Stevie Winwood and the Spencer Davis Group. So I no longer was going down to Jamaica and wheeling and dealing with records. I stopped doing that around 1966.

DANNY SIMS: [When we were recording Bob at Sony Studios,] a guy called me and said Chris Blackwell had come by the studio and he got our keyboard player to work with Traffic.

ROGER STEFFENS: It turns out Blackwell had his eye on more than the JAD keyboardist.

DANNY SIMS: Bob was signed to Sony, he was a Sony artist. And Chris Blackwell had been sneaking over to Sony Studios romancing Bob. And when we found out, Sony sent a stop and desist order to Blackwell.

ROGER STEFFENS: But Marley had already been swayed, furious over his treatment by Sony executives in London. One of the people who had "snobbed" him was a lawyer named Bob White. Marley was so incensed by the slight that he asked for a release on his contract. At this point he and Sims were still allies, so Danny went to bat for Bob against Sony.

DANNY SIMS: I got him unsigned from one of the biggest companies in the world. Nobody would let Bob Marley go after putting a year of moneys into him, putting him into a big house, giving him moneys for his band. Chris Blackwell talked about the moneys that he spent, [saying] they were impoverished—with Sony, you're going to be impoverished? They wanted Bob. The lawyer, Bob White, guess where he went? He became the lawyer for Island Records.

ROGER STEFFENS: Danny implies that there was some kind of secret arrangement between Blackwell and White to dissuade Marley from continuing with Sony, causing him and the group to move to Island Records.

DANNY SIMS: The motherfuckers—you know what they did, they set me up. Bob White was the one who snobbed him—that leaked down from the A & R staff. They liked Bob, and they believed that we was fishing, we didn't know what kind of record to put out on Bob to make him take off. It was Bob White we negotiated with. And when we found out it was White that snobbed him, they fired Bob White. There was a big shakeup with Bob leaving Sony.

It was my relationship with Dick Asher that got Bob released from the contract. It wasn't easy to get that done. We took an override. What did Sony want with an override? But my contract with Bob was up now, I'd been with Bob for five years. I asked for another five years of renewal with Bob as a writer and I got it. And an override on the records.

Did I have to bring some kind of specific pressure on CBS to let him go? Well, I think between you and me that anybody I dealt with would have brought pressure on him. You got to remember who my partner was, where I was. So that'll put pressure on anybody—except the federal government. [Danny often boasted that he was partners with the Mafia.] Cayman Music continued under my control until 2011. I sold it to some guys in London, I forget the name of the guys. I'd have to think about the fact that contract renewal is after twenty-eight years, so I would have lost it anyway. 'Cause I signed him to ASCAP. If I had signed him to a British society I would have saved myself, but I had to sell because the time was running out.

And sometimes I think about that and I think that Bob being a friend, I told him, "Bob, give me an extra five years on your contract, so that I publish every song that you put out on Island and an override that I'll split with Sony." So to this day, every record Chris has sold from the time Bob was with him, they have to pay us about 20 percent for the publishing. Half goes to Sony, half goes to JAD. And they paid that all the time on all the Island albums through *Exodus* in 1977. He made more money with me as a publisher, 'cause Barbra Streisand did "Guava Jelly," Eric Clapton did "I Shot The Sheriff."

ROGER STEFFENS: After years of trying to engineer a breakthrough for Marley and the Wailers, Danny surrendered control to Blackwell, knowing that the rough-edged artist he felt he had discovered was now ready in every way for the demands of the world's biggest stages.

DANNY SIMS: When we sold Bob's contract to Chris Blackwell and Island Records in October of 1972, Bob was ready. Bob had great training by Johnny Nash. But they both lent something to each other. Bob taught Johnny how to play the reggae rhythm, 'cause Bob played it. He was an established, polished artist who was able to coproduce with Blackwell or any other producer. He was able to use what he had learned from Johnny Nash, Arthur Jenkins and all the other great people we put him with. From 1967 to 1972 was enough for anyone to get his PhD and be able to go out on the stage of the world. I think the fact that he is the only star from the third world who is in the Rock and Roll Hall of Fame speaks for itself. [Bob has subsequently been joined there by Jimmy Cliff.]

CHAPTER 13

Island's Kinky Reggae

ROGER STEFFENS: When the Wailers signed with Chris Blackwell's Island label, it seemed that they had finally found a champion who could bring them and their music to the outside world, a culmination to ten years of dreaming of becoming an international act. He advanced them eight thousand pounds to record an album. The group returned to Jamaica to lay new material at Dynamic Sounds studio's eight-track facility.

The UK-based Blackwell had been a distant figure to Jamaican musicians, unapproachable and mysterious. Coming from a once-wealthy family, he maintained an imperious air and was accused of ripping off Jamaican artists by rereleasing their records in England without paying royalties (a charge which, as noted earlier, he denies), including many of the Wailers' earliest recordings for Coxson Dodd. The group was shocked when they first met Blackwell and he told them about payments that he claimed to have sent them, but which they never saw.

BUNNY WAILER: When we went to meet Blackwell in London he said, "Well, I've given Coxson hundreds of thousands of pounds for the Wailers." I said, "You're actually saying that?" He said, "Yes, I'm actually saying that because that's a fact. I've given Coxson hundreds of thousands of pounds for the Wailers. Not for just royalties, but for the Wailers." Me say, "Well, we never get more than ninety-nine pounds." We were never to know about the three figure—what a hundred pound feels like.

COXSON DODD: I only ever received seven hundred pounds from Chris Blackwell for using my Wailers masters. And at the same time to get them for him, he's telling them that he had paid me large sums of royalty. Because Bunny Wailer, when he saw an article come out [revealing the truth], he had to phone me and say I'm really glad I see this article 'cause Chris tell me how much big royalty him pay you, and this is why we were so mad at you.

ROGER STEFFENS: Chris Blackwell would dispute that he ever with-held royalties owed the Wailers. Blackwell has stated over the years that his relationship with Marley was a positive one, telling a 2016 interviewer that when he met Bob and the Wailers "they were trying to reach the African-American market. I could see that they had a better chance of reaching white college kids. I worked with Bob quite closely, mixing and producing most of his records. Our collaboration lasted until his death in 1981."*

The Wailers returned home with big plans, flush with a large sum of money. Eight thousand pounds was a drop in the bucket compared to the budgets of their contemporaries, similar to the weekly cocaine budget of rock stars. Newly freed from Johnny Nash and Danny Sims, they were now being backed by Blackwell, who was beginning to increase his holdings in the burgeoning reggae industry in Jamaica. His right-hand man at the time was Dickie Jobson, from another wealthy local family.

JOE HIGGS: Dickie Jobson owned Island House at 56 Hope Road in 1972. At that time, Chris Blackwell was putting me in a corner, giving me five hundred Jamaican dollars a month, easing me up and keeping me down.

ROGER STEFFENS: Higgs had recorded an album for Blackwell called *Life Of Contradiction*, but it was shelved.

---

* http://robbreport.com/sports-leisure/conversation-producer-who-discovered-bob-marley.

JOE HIGGS: When I got connected back with Island it was through Harry J, I was on his label at the time, with Bob and Marcia. In '72 Dickie Jobson was acting like a manager for me. Chris had a deal with Harry J, so I kind of came as a package to Chris.

ROGER STEFFENS: Harry J, a former insurance salesman, had begun producing records in 1968 and had significant successes in England with an instrumental called "Liquidator" and Bob [Andy] and Marcia [Griffiths]'s "Young, Gifted And Black."

JOE HIGGS: I found out later that the publishings on some of the songs I made for Harry J were coming out under his own publishing company, and I never had a publishing agreement with him.

ROGER STEFFENS: Higgs cautioned the Wailers to be very careful in protecting their rights as they embarked on an intensive work schedule.

BUNNY WAILER: We had maybe ten days' hard rehearsal. Then we went into Dynamic Sounds, the old West Indies studio, with Carlton Lee on the board and his young assistant Karl Pitterson. We started with the same instruments that we were rehearsing with, which was like next to be thrown away stuff. Sometime old instrument give a sound that no new instrument can ever give, and that was why *Catch A Fire* sounded the way it did, and no other Wailer album sounded that way. Because it was played under circumstances where some of these instruments, you had to hit them at some stage for them to start playing again.

And Family Man was a kind of genius when it came to taking old electronical things that you would automatically throw away. Family Man would take all these little things, put them together and get a sound or get something from it that maybe you couldn't buy in a store. You couldn't get new equipment that would sound like that. So you could call him a freak genius 'cause Family Man didn't go to no electronic school. He was toning the bass so that it come out clean without having to mix that much, you don't have to put it through no heap of equalization.

Carly Barrett was good at toning his drums, 'cause Carly was coming from playing pans, tin cans. So he worked to get the sound that suit the ear with that kind of rubbish kind of stuff. He was the first man I see put things in front of the drum and paste it down on it, like pad it so that when he hit it, it was finished, the sound didn't go nowhere. He was the first man who used to take off the front of the drum.

We laid the raw riddims for two days. Five each day. Then we take a break, make sure of the tracks, then we go back in a week and we voiced everything in one day, because Wailers don't need more than that. So in the space of about a month from we took the money from Chris, the album was ready for him to mix.

ROGER STEFFENS: *Catch A Fire* turned a lot of heads with its modern production techniques and lead guitar sounds, something new to reggae. Dermot Hussey heard the album early on. Known as the dean of Jamaican broadcasters, Hussey recorded a seminal interview with Bob Marley that was eventually released as a record. In the 1960s he had moved to England to take a course in directing at the BBC, and then studied another year at the London School of Film Technique.

DERMOT HUSSEY: When I went to England I was aware of the Wailers to a certain extent, but I think they came really forcibly into my consciousness when I met Bob. I'd heard the singles that they'd been putting out and topping the charts. And then of course being a follower of ska, because of the musicianship and all that, I got to realize that the Skatalites were really the backing band on a lot of those early releases, virtually everything the Wailers did on Coxsone. And then I had a chance to meet Bob personally at Dickie Jobson's house in a place called Industry in Gordon Town. Joe Higgs was there, Chris Blackwell was there, Bob was there in his denims and he was just beginning to grow locks, around the end of '72. Dickie had a copy of *Catch A Fire* and we played it.

DICKIE JOBSON: When I first met them Bob and Peter and Bunny

Sirius/XM DJ and dean of Jamaican broadcasters Dermot Hussey,
Washington, D.C., November 2014.

weren't talking. They had some quarrel before. It took several meetings
for them to agree [to let me manage them].

ROGER STEFFENS: Another witness to this period was Dr. Gayle
McGarrity, a scholar, teacher, anthropologist and international development professional, who was also a good friend of Bob Marley's. I first
encountered her while presenting a Bob Marley show at the House of
Blues in Cambridge, Massachusetts, in February 2000. Her unflinch-
ing insights into the people in Bob's circle, from the highest to the
lowest levels of Jamaican society, are noteworthy for the specificity
of her personal memories. She explained to me why she believes that
the Wailers were deliberately broken up, and spoke about the many
influential Jamaican "society" people who wanted Marley eliminated.

GAYLE McGARRITY: I went home from the California Bay Area, where

Dr. Gayle McGarrity, political scholar and teacher, who informed Marley's political understanding, at the Reggae Archives, Los Angeles, December 2001.

I was attending university, to Jamaica for Christmas in 1972. Dickie Jobson, who has always been like a brother to me, said that he wanted me to come with him out to Hellshire Beach. First he said, "Let's go to the beach," and then he said, "Oh, you know there's these guys that we're doing a record with, let's go down there instead," meaning Trench Town. Our usual haunt at that time was Hellshire Beach, which, of course, at that time was totally pristine. There was nobody there except for Countryman [who in 1982 would become the title character in a motion picture directed by Dickie Jobson] and his family, together with three or four other Indian fishermen families. I mean, you could go nude swimming there in privacy and cook out on the beach. There was hardly anyone around for miles. That day when we visited Trench Town, Peter was there, maybe Rita too, I can't remember, but Dickie focused very much on Bob, as Chris Blackwell and Dickie have always done. He introduced me to Bob and Bob was very respectful and we found a place to sit—sort of like in the song "No Woman No Cry," in a government yard in Trench Town. They brought a newspaper for me to sit on, so that I wouldn't dirty my clothes, and you know, Dickie was talking to him—technical stuff about the music business—which I wasn't really listening to. I was really just looking around at the surroundings and was just amazed at the level of poverty. Until then, for me Jamaica was always exuberant—flowers and trees, beautiful mountains and beaches and breezes—but down there, there was such a level of sheer sensory deprivation, that I remember being in total shock.

Bob was very respectful to me. He struck me as being very humble and I remember thinking, too, how interesting it was that he was so light-skinned and yet he was living in this very black, very poor environment. In those days in Jamaica, it was still mostly brown and white people in the middle and upper classes, and overwhelmingly black people in the working and poorer classes. He welcomed me and said, "Nice for you to come here." And, he added, "I'm sorry the place is so, you know, messed up and I don't have a nice place here," just very humble. Dickie said, "These guys really have a great sound and they're really interesting. Chris and I are thinking about what we can do with them." And then he showed me the *Catch A Fire* album.

ROGER STEFFENS: The album had a unique look, with curved edges and a middle hinge that allowed the sleeve to be pulled back, revealing a die-cut flame like a Zippo lighter. For the first time, reggae was being given a full-scale rock-act presentation. Indeed, Blackwell changed the name they had been using for years—Bob Marley and the Wailers—to simply the Wailers, indicating that they were a self-contained musical entity. Despite good initial reviews, the album sold fewer than fifteen thousand copies in its first run.

BUNNY WAILER: When we went back to England to promote *Catch A Fire,* because the Wailers looked so simple they say it couldn't have been us that played the music. So *The Old Grey Whistle Test* TV show was introduced to prove to the whole of Britain, because if you are going to be a flop, be a big flop and done. So they took us through stages. At first they let us record live, play and sing. Then they made us record the riddims, and then we went and voiced on top of that. Then they played the riddim track of the songs through the speakers and we had to pretend to play. On that *Old Grey Whistle Test,* you see, we are pretending. We are not playing. We recorded the entire album. And a little short guy, who said he was in the business for fifty-one years, came out and said to us, "I like your noise. You got a good noise. You're going to

Family Man Barrett and Marley in the San Diego Sports Arena
dressing room, November 24, 1979.

be the next Beatles. Since the Beatles your noise is the first noise I've heard that is a good noise."

FAMILY MAN BARRETT: I can recall the time in London at the Greyhound Club, that was the most critical club. It was uptown London. This was between *Catch A Fire* and *Burnin'* time, 1973. At that time we used to open with the "Rasta Man Chant." And what the reviewers wrote up was very pleasing. They say the first number cast a spell and after that it was musical magic—from a spell to magic.

ROGER STEFFENS: Despite the onstage magic, privately things were more and more miserable for the bandsmen. They hated the dampness and bitterly cold weather. Their quarters were spare and impoverished. And the financial arrangements they were promised turned out to be so unacceptable that the group was on the verge of splitting up for good by the end of spring 1973, once the recording sessions for their follow-up album were complete.

CHAPTER 14

Burnin' Out in London

ROGER STEFFENS: *Burnin'*,* the resonant final album by the original Wailers trio of Bob Marley, Bunny Wailer and Peter Tosh, had its beginnings in Harry J's studio in Kingston, where all the basic tracks were laid. Mixing and overdubbing took place at Island Records' Basing Street Studios in London during the spring of 1973, in between live dates the group played to support their critically acclaimed first international release, *Catch A Fire*.

BUNNY WAILER: The album should have been titled *Reincarnated Souls*, after a song I recorded for it, but because I dropped out of the group before it was released the album was retitled *Burnin'*, with "Reincarnated Souls" used only as the B-side of an English single. We were coming to England on a mission. We were going to establish Rastafarian culture and reggae music. So I knew that we had to have the Nyabinghi drums so as to make the chant so that the people would understand that we had some foundation, that this music did not come out of nowhere. The drums had just been finished out by Six Miles [in Jamaica] by a guy named Ferry. The bass was made from

* In 2004 I was asked by Island Records to write the liner notes for a deluxe rere-lease of the final Wailers trio album, *Burnin'*. It is the only time in my career that I have ever had a liner note rejected. This chapter contains information, previously unpublished, from those notes, which were refused with the accusation that they were "too honest."

the wood of the wine barrel and the funde was made from the trunk of a coconut tree.

ROGER STEFFENS: In late April 1973, accompanied by these most rootical of instruments, the Wailers—Bunny, Bob, Peter, keyboardist Earl "Wya" Lindo, drummer Carlton Barrett and his bassist brother Family Man—landed in the foggy chill of England.

BUNNY WAILER: We were taken to a dump in a commercial district owned by Chris Blackwell, on King Street, above an Indian restaurant. There was a basement where we rehearsed, which was also a dump. When we weren't cooking our food and we wanted a quick cook-snack, we would get it from the Indian store. There was not a bed in the place, there was just mattresses. Bob stayed around the corner with Esther Anderson in her flat most of the time.

ROGER STEFFENS: Anderson, Bob's companion at the time, became the guide for the Wailers during their stay, and played a vital role in several of Bob's compositions during the 1973–74 period.

BUNNY WAILER: We did twenty-odd polytechnic colleges, and one or two big nightclubs, including four nights at the Speakeasy, which was our breakthrough. We were like the biggest thing with reggae coming in town, ever since Jimmy Cliff or Desmond Dekker. The Wailers were now definitely the stars of the lot. Each night at the Speakeasy was better than the one before [despite the fact that the aristocratic crowd was virtually all white]. It was the *Catch A Fire* tour, but we were still singing tracks from the *Burnin'* album. And when there were break times, days off, we were in the studios doing the *Burnin'* album. No days off. We spent our days off in the studio, that's the only time we would get to relax.

FAMILY MAN BARRETT: I would listen to everyone's ideas, and then we'd try to take it to the tape. We would record the backing tracks, making them special; we were all there during that stage. Then the three singers would sing, and Tony Platt and Phil Brown [the engineers] would listen technically. They were always having a good time.

But the studio was kind of . . . smoky. And you never see smoke without something burning.

ROGER STEFFENS: Fams is definitely not talking spliffs here. Both Peter and Bunny spoke often in later years about their concern that their creations were not being given proper exposure in the Wailers, being passed over in favor of Bob's, which cut them out of the lucrative writer's royalties that were beginning to pile up. It was for this reason that Peter was asked by Bob to contribute the "bullshit" verse he sings on "Get Up Stand Up," giving him the opportunity for a cowriter's credit on the album's anthemic opener.

"Get Up Stand Up" was also one of those tracks on which the stunningly beautiful Anderson played a role. A successful actress who had costarred with Sidney Poitier in a film called *Warm December*, she had met with Bob in New York through a young film director named Lee Jaffe. In February 1973, she found herself hopscotching across the Caribbean from Jamaica to Trinidad to Haiti and back to Jamaica in a plane chartered by Blackwell. In a 2001 phone call from her home in Cornwall, England, Esther spoke of her early collaborations with Bob.

ESTHER ANDERSON: Bob and I wrote "Get Up Stand Up" in twenty minutes flying from Haiti to Jamaica. I was teaching Bob how to be a rebel, based on what I learned from living with Marlon Brando for seven years. In fact, I bought him a jacket just like the one Marlon wore in *On the Waterfront* when he said he coulda been a contender.

BUNNY WAILER: "Get Up Stand Up" was the final song recorded for the Wailers' final album, left for last because it was the easiest track on the album, just unison singing.

ROGER STEFFENS: Eric Clapton's worldwide smash cover of "I Shot The Sheriff" brought the final ray of attention necessary to shine the global spotlight on the Wailers. Ironically, the Jamaican radio stations favored Clapton's version over the local fellows', and it wasn't until some of Marley's friends threatened physical retribution that they

Esther Anderson, Marley's companion throughout 1973, took the pictures in the centerfold of *Burnin'*. At the Reggae Archives, Los Angeles, December 2000.

began to play Bob singing his own composition. Several people claim a hand in its creation.

BUNNY WAILER: From the start it was intended to have that kind of cowboy ballad vibes, like Marty Robbins.

ESTHER ANDERSON: The storyline came from me in my bedroom in London. It's about birth control. Bob was always after me to "breed" and have a baby with him. He kept asking me why after I'd been with him for a month already I hadn't got pregnant yet. I told him I was on the pill and this led to the line "Every time I plant a seed he said kill it before it grow"—you see, the sheriff is the doctor. It was the third song we collaborated on.

ROGER STEFFENS: More details emerged from lengthy interviews with Lee Jaffe for our book *One Love: Life with Bob Marley and the Wailers.* Lee lived with the Wailers in Kingston at the time, acting as Bob's "beard" for his relationship with Esther, allowing Bob to tell Rita and others that Esther was actually Lee's girlfriend. His account of the birth of reggae's finest anthem differs from Esther's.

LEE JAFFE: The song came out of me playing harmonica on a beach in Jamaica. Bob was playing guitar and he said, "I shot the sheriff," and I said, "But you didn't get the deputy." It was a joke, because they don't have sheriffs in Jamaica. Bob was funny, he was witty, so it was about him hanging out with this white guy, me, it was a comment about that. And yes, it came out of western movies, which Jamaicans really love. *The Good, The Bad and the Ugly* was always playing somewhere in Kingston. So they're into that whole attitude, and here Bob was hanging out with this white guy, so it was like being in some western movie with me. I remember there was these two really really fat girls dancing on the beach when Bob came out with that line. And then, it was like such a funny song, the beach wasn't that crowded, but we had a whole bunch of people just dancing to that song. I wrote down all the lyrics that Bob was singing, and I was excited 'cause I knew it was a big song and I felt I was integral to its conception. And then I came up with the line, "All along in Trench Town, the jeeps go round and round." 'Cause the police and military drove jeeps and I was thinking of the curfews that were being called in the ghetto and what it was like for the poor people, the sufferers, to live in a militarized zone and to have the basic freedom of walking in the street taken away. I think of what a genius Bob was for coming out with the line "I shot the sheriff" because, though it was funny, it was also so poignant, so relevant to the global repression. Later he changed the line to "all around in my home town" and that was better, because it made the point that these violent interventions into everyday life in the shantytowns of Jamaica were intrinsically foreign-influenced. And when I said, "But you didn't get the deputy," it was ironic and slightly self-deprecating, because what it was saying was yeah, I got the balls to shoot the sheriff, but I don't have it together to get all his backup. And this is going to be a long tragic struggle that's going to need a lot of everyday heroes.

ROGER STEFFENS: One of the album's most misunderstood songs is "Burnin' And Lootin'," after which the album is named. It was, according to Bob, "about burning illusions," not material things.

ESTHER ANDERSON: It's completely based on something that happened to Joe Higgs [the magnanimous early teacher of the teenaged Wailers, who would go on to replace Bunny during the group's final tour in late 1973]. He told me that the night before he had awakened to find the police surrounding and raiding his house in Trench Town. So I told Bob about it and said that we have to write about it. These are the kinds of things that are happening in the country, and you have to document it. "Weeping And Wailing" was the first title. We wrote half of it at Hope Road, another part in Castleton Gardens in St. Mary near Golden Spring, and finished the song in Annotto Bay. People around him were beginning to use cocaine, so that's what those lines are about when he said, "Let the roots man take a blow, all them drugs gonna make you slow, now." I added the line about it not being ghetto music. Fams worked out the entire score to go with it in the rehearsal room in Tuff Gong. When we came to London to record it, Bob changed it to "Burnin' And Lootin'" because, he said, that's what's going on down there.

ROGER STEFFENS: Bunny Wailer has another, more foreboding, take on the song.

BUNNY WAILER: When we met Chris Blackwell in the fall of 1972 in London, he told us that he had sent the Wailers hundreds of thousands of pounds for the records of ours that he had released in the 1960s [money which the group never saw]. He told us he was afraid to meet with us because he had been hearing that "you people were danger-ous people, that you were killers." So, seeing the Wailers looking at the boss for the first time, the Big Boss, is what made Bob write those lines about crossing the rivers to talk to the boss: "All that we got seems lost, we must have really paid the cost."

ROGER STEFFENS: Another cover, this of a track cut three years earlier for Lee Perry's Upsetter label, was "Small Axe."

FAMILY MAN BARRETT: It was one of our favorite songs, a big local favorite. We wanted to do it in the R & B style on the album in an inter-national style, add a little more flavor to get it across.

ROGER STEFFENS: The oldest song on the album is "Pass It On," which Bunny wrote around 1962, prior to the formation of the Wailers.

BUNNY WAILER: I should have recorded it at Beverley's at the same time [1962] Bob did his second solo record of "One Cup Of Coffee." But I was late, so I missed the session. Over the years I added new lyrics to it and it got stronger still. It took eleven years before it was finally laid. It was one of those songs that I hear when I was a very little child that I never forget. It's a kind of traditionally adapted song, the first song that I ever wrote.

ROGER STEFFENS: "Duppy Conqueror," originally recorded in late 1970 for Lee Perry, is taken here, in Fams's words, "to the next stage." A duppy is a malevolent spirit in Jamaican folklore. Bob sings about being stronger than a bullbucker.

BUNNY WAILER: A bullbucker means like a guy who bucks bulls, a guy who's so strong that he can buck bull, knock him out. So if you a bullbucker, then I'm a duppy conqueror. It's an old traditional saying, like if a man say to you, "If you think you chew 'pon iron, I chew 'pon steel!" I conquer duppy, and duppy's the hardest thing to conquer. If you think you kill ten men, I kill twenty.

ROGER STEFFENS: "One Foundation," Peter's composition, is a plea for togetherness under the implied leadership of His Imperial Majesty, Emperor Haile Selassie. Oneness, the Wailers believed, was the answer to all the world's ism-schisms, and any duality was the work of the devil, a false veil of separation that only a belief in the oneness of Rasta could lift.

"Rasta Man Chant," the album's speeded-up closer, was partially inspired by Esther Anderson, who took the original album's photographs.

ESTHER ANDERSON: I was a photojournalist with a socialist newspaper at the time, with Alex Cockburn. One day Countryman turned me on to a man who lived on the beach across from Bunny in Bull Bay, a man named Bongo Mackie. He's the dread with the goat in the centerfold of *Burnin'*. Mackie was living in a big Rasta compound with all these children. I was so amazed at all the red, gold and green there. This was a time when none of the Wailers had dreadlocks yet. I took Bob there the next day with Countryman to photograph them together. In the evening, Mackie started to play these akete drums, and they reminded me of a time I had gone to Africa with Millie Small and Brando was there. The big university in Accra gave a private thousand-drum concert for us, and Bongo Mackie's drums reminded me of these. When I heard him sing "One bright morning when my work is over," I told Bob, "You must wear red, gold and green and grow your locks and open your show with the drums." The rest is history.

ROGER STEFFENS: Let the final word on the eternality of *Burnin'* rest with Jon Pareles, the eloquent chief pop critic of the *New York Times*. In 1996, the *Times*'s Sunday magazine celebrated its one-hundredth anniversary of publication, and asked each of its critics to choose one work of art in their field that they believed would survive a hundred years into the future. Pareles chose *Burnin'*, immortalizing it with these eloquent words.

JON PARELES: Bob Marley became the voice of third world pain and resistance, the sufferer in the concrete jungle who would not be denied forever. Outsiders everywhere heard Marley as their own champion;

if he could make himself heard, so could they, without compromises. In 2096, when the former third world has overrun and colonized the former superpowers, Marley will be commemorated as a saint.

ROGER STEFFENS: Even though the work the Wailers had just completed showcased them at their best, urges to explore their own muses more deeply widened the gaps among the three of them. And the pressures exerted by the label and its failed promises became unbearable.

Karl Pitterson was a young engineer working in local studios, encountering Bob on different recording sessions during this period. I spoke with him in his new studio in Miami in 1995.

KARL PITTERSON: I was around during that time. A lot of people put the blame for the breakup on the divide-and-conquer thing, with Island Records taking the best of the group. But I think that's the way it was planned by the maker. It's part of a script.

CHRIS BLACKWELL: I realized that it wouldn't have been possible to work with all of them. And the main ones sort of at war were Peter and Bob. Bunny has always been Bunny. He stands in his own place really.

BUNNY WAILER: After the spring tour of 1973 in the UK, we went to Chris to discuss where the tour would be going next in the United States. We were looking forward now to larger venues, getting exposed to bigger markets because we had proved ourselves. If we continue to play these little gigs we wouldn't be making money. So I said, "Chris, what kind of thing you have planned for us going to America now— where are we going to play?" He said, "Freak clubs." So me say, "What you mean by freak clubs?" Him say, "Well, you know, clubs where gay guys and gals, gals meet gals and guys meet guys and freak out. Drug business, all kind of stuff—freak." We say, "What the blood-claat?" So me say, "Chris, you know I & I is Rasta. How you want to take us all in that direction? Why you want draw us down in dem kind of things? After you know say we is Rasta, we no stand for dem things. Why don't you get us cultural centers and even the polytechnic college what we just do? We stay on a trend now and we sing for children now. We no care to go sing for no freaks." Chris said, "If you don't do these clubs you are nobody." Just like that. So me just say, "Listen, Chris, 'body' is buried. I am a living being, a living soul. I'm not a body. And if where you have in mind for the Wailers is where bodies go, I won't be going. And one monkey don't spoil no show."

Well Bob jumped up and said, "What's happening, we come to talk about tour or what?" Me say, "Listen now, me bredren, you are my brother. I love you and respect you and the decisions that you make all this time. But," I said, "this one decision I have to make to protect my integrity. And you can't speak for my integrity. You can speak for me which you have done. But it's my integrity, Bob. And my integrity tell me—don't move."

So I just state, "I am not going, me bredren." The meeting end kind of. Everybody was amazed, dismayed, everybody was lost because a decision had to be made. I wasn't going, so the rest of the man would have to decide, say well, Chris, if Jah B not going we are not going either. So you better get your act together. But I was voted out. By everybody. And I know that they were heading for shit. I felt good because I wasn't going to wallow in no shit.

ROGER STEFFENS: Sebastian Clarke, who was working with the group at the time, wrote that "After waiting several months to get some funds we were confronted with a pile of papers so high, telling us that we owed Island Records forty-two thousand pounds as tour expenses. And yet before we made the tour there was an agreement that Island Records would cover all the expenses. On a subsequent visit to Jamaica, Blackwell had talks with Tosh, who became infuriated, left and returned with a machete to confront Blackwell who left immediately."

According to his biographer John Masouri, Peter believed Bob had betrayed the Wailers by siding with Chris Blackwell, and it happened because Bob was half-white. "There was an old saying that, 'If you're white, you're all right. If you're brown stay around. But if you're black, stay back.' Well that's what it had come to. It felt like he and Bunny were too black for the group now they were at the threshold of success, despite having worked long and hard in building the Wailers' reputation. Bob had sold them out right at the point where they were supposed to stand firm, although Peter felt it was time to strike out on his own in any case. 'I did not come on earth to be a background singer.' "

Peter confirmed to me that they were given only a hundred pounds each at the conclusion of the tour, which dropped its twelve final dates due to Peter's bronchitis. Years later his anger was still at fever pitch.

PETER TOSH: It was a ras-claat and pure fuckery. Well, the reason why I stopped these things too, the agreement that we had, the company wasn't living up to their side of the agreement, the respect and everything that was due, was pushed aside. And we couldn't take them fuckery there, because after having twelve years of experience of what reggae music is, the first thing Chris Whitewell told us was that it would take him five years to build us. That was after we knew all that we know, it was going to take us another five years of twelve to build us again. I want to know what else he was going to put on us. [Yet it] was not a breakup you know, is just going three different ways and sending the music in three different directions. It was just that my inspiration was growing and my cup filled and runneth over.

ROGER STEFFENS: The sadness that filled the reggae world was overwhelming, once it was realized that the Wailers, like the Beatles three years earlier, had dissolved their group at the height of their powers.

CHAPTER 15

The End of the Beginning

ROGER STEFFENS: Bunny's departure from the Wailers exacerbated the tensions between Peter and Bob, and by the end of 1973 the three would no longer tour or record together. Their final album, *Burnin'*, would receive ecstatic reviews and showcase lead vocals from each member, leaving the world to wonder what was going to happen now. A big wave had thrust them upward, only to smash the group on the rocks of dissension.

NEVILLE WILLOUGBY: By 1973, Bob had now broken in a way, he had gone and done a show abroad. It was a big thing to me. So I decided that I would like to talk to him. And a very very wonderful person who is now deceased, Denzil Laing, percussionist, who was a good friend of mine, I said to him one day, "I want to interview Bob. You know where his house is in Bull Bay. Would you come with me and show me where it is?" So Denzil came with me that day, and we went out there quite early on a Sunday morning, like about nine o'clock, and they were rehearsing already. And you know Bob isn't the type of person who fuss over anybody, he just saw us and said hello and we sat down and waited. And then he asked us if we wanted some breakfast and we had breakfast with him. They went on practicing. He asked what I wanted. I said I wanted an interview. He said well, he had to practice first. So I sat down, and we were there for hours listening to him. Hours! Hours and hours! Later on in the day, after lunch, they rehearsed right through and I stayed there because I made up my mind I was going to get it.

I discovered that about him, that he liked to test people. For instance, if you listen carefully to the interview, every now and then he would be answering a question and he'd stop in the middle and he'd say, "What did you ask me again?" And I realized that what it was, was to see if you're really listening carefully. He wanted to see if you're really that interested in him. So that when it came back to you, if you couldn't remember the question, he'd dismiss you. Not literally, but just his eyes would dismiss you.

Because I realize that Bob was the type of person, if you didn't realize that he was worth waiting for, then tough on you. That's the feeling I got from him. But if he saw that you really were sincerely interested in him and his talent, it's all right. That is why so few people interviewed him, because not many people would sit down for half a day and wait for him while he rehearsed. Because they'd say [kisses his teeth], "That bwoi feisty," you know, that type of attitude. But I saw something special about him that I've never seen in any other person, any other recording artist in Jamaica.

You could tell that he wasn't too sure about Wailers, when you asked him about Wailers. But he would say, "Yes, I'm still a Wailers," but he would say it hesitantly. But basically he was in a very upbeat frame of mind, because he saw that he was really going to get where he wanted to get. I felt that way.

ROGER STEFFENS: Third World's Cat Coore also remembers Bob's uneasy optimism in this period of transition.

CAT COORE: Bob had already done the *Catch A Fire* album, so it's mid-'73. We had backed him up before, and he had known us. We had played with him not only on stage but we had done some sessions at Randy's too with them. We did a version of "Stir It Up" and "Walk The Proud Land."

DENNIS THOMPSON: Bob experimented a lot with other musicians. He did a lot of stuff with Sly and Robbie, with Inner Circle, before they even branched out and became Third World.

CAT COORE: Bob was in this restaurant one night, the Epiphany, and downstairs at Epiphany they have a club that used to serve food twenty-four hours. And he was sitting in there. And I said, "Bob, that!"

Even before Bob got big, we Jamaican musicians used to hold him in reverence, because of the kind of songs that he did like "Trench Town Rock." They were so outrageous and just so commanding, that we used to always hold him in this presence. There used to be all these stories about him, how when him come on stage him don't sing for two minutes 'cause him listening to the band first until it get right. He had a folklore thing about him already among us musicians, stories, things about him, that he was slightly kinky, slightly off the wall. It was one of the traits that everybody know about Bob as a musician at the time. When you go and play for Bob, you don't mess around. You make sure you listen to what him say and think, 'cause the man would fly off the handle. And he just came out to me at this restaurant and said, "Wha'ppen? The man no want to play inna Wailers?" And I said, "Bwoi, Bob, too bad I see you. I just started this group. Third World." And he said, "Who's in the group?" and I told him and he say, "Oh, cool. Anyway, Wailers a go big, you know!" And me say, "You no have tell me that."

We were all talking at the end of the show and he was cussing somebody about something. You know he had a way where he just get off on something for a minute or two, and then he'd just come back and laugh again. And he said, "Bwoi, you guys have a good band, and you must keep it together. You mustn't fight among yourselves and you must always look towards what you can achieve out of it. Don't just think you're the star, or he's the star, or this one is the star." And I remember [Third World bandmate] Ibo was picking at him that night about Peter and Bunny, asking him what happened, and he was saying to Bob, "How come you just leave and gone on your own?" And Bob said to him, "How come you know I left? Suppose they left me?"

ROGER STEFFENS: In October 1973 the Wailers returned to America.

BUNNY WAILER: They toured with Sly and the Family Stone. Joe Higgs worked as Bunny Wailer, in my place, which was appropriate because I was satisfied to know that if anybody took my place it would have been my tutor, my teacher. I felt good about that.

ROGER STEFFENS: Segree Wesley was on the tour, and he sensed the possibilities of the Wailers' sound, even without Bunny.

SEGREE WESLEY: I saw Bunny after the breakup and I says, "You know something, everything start opening now. I mean, what's the matter with the group?" He says, "Man, Segree, Bobby he becoming too commercialized with the reggae, you know?" And I remember I said, "Listen, once you start go there in the international scene there's a lot of changes you have to make. People gotta be able to understand what you're saying. All you guys gotta do is try and stay with the international market. 'Cause the local market can't take care of you guys." So he said Bobby was a sellout because he was making reggae too commercialized with the kind of music he started coming out with. I said, "But if that's the music that people are willing to accept abroad, then that's what he has to do. I say it's a business; I say you guys spend too many years in this business to break up and don't go back, 'cause there are things that open. I'm in America—you'd be surprised to know how they accept the reggae. As a matter of fact, the white folks accept reggae more so than the black folks right in America." There was always that inroad fighting while the music was stepping up. But I know prior to Bob's death he did say to me, they can't stop Rasta since everything opens up, which is true. While I was in America, I really saw where the music was taking a stronghold.

ROGER STEFFENS: The popular myth, sometimes promoted by his record companies, is that Bob blew Sly off the stage.

JOE HIGGS: In that era Sly was a total influence, the in thing of the time. People came to see Sly because of what he had to say, what he looked like, his latest design. How was Bob a threat to Sly Stone? People said they can't hear us, our accent they couldn't understand and our rhythm was too slow. We weren't happening and our outfits were inappropriate and we were rebels.

All I can remember is that we were opening for Sly and the Family Stone and when he got to Las Vegas we were fired. We had played five shows together: in Homestead and Tampa, Florida, Lexington, Kentucky, Denver, Colorado, and Las Vegas, when Sly left us and our luggage on the side of the road, rejected from the hotel. Somebody [San Francisco's KSAN DJ Tom Donahue] took us to Sausalito. We made a broadcast there and did some club shows.

ROGER STEFFENS: Gayle McGarrity went to see the band in the autumn of 1973 in San Francisco at the Matrix.

GAYLE McGARRITY: We went backstage, my friend and fellow Stanford student Michael Witter and I, before the show, and I remember having a distinct feeling that this was such a special moment. It was like a transcendental event for me, 'cause when I went backstage and I saw Bob, Peter and Family Man, I remember just being totally mesmerized and feeling that I was in a spiritual kind of context, like you know, when you're feeling like you're having an out-of-this-world experience—I mean, very intense. And it wasn't just the herb! And when it started, I mean, I just couldn't believe that concert! It was a tiny little place and it was the perfect atmosphere for them. And the other thing was that they were so revolutionary and militant, dressed in military khaki stuff, and they played all of their most militant stuff. And, because we were all so into very leftist, revolutionary stages of our lives, this group just became the articulators of our deepest, most innermost political feelings.

ROGER STEFFENS: The fact that the original teacher of the group, Joe Higgs, was drafted for a crucial tour that was designed to introduce the Wailers to the black American audience left a foul taste in the teacher's mouth when he realized he wasn't going to get paid.

JOE HIGGS: Bob Marley was a user in a lot of ways. For example, here is a man who had a tour pending, his first U.S. tour, and at the very last minute, maybe a week before leaving, Bunny walked away for whatever reason. With that short a time, Bob came to me on his knees and asked me as the most appropriate replacement. He said I was the "most fitting replacement for Bunny," I can play drum, I can sing harmony. He got us to go on the road voluntarily, I wasn't offered a salary or anything. I wasn't paid; at the end of the tour, Bob said there were purposeful mistakes made by Peter on the tour. In rehearsal he was always trying to change things. If you look at the tension [on the video of a Wailers rehearsal in the Capitol Records building in Hollywood] Bob never said a word. I was not being thanked, no compensation at all.

My brother died in '74. We had no money to bury him. I decided to play the role of a madman. I went to Bob's at Hope Road and I stood up and wasn't saying anything. He looked at me, "Wha'ppen, Joe?" He called me by name. I never respond. Bob said, "Well, them finally fuck up Joe now. Joe is mad now!" Offer me spliff, banana, I never respond to anything. So he would think I was really out there in space. However, I waited for a while, an hour or so. Finally I said, "Can I talk to you a moment?" Him say, "Yes, man," and took me upstairs to the end of the rooms there. I said, "You don't really owe me any money because I never really sign a contract with you, but I told you as a member of the Wailers I never got nothing from you." Bob said, "How much I owe you?" I said, "Just give me something." Bob say, "I'll give you two thousand dollars [Jamaican]." The check had to be signed by him and Skill Cole. So we went to National Stadium where Skill was training, got his signature and the check was fifteen hundred dollars. First money I got from that tour.

I used some of the fifteen hundred to bury my brother.

ROGER STEFFENS: Marley returned from tour only to be told by Peter that he was leaving the group for a solo career. Although they didn't realize it as it was being cut, *Burnin'* would be the Wailers' valedictory collection. Its sales would at first be lukewarm.

To add to his income, Bob opened a small shop on Beeston Street in Kingston selling his Jamaican-pressed recordings. He struggled to know what to do next musically, and professionally.

Reggae's initial invasion of America had come with the triple explosion of the Wailers' Island Records debut, *Catch A Fire*; the captivating roots flick *The Harder They Come*, directed by Perry Henzell and starring Jimmy Cliff; and its irresistible soundtrack album. With Marley now seen as a potential superstar on his own, several people approached him about managing him. He ended up going with an aggressive Jamaican hustler named Don Taylor.

DON TAYLOR: I met Bob in 1973. I went to Jamaica as one of Marvin Gaye's co-managers and advisers. Basically, at that stage you don't manage a Marvin Gaye, you advise a Marvin Gaye. So I was there, I financed the entire thing for the Trench Town Sports Complex. What happened was a guy named Stephen Hill knew me since I was a kid hanging around the theater he ran. So as I grew we kept in contact and stuff. He called me one day from Jamaica and says that his son had

Danny Sims and Don Taylor at the Midem music conference in Cannes, France, April 1997, promoting one of Marley's posthumous hits, "What Goes Around Comes Around."

become a very main adviser to Tony Spaulding, who was then the Minister of Housing. Michael Manley had just won. And that Tony wanted to do something to build a sports complex in Trench Town if I could help him to get an artist. Right around that time Marvin Gaye was going down to Jamaica a lot, going up in the hills above Montego Bay.

ROGER STEFFENS: Taylor arrived just as worldwide sales of reggae music were starting to produce real money, money unlike anyone had ever seen in Jamaica for music. This would inevitably lead to grim exploitation. For example, Joe Higgs, Jimmy Cliff's early supporter, publicly lamented the treatment of the artists on the soundtrack album for *The Harder They Come*, which has never been out of print since 1973, selling steadily ever since..

JOE HIGGS: I met Jimmy Cliff in the early days. Jimmy lived near Tivoli Theatre, which later became the Queen's Theatre on Spanish Town Road. He was just in from country. There was a guy who had a barbershop on Spanish Town Road who loved to sing and play his guitar. That guy taught Jimmy Cliff lots. He trimmed me a couple of times too. I don't think Bob and Jimmy Cliff had really a link at those times. Jimmy was an early guy with Byron Lee at an early stage, with Ken Lazarus, the Byron Lee crew.

I started with Jimmy Cliff, and I have seen that he's a very, very powerful performer. I come in with Jimmy Cliff when he'd been out in the world, after the disappointment with the movie *The Harder They Come*. I heard it belonged to Chris Blackwell, who sponsored it, even though Perry Henzell produced it. The soundtrack belong to Chris Blackwell. All the participants in the movie were like in their infant stage, and there was no legal adviser in Jamaica who knew about copyright law. In those times no lawyer was interested in that or entertainment law. There was none who could defend you. You had to go to the library. There was no major deal in the music industry. All who did the movie believe they were robbed, underpaid. Jimmy Cliff said he got some money to do an album, but instead he bought a house on Lady Musgrave Road. Chris Blackwell was pissed, and told him that "I made you and I can break you."

I was ahead of most of the guys, I was the first singer that knew anything about copyrights. Because I never sold a song, and always registered it myself—the only one I never remembered to do that on was "Stepping Razor" and it took a long time to sort that out. PRS [the Performing Rights Society] helps maintain your copyright. I never sold my copyright.

ROGER STEFFENS: Marley himself was involved in a web of complex contracts involving JAD, Danny Sims, Sony and Chris Blackwell's Island Records.

DON TAYLOR: One of the things that was a problem when we were renegotiating Bob's deal with Island to get the contract that he has now, is that Danny [Sims] had a contract that was still in effect to CBS Records. Bob was put there by Danny and one of the things that we sat up there and figured out, with Chris Blackwell trying to figure out with us, was a way to deprive CBS with an override of two points, because Bob was starting out selling product now. We see he's selling those big numbers, and to try to figure out a way to not pay CBS, or get around paying CBS these royalties.

ROGER STEFFENS: In 1974 Marley started hiding his copyrights from Danny Sims to avoid paying royalties, putting songs under the names of his wife, Rita Marley, Family Man Barrett, and a friend from Trench Town named Leghorn Coghile.

JOE HIGGS: Leghorn was a student at St. George's. If Leghorn Coghile is credited with "Talkin' Blues," I'm surprised I'm not credited on several of Bob Marley's songs. "Talkin' Blues" is a song me and Bob jammed to, we made many lines. Same with "Mr. Talkative," which I helped him write. Leghorn Coghile was not a bad man or a fighter. He was a brainy boy, one of the early people who associated with Planno, who became a producer and manager with the Wailers. He was never in charge of the Beeston Street shop, as some have claimed. He had a deep knowledge about shipping and clearing, really big knowledge of customs. That was his major input into Bob's development. Very essential, very progressive. But not in charge.*

DERMOT HUSSEY: I remember once when Leghorn Coghile said he was author of "Talkin' Blues," Bob draped him up, actually. He said, "Leghorn, I hear you say you write the tune?" Bob was just asserting himself physically. So when you say draped, he held him by his pants!

ROGER STEFFENS: With the Wailers fading out, Bob sought new vocalists to back him and began composing some of the most militant compositions of his career, as the violence around him grew daily in the festering streets of West Kingston. What once seemed so promising had now, again, turned to dust. Would he survive on his own? Who was his real audience? Marley would answer those questions with one of the most important albums of modern times.

---

* Higgs does allow that Leghorn "was central in a lot of ways to getting things done for Marley. And he definitely wrote songs with Bob."

CHAPTER 16

Natty Dread

ROGER STEFFENS: In 1974 Bob released his first solo album, *Natty Dread*. Violence in the ghettos of West Kingston was raging out of control as tens of thousands of the professional class were abandoning the country and taking their vital capital with them. Huge import taxes were imposed and essentials like soap and cooking oil were becoming almost impossible to find. Democratic socialism, as envisioned by prime minister Michael Manley, had turned into class warfare, and Rastafarians were often the victims of vicious police repression, blunting the hopes that their movement would become legitimized under a Manley regime.

As Peter and Bunny took their leave from the Wailers, Bob had to make some serious decisions about his own future, renegotiating his recording contract to include Family Man and Carlton Barrett as members of what would become known as the Wailers Band in later years, to distinguish them from the original trio. A new female backing trio was hired to record and tour with him.

After the breakup, Bob became ever more politicized. *Natty Dread* was a militant masterpiece, in which he vowed to "never make a politician grant you a favor / they will only want to control you forever." He was being educated in his emerging role as a spokesperson for the disenfranchised by people like Michael Witter, an economics professor at the University of the West Indies, and by Dr. Gayle McGarrity.

GAYLE McGARRITY: The time I first remember reasoning about politics with Bob was very shortly following my return to Jamaica in 1974, following my graduation from Stanford. During that period, I worked at the University of the West Indies at Mona, at the Kingston Legal Aid Clinic, as well as at the Institute of Jamaica. I got very into Rasta, but not in a religious sense—more in a cultural and political sense. An American friend contacted me and said that a good friend of his, Yvette Morris Anderson [no relation to Rita or Esther Anderson], was living with Bob, up at Hope Road. She introduced me to Bob, which for me was like the first time really meeting him.

I remember at that time, because of my political beliefs and convictions, I saw Bob in a particular light. As the original uptown rebel girl that I was, I remember feeling that he was getting kind of contaminated by Blackwell. I'd gone to visit Chris's house in Nassau with Dicky once, and they very openly had a conversation that I'll never forget, during which they talked very clearly about the need to separate Peter—to get Peter out of the picture and to have Bob as the head of the group and to neutralize the more radical, revolutionary aspect of the group. I think Chris said something about Peter's super-black racial thing or something to that effect. Whatever he actually said, it was clearly a putdown of that side of the Wailers. And so, after I heard that, I said to Bob, "You know, I think this is really a shame, because you guys started out together, and I mean, Peter's message is important too." By this time, I think Bob was understandably getting used to being a superstar and he didn't want to hear any stuff like that. So when I would talk to him about such things, he would always look at me kind of skeptically.

ROGER STEFFENS: Peter and Bob had become increasingly contentious following the misadventure with Lee Perry in 1971. Peter blamed Bob for making bad business decisions and questioned whether Chris Blackwell was trying to break up the group and concentrate on Bob because Bob was half-white, while he and Bunny were "too black." The packaging of *Burnin'* was the final straw. Two pictures in the centerfold shot by Esther Anderson drew his specific ire. In my first interview with Peter in September 1979, at the home of my *Reggae Beat* partner Hank Holmes, he jammed his finger angrily into a pair of those photographs featuring a man with shoulder-length dreadlocks. Peter Tosh called him the Devil.

PETER TOSH: This is a great album, [but look at] all them pictures of Lucifer! When I come home to Jamaica and I see that, I was grieved. You see any of my picture there, mon? Not one picture is there for I. And yet still I sing on the album. So there was something within those fuckers was trying to keep me out. He Lucifer! The ras-claat. Yes, man, him dread[locks] drop off clean, clean, all his trimmings [referring to the long ropy uncombed braids hanging down his back]. Me ask him, "What happened to it, what happened to your dread, man?" Him say, "Bwoi, look like lice eat it off!"

ROGER STEFFENS: Whatever divine retribution may have been involved, Peter was still determined to go his own way, refusing to call the dissolution of the group a breakup.

PETER TOSH: Well, was not a breakup, you know, is just going three different ways and sending the music in three different directions. Was just that my inspiration was growing and my cup filled and runneth over. . . . One man grow mango, another grow pear.

ROGER STEFFENS: With solo careers in sight, it was time to create titles and logos for their new labels.

BUNNY WAILER: I created both labels: Solomonic and Intel-Diplo. I brought the two of them to Peter and just say pick one and he picked Intel-Diplo. So Solomonic Production was destined to be my label. I designed the two of them. Intel-Diplo is very deep. Solomon was an intelligent diplomat, so that's its meaning. I only shorted it. Either one of them would mean just the same, because King Selassie I say we have to live as intelligent diplomats among men so you have to be wiser than the serpent and more harmless than the dove.

ROGER STEFFENS: *Burnin'* gave an indication of where the group's members were headed as they stepped out on their own. The two tracks on which Bunny sang lead were "Hallelujah Time" and "Pass It On," biblically inspired lyrics of the type that would manifest even more clearly on his solo debut, *Blackheart Man*, considered one of reggae's most important albums. The verse that Bob invited Peter to contribute to "Get Up Stand Up" was its most biting, although its opening line was ludicrously misrepresented in the transcription that appeared in the album's lushly illustrated centerfold: "We're sick and tired of your easing kissing game" instead of the actual words, "ism-schism game," or—as Peter often sang live—"bullshit game." These emotions would find full exposure on his 1977 masterpiece *Equal Rights*, which was filled with anthems of liberation.

Individual interviews with the Wailers at the time helped cement the split.

DERMOT HUSSEY: I did an interview with Bob around the time of the breakup, the one that was used on *Talkin' Blues* [a posthumous early eighties release]. It created a lot of friction. Because if you go back and listen to it, he was really responding a lot to what Peter had been saying—I think he said he "throw word"—'cause he said I can deal with Bunny's position but he had problems with what Peter was saying, that he didn't get any money. To a certain extent that was true but he came to me and said, "Look, you have to destroy that interview, you know; that interview could be worth nothing as well as could value a million dollars. I want to destroy." I said, "I can't destroy that, Bob." And in fact what I did was I gave him a copy, I never destroyed it.

Peter always had a bitterness about that whole breakup experience, unfortunately, and there is something really to be said about them if they had stayed together because that group would have been phenomenal but at the same time in virtue of the personalities involved, they would have had to at some time be apart.

ROGER STEFFENS: Gilly Gilbert, Bob's personal chef, made a key distinction between Peter and Bob.

GILLY GILBERT: Bob and Peter were different. When Bob make his decisions he stuck with them. Bob don't change; he makes a decision, he just do it, and that's it man. Don't business 'bout whether your color white, or your color black or pink or blue. No racism in Bob at all. Bob just want to deal with people. Out of many come one people. He just believe in unity for all.

ROGER STEFFENS: With Bunny and Peter gone, Bob wanted to find backing vocalists for his solo outings. He decided to bring in his wife, Rita, and their friend Marcia Griffiths, together with Judy Mowatt. The stunning Mowatt says she was born to be a preacher. She became a pop reggae star in the 1960s and toured the world with the Wailers in the 1970s, gracefully representing the very best public face of Rasta womanhood. Our discussion took place in August 1981, three months after Bob's passing, at the Seawind Hotel in Montego Bay, prior to her performance at that year's Sunsplash Festival's tribute to Marley.

JUDY MOWATT: Marcia Griffiths and Rita and myself were good friends, but then Marcia said to me one day that she is doing a show

Two of the I Three, Judy Mowatt and Marcia Griffiths, tour the author's exhibition at the *Queen Mary* on its opening day, February 1, 2001, in Long Beach, California.

at the House of Chen [it's now called Caesar's Palace in New Kingston], and she would want some background vocals because she is doing a song that Diana Ross does, "Remember Me"; I can remember clearly. And Rita and myself went to the rehearsal with her and we did it. Well the night of the show she called us on to do that song with her and everybody said we should team up because we sounded so good and from then we started doing a little background vocals for various Jamaican artists in Jamaica, and Bob heard. Bob was doing this song at the time, "Jah Live." This was when the propaganda came to Jamaica that His Imperial Majesty was dead, and Bob was answering to it, and he called us in the studio to work with him.

ROGER STEFFENS: Although the three Wailers were pursuing separate paths now, they were still hanging out with one another.

JUDY MOWATT: That was the first time we worked with Bob. It was a couple of months before *Natty Dread* in 1974, and then Bob started doing the album, and he said well, he wanted us to come in the studio and work with him. But then we didn't have a name. So Bunny Wailer was there, and Bob was there, and Peter was there and we say, "Well, what are we going to call ourselves?" Somebody said, "We Three." I say, "No, you can't say 'We Three' because the I within the Three is the Almighty, so let's say the I Three, which is the I which is Rastafari, and the three of us." So everybody agreed to it, and from then I Threes was birthed in Harry J's studio [and thus the confusion about the correct name, as Judy immediately uses the plural]. And we started the album with Bob and we finished it, and the album was a success. Everybody say, "Well, boy, from you people start working with Bob—he's really gone through the door now." Because this was when he broke away from the foundation members of the Wailers—with Peter, Bunny— and we did all the albums for seven years.

ROGER STEFFENS: In recent years, Mowatt has renounced Rastafari, shorn her dreadlocks, and become a Christian preacher, appearing mainly on gospel shows. She regards her work with Marley, however, as divinely directed.

JUDY MOWATT: I've contributed my career in working with Bob which I know it was really ordained for me to do so. Because I have neglected my own career to work with him.

ROGER STEFFENS: From the time of the I Three's arrival, Marley's career took off on a constantly upward trajectory. Formerly an intensely masculine presentation, the new lineup of Bob Marley and the Wailers offered a visual and audible turn that many critics felt helped them reach a truly international level of showmanship. Three lovely young women, dressed modestly in the colors of Rastafari—red, gold and green—moved in gracefully flowing synch—the movements were choreographed by Judy Mowatt, a dancer herself—singing lilting harmonies on songs like "No Woman No Cry." This positive exhortation's sing-along chorus of "Everything's gonna be all right" helped make it one of Marley's finest and most notable compositions. His live shows began to resemble gospel gatherings with a preacher and his (all-female) choir. Segree Wesley, Marley's childhood friend, offers further insight into the lyrics.

SEGREE WESLEY: The music says in "No Woman No Cry": "Georgie, he lit the firelight." Well, this is a fact, but the fire, it wasn't logwood, it was rubber tire. Because some of the streetlights are out, you burn the tire—you know Georgie's up. But the porridge he used to cook, we drink and he never charge you a dime.

ROGER STEFFENS: Chris Blackwell released *Natty Dread* in late 1974. Island was one of the major labels in the world at the time. The LP featured a painting of Marley with sprouting dreadlocks in a burgeoning Afro style. Concurrently Island rereleased *Catch A Fire* with a similar painting of Bob with a slightly menacing look as he sucked on a giant spliff, a defiant challenge to all the anti-herb factions lining up to disparage Marley's open use of marijuana. This man was a rebel, and the lyrical content of Bob's first solo album left no doubt where he stood. Songs like "Them Belly Full (But We Hungry)," "Rebel Music (3 O'Clock Roadblock)" and especially "Revolution" were a slap in Babylon's face. Perhaps the most notorious line on the album revealed that "I feel like bombing a church now that you know the preacher is lying."

Lee Jaffe, known as "the white Wailer," lived among the original trio of Bunny, Bob and Peter from early 1973 through 1976, during which time he played harmonica on the title song of *Natty Dread*, performed live at venues including New York's Central Park, and produced Tosh's solo debut album, *Legalize It*, for which he also shot the cover picture. But Jaffe had a violent falling-out with Marley over the title of *Natty Dread*. Jaffe collaborated with me to produce a collection of his photographs and recollections called *One Love: Life with Bob Marley and the Wailers*; this interview is excerpted from the book.

LEE JAFFE: I was in a motel room with Bob, mid-1974, and it was the kind of a fight where you throw a couple of punches, but you don't really want to punch the person, so it turns into a wrestling match. Basically it was over the album cover. Me, not only did I not get credit for playing on the record, or any songwriting contributions, but other people got credit for things they didn't even participate in. We were in L.A. and had just seen the album cover at the Island Records office, which was a converted residential house on Sunset Boulevard in Hollywood. The thing that was most disturbing was that when we saw the cover, they had changed "Knotty Dread" [the title of the original Jamaican single] to *Natty Dread*. I protested that they had spelled the title of the album incorrectly, but Bob said nothing to back me up. I was stunned. When we got back to the hotel, l wanted to know if he was going to let the album come out like that, and he started to go off on me about how I was too concerned about my own credit, but I wasn't buying it. I wanted to know how the album that was called *Knotty Dread* could be released with a title that means exactly the opposite.

ROGER STEFFENS: Jaffe explained to me privately that "natty" is an "English twit with a top hat, while Rasta called their hair 'knots.'"

LEE JAFFE: It turned into us cursing at each other. It started with shoving, but I wasn't going to back down. And then it turned into a fistfight. We were about the same size. Nobody really won. It just ended in exhaustion, but it wasn't really over, because nothing had been resolved. We stopped talking to each other, and it wasn't until half a year later, when I was in jail in Kingston Central and Bob was off the island, when he arranged for me to have money for a lawyer, that I was able to forgive him, knowing that his being there for me was more important than any fight we could possibly have. For me, it wasn't the same anymore between us, because part of my desire to go play with Peter came from the fact that I had contributed so much to *Knotty Dread* without any credit, it kind of put me in the same boat with Peter. We both had something to prove with *Legalize It*.

ROGER STEFFENS: More details of this pugilistic contretemps are contained in our book. Despite Jaffe's protestations, the *Natty Dread* album received rapturous reviews. Marley was heralded as a budding superstar with a unique talent and repertoire (the polar opposite of the lightweight disco-ized pop music of that time), and a beacon for the maturing counterculture of hippies, weed smokers and political activists.

Although they were finished recording together, the original Wailers would do a handful of final stage shows in 1974 and 1975 with stars like Marvin Gaye, the Jackson Five and Stevie Wonder. The Gaye show, in particular, was a significant breakthrough.

DERMOT HUSSEY: After the Marvin Gaye concert in May 1974 that they did, everybody was blown away by it. I remember being there in the theater and we were so proud. Everybody jumped off their seat for Bob! Because Marvin, I mean, he got upstaged. Marvin had a huge orchestra, he had pulled out all the stops, but Bob and them just upstaged him. And then of course the fact that we were seeing a group of Jamaicans presenting a body of work that was so fresh, so new, yet so Jamaican in terms of what it addressed. Jamaicans were beside themselves that night. Including myself. I'll never forget that experience. It was a major breakthrough for Bob in his own country that night.

ROGER STEFFENS: Bob was settling into his new role, and a key part of his mystique was the vibe at Hope Road, his new headquarters in uptown Kingston.

CHAPTER 17

Hope Road Runnings

ROGER STEFFENS: Years before, during their sojourn in the mountains, Bunny Wailer had said the Wailers wanted a place to live together as a family.

BUNNY WAILER: Wailers them time [mid-sixties], we could never live inna nobody house or live in our father house. We never have a house where the Wailers could know say, well it's our house, our land. So we a look for that, we all a work for that, when Wailers have a house where we a go live one place, with Peter and him family, and my family, and Bob family—one, so we used to think.

ROGER STEFFENS: Bob initially seemed to be following through on that vision. When he signed with Island Records he was given access to their headquarters at 56 Hope Road in uptown Kingston, which also rented out rooms. At one point he got into a serious disagreement with Blackwell, and moved all of his music equipment out of the main building and stored it at the home he had bought for Rita in Bull Bay, along the coast. Ultimately a settlement was reached and Bob bought the house from Blackwell for a reported $125,000. Buildings behind the house became rehearsal spaces. The broad front yard was perfect for kicking ball. The main building, a modest-sized two-story colonial-style house, was gutted and a recording studio installed, and Bob and his entourage moved in. The singer had a small room upstairs where he entertained a variety of lovers, meditated and wrote his songs.

The property was just down the road from the governor general's residence, and his neighbors, the so-called elite or "Topper Norrises" of Kingston society, were appalled at the carryings-on day and night in the walled enclave at 56 Hope. It was the first time that the ghetto had moved uptown, and Marley's bass-heavy speaker boxes boomed throughout the night. The sounds were indeed disturbing the neighbors, "blowing full watts tonight," as Bob would sing in "Bad Card" on his final album.

BEVERLEY KELSO: Everything was just happening so fast. So, when Bob went away and come back he come to me again and he sit down on my mother's veranda and he tell me about getting the place on Hope Road. He said to me that a little white boy want to give him the place on Hope Road but he think he's gonna give him some money for Hope Road because he want Hope Road for the Wailers. He's buying it for the Wailers and when he said the Wailers, what he mean? He said you, Peter, Bunny, Junior and himself. The Wailers. I don't know how much he paid for it, but he come to me and he sit right on my mother's veranda. He called the five of us. That place was for the Wailers. So, he said to me as soon as all the paperwork come up he's gonna call me to sign my name on whatever. He did send and call me.

When I went there the first evening, he was playing football. He introduced me to Johnny Nash. He introduced me to this lady named Esther Anderson. And he introduced me to some other little people that was there that wasn't Jamaican. I remember that. But at that time the place wasn't fix-up like how it is now. They had a gate, it's still there and it said that this white woman was living on the other side. She could walk from that gate and come right in. But they used to hang out there. I used to see all these white people sitting around the back.

I used to go up by Hope Road but I never used to hang out up there. I didn't like the crowd and it was mostly men then. Playing football. It wasn't very open to women. So when he send and call me that evening he want me to sign some paper, but he was playing ball. But he would send and call me again. And I stood up there the whole afternoon and then I went home because Rita was there, you know? And that was it. From when I go up there that day I didn't go back.

ROGER STEFFENS: As Beverley suggests, Marley's life was changing, with a new crowd surrounding him. Life began to take on new rhythms, starting with food and exercise. Bob brought in a chef, his close friend Gilly Gilbert, a big, bearded, friendly, outgoing man whom Bob depended upon to keep him fed and fit. He began cooking for Bob in 1975 and by 1977 he was part of the entourage that accompanied Bob all over the world on his record-breaking tours. Speaking by telephone in 1994 from Gong Studios in Miami, which he operated as both a production center and record label until Rita threatened to sue him over the use of the Gong name, Gilly described Bob the man, his physical regimen, and the diet he and Gilly shared.

GILLY GILBERT: I first met Bob through his music. I was always buying his music as a kid, he was the main man for me, until I got to meet him in the early period, Wailers, I would say like in 1969. I knew the music, then I met him on Beeston Street by his shop. I was a good soccer player in Jamaica. I played all-schools, I played for Jamaica's Juveniles, represented the national team. I was an ardent and good soccer player. Bob liked my mannerism with the ball, they style me as the no-nonsense soccer player, because I don't play around. I'm all for business. And I was a physical player, love to exercise, and he liked that. Soccer and music brought us together. I tried to play some bass and a little keyboard, but I never took it that serious. But I was more interested in the business of the music, always fascinated over all the aspects of the business.

My first impressions of Bob were that he always carried himself like a star. Yes, man, I'm telling you! Him step like a king. He was ordained from he was born to be a king—in music, soccer, whatever. But God gave him music and he went and delivered. He's just the class and the youth. He's like a young prophet, something destined for this man. It inspired me. During this time he sighted the same Rastafari livity as me. Selassie I live! So we were on the right path. It was good for me to live with him and eat with him, drink with him, smoke with him, play ball.

I started cooking for Bob from about '75 at Island House at 56 Hope Road. Cindy Breakspeare was living downstairs with her brother Stephen and Esther Anderson's sister. Esther was living there before, and then her sister took over. A big yard. In the back there was an old white lady named Miss Gough. Renny and his lady, he was the caretaker. He got the inspiration from Bob too, because when we went there he was like, he never know nothing about Rasta nor no form of livity. Bob vibe just change him fully too.

In the morning him love him bush tea: It's like circe tea—mint tea, all the good herbs in Jamaica—mixed into a blend of two or three. Mint or fever grass. Porridge. Drink tea first, then porridge after; drink a cup of tea first, and then eat fruit, like suck two orange. Then we go jog, 'cause you can't jog with full belly. Then after jogging, good Irish moss and good porridge. And then we cook down the good vegetable. We always have things stirring. The fire always keep burning with food, bowl of fish tea, big pot of Irish moss. We cook down some steam fish, or fry down some fish, or cook down the good ital stew [ital means vital, natural]. My personal ital stew recipe has the best in vegetables, red bean, coconut milk, carrots, turnips, all the good vegetables. Whatever was in season at the time. Pumpkin.

Bob's favorite meal was Irish moss from the bottom of the sea, it's seaweed. Clean it first, wash it good. Sometime you just boil it, boil the fresh moss then dry it. Then, put a little water, a nice bowl or pot of water, and you boil it for a certain amount of time, then you add linseed, flax seed and stuff like gum arabic that stabilize the moss and isinglass that stabilize the moss. Then you boil it all up with all these different ingredients, down to a nice simmer, then it thick up, thick up, and your common sense says it boil and it ready. So you just strain it; and sweeten it with honey or a little milk. Then you drink it.

Sometimes we boil so much that we pour it out and we let it stay there and sit, so that every so often we go there, we can scoop out some, and we make like a mixture, like a health juice, a high protein juice. The blender's always rolling, always blending. Something always a mix and Bob did cook with me sometimes too.

Bob loved to exercise. He loved to train like us. We were hard, jogging all over: Cane River, Seven Mile Beach. Anything we do—if we run ten miles, Bob run ten miles. Tosh didn't go jogging like Bob. But he was a serious character man, and a physical man, into yoga. He exercised and trained differently from Bob, a little jogging here and there, swimming and all of that. But Bunny now was like Bob in a sense. He loved to train hard also. He was with us also jogging on the beach, running to Cane River. When we finished doing that we ate the best fish, the best doctor fish, the best sprat, with the dread named Gabby Dread. He was like an inspiration to them, because he was the man on the beach that have the steam chalice ready, and have the roast fish ready, and fish tea. On Bull Bay Beach, out on Eleven Mile.

I don't see no other entertainer right now who can step in Bob's shoes. Bob took this thing serious. He was no joker-smoker. He was something special. One of a kind.

ROGER STEFFENS: As the violence increased almost daily, a kind of civil war reached into every part of daily life in Western Kingston. Bob had friends on both sides and tried his best to avoid being forced to choose one side over the other. Being affiliated with a particular faction could put one's life in jeopardy in a country where to the victor went all the spoils. Voters on the losing side of an election could be forced from their homes and jobs—and worse.

BEVERLEY KELSO: I didn't go back [to Hope Road] until '74 at the death of my mother, right after the people there in Trench Town started the war. Everything start to get [bad], you know, the shooting, the fighting and whatever. So I said I have to move out from Trench Town now. I was looking for a place to move out, so I went up to Bob. He showed me around the place and he said if I need a place to stay and I need anywhere to live, he showed me one side of the house and said, "This belongs to you. This is where you should live." So, when shots were firing and I wanted to leave and couldn't get any place, I went up there one evening. And when I go there, [Joe's wife] Valerie Higgs, she first me [i.e. beat me to the place, got there first]—when I go up there that even Valerie was living up there. It was in the same place that I was supposed to, you know? So, when I see that, I said, you know what? I am not gonna say anything because Valerie was there.

ROGER STEFFENS: Beverley wasn't the only one made to wait while Bob played soccer or rehearsed. In September 1975 JBC anchorman Dermot Hussey recorded a landmark interview with Bob that later would be incorporated into the posthumous *Talkin' Blues* album. Despite Hussey's prestigious position, Bob tested his patience for days at a time.

DERMOT HUSSEY: Bob never said much, he was kind of shy, really. Those days were remarkable. I mean, I caught him in that period when he was just about to go solo. I was around him at several rehearsals. I saw them prepare for that *Natty Dread* tour. I was also there when they were rehearsing for the last show that they did together, the Dream Concert with Stevie Wonder on October 4, 1975. It took me a while to get the interview. In the first place I had made several attempts to get that interview, by waiting patiently, watching him rehearse. Bob used to have sessions around four o'clock, five o'clock, there'd be a serious football game played, he used to use that really to condition himself. And then as it grew dark and they couldn't play anymore they'd come off the square there, shower, get ready for rehearsal. Rehearsal used to start sometime around eight o'clock and would go on straight through till two o'clock in the morning. So I used to sort of wait patiently and in fact, Skill Cole, I have to really give him credit here because he was the one that made it possible; Bob stipulated that he didn't want to come into the radio station so I had to find a neutral place and we went to a small recording studio which was on an avenue off Hope Road and he did it there with Delroy Butler as the engineer. But he came and was in good spirits. But he was still smarting from the breakup of the Wailers.

ROGER STEFFENS: In those early Hope Road days, if one could penetrate the circle that gathered around Bob, glimpses into his creative process were everywhere. He was at ease at last, because he had found a home.

CAT COORE: For me, moments that stand out are like when he was rehearsing at 56 Hope Road, when I first saw the Wailers Band with Al Anderson and everybody, and he was rehearsing these tunes "No More Trouble" and "Midnight Ravers," just over and over and over again. I couldn't believe it. I'm saying, "How many times this guy going to sing this tune?"

DENNIS THOMPSON: Bob would do twenty tracks of "Ambush In The Night," vocals, and he'd say, "Which one you like?" It's all twenty, but we had to pick one. He never sang the same song same way twice. He do different moods, different feels. He was just prolific. That's the kind of person he was.

CAT COORE: I remember he walked out one night and he said, "What's going on with you? Wait, how come so much people around the place?" And cussing out so much people in this place, people just watching. He was smoking a chalice, him and Skill Cole. And he looked at me, there was a little kid, and he just gave me the chalice like that. What he didn't realize was that I had been smoking a bag of weed. So I just took the chalice from him, took a big sip and handed it back. And him turned to Skill Cole and say, "Bwoi, dem brown boy dere wicked, now, Ras!"

ROGER STEFFENS: Another close companion from these times was the Studio One keyboardist Pablove Black, who explained the daily routine at Tuff Gong.

PABLOVE BLACK: Me used to go watch Bob Marley get up six o'clock in the morning and me make juice fe him. And him say him want to play some table tennis. And we start to play table tennis, and him look

Keyboardist Pablove Black, Twelve Tribes member and close friend
of Marley's, at the Reggae Archives, Los Angeles, June 1997.

and him see two white youth outside, and him say him supposed to do
some interview with dem but make dem wait. And we play table tennis
for about forty-five minutes till him sweat and him go shower. Him
come out, then have callaloo and things fe give him fe eat. Seen? And
him leave and go in the rehearsal room with him guitar, ten o'clock
the morning! Him walk away into the rehearsal room and them have
a blackboard where the songs dem write, a part of the wall dem paint
black, and dem tune dem write 'pon it. And him say, "Plug in the amp
set fe me." And me plug it in, and him plug in him the guitar, and we
start play. From ten o'clock till two o'clock him rehearse, till a couple
of more man come and him cool it. Him start back about four, them
never start rehearse till about eight at night the night when every man
come. Bob Marley rehearse from eight o'clock till two o'clock the next
morning, before rehearsal done. By three o'clock man split up back,
and me and him and [Tuff Gong staff producer–composer] Sangie

Davis sit down in there 5:30 the morning, same way the man have him guitar in him hands, from ten o'clock the [previous] morning, right back round. Must know say, him no tired fe do it. And do it again. And do it again. And do it again. Him have a spirit, mon, you know that's why dem call him Tuff Gong. Is a spirit weh indomitable. If you beat him today, you haffe go beat him tomorrow. And him a come the next day come fight you again!

CHAPTER 18

Cindy Breakspeare and the 1975 Tour

ROGER STEFFENS: The most glamorous resident of Hope Road when Bob took over was a young white Jamaican woman named Cindy Breakspeare. Bob formed an immediate attraction to her, but she initially rebuffed him.

Cindy was crowned Miss World in 1976. In the year of her reign, Bob spent much of his time in exile in London with her, eventually fathering their child, Damian, known as Junior Gong. Their public relationship led to bizarre tabloid headlines in the UK which referred to Marley as a "wild man" and the couple as "Beauty and the Beast." But their time together actually began much earlier, and lasted longer, than many people realize. Interviewed in 1994 at a time when both she and their young son Damian were aspiring professional singers, having toured most recently with Bob's mother, Cedella Booker, Cindy proved to be gifted with a lightness of being that was at once charming and compelling in its frankness. Many of Bob's closest friends insist that she was the great love of his life.

CINDY BREAKSPEARE: I think I must have been about seventeen when I heard Bob for the first time, and I think that was when I really fell in love with reggae, like so many other people. It was *Catch A Fire* time. I just couldn't take the album off the turntable. And we went between that and Marvin Gaye's *What's Goin' On*. I saw Bob and Marvin play at the Carib Theatre.

As a child I always kind of had a rebellious nature and I left home

Cindy Breakspeare, Miss World and Marley's companion in his
final years, in Kingston, Jamaica, January 2003.

early. I mean I moved out on my own with my brother and a friend really early, so I was able to make my choices. My parents divorced when I was about seven. And even though I ended up living with my mother up until I was about seventeen, in 1971, she just informed us one day that it was time for us to find our own digs and make our way in life. So my brother Stephen and I ended up at 56 Hope Road. And then I moved away for maybe six months or a year, and then I moved back there a second time, which would have been '75.

And I worked! I did a multitude of different things. I sold jewelry, I sold furniture, I worked at the front desk of the Sheraton, I ran a restaurant, I ran a nightclub. Whatever came along that looked exciting, I did it.

In '75 Bob was about to buy the house at Hope Road from Chris. Bob was there all the time, he and his crew, and he was basically living upstairs. We were the only outsiders who lived there, nobody else was living there at that time, because Dickie Jobson had cleared it out on the basis that he wanted to make the whole place kind of commercial. He never went through with it, and we begged him to let us have the apartment back, 'cause we liked being there so much, and he agreed. So we hastily moved back in.

I used to live on the ground floor there at Hope Road, and this was in the very early days of our relationship before I was really sure if I was going to enter into a relationship—because I knew from the first time that I ever spoke with him at length, that a deep relationship would change my life permanently. And he would go by the door and kind of glance sideways to see if anybody was around, and attempt to engage me in conversation, and of course it would always be philosophy and talking about how you see yourself, how you present yourself as a woman and all the things you should and shouldn't do, because of course doctrine was everything then. And he would sit on the steps out the back of my apartment there with a guitar and sing. I remember hearing "Turn Your Lights Down Low" just like that. And he wasn't a man of words on a one-to-one basis, you know, not a lot. And certainly not when he was just getting to know somebody, he was very shy that way. And gestures were very innocent and very boyish. He would offer a mango as a gift, or simple little things like that, which I thought were very charming, especially since I had been involved with people whose style was quite different. I found it very disarming.

People have asked if I believe that he wrote "Waiting In Vain" for me. But I don't know what to say. I mean, I would love to, why not? There's a line that "it's been three years since I've been waiting on your line." Well, it took a while! Not three years, but it took a while. But I can say that when that record came out, that was certainly one of the finer times in our relationship. 'Cause you know relationships do go through changes and stresses and strains, and you have times when you're closer and times when you're not so close. There were separations and all the pressures that were being brought to bear. But definitely, I mean, when I think of it, when we were in England together on Oakley Street after the shooting attempt and all of that, when I was actually Miss World, those were some very very close days, very very very close.

ROGER STEFFENS: Bob's relationship with Cindy unsettled some of his oldest friends and collaborators.

BEVERLEY KELSO: I had moved out of Trench Town because of the violence and I was living now in Forest Hills, that's the foot of Red Hills. So, Bob send somebody to my job and call me and said he want me to sign some papers. So I went up there with a friend one evening. And that evening when I went up there I couldn't go in because Cindy she take over. It was all white people. I couldn't go inside to see Bob anymore. And so I talked to her and I tell her who I was and Bob came out to me. When Bob came out to me, Bob didn't know who I was. He was just looking at me and gazing. He was just like in another world, looking on me and gazing and, "What your name? Who are you?" Yeah. And I said, "What?" My girlfriend was just laughing and I start to cry. And I said, "What happened to Bob," you know? I start to cry. I was living at Forest Hills and I feel down and I actually walked home to Forest Hills that day.

That was the second time he wanted me to come to him and sign some papers. He sent back and called me a third time. I didn't go. I didn't go because of the condition that I hear Bob was in. I tell a guy that Bob must go and (bad word), you know? And the guy said, "What? You cursed a bad word? Say it again!" And I tell the man, I said, "I'm not going to," and I didn't see Bob again.

I want people to know that the fact is I didn't like the way they treat the whole group. Bob, then, I mean, we start from nothing. We start from nothing. None of us didn't have a thing. And to see them reach somewhere in life where they're handling money and it's like Bob was on a different level by himself, you know? They didn't remember. It's like they don't remember—they remember where they're coming from but they don't remember who they start out with.

ROGER STEFFENS: Whatever Beverley's reservations, Bob was headed for higher heights (or "irie ites" in Rasta parlance). His debut solo tour of North America and Europe in 1975 would introduce him to much larger audiences, many drawn out of curiosity by the monster hit cover version of "I Shot The Sheriff" by Eric Clapton. An art director, Neville Garrick, was hired to light the shows and paint huge stage banners with pictures of Selassie and Marcus Garvey, the 1920s' Jamaican national hero and early apostle of repatriation to Africa. The record company finally took notice of Marley's true potential.

I caught this tour in the Bay Area, where Bob played a series of solo sold-out dates in San Francisco's tiny Boarding House club. So great was the demand that promoter Bill Graham, on just a few days' notice, booked the giant Oakland Paramount Theater for a show that was almost completely sold out on word of mouth. It was my initial exposure to a man whose music I had become enamored of two years earlier. I had seen most of the fifties and sixties legends live, from Buddy Holly, Chuck Berry, Bo Diddley, Nina Simone and Jackie Wilson to Janis Joplin at the Fillmore in 1967. But no artist had ever captured me quite as strongly as Bob did that night in Oakland, windmilling his Medusa-like locks, then standing still and mesmerizing the audience, eyes squeezed shut in ecstatic concentration. I sat next to Moe, a well-known Berkeley bookstore owner, who had been told by one of his employees not to miss this unprecedented spectacle. "What the hell's he saying?" Moe kept asking me, but it really didn't matter then if you knew what his words were; he could have been chanting in Swahili for all the audience cared, so powerful was his presence that night. Joining the group on Bob's first solo tour that night was Tyrone Downie.

TYRONE DOWNIE: When I'd just joined the group in '75, everybody was so serious. Bob was so serious, Peter and Bunny had left, and everybody was serious. Skill Cole was there and all of these dreads, and I was a little kid, very naive, and I wasn't used to the aggressive attitude. And always hearing "screwface," and always "bumbaclaat."

I wasn't used to that, so I was scared at times. Terrified, actually, of everybody. They were confusing. I mean, Family Man was saying to play in a certain way, and Bob was saying to play another way. And I was getting really confused at one point. Then I get to find out that it's just like some dogs—the bite is not as heavy as the bark.

Al Anderson is the one who actually pulled me to tour with them. I used to record with the Wailers, but I never used to get any money. I used to get a spliff, some ital juice. You're supposed to just be happy with that! And I left school to play music! I said, "God, if I'm gonna be playing this thing, at least I have to make a living!" So I couldn't take the ripoff of studio work in Kingston, and I left and went to play in hotels on the north coast. And then I got sick of the north coast after a while and came back to Kingston to play at the Sheraton, which is where Bob came with Cindy Breakspeare one night. It was just before she became Miss World. They were dancing and I was singing this song by Billy Preston, "Nothing From Nothing Leaves Nothing." And Bob came up and say, "Hey, mon, I want some a dem vibes inna de band, 'cause we a go 'pon tour, we a get international now, we a break a foreign." And me say, "Wow, if these guys don't pay me in Jamaica, why are they gonna pay me when I go thousands of miles away?" I was still unsure, reluctant to do that. And then Al used to come to the hotel. I think he had some girlfriend staying there. So he'd come there every night and listen to the band. And Al said, "Tyrone, you have to come, man! Leave this hotel thing here, you don't know what you're missing. You don't know how big this thing is gonna be!" And he was saying it from then, even knew it more than anybody else in the band.

What really made me leave was the Jacksons were doing a gig with Bob at the Stadium, and I asked my bandleader, who was Jackie Jackson who played on all those Toots records, if I can go and do it. And I'll get Robbie Lyn to sit in, who plays with Robbie and Sly. And he said, "Sure, if you can get Robbie in." I asked Robbie; Robbie said he would sit in. It was a weekend. And when I went back Monday, Jackie says,

"Don't come back. Go stay with the dirty Rastas." And I said, "Well, jeez, I mean—well, maybe I'll do just that!" He lived to eat those words, because he came back a couple of years after that, when he wasn't doing much touring, and wanted to buy Family Man's bass amp. So he was asking me to ask Family, and I said, "No, why don't you ask him yourself?" I just had to see that, you know?

Bob wanted two keyboardists in the group because on the records there is more than one keyboard part. In early Island days they had Touter Harvey, Wya Lindo and Winston Wright. And myself. And the thing is we wanted to try and get back the same record sound. And that first tour I was playing everything—organ, clavinet and piano. Marcia was pregnant, so with Rita and Judy, Al and I just made it the I-Fours!

ROGER STEFFENS: The tour wasn't easy on the musicians.

TYRONE DOWNIE: Al Anderson and I had left after the '75 tour because I couldn't stand it. Al was in America, and he wasn't used to it either, being from a kind of middle-class family background. He was really fascinated. He wanted to be involved in the challenge and the adventure, but when you're not used to dealing in a certain way and people come on to you aggressive all the time, sometime you get turned off, and you don't want to be there. And that's how we felt after that first tour. The music was good. Bob Marley was great. But if you gonna play with people, at least you want to feel comfortable. So we did this interview in *Black Music* magazine in England. Carl Gayle was the journalist and the writer for reggae. And he interviewed us on a train on the way from somewhere back to London. And we just both spoke out. So when we realized that we actually expressed ourselves and said what we really felt, we both asked each other [whether we should stay with the group].

ROGER STEFFENS: Al ended up leaving for a couple of years. Following that successful summer 1975 tour, Bob returned to Jamaica for one final performance with his former partners, and Tyrone came aboard for it.

GAYLE McGARRITY: I saw a wonderful show at the National Stadium when Stevie Wonder came to Jamaica, on October 4, '75. That was the last show that the Wailers, all three of them, did together. And the I Three were part of that show, too, so it was truly unique. That was wonderful. In fact, I went home with Bob after that. I remember feeling like a real queen, because he was like, "Wha'ppen Gayle, ya'ave a ride?" And I was like, "Oh no, I can get a ride." He was jealous, and he was like, "I'll give you a ride." And he came to the house, which was my maternal grandparents' house called the Moorings on Seymour Avenue, not at all far from Bob's residence and studio at 56 Hope Road. That was when he said to me that he wanted to buy the house and we sat up and talked till really late that night.

ROGER STEFFENS: One of the topics of discussion was the shameful treatment of Bob by his father's family.

GAYLE McGARRITY: I don't remember through whom it was, but I met this guy who looked so much like Bob. And then somebody said his father was Bob's father. Then his wife said how when they went to Spain on vacation once, when they registered and they signed the name "Marley," the guy came out and said, "Wait a minute, you're from Jamaica and your last name is Marley, are you related to Bob Marley?" And her husband said, "Yeah, he was my half-brother." And they let them stay at the hotel in Spain for ten days without paying for one thing. And I thought that was disgusting because they had treated Bob like shit, you know what I mean? And now that he's dead, they're getting over on his name. Again, I thought that was an example of Jamaican obscenity. But they did it. I would have insisted on paying just out of conscience, but they didn't have any. Certainly I know that Bob went to his uncle after his father died, trying to get money to do a record, and they threw him out of the office and that after—this is what the sister-in-law told me—she said that she can't believe white Jamaicans sometimes. She said that he threw him out of the office and then right after he threw him out he said, "Boy, that's definitely my brother's son. Did you see those cheekbones?" They're really full of shit.

ROGER STEFFENS: Now that Bob had an international audience, he was keenly aware that he had to learn more technically so he could gain full control over his material.

DERMOT HUSSEY: He came to my house and had dinner with Cindy Breakspeare because he said one time, "Look, I want somewhere fe go, a dating this daughter here." So I said, "All right, come up and have dinner." It was a fabulous night. He was cool and enjoyed himself. Cindy was this beauty. Bob was very easy, very easy. He would talk a lot about music. I remember he was very concerned about getting the music to an international level. I remember once he was saying, "Why does a Jamaican record sound so different to one that's released in America?" In fact, that whole roots rock reggae was him making a decided attempt to raise the level. "Play I on the R & B." He was very concerned about that and he used to talk a lot about that. He used to talk about Africa, he used to talk about Ethiopia. He used to talk about eventually going there, he wanted to open a studio there. And he used to talk about Rasta. In fact, he said, "Dermot, why you don't locks?" So he did proselytize, yeah, a little bit! "If you just locksed." I and I used to just laugh.

ROGER STEFFENS: With momentum building, it was time for Bob to create an album that would help him crack the black American audience. The result, *Rastaman Vibration,* would become the biggest hit of his lifetime, and his only top ten record. But others were about to try to capitalize on his fame in nefarious ways, with lethal results.

CHAPTER 19

Rastaman Vibration and the Fatal Reissue

ROGER STEFFENS: Dennis Thompson joined the Wailers touring company in 1976, as Bob recruited new members to replace Al Anderson and enlisted an accomplished engineer.

DENNIS THOMPSON: Bob told me he always wanted me to be his engineer. At Randy's Studio everyone talk about going on tour, but nobody ever go anywhere. Bob said, we're going on tour, why don't I come. I said, "OK, come and get me when you're ready," never expecting a call. But it happen in such a funny way.

At the end of 1975 I was in the Virgin Islands and I was watching the Manhattan Transfer TV show and here comes this big announcement, "The Trench Town experience, blah, blah, blah," about Marley and the Wailers. I said [to Bunny Wailer], "Jah B, Bob Marley is on TV, nice man." But I said it don't sound right. Congas playing and his hands moving and you don't hear nothing, and drum sound funny because you got one mic sitting in the middle. I said it was a cheap little way of doing it. A guy said to me, "You see a problem, go and fix it." I said, "I'm going home in the morning." I went home January 1, 1976, and I ran into Allan, Family Man and Carly January 3rd. That was that. From the beginning of 1976, I was Bob's engineer.

DON TAYLOR: What happened when I got Bob, he had learned from Scratch, his greatest influence in laying that heavy rhythm track was Scratch. He learned from Johnny, he learned from everybody he came up with. At that time he was still in the developing stage, he learned enough to lay the tracks. After he laid the tracks, he was basically lost. This is where Chris Blackwell again used him. In addition to having the 6 percent contract for his first couple of albums before I came in, because Chris know that he couldn't mix the tracks, Chris put into the contract that he would mix the tracks as the executive producer, and get 2 percent back. So Bob made four! When I came in I saw that all Bob needed was the experience. So on the first album we did, *Rastaman Vibration*, I brought him up to Miami. King Sporty gave us a white guy for engineer.

DANNY SIMS: Alex Sadkin! Me and Bob Marley with King Sporty discovered Alex Sadkin working as an engineer at Criteria Studios. That's where Bob started to learn how to mix. Bob would never work without Alex.

SEGREE WESLEY: Among the songs from that period that I really admire is "We're Gonna Dig Them Crazy Bumpkins Out Of Town" ["Crazy Baldhead"]. 'Cause there was a meaning to it. When I went to Jamaica Rita told me, she says Segree, wasn't it true they used to rehearse up on the Hope Road? Said that the neighbors even called police down on them. And they just kick a soccer ball outside. And of course, they see these bunch of longhairs and these people not used to that. So they call the police. So Bob went in the toilet on the toilet seat and that's where he penned that music. We gonna dig them crazy bumpkins out of town, I and I build a castle. So you have to hold down on the noise because the people, they knew who the Wailers were, but the people were complaining. And Bob wrote about that situation. You see, the thing about him, he writes just about everything that he has been through. I mean, it's reality more so than fiction. Most of it, in regards to who may say they actually penned this, Bob had to have an input in it because it always reflected what he has been through.

ROGER STEFFENS: *Rastaman Vibration* was set up to be a major release, with advertising and exotic promotional materials. A thick, burlap-covered box was sent to reviewers containing the record, a press book and a large burlap sack with Bob's picture and the album's title printed on it, created by the Wailers' new art director, Neville Garrick.

NEVILLE GARRICK: I hooked up with Bob in 1974. It was a natural mystic! I was working for the *Jamaica Daily News* as the art director, and when Marley did the show with Marvin Gaye in Jamaica I took some photographs of that concert. I was thinking of doing some posters of Bob, because they were good. So I took them and I showed them to Bob and he liked them, so we decided to produce the posters together. That was our real first connection in me, really, working with Bob.

But before at the newspaper I'd taken my feature writer there to do a story on the Wailers which was on the cover of our Sunday magazine and five pages inside. And from then the relation started to grow. I eventually got frustrated working at the newspaper as an artist, so I went to Hope Road and I got together with Bob, saying, "Well, you're

Neville Garrick, Bob Marley's art director, at his studio
in Kingston, Jamaica, August 1988.

a musician, and I'm an artist, and we feel the same way in terms of black people's redemption, the cultural identity leading to Rastafari." So sight and sound just combining from then, and it was a beautiful experience for me.

Regretfully to say, *Rastaman Vibration* was my first album cover that I did for Bob and it was the one that was the most heavily promoted album out of any of Bob's. I say regretfully because I think that the next one, *Exodus*, should have been promoted more than the other ones, instead of this one being the heaviest campaign Bob ever got in America. Basically I'm saying the promotional dollar that was spent on *Rastaman Vibration*, if it had increased with the albums to come, I mean, like whew! Bob would be further than where he is really in the ears of people.

I came out to California to do the finish of this album, while the band was still in Criteria Studios in Miami. And when I took back the first printed proof with the embossing, we were using it to clean the herbs. And with the grooves in it, the seeds would roll off, and the herb would stay right there. So, somebody in the studio say, "Hey, this jacket is great for cleaning herb." And Chris Blackwell said, "Hey, put that on the album!" And that's what I did. That's how it got there. Simple like that.

ROGER STEFFENS: The 1976 tour introduced a new lineup to the Wailers band , absorbing two prodigiously talented lead guitarists into the fold. From Jamaica Bob invited the Soul Syndicate's Earl "Chinna" Smith, known as Melchizedek the High Priest, to join Donald Kinsey from Gary, Indiana, a precocious bluesman. They would bring a much bigger sound for the larger venues that the group would now play.

NEVILLE GARRICK: I ended up onstage as a musician as well, in the daytime when I wasn't running the lights. That was really due to Bob's encouragement. Bob was a person like this: Bob strived for perfection within himself, and he wanted everyone around him to grow in the same way. He once said to me, "All you do is just draw and take picture and t'ing, mon. Learn to play some instrument, just get involved totally, then you will really be a part of the music, so you really interpret it because you now become the music." So it started up with a few percussions, and Family Man and Carly really show me two things, some funde drums and play different little percussion sound and I added my own little spice to it. I played percussion on *Exodus* and *Kaya,* most of the others, a few licks here and there, but being the person who wrote all the credits for the album, I didn't feel like crediting myself there, "Neville Garrick: percussionist," because that wasn't my portfolio. Or "Neville Garrick: background vocal," although I did some. It was just a privilege for me.

ROGER STEFFENS: Garrick created radical changes in the way reggae was presented on stage. At the Reggae Archives in the summer of 1990, he revealed the technical secrets of his lighting effects and the reasons behind them.

NEVILLE GARRICK: I can tell you Rosco 822 was the red filter I used. People would use more like 819 because it's orange. But I had the Rasta colors of red, gold and green to work with. I would say that, without no apology, I revolutionized the lighting business with green. I used 874 green, and when I started every light man said how the hell can you use that because green made people look dead. And this is Rasta and green got to work for me! And all the rock groups now use that 8-rahtid-74 ["rahtid" is a Jamaican swear word] which them used to think I was mad for all that. I was coloring the music. I wasn't going off what the books say. It was all a feeling, vibes business. I didn't come out of no school of lighting.

I knew the lyrics. I was trying to enhance what they say. If him talking about water, it going to be blue, I'm going to have a wash blue in there. If him talking about sun shining, him going to have sunshine. If it's a green vibe, if it's something melancholy, you have lavender.

And red if it's something like "Burnin' And Lootin' " and cut through with yellow and make fire and them things. It was a whole tricks. So I used the color to represent something.

In the early days, I went through plenty of criticisms in my life in innocence because I wasn't approaching like how these [others did]. Bill Graham called me on the intercom once. And I didn't even know who Bill Graham was. On the intercom while I'm lighting the show I don't want to talk to people. But he wanted to talk to me on the intercom: why am I fuckin' flashing the lights so much? I say, "Who is this fuckin' Bill Graham? I don't know Bill Graham." Them say, "He's the promoter." I just say, "Mr. Bill Graham, reggae is another bag!" and just slam down the phone. Them don't know reggae lighting more than me, because they never had no reggae lighting before, so therefore I had the opportunity that whatever I did *is* reggae fucking lighting.

Several photographers at that time used to say, bwoi, my colors, if I can help them. That's why I even started to put Car 54 immediately over Bob's head and don't put no gel in it, so I could just keep it up a little bit. And sometime I would just solarize it a bit and some light coming from there. But all I was doing was like to help the photographers. Because after all I want them to take good pictures and Bob get more promotion!

ROGER STEFFENS: In the summer of 1976 Columbia Records released an album of early Coxsone ska-era tracks called *Birth of a Legend*. Coming at the same time as *Rastaman Vibration*, the album shocked people who had only heard Marley's more sophisticated Island material. It was a highly controversial project, with recent overdubbing, and one which caused great concern to Coxson himself, who felt he had been conned by a man with mob connections.

COXSON DODD: On the CBS *The Birth of a Legend* album I think Ernest Ranglin did some guitar overdubs. If there was any piano dubbing it would be Jackie Mittoo. What I think we did was to improve on the top ends because it was a bit bassy with no top, so we added like hi-hats and little drum here. I did them with Tom Walton at my studio in New York. And when the *One Love at Studio One* album on Heartbeat came out we went back to the original mixes.

The Birth of a Legend came about with Nate McCalla who was with Roulette Records, and Morris Levy. Nate was a Jamaican and he came to me and really admired the sort of material that we had. So he came up with this idea that he would be able to market the album in America here, which I agreed. I collected five thousand dollars advance on the transaction. But the check was returned. It wasn't honored. And ever since I've never collected a penny from nobody. When I got in touch with CBS they was putting me on to Shakat Music, but Shakat Music doesn't exist anymore because it was operated by Morris Levy and them and whatever it is, and there was something with the government that I figured, more or less, that the government must have frozen some of their assets and things like that and demand that they leave, because they were all crooks.

ROGER STEFFENS: Levy was a convicted racketeer who, at the time of his death, was facing ten years in prison for extortion.

COXSON DODD: He even went as far as—this is how McCalla died, he was found in his bathtub with his throat slit.

ROGER STEFFENS: A subsequent pressing was released by CBS, despite Coxson's attempts to prevent it. Promotional materials claimed that the album contained the original master tapes with no overdubs.

COXSON DODD: I doubt that, because I brought back the original tapes and left CBS with the overdubbing. I've never collected a penny in my life from CBS. This is so sticky, because I had a lawyer working here with them, but Chris finally got to them. Because it seem as if Chris would prefer to really do something under the table instead of coming up front. Instead of really taking this chicken feed that Chris and Trojan really want to offer I prefer to let the world know what is happening and leave the rest to God.

ROGER STEFFENS: Marley was beginning to make serious money, and vultures circled more frequently. But there was a tour to do, and Marley spent most of his energy preparing for it. During the American leg, his mother, who had left Jamaica in 1962, saw Bob on stage for the first time ever, in Philadelphia. It was one of the very few shows in which Bob spoke between several of the songs, motivated no doubt by the presence of his extended family.

CEDELLA BOOKER: Philadelphia, 1976, that was my first sight of seeing Bob perform. It start from the house in Delaware, he sent a limousine to pick us up. It was around ten of my family, my sisters, my brother, my nieces. And on the way going on, I just feel, to go and listen to my son perform and everybody so excited about it, you hear them a talking all over, I tell you I was excited myself! Oh my, that night, it bring joys, it bring tears, everything really. When I sit there and look at Bob, according to the glaze of the light, they put that light on him, when I see sweat running down it looked to me like blood! He was highly in the spirit.

ROGER STEFFENS: Bob was indeed becoming more spiritual, influenced by Skill Cole, who was now an official with the Rasta organization known as the Twelve Tribes. They believed that the people of the world were divided among twelve tendencies of mankind, indicated by the house or month in which they were born. Bob, born in February, was in the House of Joseph. On the back cover of the *Rastaman Vibration* album is written, "Joseph is a fruitful bough."

NEVILLE GARRICK: Yes, yes, yes! But it does not necessarily indicate his coming out in support of the Twelve Tribes of Israel. Skill Cole was one of Bob's very close friends. Skill was in the Twelve Tribes, and Bob, because of closeness with Skill, was more dealing with other of Skill's bredren who were in the Twelve Tribes. But Bob always dealt with every group in Jamaica who were dealing with Rastafari business.

ROGER STEFFENS: The quote went on to say, "The archers have sorely grieved him, and shot at him, and hated him." Soon after the group's return from the 1976 tour there would be a dramatic attempt on Marley's life. Some saw the biblical quotation as prophetic.

NEVILLE GARRICK: Bob called for a meeting of all the different houses of Rastafari to meet at Hope Road, and really get together, because he wasn't dealing with this division business, like Presbyterians and Mormons, and all that, because we're not about that. And the same day, a queen bee flew into Hope Road and the beehive is still there! Bees are a symbol of wealth and prosperity. So, as I say, is prophecy.

CHAPTER 20

Ambush in the Night

ROGER STEFFENS: Bob's life came within inches of ending on December 3, 1976, when a carload of assassins drove into a suddenly unguarded Tuff Gong at 56 Hope Road and opened fire on everyone in sight. The Smile Jamaica concert, headlined by Marley, was to take place two nights later, and the atmosphere in the city was tense and filled with violence.

Charles Campbell, a PNP government official in 1976, told me at the Reggae Sun Ska Festival in France in 2011 that it was he who had come up with the idea six months earlier, in June of that year, for a kind of concert of national unity. He wanted Bob and others to perform in a free public event. Others have claimed that it was Bob himself who approached the government for permission to do such an event.

Author Stephen Davis wrote one of the first, and best, biographies of Marley and studied the shooting extensively.

STEPHEN DAVIS: Stevie Wonder had done a concert the previous year in aid of blind children in Jamaica. Bob wanted to do something like that, a benefit concert. It was set up for the National Heroes Park. It had no political overtones, except, of course, the fact that there was a huge battle for the soul of the nation; it was an election year. And Bob had supported the PNP in the past. Then Manley called for elections right after the concert was announced, so it would look like, at the height of the battle for Jamaica, that Bob Marley and the Wailers would appear to support the PNP. Now obviously, to do a concert like that, it might be a bit naive to say that there was no politics involved in this in the beginning. Because even to mount a small concert in Kingston, you had to have approval of the government. To do a large concert like Bob wanted to do, it all had to be done almost directly through the prime minister's office. So there was politics involved from the beginning. So for all intents and purposes, and indeed appearances, it looked like this was a benefit for the People's National Party, which was Michael Manley's party.

ROGER STEFFENS: Jeff Walker was the West Coast director of publicity for Island Records, based in the label's Hollywood headquarters and responsible for all publicity for Bob as well as all of the Wailers and Island's other reggae artists. He and his wife, photographer Kim Gottlieb-Walker, spent a great deal of time in Jamaica in 1975 and 1976. I devoted an entire four-hour *Reggae Beat* broadcast to the Smile Jamaica events in 1985, and interviewed both Stephen Davis and Jeff Walker on it.

JEFF WALKER: Although there were efforts made on the Wailers' part to divorce it from politics, it was specifically announced as co-sponsored by the Ministry of Culture. Bob was conscious that it could be interpreted politically. I think there was a certain amount of that he was willing to go along with. But he did not want to be swept into something where he was going to be used. The lineup was not just Marley. It was a lineup of the top bands of the time. So it was An Event. And I believe that the political forces, more or less, were behind the scenes and manipulating that event into something that might, they thought, be helpful in the long run. The elections were announced after the concert was already set and there was no way Bob at that point could say, "I'm gonna cancel the concert," because then it would be interpreted politically.

ROGER STEFFENS: The name of the concert would be Smile Jamaica,

taken from a recent Bob Marley hit. Artist Neville Garrick did uncred-
ited backing vocals on the tune.

NEVILLE GARRICK: I know of two versions of the song, a fast one and
a slow one. I remember one he did with Lee Perry, which was the faster
one. Sometimes Bob made songs for the Jamaican market, for there,
how the people pick up sound there. And then the other one we made
was not at Lee Perry's four-track studio: it was at a multitrack studio,
probably Dynamic, the international "Smile Jamaica." Something that
we feel had more refinement there. Almost calypso. It was just wid-
ening the audience. One was for a specific audience, and one was for
the world. And remember when "Smile Jamaica" was released, what
happened after that—Bob was shot.

ROGER STEFFENS: Some people thought it was a simple tourist song.
Others felt that what Bob was saying was, "Hey, buddy, you better
smile! Smile, you're in Jamaica, dread!" It's more of a threat.

NEVILLE GARRICK: Not even more than a threat. Is a time Jamaica
is into a lot of political and economical problems, at the time, the '76
elections. And Bob was always speaking to the problems of the people.
I'm not saying that he was saying, "Smile, it's cool." Because if you
listen to the song, he says, "Pour some water in the well," you know like
drought, we need help. But as long as you're here, try and smile. You're
in Jamaica, do it with a smile, but move ahead. "Hey, natty dread, flash
your dread and smile!" Don't screw them. Like everybody say, "Oh, [in]
all the songs, Bob is a prophet of doom, and Bob is just saying, 'Boy,
it's going to get real bad.' " So this was really uplifting for the time. A
lot of people saw it differently and figured this was a sellout. He did
it for the government to promote tourism or something. But it wasn't
about that. In fact, it would be the best thing to use now, I feel, within
a tourism thing, to say it. Because I even suggested one time, I said,
"Why don't you have that at the airport—'Smile, you're in Jamaica'?"
It would be great for the first thing you hear when you get there, and

start playing some Bob Marley records when you're in Jamaica, instead of Connie Francis and Nancy Sinatra.

ROGER STEFFENS: The Smile Jamaica concert was meant to give people a positive sign that Rastafari was a way to unite them for a better life. Many others besides Charles Campbell and the PNP were involved in organizing the event. Bob's recent connection to the Twelve Tribes branch of Rastafari was cemented by his friendship with people like his football hero Skill Cole and keyboardist Pablove Black, who were key members of the Twelve Tribes.

Black, Rasta elder, acclaimed Studio One player and bandleader, medical student and healer, would arrive at his friend Bob Marley's side shortly after he was shot, and would spend the next two tumultuous days with him. In 1998, for the first time, Pablove Black gave an eyewitness account at the Reggae Archives in L.A. of that historic weekend. He began by explaining the importance of the Twelve Tribes at the time of "Smile Jamaica," acknowledging the danger for musicians of being associated with either political party.

PABLOVE BLACK: Twelve Tribes run music business in Jamaica! Because we was the only ones who hold the culture. Everybody else had switched [to us], even Bob had to become part of we. But three months before the election I don't do anything for any politician on any side 'cause you get marked. Me just say I'm not doing that show [the Smile Jamaica concert], and them carry it to a brother named "Scree" Bertram, Arnold Bertram, who was a government minister. We know him from calypso days. Him used to run music and him carry it now as the government man, and start print up poster. Before Bob agree to do a concert, them a print poster with him [on it]. But every time them call, him say, "Me never make no arrangement fe do no show fe oonoo [all of you], you know." 'Cause them did print it fe go on at Jamaica House [the prime minister's residence]. And him say him not going to do it there, him no want it connect him now with that political party [then-prime minister Michael Manley's PNP]. And them move it now down to the Heroes Park Circle. But up to the night before the show, nobody no know if him a go do the show or not.

ROGER STEFFENS: Dr. Gayle McGarrity, a keen political observer, explained Marley's political leanings at the time.

GAYLE McGARRITY: He was always seen as, and I think was considered by most who knew him well, as being more on the PNP than the Labourite, i.e. JLP side, as he had lived in Trench Town, and Trench Town was always more PNP. That was the way it was in a society in which tribal politics and warfare was the norm. But he did have some friends in Tivoli Gardens, which is JLP turf. I remember some of those really seedy characters that would hang out at Hope Road, like Tek Life. Lovely name, right? I remember a lot of those guys being Labourites, and, in fact, a lot of people feel that was why he ended up being shot up at 56 Hope Road, because he had both the Labourites and the socialists hanging around there, and it was easy for people to know his movements.

Now, many of the uptown people that Bob started to associate with are people I grew up with. The uptown social elite circle was, in those days, a small one. I'm not being a hypocrite, but many of these Jamaicans were essentially fascists. These were people who did not think twice about shooting to death black trespassers on their estates, secure in the knowledge that they would never even be charged with a crime, let alone serve time in Jamaica's notorious prisons. We're talking now about the really ugly side of white–brown Jamaican society—the very Babylon that moved Bob to take up his lyrical ammunition to destroy. And the fact that Bob was beginning to mingle, albeit probably to a limited degree, within these circles, was probably a reflection of his love for Cindy.

I noticed him beginning to make different kinds of decisions about how to spend his spare time, which was precious to him as he was always very disciplined and hardworking. I overheard some white

Jamaican uptown types talking in Jamaican patois about how Bob was going to be made to pay for hanging out with this white girl. And when I told him, Bob just laughed. He said, "You know, I never thought of you as the type to be jealous and I-man no fear no one. Jah protect I." But I continued trying to convince him of my fears, saying, "You know, they're talking about this and that." He would just brush it off, with comments like, "Miss World! I could have Miss Universe!" But I kept on trying to tell him what those who simply wanted him to disappear were saying. It was only about a week after the last time that Bob and I spoke about such matters that the assassination attempt at 56 occurred, so the whole thing began to feel very scary to me, too, and I didn't want to be caught in the middle.

ROGER STEFFENS: It wasn't just Dr. McGarrity who was feeling the scary vibes. Norman St. John Hamilton was the manager in 1976 of the I Three and solo star Marcia Griffiths.

NORMAN ST. JOHN HAMILTON: Although Bob Marley's music was an integral part of my life and "uplift-bring-ment," I never met him until the summer of 1976. It was after his concert at the Beacon Theater in New York City while he was on the *Rastaman Vibration* tour. The "natural mystic" that evolved from the stage that most memorable night changed my life forever. My plans to attend the London School of Economics to pursue a law degree were dashed; I became manager to Marcia Griffiths and thereby became intimately involved in the business of reggae.

Bob and I had a mutual respect for each other—as did Don Taylor, Bob's manager. I stayed out of their business; they stayed out of mine. I set up Marcia's tours without conflicting with Bob's, with one exception. When I learned that then-Prime Minister Manley had insisted that Bob do a concert in Heroes Park, Kingston, I was very apprehensive, I smelled trouble. I told Marcia that I had scheduled her for two shows, Friday and Saturday night of that weekend. I told her she had to come to New York on Wednesday for rehearsals. Reluctantly she arrived on Thursday, stating Bob's annoyance that I had never created a conflict before.

I explained to her there was no show arranged and I wanted her out of Jamaica because I was afraid for her safety. She was relieved and mentioned that she dreamed "that a hen was walking with three chicks; someone was throwing stones which hit the hen and one of the chicks." The rest is history. One of the victims at Hope Road that night was a young man named Griffiths, no relation to Marcia.

ROGER STEFFENS: Friday, December 3, dawned hot and humid. Members of the Wailers Band gathered at Tuff Gong late that afternoon to rehearse for the upcoming concert.

STEPHEN DAVIS: Tuff Gong House was an old tropical mansion on Hope Road which is in uptown Kingston, and it was owned for years by a Mrs. Gough. She was apparently a very interesting woman who was a white Jamaican lady who was married to a black Jamaican man, and apparently ostracized by Kingston's white community for that transgression. So she sold it to Chris Blackwell. It became a set of flats where a lot of people I knew, like Dickie Jobson, lived as apartment dwellers, until Bob sort of took it over around 1974. Now it has a big concrete block wall around it that Rita Marley built. But then it just had a sort of iron gate around it. It was fairly accessible, anybody who really wanted to drive in could just drive in. And it had a big mango tree in the back. And the front yard was paved. It was a large place. It must have had a dozen bedrooms; it was that big. Just a big tropical mansion. At that point, Don Taylor had taken out the sash windows and put in sort of louvered windows to replace them. The whole place had been gutted and was being rebuilt.

ROGER STEFFENS: The openness of Tuff Gong House was well known. Musicians and others would come and go at all hours.

PABLOVE BLACK: The week before I see two guys come to Tuff Gong, come a Hope Road, and me know two gun-hawks [hit men]. Them come the week before. One of them never know it was me, and him come in and say, "Wha'ppen Bob?" And the next one a draw him away. But the next one know me and him say, "Wha' you a do here?" Me say, "Wha' you a mean? Me is a musician, you know. Me there anyway." After the two of them leave me feel a cold spirit, and me just take me time come out and walk go up Hope Road, walk up to Twelve Tribes. And from that, me never go back there.

JUDY MOWATT: I had a vision a few days before the shooting. Marcia left; she didn't feel too good about that concert. Like she had a premonition that something could happen, or she heard something and she left the island. Rita and myself had been going to rehearsals. So one night I went to my bed and I dreamt that this rooster, it was a rooster with three chickens, and the rooster got shot, and the shot ricocheted and damaged two of the chickens. I even saw like one of the chicken's tripe inside, the intestines come out. And I didn't like it, and I told it to Rita and Rita knew about it. But we were looking out for something. Because usually, how the Africa woman understands, a lot of times we depend on our dreams. We know that when you dream, if it's not so, it's close to what it is. So we were expecting something to happen. And then again, I went to my bed. I never mentioned this—but I went to my bed again and I saw in the newspaper where Bob sang that song "Smile Jamaica" and that was the song that created a controversy because of certain lyrics that he had in it that was like a then political slogan: Regardless, you control your state of being, so smile, because the power's ours. The victory's ours.

ROGER STEFFENS: The forebodings came true in the midst of rehearsals around 8:30 in the evening. Two white Datsun compacts drove through the gates of Tuff Gong, from which the longtime guards had mysteriously disappeared. The exact number of gunmen who came leaping out, guns blazing, is a subject of controversy. There could have been as many as seven or eight, armed with machine guns and pistols, some reportedly containing homemade bullets. They went room to room, often firing wildly.

TYRONE DOWNIE: At the moment when the gunmen broke in, we were rehearsing "I Shot The Sheriff." Bob had stepped out, 'cause the horns weren't on that record and the horn players wanted to play on it. So we were working all the horn parts, and Bob got bored from hearing the "da-da-da." He came out of the rehearsal room and went into the kitchen to get a grapefruit or something. Don Taylor had just arrived and went round there to talk to him. Thank God they both went round there! Because right after that was just pure shot you hear start fire outside. And all of a sudden you see a hand come through the door like, around the door, and start firing this .38.

At first it was blindly. I mean, when I saw it happening I couldn't believe I was actually witnessing this. And then when we really realize that that was a gun, and someone was firing, we all hit the ground. And just headed—the only way we could go was toward the bathroom. And we all went in there, and we were waiting for them to come in and finish us off, me, Family Man, Carly, the horn players Glen DaCosta and Dave Madden. Donald Kinsey came out of the rehearsal room too. Carly was just sitting around the drum. Family Man was standing with the bass. It was a small room, so everybody wasn't in there at the same time. And were waiting and then Bob runs in, and then I said, "Oh, shit! This is it! They gonna come in here and just finish us off!" And what was going through my mind was, what's going on! Who did this? Maybe they followed Don Taylor here, 'cause he was a gambler. There were so many things running through my head. Skill Cole was in some problem with horse racing, and we were just waiting. And then we heard a car driving out, which was Rita, and then a shot fired. And then after a while the shots stopped. And then they left, and Rita started asking, "Is Bob OK?" At that time she had a bullet in her head. So I was saying, "Has anybody seen Stephanie [Rita's daughter]? Is she OK?" And Bob said, "Shhh!" And he had blood on his shirt. We were all in the bathtub, like four or five of us in the bathtub! When I came out of the bathroom and I saw Don on the ground, he was covered with blood, his eyes were wide open and I say, "Shit. Don is dead!" I just say, "I'm going home, fellas." I walked to Half Way Tree. I wanted to get out of there! I just wanted to leave that place because I just did not know what had happened and why.

STEPHEN DAVIS: The Wailers' guitarist, Don Kinsey, who was in the room with Bob when he was shot, said that it was just the three of them in the room. It was Don Kinsey, Bob Marley and Don Taylor. And Don Kinsey says that the gunman came in with this automatic weapon, looked at Bob, and obviously could have killed him, because Bob was just standing there in a corner. And that instead of aiming the weapon and shooting Bob, he aimed in a sort of vague, general direction, very lightly grazing Bob across the chest. The bullet then lodged in his left arm. Obviously, Don Kinsey insists, if this man had wanted to kill Bob, he would have. Instead, Don Taylor got five bullets.

JEFF WALKER: I have to agree with that in the sense that the firepower these guys apparently brought with them was immense. There were bullet holes everywhere. In the kitchen, the bathroom, the living room, floors, ceilings, doorways and outside. I was there a half hour after the shooting, before all the blood had been cleaned up. And there's just no question that if there was going to be carnage, there could have been carnage.

ROGER STEFFENS: As threats against Bob's life had become frequent following the announcement of the concert, protection had been arranged with a loose confederation of gang members and others, known as the Echo Squad. They disappeared from Hope Road shortly before the attack occurred.

STEPHEN DAVIS: This whole Echo Squad business, supposedly surrounding the house. I've heard that this was actually a couple of cops in a white Toyota out front, and that this was the extent of the so-called Echo Squad.

JEFF WALKER: I heard about the shooting with Blackwell when he got a phone call in the Sheraton. We were in Jamaica with a film crew, and I'll just preface this by saying this was a period of time when music on television was just beginning to have some sort of impact on the marketplace in America. And I felt very strongly, because Bob toured so rarely, that we needed to get him on film. And the Smile Jamaica concert was an ideal way to do that. But we weren't going to film it ourselves. It was a conglomeration of filmmakers from New York, along with Perry Henzell, under the supervision of Peter Frank, who was responsible for that Wailers appearance on *The Manhattan Transfer Show* the previous summer. It was essentially Peter Frank's film crew. I went down and joined Peter Frank's film crew and Perry met us once we were in Jamaica. At any rate, we were discussing the plans to film some events around Jamaica the day before the concert when we heard that Bob had been shot.

ROGER STEFFENS: Those who came to kill Marley met a variety of fates. There are continuing allegations of their alliance with American intelligence agencies, spurred by an unlikely coincidence regarding a key figure in the crew that came to film the "Smile Jamaica" concert.

CHAPTER 21

The CIA and the Assassination Attempt

ROGER STEFFENS: Carl Colby, filmmaker and son of a former director of the CIA, has been the object of rumor and speculation ever since it was revealed that he was one of the cameramen who shot the Smile Jamaica concert, held in Kingston two nights after Bob Marley and his colleagues were shot. Surprisingly, Colby, a documentarian living in Los Angeles, was unaware of these allegations; no one had ever interviewed him on the subject. It wouldn't have been hard to track him down. In fact, I found him in the Beverly Hills phone book, and a few days later he came to the Reggae Archives for an interview, conducted on the twenty-fifth anniversary of those troubling events, in December 2001. To give these words their proper emotional context, note should be made that no discussion of specific questions was held before the interview began. Colby's rapid-fire speech and instant responses characterized 99 percent of the conversation, which was also filmed. On a side note, as a Vietnam veteran, I found it fascinating to compare notes and hear of his childhood in Saigon. I began by asking if he had ever been a member of the CIA.

CARL COLBY: I was never recruited by the CIA. No, I would be the worst possible person to be. I'm the son of the CIA director, they already know, they'd think that I was anyway. I wouldn't be a good agent. I wasn't interested in that. I studied philosophy, I was a filmmaker, I'd started making documentary films when I was at Georgetown. I was also very interested in art and all of the interest that I had in politics

Documentary filmmaker Carl Colby with a copy of *The Beat*'s cover story
"The Night They Shot Bob Marley," Los Angeles, December 2001.

was sort of dissipated and I became very interested in journalism and particularly documentary filmmaking. So I started making films about artists. I had a good friend at the time who was the sister of Peter Frank, a Harvard-educated wild man in New York who had started a company called the Video Lab with two other characters, and I joined forces with them, probably in October '76, and I moved up to New York. I met Chris Blackwell and we'd all go roller-blading out in Brooklyn at this roller emporium, which was really crazy. Yeah, Blackwell was out there with his girlfriend at the time. Anyway, he was a great guy, very relaxed, and we all went to this Ray Barretto concert at the Village Gate and I remember that very well because I met Perry Henzell for the first time and I'd always loved his movie *The Harder They Come,* because obviously I loved filmmaking. I'd probably seen it five or six times. Anyway, I liked Perry right away. You could see he was of the same ilk as Chris Blackwell, they're both white Jamaicans and sort of landed gentry, but at the same time incredibly aware of what the culture was like there. And they started talking about reggae and about this reggae concert coming up, Smile Jamaica, with this Bob Marley person. I thought well, this is the most incredible thing of all, I've got to be involved in this. And so Peter said, "We've got a really low budget and Perry's going to direct this, but it's mostly about the concert, so we'll all go down there, you and Fred Brocetti. I don't really know why we ended up going instead of other guys, but we were all part of a little team, we'd just built this company together and I think we all just felt, let's go, we'll hire a few cameramen and we'll just go, we'll just wing it. I remember taking all this equipment and the soundboard—Peter had everything and we flew down on Air Jamaica. We were all drinking rum drinks on the way down, thinking this is going to be fun. It's gonna be Bob Marley, we're going to a concert and we're going to Kingston.

We must have gone down on the Friday—I remember we arrived in the afternoon, because we were unloading all the equipment and for some reason I'd been given the responsibility of the carnet, which is the customs documents. It's about $250,000 worth of equipment, the soundboard, all the cameras, etc. You've said it is mine to begin with, you didn't buy it there, so you don't have to pay duty on the way back, so I had the responsibility for that.

So we arrived and we're unpacking everything, unloading, about ready to go to the Holiday Inn in Kingston and we're just getting into the car and someone said Bob Marley had been shot. And so everybody just panicked. My God, what do you mean, shot? First of all, what happened to him, is he okay, is he dead, how could he have been shot? Also then, is there gonna be a concert? I mean, is it all called off? What's gonna happen? Should we leave, should we stay? We had just gotten there and I thought well, we're here to make a movie and if he's been shot maybe there will still be a concert, but maybe not, but we're here. At least let's stay for a few days and see what's gonna happen, what's going on. So there was a little of a debate about that. And I thought, shot for what? That was really my question: he's a musician, why would he be shot?

At the same time, Peter Frank, I can say at that point, was pretty nervous and he had all this equipment, so he basically arranged to ship it all back, immediately. Almost all the equipment he was gonna ship back because he was panicked about the value of the equipment. A lot of the equipment was not there when we needed it the next day. The soundboard I think was shipped back, which was critical to the concert. They must have found another one for the actual concert. But our cameras were taken.

PABLOVE BLACK: I was riding on the back of a bike, going down Shortwood Road, when I heard Bob was shot. Police pull me over. Me and Stereo, who have Mix Dat Studio in Atlanta, riding fe go to Elliston Road fe pay dues, 'cause the Twelve Tribes have dues every Friday. Friday night the shooting happen. Me no forgot nothin'. And we halfway on a red light, and police pull we over and when he look at me he say, "I think they just shoot you." 'Cause the police take me for Bob Marley. And is a police tell me that they just shoot Bob Marley up a Hope Road.

JEFF WALKER: Chris, Dickie and I went straight over to Hope Road. On the way to Hope Road we heard the first reports of the shooting over the radio. In terms of who could have done it, whether it was related to the concert, and what we were going to do now, that did not come up until later. We were shocked, and it was like, what else could we do? We went over to Hope Road, and the extent of the barrage—it was just amazing! The gates of the iron fence were crashed in. That was the only evidence of any kind of forced entry, so it obviously had been closed. I don't think it was locked, but they just went right through it. I was not there during the shooting, so I don't know how many cars, how many people. But the people who were still there described it as just one car and maybe seven guys, all armed, and thought that the oldest of them looked seventeen and were as frightened as the people who were being shot. They seemed to be firing wildly, and came in and did their number, and left very quickly. So in terms of the event, we only saw the aftermath. Tyrone and Family Man were still there. I don't think there was any imminent sense of danger. The police were there at that point. We made arrangements with Family to come back because we wanted to see them the next day.

We went to the hospital at that point. Manley and many other VIPs were down there. Don Taylor was still in critical condition. After Marley had been checked, he basically came out and sat with all of us. There was a throng of people: Manley, Blackwell, Jobson among them. Bob was sitting in a corner; there are pictures of him holding up his arm with the blood on it. We were waiting to see what Rita's condition was. She certainly came the closest, you would think, aside from Taylor, to being fatally, mortally wounded. But it was a graze. And this was apparently a near point-blank gunshot.

STEPHEN DAVIS: There was another guy named Louis Simpson, who was very badly wounded and apparently hasn't recovered to this day. He had some nickname, he wasn't known by that name.

JEFF WALKER: After he was released from the hospital Bob went up to Strawberry Hill, which was Chris Blackwell's hideaway in the Blue Mountains. Only a handful of people knew where Bob was.

STEPHEN DAVIS: This was a house up on top of a mountain in the jungle really. I remember there's something on the first Third World album that was recorded up there, just jungle sounds. It's just a really remote, beautiful place.

ROGER STEFFENS: With almost all the cameras brought to Jamaica to film the concert having been sent back to the U.S. by producer Peter Frank, Colby and others of his crew left the airport for their lodgings in Kingston.

CARL COLBY: [However, Peter] didn't want to take certain cameras. And then we ended up with a few of our things and then we went to the hotel and woke up the next morning with Countryman dancing in my room! And all these other characters were in my room. I was in a room with Fred Brocetti. The whole room was like full of smoke and everything. It was a pretty wild atmosphere in there.

Then Perry Henzell shows up, and he says, all right, I've got a plan—we're gonna do this, this, and this. At that point we didn't know where Bob was, we didn't know anything. So this was the Saturday and I could see already that there was a little bit of friction between Island Records and Perry Henzell. It appeared to me that Perry Henzell, having made *The Harder They Come* and being Jamaican, was very caught up in the Michael Manley vs. Edward Seaga political campaign, which was at fever pitch at the time. Anyway, that day was a bit confusing because we didn't know what we were supposed to do and I saw that there was a conflict between, let's say, Island Records and Jeff Walker being their representative and Perry Henzell and his vision of what the movie was gonna be. And I think what happened is that, in my mind, it was pretty clear because I was getting conflicting orders—I mean, literal orders: one would say let's go and shoot this and the other would say let's go and shoot that, so suddenly it came down that I think Perry Henzell wanted to make a film about the political scene in Jamaica, and I think Island did not want anything to do with the political story. My sense was that they wanted to shy away completely from any politics because Blackwell is Jamaican; he's doing business with England, he's doing business in Jamaica, he doesn't need to be making a film or any of that sort of thing that's critical of the government or that even mentions the government or needs to be about those political issues.

So Saturday morning I remember we go down to have some break-fast. I remember this battle was going on, because Perry Henzell said, "Let's go out today and start shooting the film." And he's the director. And he's also somebody I've heard of and respect, so at the same time Jeff was saying, "Well, let's not do too much of this political stuff." He said, "No, I'm gonna make a film using this as a metaphor and it's Bob and his hopes and dreams for Jamaica and my hopes and dreams for Jamaica and this battle, really, for the hearts of Jamaicans and Manley and Seaga and how these are the two forces that are conflicting and it's got great tension, and the island is this beautiful, bucolic island in the backdrop, and so this is the story. And it'll be a political story with Bob kind of giving it energy. Otherwise, it's just a rock star, just a concert, I'm not interested." And I thought, this is not just an act he's putting on, he really fervently believes this, but then I thought, well, how come you don't jive this with Chris Blackwell, isn't he the guy that hired you?

PABLOVE BLACK: After the shooting we go to Twelve Tribe headquar-ters and we sit down and we take conference, and Dr. Pee Wee Fraser go check him, Mikey Dan go see what gwan. Them say, well, them can't find no man, all of the man them wha' Bob used to pay fe protect him, every man scatter! That man called Frowser, everybody, the whole of them man and Tek Life.

Bob is a member of Twelve Tribes of Israel. Any man touch him, touch the Twelve Tribes of Israel, 'cause you touch Joseph [Bob's name in the Tribes' monthly system of identifications]. So is twelve people vex with you, twelve people who are born twelve different month. That mean, if we did want to know who, we just keep a conference and make the twelve man from twelve different month check it out and we find out all of who do it. We become directly responsible fe him now, 'cause him say all of them he pay fe guard him, run gone. So me now find myself 'mongst Binghi Roy who is the sergeant of arms. And Gad [leader of Twelve Tribes] say fe go guard it. Plus Pee Wee and couple of more man. A next youth named Little D, who went into Ethiopia.

About eight of we go a Strawberry Hill [Blackwell's home above Kingston, where Bob took refuge].

When Bob come now, him just take charge and we patrol the yard a nighttime. Is four of we a patrol, position north, south, east and west, to cover the four corners. Daytime, him there down in a dungeon, like kind of big castle, a slave-master house. Built that you go round some corner, there are groves for privacy. And we were mostly downstairs in a bottom room. Any man what come to him, we screen him first. All kind of photographer and man come up, and we screen them. If a guy joke, we just say, "Down the hill!" and him go down back. Pure screening we do fe him. Nobody no approach him so easy after that. Him a say, boy it funny how all the man what him pay fe protect him, when the time come, him no see none of them! Some bad men, Frowser and them man. But Strawberry Hill is an enclave, it's a very private place. Not really well defended, but kinda way up there so no man can come through without we know.

Bob was apprehensive. Any sound outside him woulda lock off the light. Him get quiet at first. But you know Bob is a man any time him come in yah, any time him see every man cool, him start crack back him joke and thing. Him a jovial man. But every now and then you see him get back like him think to himself who the blood-claat do that? Him was apprehensive more than afraid that it might happen again, 'cause him probably never believe it woulda happen in the first place, you know, say a man woulda really do that.

CHAPTER 22

Smile, You're in Jamaica

ROGER STEFFENS: Having gone into hiding following his release from the hospital, hours after the shooting, Bob was surrounded by friends and associates from the Twelve Tribes, listening to everyone's point of view on whether he should do the concert and risk being shot again at the open-air event.

CAT COORE: Third World had been hired to play on the Smile Jamaica show. There was a guy named Jeff Walker who was in Jamaica who was hanging out with all of us, Third World, Bob Marley, Jacob Miller. He was moving through all the camps of Island artists. And he was really down on this thing that the show must go on, it must go on! Because if the show doesn't go on, then the guys who came for Bob would have won. So the show must go on.

JEFF WALKER: I joined him late the second day. He went up alone that night. I went up the next afternoon, and kept going back and forth to Kingston. The day after the shooting, in the morning, we went over to Hope Road with a film crew. Family Man and Tyrone took us around the site and pointed out the events of the night before and described what happened on camera. It was three years before Bob got to see any of the footage that was taken that night.

ROGER STEFFENS: In the footage of Family Man back at Tuff Gong the day after the shooting, he is seen putting his fingers into the bullet holes. In late November 1979, during Bob's final visit to Los Angeles, I arranged for screenings of Jeff Walker's footage. There was a crowd of about fifty, including the band, in the large living room of the bungalow at the Hollywood Sunset Marquis in which Marley stayed. As that scene appeared Bob started to laugh, and the whole room stilled, absolutely stunned and unable to comprehend what Bob was finding humor in. In June 1977 Blackwell had insisted he did not want any of it to be released publicly because it was "too political."

JEFF WALKER: The only humor inherent in the situation I think was Family's relation of the events. And the "Boom Boom!" and acting out everything that happened, and ducking, and so forth. And seeing it three years later. And this was the intensity of the morning after it all happened. The basic events of that day had been spent with the barrage of press inquiries that were coming in from around the world, and all the wrong stories and rumors that were getting out about people's conditions and the fact that both Rita and Don [Taylor] were still in the hospital and that Don was in surgery and in critical condition. After Taylor was jet-lifted to Miami the next morning, it was then that I went up to see Bob.

At this point, Chris Blackwell had left the island. He and Dickie chartered a jet and were off to New York the same evening. He was not there the next morning. But I was in touch with Chris in New York, calling him on the phone, in order to arrange a jet to take Don Taylor and Bob off the island. He arranged from New York to have a jet come to Kingston.

ROGER STEFFENS: Walker says he does not resent Blackwell's departure.

JEFF WALKER: Obviously, there was some sense that there was something pending. I think the only problem I ever had with the fact that he left is that we were never offered a ride out if we wanted it. None of the film crew.

CARL COLBY: [On Saturday] Jeff rode around with us a couple of times in the car and he'd sit in the backseat like, "Oh God, we're shooting this political stuff." He was like, "We're not gonna do this. This is not what we want to do." And we got back late that afternoon and I don't remember what happened that evening, just everybody was pretty tired. So the next morning we got up and I asked Peter Frank, "What are we doing?" And then suddenly Jeff said to me that we're going up to Blackwell's house, we're going up to where Bob's hiding out. And I remember I said, "Well, what camera do I take?" Peter said, "Well, you're not taking the good camera." And he didn't want to go. He said, "I wouldn't go up there if I were you." And I said, "What are you worried about?" And he goes, "Well, he was shot at, I don't know who's up there." And I said, "Well, this is the movie. I mean, we came down here to shoot a movie about Bob Marley and I haven't even seen him. Why wouldn't we shoot a scene with Bob Marley? I mean, what are you afraid of? I don't care." And I remember being very irritated and I said, "All right, so I'll take the other camera."

Perry Henzell gave me the camera and it was like an old, mildew-filled, humid, velvet box and a couple of lizards run out of the box. And I thought well, at least it worked. And then there was a sound man there, so we went up the mountain to do this. And I remember Peter didn't go, nobody else went. It was just myself and a couple of guys and I think, I'm not sure if Fred Brocetti was there—he must have been there because he was shooting with me.

So what I ended up doing was going up the mountain in this car, I guess late morning sometime. Perry didn't go. Which is another part of this thing that bothered me, because I thought to myself if you're gonna make a movie about somebody, particularly one man, or one legend, or one great charismatic character, you better know this guy. Like what I did with George Hurrell, or a lot of other artists, Franz Kline, Willem de Kooning. I've done a lot of films about a lot of artists: you've got to get to know their whole world and understand them. And I always thought with Bob I was halfway there, because I was such a fan and I kind of understood what he was about coming from the third world and representing a country like that. I'd spent only about six months of my life in the United States before I was twelve years old, so to me America was like a foreign country.

So we get up there and it's Chris Blackwell's estate. It's very beautiful, the Blue Mountains, and we arrive and it's kind of overgrown and these guys did jump out of the trees with machetes, "Who are you guys?" and this and that, and it's like protected and all of that. I'd already heard rumors because the day before we'd gone by Hope Road and there were bullet holes in the walls and a couple of guys recreated the whole shootout for us and told us what went on when and who must have come in and who fired at whom. Saturday afternoon, I remember also talking to Family Man and the other Barrett brother, I believe, Carly. And another fellow was there, talking about what happened. There were bullet holes, someone must have come in here at some point and shot at these guys, but for what and for what purpose?

So that had happened the day before. Anyway, we get up to the house and these guys jump out of the trees with the machetes and that didn't really bother me because I thought they're protecting Bob. I thought the only thing to say was the truth—we're here from Island Records and we're doing a project. I realized that there were a couple of magic words that opened a lot of doors. So saying "Island Records," the machetes just immediately dropped. So then we go in and we go up and we see Roberta Flack come around after a while and she was nice, and we stand around and there were a few other musicians and friends sort of around. We were there all day. At one point I saw Bob, he comes walking around and it seemed like there were some women and Bob talking on the lawn, quietly, and Bob was sort of relaxed, almost tired—world-weary almost, kind of like he hadn't expected to be shot at, as if he just wanted to go to sleep, very tired, very worn-out almost, a lot of stress involved with these things happening. The energy was very low, it seemed, he was sort of tired and haggard, almost. So I didn't want to bother him or anything, and he was speaking to them, and at some point we joined up and started talking to him and we asked him if it would be OK to ask a few questions and he said yeah.

We did a whole interview on film. He was sitting in this low easy chair and smoking and kind of relaxing, just talking about all sorts of different things. I was asking him a bunch of questions about this and that and his music and New Orleans and Detroit and the radio, and where'd you get this. Remember I listened to every album a lot and I loved the music and I knew a little bit about Jamaica and I knew a little about the political situation, so I asked him a lot of questions and Fred was shooting it. Then we'd stop sometimes. He'd say, "All right, man, that's enough already," and he'd wander off and he'd come back and we'd talk.

ROGER STEFFENS: In the chaotic aftermath of the shooting, opening lines of private communication was essential.

JEFF WALKER: We needed to communicate with Bob, did not want to take the chance on phone calls being overheard. And it dawned on us that we had this whole walkie-talkie setup that we brought down to do the filming with. I was determined to take a walkie-talkie up to Bob so that we could stay in touch with him. That was the night before the concert.

ROGER STEFFENS: When Jeff Walker arrived that evening and walked onto the property, a Rasta with a machete dropped out of a tree in front of him. It scared the hell out of him.

PABLOVE BLACK: I wonder if it was Little D, that? Is a whole house, and the land is like maybe about two acres around it, maybe more. Four a we cover it, that we walk and meet one another, walk back and meet the next man at the corner. That's how we a cover the four corner them fe the first night. Right through till sun come up. The other guards were Little D, Binghi Roy and one more. 'Cause is two man me a meet whole night. The next man me no know who.

JEFF WALKER: I think there are some mentions in Stephen's book about Rastas in trees with machetes. I met one firsthand as I walked from the car to the house at Strawberry Hill. He literally dropped out of the trees in front of me with a gleaming machete poised. I remember his teeth, and the gleam on the machete, were just absolutely bright from the moonlight. It was incredible! I raised my arms and said, "I'm with Bob." And I was escorted up and Marley said, "Yeah, he's OK."

ROGER STEFFENS: Jeff Walker had arrived in the midst of a council of Twelve Tribes elders.

JEFF WALKER: The night that I brought him the walkie-talkie was the night of the council—there were some Rasta elders, some people from the Twelve Tribes. Cat Coore was there. Cat was really the only one there that I knew. At this point, most of the Wailers had scattered. Don was in critical condition. Rita was shot and still in the hospital. Bob was not at any point entertaining coming down to do a concert, that second day. The discussion and the decision-making process began that night, after Don had been evacuated from the island, and after we knew Rita was going to be all right. The overwhelming sentiment at that point was that Bob would be crazy to go down and perform. Everybody, particularly the elders, the more conservative Rastafarians, were very much against Bob going down to perform. They urged him to stay up in the mountains.

ROGER STEFFENS: Among those who had come up to Strawberry Hill to consult with Bob was the founder of the Twelve Tribes organization, a man known as Prophet Gad.

PABLOVE BLACK: Gad come look fe him now. And Gad said, "What you want to do?" And him said, "I don't know yet." And Gad said, "All right, if you gwan to do the show, we there with you. If you decide you don't want to do it, we still gonna support you. Any decision wha' you make." And then when him leave, we now with Bob and say, "Anything weh him say."

CAT COORE: So the night before the show, all of us went up to Bob at his hiding place in the hills and we say, "How you feel about the show?" And there were a lot of guys around Bob at the time and everybody was telling him this and that, and "Bwoi, a perfect assassination attempt, the man them try to kill you already and you must understand that." People talking real truth to Bob still, most telling him not to go, and no one could really say that they weren't giving him good advice. Because even I was feeling at the time that it was crazy for Bob to head out and go to that show.

JEFF WALKER: Basically everyone took turns talking to Bob and giving them his opinion, and I really at that point felt that I had no choice but to get up and put in my two cents. Standing on the outside looking in, I could not see any alternative than for him to go down and perform. I pointed out to him that if this concert was canceled, that everything they had intended to do by shooting him would have been accomplished and that would have been to stop the music. And he said, "There's no way I'm going on stage without a machine gun." And I remember this very vividly, because the line I gave him in return was, "Your guitar is your machine gun." And that got a round of laughter. And it was probably the truly corniest thing I've ever said in my life but there was a certain element of truth to it. And I said, "I know it's easy for me to say, Bob, but I don't see how you cannot go ahead with this concert. And if it means anything, I'll stand up there on stage also." Which I did, and which everyone else who was there that night did. If there was a risk to be taken, we were all there on stage, within a ten-foot circle around Bob.

I think at this point he was beginning to lean toward going ahead and performing. This is just an instinct. Because he agreed that whatever might happen, we could come up the next morning with the film crew in order to record whatever events might take place. We even signed a hastily written agreement to guarantee he would retain control and approval of any sound recordings. So he was at least considering playing. This was the day of decision, leading up to the concert that evening. It was during this period, in the afternoon before Rita came back up, where I think we were all pretty well convinced that Bob was going to do the concert. Then Roberta Flack showed up, literally out of nowhere, and urged him not to perform, not to take the risk.

ROGER STEFFENS: Accounts of Flack's effect vary from witness to witness. Credit for Bob's final decision has been assigned to several different people, one of whom is PNP official Tony Spaulding, one of the organizers of the concert.

JEFF WALKER: It's been said that a Jamaican government official named Tony Spaulding came up to Strawberry Hill and talked Bob into playing. I don't think it was so much that he talked him into it, although Tony Spaulding did show up.

JUDY MOWATT: The government minister Tony Spaulding kept insisting that Bob should do the show after the shooting.

PABLOVE BLACK: Up to when Spaulding come, we don't know what Bob a go do. And when him look 'pon me and say, "Bwoi, me a just do this show here, and get dem man here offa me back." You know, him realize it never woulda go away.

CAT COORE: As the night came, as the feeling of the people became more sympathetic towards the shooting, people were in the streets saying, "Bwoi, if I ever see that man [the gunman] I just kill him!" You realized how much the country really cared for this man. Then I realized that there really was no need to be any fear and that no one would try to do anything in a crowd like that to him. So we [Third World] decided that we were going to do the show.

JEFF WALKER: Around this point, the director Perry Henzell, who was up there with us, did not want to wait around any more for Bob to make up his mind, and decided to go down to the concert site. So we were left, unfortunately, with a defective camera, which we didn't even know was defective at the time. And this is where the various intrigues with the walkie-talkie are concerned. There was a walkie-talkie down at the concert site, and there was one with the Russell brothers, Greg and Compton, the pro tennis players, who were going around the island trying to find whichever Wailers they could. Periodically we would get a call on the walkie-talkie and someone like Don Kinsey would be there and say, "OK, I'm going over to the concert site." We managed to gather everybody but Family Man.

Throughout this day we were getting news reports, we were getting communications from the concert site when Cat Coore went down and felt the vibes and saw the huge amount of people—because it just started growing and growing. At about six o'clock there were fifty thousand people there, waiting for Bob, convinced that he was going to show up, although there still hadn't been any announcement made that there would be a concert.

CAT COORE: The prime minister called us at like ten to nine and said, "I'm on my way to the park now." Sort of saying under his breath like, "I hope you're on your way to the park also." This is in the evening, like when the show was supposed to start. Nobody knew if the show was going to happen or not. Everybody was saying it's gonna happen, it's not gonna happen. Sixty thousand people gathered down there. The prime minister said, "Something's got to happen. If I even have to just go there and talk, something gonna have to happen." So we say, "You know, this true. Let's go do this show. 'Cause everybody going to be safe, no problem. Jah just going to protect."

JEFF WALKER: We listened as Cat and Third World went on and played. We listened to the crowd through the walkie-talkie, the reactions and so forth, and Bob began nodding. I think now we were really rolling towards him going down. When we couldn't find Family Man, after Third World had played, Cat got on the walkie-talkie and offered to play bass.

CAT COORE: What we had decided to do was use one backline. We'd use Third World's bass and guitar amps. In other words, we wouldn't have a set change or anything like that to go down. So while we were down there playing, the walkie-talkie was on. Somebody came up and said, "Bob is on the radio and he wants to talk to you." So I took the radio and say, "What's going on?" And he say, "How it stay down there?" I said, "Sweet, mon. The place a rock, and them a wait fe you, star." And him just kind of laugh and him say, "Oonoo play already?" So I say, "Yeah, we played already." "So who gonna play now?" I say, "Well, there's nobody here to play now. So is either you're coming or you're not coming." So him say, "All right. Mek me talk to such and such about it." I don't know who he was talking to, but they spoke on the radio awhile, and then they started asking about if the police commissioner was there, and that's when they send the police guys to pick him up. That was involved with Tony Spaulding and some people who were instrumental too. 'Cause Tony Spaulding went up to Strawberry Hill and started from that angle, saying, "Bwoi, you have to go do the show." Eventually, Bob came.

ROGER STEFFENS: Back up at Strawberry Hill, momentum started to build to a fever pitch. In 1991 backstage at a show in Ventura, California, Rita Marley revealed to me that when she was brought to the hospital with a bullet in her skull, she was told it was inoperable and that she had to remain in bed. By Sunday afternoon, she said, she couldn't stand her inactivity any longer, and she fled the hospital and stole a car from the parking lot to drive to Bob's hiding place. This has not been confirmed; others say she was discharged normally, and others recall Judy Mowatt escorting her to Strawberry Hill.

JUDY MOWATT: I went to the hospital on Sunday evening when Rita was discharged. We decided to do the show with Bob. Rita appeared in her hospital duster and her head was bandaged.

JEFF WALKER: Rita only turned up there a short while before he went down to play. Bob had decided to go, and Spaulding came up with an escort to get from there to the site directly without running into any problems along the way. As far as that goes, he came up with two other cars as an escort for Bob down to the concert site. Rita, in the meantime, had returned. Her head was in a bandage, she was still in a dressing gown, and not having been there for the whole proceedings of the day, or exposed to any of the events, was absolutely appalled at the thought of him going down to perform, and was against it.

ROGER STEFFENS: This led to a moment of disagreement between Bob and Spaulding.

JEFF WALKER: If there was any discussion, or disagreement, between Marley and Spaulding at that point, I think it was because Bob had just encountered Rita and her desire that he not go down.

CARL COLBY: At some point we went outside and there was this incredible view of Kingston from there and the sun was setting and there were these four or five friends of his, maybe band members and whatever, Rasta, dreadlocks and all—it was just an incredible shot. He was holding, in a sense, the whole weight of their legend on his shoulders and around him and you could almost feel that he wanted a more light environment, he wanted something a little happier, a little lighter, not so everything was heavy. He spoke about that. He spoke kind of about fate and how things are in the world—not pessimistic, but rueful—he reminded me of Bob Dylan. A lot of sense and a lot of world—lots of experience, like a wise man way beyond his years, far older than his age. At some point he was outside and then this car shows up and we were talking also about how you gonna do the concert and everything, and he goes, "Oh, you know, whatever." And that was when Rita was like, "You want him to do the concert, he's not gonna do the concert. He got hurt and everything." I remember he was sort of cradling his arm a little bit, he didn't seem particularly injured to me, it's not like he was in bed with wounds and all, and he just seemed haggard and tired.

But something started creeping over me which was kind of interesting and that was that he, I got this sense of that this is a performance, that this is all part of this incredible build. It just sort of hit me that this, wait a minute, he's thinking, he's feeling, he's building. Because when we were all gathered at the edge of the lawn, he was standing out on the lawn and you could look down with the other guys and you could see this whirling dust. It was late afternoon, you could see this dust now just whirling out there and that was Heroes Park. You could see down the mountain, and you're high up, a couple of thousand feet up at least and you could see down there this teeming mob, huge clouds of dust coming up, there must have been tens of thousands of people down there. So we were like, "Look at all those people there, mon, they're there and they're waiting for us." Bob was like, I don't know. He didn't really *really* want to do it and it was, is he fearing for his life? Is it the last concert he'll ever give? Because if he shows himself publicly, he's gonna be a target again, and yet you could almost feel it was like the ultimate kind of dream. It's a strange feeling to have this group, you could actually see them begging for him to come.

And then this car pulls up and this guy gets out and he wasn't wearing a uniform that I know of. It seemed he was a Jamaican police officer, I mean high up, maybe an army officer or police officer. He identified himself as a police officer and he had a couple of guys in the car with him and he came right up to Bob and the others and said, "You gotta play this concert. You have to play the concert." And I was thinking, Jesus. And they were like, "I don't know." And they were like, "Now, we gotta do this, we have ten thousand people there, we got a situation," whatever, and they were a little oblique about it, but they were like, we gotta play the concert, man. And Rita was like, "I don't know if we want to do this." And all of a sudden Bob just kind of looked up like that, and it's like he had finally found a little bit of energy, like he had finally woken up that day, and it was like, "Let's go." And I thought it was really interesting. It was like the police saying, you perform at the concert or there's going to be hell to pay—I don't know what, but there's gonna be hell to pay: we've got a riot on our hands. And maybe we can exert some pressure on you. Now night was falling, and it was like, let's go. And it's like he found energy.

JEFF WALKER: The decision made to actually go perform seemed almost instantaneous. And Spaulding was there. Rita did not even have time to get dressed. She threw a robe on over her dressing gown and a wool hat over her bandages and jumped in the car with Bob and Spaulding.

PABLOVE BLACK: Me haffe go in the car with him, you know, 'cause Pee Wee said this man here haffe travel with you go everywhere, you understand.

CARL COLBY: All of a sudden he gets in the car and I get in the car with him and he's in the backseat and Fred Brocetti's on one side and I'm on the other side filming him—Fred's actually driving, and a police officer gets in the car with him. Anyway, he starts loading this .357 Magnum, putting in extra clips and everything, seriously, and Bob was just sort of relaxing in the backseat, kind of like nodding a little bit. I remember with so much chaos around him, the policeman loading a weapon and the guy's driving like 80 miles an hour and the cameraman, we're kind of jostling like that; the car's going down a road we came up around 30 miles an hour, the guy's going like 70 miles an hour and you know the roads up there, sheer cliffs, and it was like honking and honking and honking, and escorted by another police car in front of us with sirens going and I don't know who else in the back.

JEFF WALKER: They went down as the center car in a three-car entourage. In the first car was police, Bob was in the second car and I was in the third car with the walkie-talkie. I was with the Commissioner of Police and watched him as he opened a case on his lap and assembled the gun that was inside. I called down to the concert site and said Bob was on his way, and we heard the cheers coming out of the walkie-talkie. There was an announcement and we heard the crowd over the walkie-talkie, that incredible reaction. So we were rushed to the stage and there were just throngs and throngs of people. It wasn't very well lighted. It was sweeping spotlights. The military and police were not evident to the point of there being an obvious force there at all. It was just fans. And I think that was evident. Bob was literally swept along shoulders onto the stage. And we, with this damned defective camera in the car behind him, tried to get through the crowds and follow Bob to the stage. This is true *cinema vérité* now. This is handheld cameras in the midst of a throng with two terrific and courageous cameramen.

CAT COORE: When he came down, a mass crowd just carried him in. He was in the middle of a mass of people, and the mass was just moving. One of my friends lost his left shoe during the mass—never found it that night, walked around with one shoe.

CARL COLBY: They plow our way through Jamaica going really fast, we plow our way into this crowd and all of a sudden I realized the concert had started. You could see the musicians were already on stage, I guess Family Man and the others were there already and they started with this rhythm and I remember following him up on stage and then turning around and it was like, "Shit!" It felt like there were forty thousand, fifty thousand people, like they were—this is not a rock concert, this is like a religious experience, like they'd seen God or something. And he stands up like that and only he, I would say, of any musician I'd ever seen, had the ability to stop time and then take it to 33, to 45, to 78 [vinyl record speeds] and then down to zero, right? And especially with the two Russell brothers acting as the rhythm section. And it was like some kind of a new gospel.

PABLOVE BLACK: So we go down there to the site and when him look him say, "But, me no even see none of my man dem." Third World were there, a wait fe back him. Tyrone haffe take way the bass, a bass Tyrone end up a play, from [Third World member] Richard Daley. Willie haffe jump outta him jump seat when him see Carly a dive a come! And nobody never know where Carly come from, you know. Carly must a been there somewhere and hear 'pon the radio say, "Bob Marley there a park!" And him just bolt, haffe come!

JEFF WALKER: Everything had originally been set up to actually do a professional shoot of the concert and to this day I don't really understand the events that took place. But when Perry Henzell left us up at

Bob's, he was convinced that Bob was not going to perform. He went down and told Peter Frank that there was no way Bob was going to perform, and he just might as well strike. And they literally took down all of the mics, all of the cameras that we had. And when I found out about that, and I was speaking to Peter via the walkie-talkie, I told him, "Bob is going to be there. I'm absolutely convinced he is going to be there." This was about forty-five minutes before Bob actually showed up. He rushed back over there with what equipment and crew he could muster in that short time, to get hooked back up. So the concert footage is handheld guerrilla *cinema vérité* when it could have been state-of-the-art.

CARL COLBY: And all of a sudden Bob says a few things. Maybe I got the chronology wrong but I seem to remember that he didn't just start playing right away, maybe I'm wrong, but I think he said a few things to the crowd. Because I do remember explicitly where he actually said, it may have come later, but I thought it was at the beginning where he actually said to everyone, "Greetings," or something like that, and they were all aaaaahhhh, unbelievable crowd, and it was like he had them in the palm of his hand and all this energy now, this guy who's been like this all afternoon, all of a sudden this unbelievable energy. And then he ripped his shirt off and he said, "They tried to do this to me; they shot me here and they shot me here and they grazed me here," with his shirt off, and it's like you're seeing Jesus Christ on the cross or whatever, and, "They did this and they did this, but they can't stop me." And he starts dancing like that and he went on for like an hour, he just started dancing and dancing and went into some song. I remember at one point I'm filming like five feet away from him, shooting, but then I realized I think I better sit down.

I had this NPR camera now; I switched off with this other camera and I had this guy loading the camera for me so I think we started shooting as soon as we got up on stage and I'm not sure whether or not we got all of what he said to the crowd or not, but I remember swapping out at least three or four loads and unfortunately because of the nature of the equipment, they would jam sometimes. Fred did a really good job of shooting right here on him most of the time and I was on the other side to get coverage. Somebody else shot too. We were on stage for the whole time he was singing. I do remember looking around one time and thinking maybe it's not so smart to be standing right in front of him. Last time he was anywhere, he got shot at. Especially me wearing a white shirt and white pants. It was like a rally of some sort. I don't even remember Manley being there.

ROGER STEFFENS: That night at the Smile Jamaica concert, on film it looks as if there must be two hundred people on the stage. Manley was sitting on the roof of a Volkswagen bus with his wife and their little child in plain view of everyone in the crowd about ten yards away. Over the years I've talked to around twenty people who surrounded Bob that night, such as Elaine Wint, the emcee, and every one of them has said that they were up there primarily to put their bodies on the line, just as Bob was about to, so that if anybody tried to shoot Bob, they were going to have to take a lot of other people out with him.

CAT COORE: Everyone felt that way on the stage! That night I played bass on a couple of tunes because I was so into his music at the time that I knew every lick. I used to sit down in my house and just listen to *Catch A Fire* over and over again. So then I played lead guitar for half the set with Marley, because by the time Donald Kinsey came I just gave him the guitar 'cause I didn't know any of the tunes he was playing. I was playing bass on the first two tunes, then Tyrone Downie came, and I gave Tyrone the bass. Tyrone knew the bass lines. And Fams didn't come till late. But Fams did eventually come, and Carly Barrett. Everybody just started coming in one by one when they heard Bob was there, they just started. Kinsey was really scared, mon. I think that moment in his life was one he'll never forget.

JEFF WALKER: [Bob] couldn't pick up a guitar since he was very heavily bandaged around his chest and his arm. The band was part Wailers, part Third World, there were Sons of Negus there; the Cimarons' trumpet player was there on stage, Don Kinsey on guitar. Actually Cat Coore played lead guitar for a while until Don showed up and then took over bass.

PABLOVE BLACK: Him all a sing, "Never let a politician grant you a favor." Want to see the man dem, everbody dem a frown up! The drummers were Greg and Compton Russell, them two brothers who were employed to Blackwell. Them is Blackwell man and them come ease 'way Seeco. Them ease 'way Seeco! With them two red, gold and green with the colors upside down! Me never forgot them, mon, them play the congas! Yeah, that a joke!

ROGER STEFFENS: Black was appalled that the tennis-playing non-musician Russell brothers had pushed out Bob's old friend, percussionist Seeco Patterson.

PABLOVE BLACK: That show, there, now Carly come. Me never see Fams. The whole night me never see Fams, 'cause when me look at Tyrone, me see him play bass. And Ibo a play keyboard, 'cause was Third World. Cat Coore on the lead guitar.

JEFF WALKER: There were so many people on stage that Bob had hardly any room to perform; he was in a very tight circle. Manley was sitting on the top of a VW van not ten yards away. Totally exposed. Everybody there was completely exposed. There were some military people onstage, unarmed, with walkie-talkies, and the spotlights were sweeping the crowd, and so forth. But I don't think there was any fear in anybody's heart. This was obviously the event that things were sweeping towards over the last three or four days. And Bob, even at the point when he decided to perform, said he'd "just do a song or two for the people." Then he went on to perform for an hour and a half, and it was the most intense performance of my experience with him. Never once picked up the guitar. Sang. Just sang. He was like a dervish that night.

ROGER STEFFENS: Every song had nuances pertaining to the shooting, whether you realized it or not at the time, with lines like "One good thing about music, when it hits you feel no pain," right up until the final number of "So Jah Seh," which he had rarely sung live before, in which he wails, "If puss and dog can get together, . . . why can't we love one another?" as he shows his wounds to the audience. It was, in my opinion, the most unprecedented and incredible moment in twentieth-century popular music history: Bob standing there with the bullet in his arm singing a cappella in front of eighty thousand people, just days before a pivotal national election, beside his wife who has a bullet lodged in her skull. What can you possibly compare that to?

JUDY MOWATT: The night of the Smile Jamaica concert, it was powerful, as if when you give your life as a sacrifice, and you never cared what would happen, because you know that's where and when we prove the power of the Almighty. Because we know if Bob was to die then, Bob could have gone, it was the hands of the Almighty kept him.

JEFF WALKER: At the beginning of the concert he said, "When I agreed to do this it was for the people, and there were no politics." He made that clear at the beginning of this concert. At the end of it, eighty thousand people were there. It was one of the most deafening and intense crowds I've ever witnessed. Bob first of all rolls up the sleeve of the arm that the bullet penetrated, and points to the bandage. Then he opens up his shirt and points to the wound on his chest. Then he basically pulled out make-believe six-guns, went bang-bang-bang, like the cover of *The Harder They Come*, and then went "I'm OK" with his thumbs up and he was hurried off the stage and into self-exile for almost fifteen months.

CARL COLBY: I felt that he was absolutely just in touch with another— with like the righteousness of it all. It was sort of in the presence of somebody really extraordinary and the other thing about it is that a lot of people don't understand. They think that charismatic people are full of energy and have a sort of energy sparking off them. In a way, it's not.

He was bringing in, he was a very enveloping person, to me, you could almost feel that there was a rhythm about him. He would take you in. He was a good friend. He had no fear. He wasn't fear-driven. But I thought it was interesting that he was so interested in fate. "Things will be." It's like there was a weariness about him, there was a mortality about him that I almost didn't want to see.

PABLOVE BLACK: When the show end and Bob leave, a me and him haffe go back inna de car, go up back. A me travel as him decoy, when the door open and me come out as Bob Marley! 'Cause them time there him scared, you know. Him tremble and say, "Suppose a man take a next shot offa me?" And me haffe go up front and hold it. Hear what happen now. Before the show when them was coming down them turn on the siren and it was attracting attention and we haffe tell them no, don't do that. All when he go up back too, them want to turn on the siren fe go through fast, but that only attracting attention to we, and we haffe make them lock off that.

JEFF WALKER: The intrigue of the next few hours, as we then realized that one of our walkie-talkies was missing and we had arranged for a jet to come back for Bob. We were worried that someone over the walkie-talkie would hear what his plans were, when the plane was coming. We didn't want to communicate over that anymore. So that night after the concert, I went back up to Strawberry Hill in the middle of the night to tell him that the jet was going to be waiting for him at 6:30 in the morning. And I went down ahead of him, in a car with three or four members of his entourage essentially as decoys to make sure that no one had known of the plans. We got down to an airstrip, down at the back of the airport. There were soldiers on the outskirts and a few jeeps with armed guards in them that we looked at through binoculars, so they knew something was going on. Bob arrived with Neville Garrick about forty-five minutes after we arrived and had communicated back up that all was clear. Bob came down and took off. The plane came back a couple of days later for Rita and the kids.

STEPHEN DAVIS: Neville Garrick said when they arrived in the Bahamas they were only given the most conditional of visas and they had to go back to customs every day and renew the visas. When Bob arrived in the Bahamas, they apparently asked if he was applying for political asylum, and he said no, he was just a tourist.

TYRONE DOWNIE: I didn't go to the Bahamas with Bob. I didn't know where they were. I didn't know they left or nothing; I was on my way to either Canada or the U.S., because my girlfriend was living in Montreal. But I didn't have any Canadian visa or U.S. visa. And I just wanted to leave, and the only place to go to was the Bahamas. So we went there and the night we got there, we were having dinner in the hotel restaurant. And the waiter comes up and hears me, my accent, and he says, "You're from Jamaica, yeah?" I said, "Yeah." He says, "Do you know there is a studio here, this white guy has, that he produces a lotta reggae." And I say, "Oh yeah? What's the name of the studio?" He said, "It's Compass Point." Then I had never heard about Compass Point or that Blackwell has a studio there or even lived there. He never brought it up. So I go, "OK, I'm gonna check this out." And I say, "It must be Chris." So I look in the phone book for Chris Blackwell. There was the number! And I called, this same night. I called and who answers the phone! Bob Marley! "You can run, but you can't hide." Right? And he said, "Where are you?" I said, "I am here!" And he say, "Well, come on over!" And we just checked out of the hotel and went over to Chris's house and started working on "Time Will Tell." When I got there, they were drumming and playing that. That was the first time I heard, "You think you're in heaven, but you're living in hell." Yeah, I felt it strong too!

CHAPTER 23

Who Shot Bob Marley?

ROGER STEFFENS: Rumors began circulating immediately as to the motive for the shooting. Bob's manager, Don Taylor, had a bad gambling habit, and was said to be deeply in debt to some very unpleasant people. Bob's closest friend, Skill Cole, was reported to have been involved in fixing a horse race, and was eventually barred from the local racetrack. Some claimed that Bob was daily paying off the claims against Cole, or even Taylor. But perhaps the most prevalent thinking was that it was a political hit based on a rumor that "the big boss" had said that "this concert must not be allowed to take place." Fingers pointed toward Edward Seaga of the JLP. To bear witness to any of these theories even now, more than four decades later, could lead to serious repercussions, even death, from forces aligned with the successors of those who came to kill Marley. Several people were unwilling to speak on the record. Tyrone Downie, Wailers keyboardist, spoke to the questions on my seventh and final annual Bob Marley special in May 1997 on *Reggae Beat*.

TYRONE DOWNIE: Who shot the Wailers? Well, so many things have been said. They say it's racehorse, they say it's Skill Cole. They say it's JLP. It's hard to say. I heard that all those guys have died and I heard that some of them have been hanging out with us on tours afterward, which is kind of scary. They confessed to Bob!

ROGER STEFFENS: In one of the first of the interviews Bob did after the attack, he said, "Ah, I don't know who did it." In 1977, an English journalist asked the same question and Bob replied, "Yeah, I know who did it. The Devil." And then, just before his final illness, he revealed, "Yeah, I know who did it. But top secret that."

TYRONE DOWNIE: Of course he knew! He didn't look like he didn't know. So after the concert two nights later, I said, "Well, I still don't know what is going on. I don't know who it is or what it is." I just felt like our lives were still in danger.

I think in any prolific leader, any spiritual teacher, poet, whenever they die, it's fishy. Not to say that they were dead before their time, because their time was when they were alive or they wouldn't have been recognized before their time. But I just think that's why Bob didn't want to be no big star or no prophet because it's like asking for trouble.

JEFF WALKER: To this day I don't know for sure who shot Bob Marley. The day that it happened we heard a lot of people accused of it. And I think subsequently over the years that the most credible story involved people after Skill Cole, as opposed to any nefarious political goings-on.

STEPHEN DAVIS: I don't know either. I do not trust any of the accounts that have been published, to tell you the truth. What I heard from the beginning was that there was a racetrack scam involving Skill Cole. And that the attack on 56 Hope Road was aimed primarily at Skill Cole and Bob, who according to these sources had financially backed the scam that so offended whoever took these shots at him. It's significant, of course, to notice that Skill Cole had disappeared from Jamaica shortly before the shooting, and did not appear again in Jamaica till 1980. That's almost four years. But, you know, everybody was accused of it. Seaga was accused. Even Michael Manley was accused, as an attempt to get sympathy. Jamaicans at the time pointed out very significantly that no one had been killed and that may have been very purposeful.

ROGER STEFFENS: It was said that almost every day people from the Jamaican mafia would come by Tuff Gong and Bob would give them money to pay off Skill's debts. At the time of the shooting, Skill had gone to Africa for a brief visit, and circumstances there led him to coaching an Ethiopian soccer team and staying for more than three years in that country. He was among those who were in Shashamane, Ethiopia, during Bob's visit there in 1978, and he remained in almost weekly contact with Marley throughout this entire period.

STEPHEN DAVIS: Since the only one who was really terribly wounded was Don Taylor, it was also reported and theorized that there was some problem with Don Taylor's gambling debts, and that Don Taylor may indeed have been the target.

ROGER STEFFENS: In later years, Taylor claimed he had thrown himself in front of Marley to prevent him from being shot. In 1978, in a New Zealand documentary, he told a completely opposite story: that he'd had no time the think when the gunman came through the back kitchen door at Tuff Gong and immediately shot him five times in the groin.

JEFF WALKER: Don Taylor was not shot while trying to prevent Bob from being shot. No. That was a moment when Don literally happened to walk in front of a spray of bullets. No one was expecting an attack at that point. It literally came out of nowhere.

ROGER STEFFENS: Because most of the gunmen have been identified as members of gangs controlled by the JLP, others claim that Edward Seaga, head of the JLP, had to have known of the attack in advance. One of the shooters identified by several eyewitnesses was a notorious JLP enforcer named Jim Brown.

PABLOVE BLACK: See Jim Brown now, Jim Brown is a longtime bad man, that man there wicked! Jim Brown a Labourite fe true. But I cannot say they were Seaga people who came to kill Bob. I can't say that. 'Cause the political climate in Jamaica, a man will be for Seaga this election and the next election him switch and gone over the next side. Basically a politician is a traitor, at odds, so he will swing anywhere the money is. Anywhere!

ROGER STEFFENS: The deeper one gets into the political story, the more complicated things become.

PABLOVE BLACK: You see, the same man what shoot Bob, Bob used to give them money too, fe protect him. The same set of man them, 'cause Bob did give money to the two side, PNP and JLP bad men get money. Them only want hear Bob Marley come, and have a little bag over him shoulder, man ride from all part of the ghetto, come look for Bob Marley. In no time, is thirty thousand dollars that him give way. That a nothin' to him.

AL ANDERSON: Every day!

PABLOVE BLACK: Yeah, nothin' to him to just give away money so.

ROGER STEFFENS: Today, the preponderance of evidence seems to indict the Seaga forces, although doubts remain about the other main theory.

STEPHEN DAVIS: Not if it was a racetrack thing. Not if it was a problem with fixed races at Caymanas Park. Seaga wouldn't be involved with that necessarily. I asked Michael Manley. I said, "Who shot Bob Marley?" just as you're asking us, and he said that the police spent the next week trying to trace the car that the gunmen had used, back to Tivoli Gardens, which was Seaga's constituency down in West Kingston. And they couldn't. And that it was, in Michael Manley's words, "an extremely professional and well-organized job, and perhaps to the fact that no one was killed."

CAT COORE: Bob got on stage, he did a great show. Very, very meaningful show. And in a way, that really helped to bury the opposition to Michael [Manley] for that election totally. Because when people thought to themselves that if Bob was doing a show for the PNP, as they were accusing him of, the PNP wouldn't go and shoot him at that time. So the obvious thing to think [was that the shooters were from] the JLP, 'cause we don't have more than the two parties. So whatever took place, whatever personal things, vendetta, was taken out on Bob, I don't really want to speculate about, but it reflected badly on the political system at the time. 'Cause it made it seem as if one party was fighting very hard against the next one, to the point where they would attack Bob Marley. That is how it looked at the time. And it was a very sad time for Jamaica. And when the One Love concert came sixteen months later and both Michael and Eddie [JLP leader Edward Seaga] came onstage and were reunited with Bob, the country sort of felt really good about it. It's unfortunate, because Eddie is a man who also care for and love Bob very much. I really feel that way because there's no Jamaican who don't love Bob Marley to the ground. I'm talking about the most uptown Topper Norris Syrian woman or white Jamaican woman—they love Bob Marley. Because anywhere they go in this world, they have to deal with Bob Marley.

ROGER STEFFENS: Don Taylor alleges in his autobiography that he and Bob were taken to Trench Town at an unspecified date afterwards and watched as two of the supposed gunmen were hung. There has never been any independent verification of this, and knowing Bob's tendency toward mercy, it is highly doubtful. Several of his closest associates have told me off the record that the hanging rumor is nonsense.

Yet the mystery remains. Further rumors abound, most especially the never-ending story (fictionalized in the recent Booker Prize–winning novel *A Brief History of Seven Killings* by Marlon James) that Carl Colby was responsible not only for somehow arranging the shooting but also for giving Bob a poisoned boot that allegedly gave him cancer, a notion shot down continually by doctors who have studied the allegation. When I confronted Colby with these allegations he was astonished, as he had never heard any of them before our interview.

CARL COLBY: When I looked at what I saw—and I've seen military people in action and others and it did not seem like anything particularly professional—it seemed like more either like a robbery, or a thing you'd do momentarily, you know, you're opportunistic; there's an advantage, you try to take it, you try to shoot at so and so and then, boom, you leave. A massive act of intimidation. And the other thing I felt, there was a rumor that there was a gambling debt—that was the big rumor all that weekend. The other rumor was that maybe it was political because of what was going on. I didn't really understand that, because why shoot at Bob? Who are you gonna hurt by killing Bob? Or shooting at the band? If you're gonna kill somebody, you do it methodically, you don't just come in and pam-pam-pam! Wild West like, bad shots and no follow-through! If somebody is a professional, they continue, they stay and they do the job and then they leave. Because why? Because they don't get paid for missing.

ROGER STEFFENS: During my interview with Carl Colby, I read him a passage from a book by Alex Constantine which had been excerpted in a magazine, as I wanted to give him a chance to respond. "Only a handful of Marley's most trusted comrades knew of the band's whereabouts before the festival yet a member of the film crew, or so he claimed, reportedly, he didn't have a camera, managed to talk his way past machete-bearing Rastas to enter the Hope Road encampment"—it wasn't Hope Road, as we've seen— "one Carl Colby, son of the late CIA director William Colby. While the band prepared for the concert, a gift was delivered, according to a witness at the enclave, a new pair of boots for Bob Marley. He put his foot in and said, 'Ow.' A friend got in there and he said, 'Let's get in the boot,' and he pulled a length of copper wire out. It was embedded in the boot. Had the wire been treated chemically with a carcinogenic toxin? The appearance of Colby at Marley's compound was certainly provocative."

CARL COLBY: Frankly, I'm outraged that anyone would accuse me of doing anything to harm, much less lead to the death of, the incomparable Bob Marley, whom I consider to be one of the greatest musicians and artists since the birth of the cool in the 1950s. First of all, the truth is that I was a professional documentary filmmaker, brought down to Jamaica from New York by Chris Blackwell and Perry Henzell.

To address this false and extremely inflammatory accusation directly, I was up at Chris Blackwell's house in the mountains above Kingston as part of this filmmaking effort. I was accompanied by Island Records publicist Jeff Walker. We felt that we had been commissioned by Chris Blackwell to make a film of the Smile Jamaica concert and about Bob, so we simply wanted to follow through and do our jobs. I had plenty of experience with unusual and somewhat unstable situations as a young boy, including living for three and a half years in Saigon, so the thought of going up to talk to a famous reggae musician like Bob, whom I admired greatly, was not something to be feared. I was excited. I was going to meet Bob Marley and it was my job to shoot a film about him—so I went. And, by the way, no one there knew who my father was—and by that time, December 5, 1976, my father had resigned from the CIA. He had been fired by President Gerald Ford. So, my word to this Alex Constantine is, please check your facts first—and your sources; simply shoddy, piss-poor journalism in my opinion and an outrageous defamation of my character.

The story about a boot being delivered is pure nonsense. I never saw or heard about any boot being delivered to Bob. And anyone who was there would know that Bob was in no mood for hijinks or in any way interested in boots. He was recuperating from some serious injuries and yet he was gracious enough to talk to Jeff and me about his music, about Jamaica, about the politics, and about himself—his hopes and dreams for Jamaica and for his people. He was not that accessible when we first got there. Yes, there were a few machete-wielding guys guarding the compound when we got there, but Jeff simply said we were from Island Records and the door was opened. Again, remember Island Records was Marley's record company—we were welcome. It took a couple of hours just hanging around to get to the point of approaching Bob and getting him to talk. Remember, he'd been shot—and he was recuperating, and he was exhausted.

ROGER STEFFENS: The bullet was still in his arm; he went to the grave with it.

CARL COLBY: And he's standing there—I didn't know that. I didn't know that one had lodged in his arm. As I said, he was exhausted and the pressure of the concert, the pressure of the political campaign, and also I had a sense that times had changed. There was this heaviness about him and about the world around him and I think he kind of resented it; he didn't want to be part of it anymore. I felt that he wanted a more—lighter, Kaya kind of world, which came later, and it was great to see that, when that came later. He had to have a lot of strength. I remember feeling how I really admired this man—this thin, lithe, reedy, intensely alert, and yet humble man standing before me—this creator. It must have been very hard for Bob to come up like that, to be him and to take on all of that—to take on all the wishes and hopes and dreams of the world, of the oppressed world and particularly all the aspirations of the Jamaican people, particularly the Rastafarians, who were all trod upon and who were looking for a way out, not an escape, but looking to build, you know, and yet they foist it on Bob. Every American rock star had rejected the mantle. Nobody took it on, did they? They didn't have Bob's strength, they didn't have Bob's courage, they didn't have Bob's vision. In the end, it's that—Bob had a vision, and though he is not with us any longer, his vision lives "on and on and on," to quote the mighty Bob Marley.

ROGER STEFFENS: Another rumor was that you told someone while you were in Jamaica that you could have an army of U.S. troops in Jamaica in twenty-four hours with one phone call.

CARL COLBY: What! No, my dad was out of the CIA. No, why would I say that? No, and I think anybody who'd believe that would be a little bit stupid. Who are these people who write these things? Did I ever have any experience with police forces, armed forces? Yeah, sure, some twenty-five-year-old kid's calling up, he wants a lot of troops sent down. Yeah, we'll get right on it! But you have to be aware that any time I hear about that kind of thing, my whole family's kind of programmed to turn off that sort of thing. I mean, my father had a listed number when he was director of the CIA. We didn't care about it. Maybe I'm cynical to say I don't really believe in conspiracy theories. I've seen from the inside these guys aren't—people are fallible, they're not all that confident.

CHAPTER 24

Exodus to London

ROGER STEFFENS: Following his time in the Bahamas, Bob flew to the UK to be with his love, Cindy Breakspeare. There he began recording material for his next two albums and preparing for what would have been the largest world tour ever undertaken by a reggae performer.

CINDY BREAKSPEARE: I was in England the night Bob was shot. I had just been crowned Miss World and I was supposed to go do some work that night, and I flatly refused. Because once the news of our relationship hit the newspaper, I mean, it was just amazing. Some of the front-page newspapers: "Miss World and Her Wild Man" and all that stuff. They really went wild over it, let me tell you. So you know there was a lot of talk about it. So for me now not to turn up for things I had been booked to do at the very time that he had been shot! It was just a big drama. It was very hard on me because I really was concerned and I couldn't make contact and it was rough, yes. We went to Nassau for Christmas that year. Then to London, to Oakley Street, where everybody lived for the time that he spent after he left Nassau and he went to England. We were there for about a year, I'd say. It was very central, right in the middle of London. Lovely place.

ROGER STEFFENS: Bob was anxious to maintain as low a profile as he could, despite living with the reigning Miss World. He gathered the band together, and made contact with a few of his longtime friends both from Jamaica and from his previous stints living in the city. Bob was a hero to the expat Jamaican community, many of whom had been lured to Britain with the promise of jobs in the 1950s, and whose first-generation British children recognized in Bob a Jamaican who had already achieved significant international renown. His status at this point, as one who had just narrowly escaped a point-blank shooting, was almost mythical.

Dr. Gayle McGarrity was aware of the effect Cindy had on Bob both politically and emotionally. She had seen their relationship develop from the start, when Cindy and Bob both found themselves living in the Hope Road house.

GAYLE McGARRITY: Cindy lived downstairs at Hope Road with her brother Stephen, whom everyone called Reds, who was a good friend of mine, and whom I actually dated for a while during this period. Then one day I'm coming over to check Bob at Hope Road and there's Cindy, lying out on the back lawn, dressed in some shorts, and Bob is there talking to her and clearly a courtship had begun.

Now, Bob had actually already confided in me that he really checked for Cindy. I was working at a club called Dizzy's, which was up at Liguanea and was managed by Reds. And I was working there for a while, and so was Cindy. Sometimes Bob would come and say to me, "I really like that girl, you know, Gayle, I really want you to help set me up," and stuff like that. And I would say, "Do you know that she works with the JLP, and do you know that she's against everything Manley's doing?" Bob was Bob, and he didn't give a damn about that—he just liked her.

But all of that stuff started putting a slight wedge there between Bob and me because Cindy, as a staunch supporter of the JLP—the party which reportedly financed her participation in the Miss World contest in London, following then prime minister Michael Manley's announcement that the government and people of Jamaica would not be sending a contestant that year as a protest against the participation of a contestant representing the apartheid regime then in power in South Africa. As the most prominent leader of the international boycott of the apartheid regime, Manley was adamant that Jamaica should send a strong message to the world that we would not participate in a contest in which South Africa was to be represented by a contestant who had been chosen from an exclusively white pool of candidates and who, furthermore, had made official public declarations of her support for white minority rule in her country. Cindy was always talking—as were most members of the upper middle classes—about the Communists this, and the Communists that. That fed into the distaste that Bob already had for the Communists, and I would say politically he may even have been swayed a little to the right of the Jamaican political spectrum as he came closer and closer to the white and brown Jamaican elite, through his association with Cindy. Because once Cindy responded positively to his courting, that went to his head. As a sufferer from an impoverished background, a young man who had lived on the rough streets of Trench Town and been through hell, who had been mistreated by both his father and his mother—as far as I'm concerned—and had been through "nuff sufferation," Bob now had this beautiful girl—whom many both in Jamaica and beyond Jamaica's borders, as well, wanted—as his woman.

I think that really affected him politically too, and he got into a lot of things that he wouldn't have got in before, and very often when I'd go over, he'd ask me what about this girl such and such, referring to uptown, elite, brown Jamaican girls and he would say, "I want to meet her," and "Can you set it up?" The reasonings on class struggle and Africa continued, but those close to him understood that he was getting familiar with the idea of being an internationally acclaimed superstar. That's when he started singing more of the songs like "Waiting In Vain," "Is This Love?" and "Turn Your Lights Down Low." Which were beautiful songs, but he was clearly into his lover-boy period mode.

ROGER STEFFENS: These songs would form the core of the new recordings he began working on in London, which produced both the *Exodus* and *Kaya* albums. Engineer Karl Pitterson recalled in 1995 at his studio in Miami what it was like working in London on *Exodus*, the album that *Time* magazine declared "the album of the century."

KARL PITTERSON: It was really cool. The album was recorded between two Island studios, the Fallout Shelter at St. Peter's Square and the other at Basing Street Studios at Ladbroke Grove. And to add a little bit more to it—Bob was involved with Cindy Breakspeare because that was at the time that she got crowned Miss World. So for him to deal with this world beauty queen it only added to the whole thing and it made him even more popular. 'Cause remember he made front-page news,

Master producer Karl Pitterson with one of Bob Marley's
mixing boards, Miami, May 2001.

television news—"the Beauty and the Rastaman" how it was termed at the time. But, hopefully, not in a negative manner.

And *Exodus*, the music, the lyrics, they were on a wider scope now. Because Bob and the Wailers were appealing to a wider cross-section, wider market. So they had to go into a different way of putting their music out to the public. Instead of just catering to the Jamaican community, or mainly the sufferers, now they were dealing with like a blue-collar up to white-collar thing for all those people who think that they were being held back. It makes no difference whether they were with a giant corporation, they started relating lyrics from his songs to their situation. And I think that's where it started to get so wide. That was like—oops!

All the songs were done at the same sessions, *Exodus* and *Kaya*. We'd work from three in the afternoon until six the next morning. But it was cool. And back the next day. And there was a lot of preferred smoking material. The studio was smoky. We recorded the basic tracks first, then the overdubbing part where other musicians would come in, like Rico Rodriguez. And the band members would do theirs. Then the backing vocalists. Because from the beginning you'd have a rough vocal from Bob. And then he'd come in and do his lead vocal. With the mixing process now, Bob wasn't there on all. Dick Cuthell, Fams and I did it mostly. And it was at this point in the session that Chris introduced Junior Marvin.

ROGER STEFFENS: Bob was now playing much larger venues, and felt he needed someone in the band who could do the kind of theatrics that he normally eschewed, and rev up the audience. Along came lead guitarist Junior Marvin, real name Junior Kerr Marvin Hanson, a black man born in Kingston. The lean and lanky Marvin spoke with me on the morning of March 4, 1987, in his Sunset Strip hotel room while on tour with the Wailers Band. Al Anderson had just stuck his head in the door to say that as he was having breakfast in a nearby coffee shop, he looked at the table across from him and there sat the Wailers' prime nemesis Chris Blackwell, president of Island Records. At that point the band had received no royalties in over four years, despite millions of sales worldwide. A complicated litigation was in process.

JUNIOR MARVIN: I went to England when I was nine years old. My family name is Kerr, and we were Scots African. My great-grandfather came from a place called Mount Charles, and apparently he owned the whole area. All my cousins, my father, my uncles, all of them had piano lessons from when they were three years old. My mother moved to London. My father went to the U.S. and then eventually got together

Wailers lead guitarist Junior Marvin in the Recher Theater dressing room, Towson, Maryland, February 2000.

with us in England. My father played classical piano and then branched out into jazz. I started to play guitar not for the music but to impress girls. I was deeply affected by watching a young American gigging in local clubs, who played with his teeth, practiced fourteen hours a day and never went anywhere without his guitar. He was a child of mixed-blood parents, and in many other ways reminded me of Bob Marley. That was Jimi Hendrix. I'm a believer in that mixed bloods produce magical people.

ROGER STEFFENS: Eventually Marvin got good enough to audition for Jeff Beck, who turned him down by telling him there wasn't room for two guitar greats in one group and that Junior should start his own band immediately. He did, calling the band Hanson and releasing two albums on Manticore. He played on Steve Winwood's debut album and eventually began sitting in on reggae sessions, including Toots Hibbert's seminal *Reggae Got Soul* album. One day in early 1977, Blackwell brought Marvin around to the London digs of the Wailers, who were then rehearsing for the *Exodus* and *Kaya* albums.

JUNIOR MARVIN: We jammed for three hours straight before we said anything to each other. Then we looked at each other and laughed, slapped five and Bob said, 'Man wan' come play with I?' And I said, 'I'd love to!' And I was a Wailer. *Time* magazine chose *Exodus* as the album of the century. I feel very honored to be part of that album. And I fought for that album. They mixed the album, and I and I didn't like the mix and everybody said, "Get rid of him." And Chris Blackwell stood up for me and Bob stood up for me and we remixed the album, spending sixty thousand pounds, which is like a hundred thousand dollars. And Bob took the chance, and it became an instant success, staying in the British charts for over two years. So I'm very proud (a) that I spoke the truth about how I felt and (b) that it paid off, thank God.

Chris Blackwell wanted to get a fine sound of guitars in the mix, more upfront. Because Europeans and Westerners responded to guitar. And reggae basically never had a lot of lead guitar until Al Anderson came along and added another dimension. And then I came with my thing. And the layers that were put together were to maintain the roots, but have a little bit of the fine top-end coming across. I remember when Bob was doing the vocal on "Running Away" he was very relaxed that day and Seeco used to give him ideas about scatting. We all used to talk, and Bob and Seeco used to have little talks, and myself and Bob, Bob and Tyrone, and Bob would take ideas from us and put them together. He'd work on it with his rhythm guitar—work on it, work on it, work on it—and eventually he'd just come in and just do it—bop!—like that. Sometimes just one take. Nowadays, people do fifty million takes and take one line from this, one line from that. Bob had a talent where he could just go in, and if everything was right, he'd get it!

ROGER STEFFENS: One of the keys to the brilliant sound achieved on *Exodus* was the contribution of the British sonic innovator Roger Mayer.

JUNIOR MARVIN: Roger Mayer had wonderful ideas. He made pedals for Jimi Hendrix that no one else had. He worked with Ernie Isley and Stevie Wonder. And when I went to work with Bob he gave me a couple of special pedals. One was called the Octavia pedal, which gives a low harmony and in-between harmonies to the guitar sound, sounding out of this world. It split the note into two and you get other vibes in between, low, high and in the middle, like you were playing three guitars at once. He worked on the guitars to get the maximum harmonics out of them, in tune with the keyboards. Roger took Bob's guitar apart and gave it that real authentic sound that it had. If you listen to Bob's previous albums, they were all a bit out of tune, so Roger made sure that all the guitars were in tune with the keyboards. You could hear Bob's scratch coming through clearly. Each of the lead guitars' notes were perfectly in tune. He gave us distortion pedals too, which were unique, very original; no one else had that sound.

ROGER STEFFENS: In many of the videos of the Wailers in the 1970s you can see Bob go over to Junior and appear to be saying something like, "What a dead crowd, get these people on their feet." And Junior would come up to the mic and start a chant, or he would start to clap with his hands above his head.

JUNIOR MARVIN: Well, we were very close. Bob, Seeco and myself used to hang out a lot at that particular time. Bob and Family Man were very close, they used to hang out at one time, and then it kinda shifted and became me and Seeco he hung out with. And it would shift to various members. So the three of us used to hang out and I was the new kid on the block. And the two of them used to jive me a lot. And if you made even the slightest mistake Bob would pick it up. And of course I used to make one or two mistakes which weren't really obvious to the general public, but Bob would hear it and tilt his head to my ear and go, "Wh'appen?" I remember one time we were doing the One Love Peace Concert in Jamaica. It was my first show in Jamaica. You know, coming forward to Jamaica after growing up and going to school in England. Coming home. It was like, to do that concert was the ultimate! I was so excited that night that he was doing a song ["Jamming"], and I played one note wrong, just bent it a little too the wrong way, and Bob said, "Wa-wa-wa-watch what you're doin'!" So he was very disciplined, he was a workaholic. And he wanted everything to be perfect, and that's rubbed off on us. He didn't just say things, he practiced it as well. We used to love jamming, we could play for hours. That's how he wrote his songs, too.

When I first joined the band I was like a soloist and I used to solo a lot. And they used to sit back and watch me solo for two or three hours! Look at this kid, you know? And it was fun, it was great, because they gave me great opportunity to express myself and be part of everything that was going on. And they gave me time to fit in, practice to get it right. It was very hard work. Bob never let up on you. He always gave you the impression you could do it better. He brought the best out of you. At one point we had two lead guitarists, Al Anderson and myself. Al would play lead on the songs that he played lead on the album and I would do also the same. But it was also competitive. And Bob knew this, he would play us against each other as a joke and made us try harder to be better and better.

ROGER STEFFENS: The joy of hearing live tapes of Bob is how different a song's length could be from night to night.

JUNIOR MARVIN: The key to that was that rehearsal. In the band, everyone knew everyone's part. I know Family Man's part, I know the piano part, I know the drum part. Likewise, Carly knows guitar part, he knows vocal part. We knew the song inside out. We still try to do that. We could ad lib because we were so close, we were like one mitt, you felt very solid in this way, very confident, because you knew that if you made a move everyone would move with you. Whenever Bob moved this way, we moved with him, he moved that way, we moved with him. So it became a unique chemistry and I think that's how it worked. My favorite show was my first, in Paris, 1977. Everything was fine! After the third song Bob came over and slapped five on my hand and I said, "Hey, this is it." It was beautiful.

FAMILY MAN BARRETT: What I remember of those times is that Bob sometimes goes into like a trance.

JUNIOR MARVIN: Spiritual trance. It's like we're instruments of God and things echo through us as musicians. It's a gift that God's given you and He's echoing through you. It's not something you own, you possess. You channel it. And at times you will find that when everyone is very solid and together, these things will come out as an extra gift. It's like, you've done the homework, you've done the practice, you've come to the reality of the thing, and God's decided to give you the extra spice. And it comes out, it happens now to us a lot, it comes out, you don't plan it, you don't organize it, it just comes as an extra gift from God, and when it comes it's magic.

CHAPTER 25

Blackwell, Bob and Business

ROGER STEFFENS: Life in London, the self-proclaimed World's Greatest City, was not just about making music and hanging out with his fascinating lover. A gigantic world tour was organized that included not just Europe but North America, Asia and the South Pacific as well. It would be in support of a major statement by Bob, released by Island in late spring 1977, an album filled with anthemic words that would alter and illuminate our times. Crucial additions were made to the lineup of the Wailers, and their sound matured. But misfortune lay afoot too, and Bob's life would be forever changed by an accident in Paris at the start of the *Exodus* tour.

Among the additions to Bob's entourage was Charlie Comer, a florid-faced Liverpool Irish publicist—and my mentor, in many ways. He had run the below-decks gambling on a Cunard liner as a teenager, managed a Mob bar in Puerto Rico, worked for Brian Epstein before he discovered the Beatles, and then flew in the same helicopter with them into Shea Stadium. Charlie's company was called CB Enterprises, echoing other crucial CBs in Bob's life: Cedella Booker, Chris Blackwell, Cindy Breakspeare and Carly Barrett.

Charlie's famous clients included Frank Sinatra, John Lennon, Mick Jagger, the Chieftains, Stevie Ray Vaughan, Richard Harris, Peter Tosh and Bob Marley. He swore he would never speak about them on the record. At the end of 1999, however, the doctor treating his diabetes sent him to warm L.A., where he spent a week at our home. Packed and ready to fly back to New York City, Charlie rather reluctantly allowed himself to be coaxed into an interview. Because he knew them both so well, I asked about the differences between Peter Tosh and Bob.

CHARLIE COMER: Peter always wanted all the journalists to know— did you get my last answer, did you understand my patois? Bob never took that time because he obviously thought that his message was strong enough that they better well get it or they'll miss it. Peter I liked right away. I think it was his honesty. And the other thing was, he always spoke the truth. And I liked Peter's humor. Peter depended on me to get publicity, getting television. On publicity he was very,

Marley's primary publicist, the irascible Liverpool Irishman Charlie Comer,
New York City, February 1998.

very good. He wanted his words to get out. He wanted to be in the biggest instances, in television, radio, newspapers, magazines, whatever. Because he said people always believe everything that's in magazines and newspapers, which of course, in Jamaica, it was true.

I always told Bob and Peter if we were doing press conferences, this is what you should try to tell people—something that *you* want to tell them. And I told them when you're doing television shows, don't give a fuck what the question is, you just say what you're on there for! A new record, a new movie, a new TV show or a new video. And I said no interviewer can stop you from saying what you're going to say. They've got to actually go on a different track and pretend that they've been asking that question, otherwise they look idiotic. But Peter was very determined to get what he felt and what he believed in out to people. Bob could be very devious, especially with the fucking press. And I used to say to the white press, "Listen, if you don't understand him, ask me. I'll tell you what he says afterwards."

ROGER STEFFENS: In light of the money problems experienced by the Wailers Band after Bob passed, I've always been interested in memories of the financial arrangements Bob had with the individual members of it. Tyrone explains the feelings of all of them when they are asked about who was responsible for the songs as they appeared on the record.

TYRONE DOWNIE: The Wailers Band were really co-creators of Bob's music, like "Jamming," which was my song. All Bob did was say the "jamming, I want to jam it with you," but every one of those verses were mine. And "Waiting In Vain," I wrote half of that. "I been waiting on your line / And the waiting feel is fine." Bob doesn't write like that. And "Rastaman Vibration." I came in one day and said, "Rastaman vibration is positive." Al will back me up on that.

Bob would split the money that he made on tour, 50 percent to the band and 50 percent to him. Record publishing was Bob Marley Music. My name isn't Bob Marley! Then I didn't realize, while we were writing the song, I didn't know what publishing was. And I thought when you played with a band or when you played on a record, you got your money, that was it! You got paid. That's how naive a lot of Jamaican musicians are.

ROGER STEFFENS: Chris Blackwell was reaping the benefits of Bob's ever-increasing success as Bob took control of producing his own product—on which, nevertheless, Blackwell was still taking a production override royalty. He himself has said that he and Bob were never friends, just work associates. Yet he found it expedient to use his perceived closeness to the burgeoning superstar Marley to gain entry into the highest levels of international society. To his credit, it is generally agreed that Bob might have never reached his unprecedented level of success were it not for skillful promotion by Blackwell, who was actually taken aback at how big Bob had become.

In 1988 Don Taylor spoke at length about Chris Blackwell's relationship to Bob during the *Exodus* period. By 1988, U2, another Island act, had become one of the biggest bands in the world.

DON TAYLOR: Chris Blackwell has gone on a crusade to deteriorate Jamaican music and Bob Marley as the greatest reggae band, strictly on a business thing, to make U2 the greatest thing. It's a fact! It's a fact. The guys from U2 told me in Paris, the manager from U2 told me this January [1988] at the Midem convention that the biggest influence, that his group spent eighteen months listening to Marley product before they made their first record. That Chris Blackwell sent the tape and had them study Marley's records before they made their first record.

You must understand Chris Blackwell. When I met Chris Blackwell for the first time and start to analyze what does Bob mean to Chris Blackwell, Chris Blackwell never intended for Bob Marley to be this big. Because of the way we redid the contract, where we took control, Chris Blackwell had to call me for the OK to do a single for everything he did. That's the way the contract read.

What happened, what Chris wanted, Bob had become by his third or fourth record for Island, he had become a darling of the jet set, which

Chris Blackwell runs it. Kennedy's young boy, John, he ran behind us the whole tour. Bianca Jagger, Mick. Bob had become a beggar of the jet set. And what proved it more than ever is that when we played Paris Chris Blackwell threw his big jet set party and everybody jetted in. And Bob was so important to the jet set crowd, that Bob was his way in to a lot of these people. For a long time he didn't say he owned Island Records; he said he was Bob's producer. That was his way in to a lot of people! There was a time when the only product Chris Blackwell had selling in Europe was Bob Marley. Nothing else he had selling.

ROGER STEFFENS: As the deadline for the release of *Exodus* approached, cover artist Neville Garrick felt stymied. His original conception had been rejected.

NEVILLE GARRICK: As Bob's new art director, *Exodus* now, this one was a real experience for me. Actually, most of the time, all my first ideas are usually accepted, like bring it and show Bob and say, "Skipper, how you think?" and him say, "Show everybody in the band." And if everybody say cool, him say, "Cool, that's it, go on." Well, in England I work three months on this *Exodus* design. I still have this design. It was the map of the world with Africa showing foremost and the Wailers were playing, like a group shot I took of the band with a fisheye lens, had them all playing drums, they were chanting, inside Africa. And the world had wings, like it was flying through the Red Sea parting. The inside was like comets coming out of space with each member of the group coming through space like that. I don't want to call no names, but a couple of people, I guess, who Bob considered their opinion that time, probably didn't like a picture of Bob on it and said they didn't like it. And Bob say him don't like it, do a next one. Well, I'd spent about two months, and I really felt frustrated in a way, you know, like whew! What I do now, airbrush work, and you know was a lot of time. Anyway, this was the first one, so I just go to the board again. So I decided to come with no Bob Marley and the Wailers on the cover. Exodus. We just left Jamaica, the mystic is there, no one know where we gone. Exodus, we're going home. Blank. Just the word. Because I thought, the title is so strong, why try to interpret it? Just write back the word. So I took Amharic [Ethiopian] letters and turned them upside down, sideways, because you don't have "ABC" in Amharic, to write out "E-X-O-D-U-S." Well, short time after that I found I almost spelled "Ethiopia" unknowingly. This was told to me by Asfa Wossen, the Crown Prince of Ethiopia.

ROGER STEFFENS: Marley had several encounters with Ethiopian royalty in exile. He felt extremely close to them and protective of them, as he believed they were blood relations of a true and living God, and gave large donations to them. In Ethiopia, three years after Haile Selassie was overthrown, one could be imprisoned for possession of a picture of His Majesty. Bob's support for freedom movements throughout the continent was in sharp contrast to his unwavering support for the Ethiopian monarchy, whose lineage stretched back to King Solomon.

In London in 1977, he met with the exiled Crown Prince of Ethiopia and was given a ring that belonged to Haile Selassie I.

NEVILLE GARRICK: Asfa Wossen, the Crown Prince of Ethiopia, was the man responsible for giving a ring of Haile Selassie I's to Bob. I was the only one there with Bob when Bob got that ring, outside of the Ethiopian family. He told Bob he had something for him in recognition of the work Bob had really done for Ras Tafari, his father, in preparing this message. And he gave him this ring with the Lion of Judah carrying the flag on it. And he placed it on his finger. Now, my knowledge of this ring is that the Ethiopian royal family has a set of rings which belongs within the Royal House of Judah, that only members of the royal family are given. I don't know about it being the direct ring that His Imperial Majesty wore, because he still wears it as far as I know.

ROGER STEFFENS: The spring-in-exile period was a busy one. The recording and release of *Exodus*, the plans for the biggest reggae tour in history, along with much-needed time to decompress from the assassination attempt and be with the woman he loved best—all this came

together at once. Thankfully, Cindy brought a new peace and direction for Bob, lovingly caring for him in the midst of many competing
demands on his precious time.

Bob's spectacular European tour-ending performance at London's
Rainbow Theatre in early June was captured on film and played subsequently as a theatrical feature in European cinemas. The new songs
from *Exodus* were accompanied by arena rock antics led by new lead
guitarist Junior Marvin, whom Bob had encouraged to be broadly theatrical for the mostly white audience.

CINDY BREAKSPEARE: I went to the Rainbow shows in London, one
or two. But to be honest with you—I'm going to tell you something
funny—those were not the times when I enjoyed Bob musically. I used
to enjoy him when he was just writing songs and they were just coming
together and he'd be sitting in a room with a guitar and somebody else
would pick up a pack of matches and somebody else would pick up
something and start to knock the dresser and somebody else would
start to hit the bottle in their hand with their ring and music would just
come together and happen. And those to me were the moments that
were special. Actually, we were lucky in that we did have a lot of time
in Oakley Street, for some reason. I guess because we were both based
there and we would come and go. You know, I can remember cooking
liver at three in the morning. Now and then he would have a bit of calf
liver. Because it's good for you. It has a lot of vitamin B in it, a lot of
pregnant women who are vegetarians become anemic and they are told
to take desiccated liver pills, so why not sit down and eat a nice piece of
liver? So ridiculous to be extreme about things. He wasn't dogmatic.

CEDELLA BOOKER: One time he told me, he said, I never go to bed till
three o'clock this morning. And I said, and you get up early. He said
more time is only two or three hours' sleep he take and that is enough,
because he was always busy doing what he have to do. Because if you
have work to do you can't put sleep before, you have to go and do what
you have to do.

ROGER STEFFENS: Despite having a personal cook, who maintained a strict ital diet, Bob's health took a blow as he prepared for the world tour in May 1977. He began to look tired from the stresses he faced in the aftermath of the assassination attempt. In retrospect, several of those closest to Bob felt that constant attention from people helped kill him.

GILLY GILBERT: I think he needed some space too. I myself sometimes I wondered why he don't even take a vacation and go somewhere and just hibernate. And have just certain amount of tranquility. But I mean, he was for the people and I guess he wanted to reach to the people. He didn't want to stay away from people. He never talked to me about death. He just got his work to do, and Rasta never die. Rasta live. Although we know we gonna die someday, we just chant that chant at all times: Life.

CHAPTER 26

The Bloody Toe in the Paris Match

ROGER STEFFENS: The first leg of the ambitious globe-circling *Exodus* tour planned for the summer and fall of 1977 began in France. Bob suffered a serious injury when a French journalist accidentally stepped on his foot in the heat of a soccer match. This would lead to an awful discovery that would eventually stop the tour in its tracks.

GILLY GILBERT: Right before the *Exodus* tour began he hurt his toe in Paris in '77. For a couple of years before at least, he had a bloodshot toenail that he never did anything about. Until he was stepped on, he never limped or anything like that. It was the guy stepping on him that aggravated it. Then he toured for about a month, six weeks. He was hopping and skipping and doing his thing with his bandaged toe during the '77 Europe tour. He was like a raging lion. They gave him a cap to put on it if he was going to play soccer, like a sponge thing. He played after, he played hard soccer. Then while he was recuperating Bob got his foot messed up again, he was playing soccer right in front of his house, like scrimmage.

JUNIOR MARVIN: Bob first had the injury in Jamaica, playing soccer. And, he looked after it himself, and it started to get better.

CINDY BREAKSPEARE: Well, the foot was just a simple case of stubbornness where he would not give it time to heal. I remember all the time we were there at Oakley Street in London he was soaking it in various solutions, and applying ointments, all of which were supposed to help it to heal. And it was coming on okay, and then I think he went to Paris and played a football match there, and somebody stepped on it with the damn football spikes. That just set it off again, and I think it's just purely and simply a case of the cells not getting a chance to heal.

JUNIOR MARVIN: They had a soccer match in Paris, and one of the players stepped on his toe with a spike, and it went right through his nail. He had to have it bandaged, and he had to wear sandals for the rest of the tour.

ROGER STEFFENS: Dr. Carlton "Pee Wee" Fraser was not only one of Bob's closest friends during his international touring years, but also his personal physician.

DR. PEE WEE FRASER: Essentially it was a past injury. The first history of that injury was associated with a football incident at Boys' Town. I guess everybody just take it as a simple superficial injury and some-time, probably about three years after, we had a reoccurrence where he had pain and swelling. I think the first instance subsequent to that was in Delaware, where it was mentioned. I think the doctors misdiagnosed it as a fungal infection, erroneously of course. It went on, knowing that its return was imminent and its symptoms.

And then sometime in France [spring 1977], when he suffered a crushing injury to the same toe, stepped on by an opponent wearing iron-studded shoes, he stopped playing and the persistent pain war-ranted a doctor's intervention. Whether the injury to the toe was the initial circumstance which promoted the symptoms, i.e. the noticeable pain, or whether there was an earlier lesion under the nail which might have been overlooked, he did some "refashioning." This is the toe seen bandaged on the *Babylon By Bus* album jacket, that was subsequent to the intervention by the doctors in France.

Now, unfortunately, I think what the doctor should have done at that time was an excisional biopsy. In other words, remove the entire lesion and send it for study, which was not done, and it wasn't until he went to England and then I think it was Chris Blackwell who actually took him to someone at the Royal College of Surgeons. That's when he had the first real diagnostic approach. What they actually did that time was the incisional biopsy and then the biopsy showed that it was melanoma. I think it was classified as grade three, which meant that it had actually invaded dermis and tissue, then that's when everyone started getting very aggressive about it.

JUNIOR MARVIN: After the tour, he was sent to a Harley Street doctor by Island, by Chris and his assistant Denise Mills. The doctor told him that the toe had become cancerous and he would have to amputate it. Of course, once you amputate your toe, you lose your balance. So Bob wasn't very happy about it, because it would have been damaging to his career at that time.

ROGER STEFFENS: Dr. Fraser says specialists in London were advising something much more aggressive.

DR. PEE WEE FRASER: The surgeons at the Royal College of Surgeons were entertaining disarticulation of the hip [meaning amputating the leg]. Because at that time there was no MRI or CT scans—it was just routine where radio-opaque material was injected and scans done to locate hot spots. They thought that disarticulation of the hip for the extremity that was involved would be the best procedure, but [in my view] medical science did not support that. In fact the routine approach to lesions of that type, especially in the extremity, was to first of all discern if there is any lymphatic spread in the contingent areas and then according to the lymphatic involvement you would know what type of surgical approach to take.

At that time when we actually got to Cedars in Miami the investigation did not reveal a lymphatic spread. Although we know that more than 80 percent of melanomas that are classified at that level usually have metastasis, there was no clinical documentation that there was metastasis in Bob. But the literature supported at that time that you should seek clear margins in the area if that was possible. Then you do the excision of that particular area.

ROGER STEFFENS: In that period, according to Dr. Fraser, there was a new wave of immunotherapy which called for cutting off the cancer and then doing a skin graft around the affected area.

DR. PEE WEE FRASER: I think, if I can remember clearly, the histological studies of Bob's particular lesion showed an increased incidence of lymphocytic response in the area, which was thought at that time to be a good sign to introduce immunotherapy.

CINDY BREAKSPEARE: As we all know now, melanoma is just a really unpredictable form of cancer. And although it's a skin cancer you never know what it's going to do. When the cancer was diagnosed, the doctors said they wanted to remove the toe. But that was vetoed, because your big toe is very important for the balance. So they decided to go with a graft. And I mean that healed beautifully. It healed really, really beautifully, and he used to take good care of it and everything. It really healed well and he wouldn't allow it to get injured in any way. The skin over it of course was very tender, having been taken from the leg, the upper thigh area. So it wasn't quite like the skin that would be on the toe. It was softer. It wasn't hardened or calloused. So one needed to be careful, what shoes you wore and everything, so nothing irritated it and rubbed on it too much, but it healed beautifully.

JUNIOR MARVIN: I think he was convinced not to cut his toe by various people, namely Don Taylor, and in fact to graft the skin rather than cut it off, which turned out not to be a good idea. On return to Jamaica for the One Love Peace Concert, doctors there advised him that the grafting of the toe would be sufficient, and he wouldn't have to cut his toe. And from that point onwards, I don't know what happened.

GILLY GILBERT: The skin graft was in early '78 in Miami, or late '77. He thought it was cured at that point, 'cause it healed. They gave him a cap to put over it if he was going to play soccer. He played after, he played hard soccer. It was like a sponge thing. He never talked about it over the next two and a half years. At the start of the U.S. leg of the '80 tour he had an exam that he passed. To this day I just can't understand.

Bob played soccer in Australia, Zimbabwe, everywhere we go and he was playing like a champion. Even before we went on the U.S. tour in '80, we had a send-off soccer game in southwest Miami here against a Haitian team, Am-Jam United, my team in Miami. He was running well like anybody else, he was kicking the ball like a bullet. If Bob was feeling pain I would have seen it while he was playing.

ROGER STEFFENS: There's a deeply held belief that "Rasta no deal with death." Even speaking of its possibility, in a world of word–sound– power, is to be avoided. Rastafarian elders were giving Bob advice about his illness, decrying Western medicine and promoting Rasta teachings and herbal remedies. Others close to him had no knowledge of the disease.

DANNY SIMS: It was strange how I learned about Bob's cancer. This is only hearsay now that came from Allan "Skill" Cole, 'cause I didn't talk to any of the Jamaica people, and Allan was constantly my friend. Allan told me that Bob was playing soccer and hit his toe and that Chris sent him to a doctor in London. And that he then discovered that he had melanoma cancer. That's because when his toe was hurt he didn't think it was cancer. The Jamaicans then weren't dealing with cancer. So they kept that away from me. Oh my God, 100 percent away from me!

Don't forget now, I'm a nutritionist. I did *The Beverly Johnson Guide to Health and Beauty* book. And all my family had cancer; it practically runs in my family's blood. So we in America knew a lot about cancer, as laymen. And so then I said, "What happened?" And Allan said, "He came to Miami to Cedars of Lebanon Hospital and the doctors there said he had to cut off half his foot."

I didn't find that out until the accident in the park three years later. Nothing. Because let me tell you something, not only would I have told him to very happily cut off all traces of the cancer. Half his feet, with the technology today with the war, you can get the kind of extension to really move. Bob Marley moving on stage didn't have a lot to do with his feet, as much as it did with his whole body, his head, his hand. I don't know why they wouldn't tell me, I don't really understand. Even why Mrs. Booker wouldn't tell me. I didn't see him in '77. When I saw Bob again he came to my house and he took Betty Wright on tour with him in 1979. I knew nothing about his illness; they kept that a very big secret. Maybe because it was cancer and Jamaicans were not accustomed to that.

ROGER STEFFENS: Marley would cancel his entire U.S. tour in 1977. There would be rumors later that French doctors injected melanoma into Bob's foot, or that Marley's cancer was the result of the CIA somehow "dosing" Bob with the disease. Both of these allegations have been debunked by many medical specialists. Here Dr. Lowell Taubman, longtime reggae collector, writing in *The Beat*, explains the disease in medical terms.

DR. LOWELL TAUBMAN: Bob Marley died of metastatic malignant melanoma which originated on the big toe of his right foot. In non-medical terminology, melanoma is a skin cancer which, if caught early enough, is usually curable with aggressive treatment.

It has been proposed that Bob Marley was injected with melanoma. According to the present medical literature, malignant melanoma cannot be transmitted by a needle injection. Melanoma also does not arise from injuries.

ROGER STEFFENS: Let Marley's white cousin have the final word, which points to a probable genetic basis for Bob's illness.

CHRISTOPHER MARLEY: Our white Marley family has had a long history of skin cancer and at least one prior case of melanoma.

CHAPTER 27

The One Love Peace Concert

ROGER STEFFENS: In the elections held shortly after the Smile Jamaica concert, Michael Manley was overwhelmingly reelected as prime minister of Jamaica. One of his first actions was to put some of the leading gunmen from both political parties in prison. Bucky Marshall (PNP) and Claudie Massop (JLP) shared a cell. They began comparing notes and soon realized that they were both being played by the political class in Jamaica in a game of divide and conquer. It's as old as the Bible itself: keep their proxies fighting among themselves in the lower ranks, and they won't drive up to Beverly Hills and attack the real enemies of the people. So these two vicious gunmen declared a truce between themselves. And when one of the other prisoners from their cell was released, he brought the news back to the war-ridden ghettos of West Kingston and a spontaneous peace movement broke out.

At the end of 1977, Massop and Marshall were released and headed to England to beg Bob to come back home and headline what they hoped would be a "One Love peace concert," named after one of Bob's most alluring songs. Knowing that he was talking to people who had allegedly been involved in his assassination attempt, he was highly reluctant. Then finally he assented, agreeing to return once his safety was guaranteed.

When he landed in Jamaica at the end of February 1978, he sat for another interview with broadcaster Neville Willoughby. The Tuff Gong headquarters was bustling with a variety of armed men—murderers, police, gang members—and a constant stream of foreign press.

NEVILLE WILLOUGHBY: When I interviewed Bob in 1978 I could tell there was something different about him from '73. He wasn't this sort of happy, sort of bubbly type of person he had been in '73. I never saw him laugh again in '78. But when he was talking in '73 he would laugh at things, make jokes. Never did in '78. And I think it's probably because he was sick and we didn't know. Never can tell, the man might have been in pain. I don't know.

JUNIOR MARVIN: Bob came back to Jamaica about eight weeks before the concert. I went to the airport to meet with him. And the airport was rammed with people. There were buses, and all the Rastafarians were there and [ska star] Prince Buster was there. I remember everyone jumped the barrier to get to the plane. Just like when His Majesty came. And I decided to jump the barrier too, with everyone else, not even thinking about it, and ran towards the airplane. When Bob came down the stairs, he was engulfed by the people. I was right behind Prince Buster, and Prince Buster grabbed Bob on his right, saying, "Bob! See me here! See me here!"

That's when the picture was taken that was on the front page of *The Star*, with Buster with his arm around Bob. All you see of my picture is my hair. Very short locks. Right behind Prince Buster. And Bob ran, and Ziggy wanted to get to Bob, and he ran to his father. Bob grabbed Ziggy, and they grabbed Bob, threw him in a car and drove off with him. He didn't even go through customs or anything. They just grabbed him and took him off down to the racecourse because they had a gathering there. The people were invited to come to the racecourse and meet Bob. To show that Bob Marley was back again in Jamaica, he was home, home to greet his people, and he was thinking positive, he wasn't thinking negative about the shooting or anything like that. And we drove to the racecourse, and there were thousands of people there. The great Nyabinghi [a Rastafarian drumming festival and ritual, also known as a grounation] started before Bob arrived, and it was going right through. Twenty-four hours nonstop. It was downtown, near Parade, in a kind of broken-down area, not far from Tivoli Gardens and not far from the waterfront. A lot of Rastas live in that area, right near Seeco's house, near Love Lane. And, myself just returning to Jamaica, I didn't know A from B about Kingston. I'd been away since I was nine years old. Everything was new to me, it was great, it was very exciting. I'd go anywhere. I was very innocent to all the things that were going on politically. To me it was just Rastafari and love.

We arrived at the Nyabinghi at nighttime. There were a thousand drums playing. There were chalices everywhere and herbs being smoked, and a lot of prayers were being said and a lot of chanting. A lotta lotta chanting. It was a real beautiful experience, because I'd never been to a Nyabinghi before in my life. And it was like I was back in the biblical times, 'cause I saw all these elder Rastafarians, and they were all so humble and very positive to one another. I really felt a lot of warmth and love in my heart for these people, because I said, "Look at the world, there's people making bombs and ammunitions all over. And these bredren here, almost like Moses and people like that, chanting for the world to be at peace." Continuous chant. And having the faith 110 percent. That was a great experience, I'll never forget it. The whole experience of Bob coming home to Jamaica, and the people greeting him, and the Nyabinghi, and the eventual One Love Peace Concert. It was an example for the whole world to follow.

ROGER STEFFENS: Filmmakers, most especially documentarians, often depend on the luck of the spontaneous and memorable moment. For Jim Lewis, one of those serendipitous instants came during the filming of *Heartland Reggae*, a musical anthology that remains one of reggae music's landmark works. Its climax features Bob Marley uniting prime minister Michael Manley and right-wing opposition leader Edward

Seaga in a gesture of peace under a full moon before some forty thousand people. Neville Garrick has compared that electrifying moment
to Christ on the cross between two thieves. After Bob had viewed the
footage of Manley and Seaga joining hands with him onstage, journalist John Sutton-Smith asked what was going through his mind. Bob
replied, "I-man no politician. But if I-man a politician, only one thing
for me to do. Kill them both!"

JIM LEWIS: I'm Canadian, more or less a long-form documentary
filmmaker. I found myself in the Caribbean after a live-action film that
I was doing was aborted, and I started looking around for something
that seemed topical. Reggae music made a lot of sense to me in '77. So
I decided to do a TV pilot for reggae music, like *American Bandstand*
except of reggae, for the local Caribbean audience. I made this half-
hour show called *Jamming*, which was played on the public network
once. Then I thought I'd get more into reggae, and so the only thing to

Canadian film director Jim Lewis with a Japanese laser disc copy of his film *Heartland
Reggae,* a.k.a. the One Love Peace Concert film. Vancouver, Canada, July 2000.

do was to go down to Jamaica. I first went down there around September '77. The One Love Peace Concert wasn't until April '78. I decided to try to film it as soon as I heard about it. My partner Billy Mitchell encouraged me to go back for it. He went down ahead and negotiated with the various factions. He seemed to think it would be OK. He was confident we could resolve everything. It was more like guerrilla film-making than anything organized. I remember Billy telling me that he had been taken to some kind of bunker deep in one of the ghettos, and this is where he negotiated with the warlords of one side. He was amazed at the sophistication, the electronics, in the middle of this so-called ghetto, that they had. But we didn't know if we'd get to film until the last minute. We didn't even know who was actually running this thing. Ultimately we had to assume that Bob Marley's people were running it, so we were dealing with Bob and his representatives, and that didn't really resolve itself until he was walking onto the stage. Don Taylor was very instrumental in all these runnings, and he seemed to be the guy who could say we could film Bob for X amount of contingencies and conditions. Obviously I agreed to everything, I thought it was worth it to film Bob.

ROGER STEFFENS: The historic One Love Peace Concert took place in the National Stadium in Kingston on April 21–22, 1978. Bob came out after midnight.

JIM LEWIS: We had four cameras. One position had to be built; two others were at either side of the stage and one small camera roved in the audience. The scaffolding one was the so-called wide-angle shot, in the crowd in front of the stage. I remember the last-minute negotiations in the sweaty locker rooms under the stage. Diane Jobson, the Rasta lawyer, was being a real stick-in-the-mud. Suddenly, somebody came running in and said they were taking all the cameras down. It was still light outside so it would be about 4:30 by now. Everything had been set up and in place. Two of the cameramen came to me and said they were ready to quit. Eventually, I came to an agreement with Don

Taylor. It was pitch-dark by then and the show was well under way. We didn't really resolve anything, not even any handshakes. We agreed to get it filmed and then deal with legalities afterwards.

ROGER STEFFENS: Bob's publicist, Charlie Comer, was on stage.

CHARLIE COMER: We were surrounded by guns, all brand-new guns! Hundreds and hundreds of them, machine guns! And I took Mick Jagger down there and we were on the side of the stage. Manley and Seaga were there, but they weren't in the first seats, they were in the second row for protection. All the fuckin' press were in front of them, they were gonna get shot first before the prime ministers, that's for sure! Because I remember the *Montreal Gazette* journalist Garry Steckles saying to me, we felt like sitting pigeons. But Michael Manley had a real poker face and so did Seaga. They weren't giving anything away.

JIM LEWIS: We had to agree that the Peace Council [representatives of each of the warring factions in the ghetto] would take possession of the film rolls as they came out of the cameras. They assigned guards to each camera and they were handed the rolls as each one ended. They then handed them to another person, and they quickly disappeared. I hoped they would manage to keep track of them all, which they did. We also agreed that the Peace Council would control the exposed footage until we sorted out the revenue split from the movie. There were about seven guys, two principally, a JLP and a PNP. It was scary because these guys were notorious.

Once we were given the go-ahead we had Tony Marsh on one camera and John Swaby on another. I think Randy Torno had the handheld camera in the audience, and I had one stage left. There wasn't much of the show left by the time we were ready. There was no special lighting for us, we just had the stage lights. Bob's lighting fellows wouldn't really make the concessions to the lights that the filming called for.

ROGER STEFFENS: The all-star bill for that evening included the Meditations, Althea and Donna, the Mighty Diamonds, Culture, Trinity, Jacob Miller and Inner Circle, Big Youth, Beres Hammond, Ras

Michael and the Sons of Negus, Marley and his former partner Peter Tosh, whose tumultuous scene-stealing act was third from the end of the eight-hour show.

NEVILLE WILLOUGHBY: Peter Tosh's performance—everybody was taken aback. When he took out his spliff and started blowing it all over the place and at these police who were around, I said, "What's gonna happen?" Nobody did anything. When he started, I think he used a few curse words. I thought he was going a little overboard and that bothered me. I was very glad when Bob came on, because I said, "Wow, that was hard!" Hard to take, you know, it was rough, it was rough that night, very rough. 'Cause I was watching the Minister of Security and that type of fellow, I was watching the policemen to see what they were going to do, 'cause I was quite worried, because I thought Peter is doing some things that I thought were a little bit too much. So it was bothersome for me.

CHARLIE COMER: I loved when Peter said, "I don't want peace, I want justice," and actually took a spliff and blew it right in their faces.

JIM LEWIS: We rehearsed the day before, when Peter Tosh and a few more acts rehearsed. As we had already got our footage of Peter and the others we had no intention of shooting anyone else except for Bob Marley. There is nothing of Peter at this concert in the film, though it is assumed that his footage was shot at it. Many articles refer to it.

When the emcee introduced Bob, he seemed unsure how to introduce him. He said that Bob had "carved out a nice niche for himself in Jamaican music." What kind of a triumphant return from exile is that, right? The key was the audience's vibes. You have to remember that when he hit the stage the people had been there for over six hours. Then he got there, performed, and gave them more than they ever could have wanted.

JUNIOR MARVIN: I said to myself, Jah must have planned this, because to go home, playing with Bob Marley and the Wailers, the Rolling Stones of Jamaica, and playing at the peace concert—I couldn't believe it! I thought, hey, to be part of this, of something that's promoting peace, such a positive thing. I had to thank Bob a million times over for involving me in such a thing. It was a really beautiful experience, and I'll never forget that. To play in front of your own people, on a project which is bringing governments together, bringing all the people together, using all our positive energy, with Bob at the forefront—it was amazing.

JIM LEWIS: We were fortunate: the right time, the right place, with experienced people. Asking what I remember about being on that stage with Bob then isn't a terribly fair question because when one is acting as a cameraman one isn't terribly aware of anything other than what's through the eye. To be honest, it was knowing that something very special was happening, and it was knowing that something even more special was imminent, namely that the two political leaders were going to come onstage. This was an unprecedented move, and only a limited number of people knew that. It felt anticipatory. I have been onstage with rock 'n roll stars and filmed the vibrations and enthusiasm, but this was very different. Even the nasty bodyguards were grooving by the end of the night.

Of course, there were times that I was aware of the vibes. I would say that it was, like, on the edge. The audience vibes were very positive and they were going with it. But, on the other hand, they were also in check because anything could have happened. I felt this kind of elation, but reserved. It was very different, a non-joke concert. No one was clapping for the sake of clapping. If you clapped you meant it. Then it was over, everyone went home. I remember walking out of there that night with the crowd, and it was like Woodstock in a way.

NEVILLE WILLOUGHBY: There's no doubt to me the high point of Bob Marley and Peter Tosh was when the One Love Peace Concert came on at the stadium. I was one of the emcees, with Errol Thompson. But I remember when I was leaving, Bob had introduced Manley and Seaga onstage and after all that was done he was continuing singing. And I decided I was going to leave before the crowd even though I was the emcee. Because once he took over, at a certain point, he did the rest of the show himself, he didn't need an emcee again. So I walked across the stadium, and I walked to go through the tunnel and stopped over by the exit and turned around and when I looked I saw the most astonishing sight. First, it was a full moon night and it was like a picture. There was Bob in the middle of the place, and I mean, the man actually looked he was climbing in the air from where I was standing in the exit. And I stood there, I didn't leave until he had finished about two more songs. "Jah Live" and "One Love." Though I stayed and then left as soon as I saw the crowd start to move, because I wanted to get out before the crowd. But that I'll never forget, standing up there looking back at Bob in a spotlight, and he had a way of moving as if he were almost climbing in the air. And from that distance I watched it and then the moon above, it was a beautiful sight, I remember that very distinctly. Most fabulous show I've seen Bob do, it was really a show!

JIM LEWIS: I never saw the film again until I met Bucky Marshall at Toronto International Airport some time later. I had to find the airfare to get them, Bucky and Claudie, to Canada. I did that by putting an advert in a Jamaican reggae newspaper. I said that a major motion picture about the Woodstock of reggae needs money; call this number. Somebody called, and I asked them if they could pay for flight tickets for Bucky Marshall and Claudie Massop. It's gonna cost $780; if you don't do this the film may never get finished. And this person who I'd never met or spoken to before went and bought the tickets. Her name was Mary Pever. She showed seriously good faith. It turned out that Bucky Marshall wasn't really his name, so when he went to claim his tickets she even had to get new tickets in his real name, Austin Marshall. So the lads came up here. We had never actually met in all of the hubbub at the concert.

Bucky Marshall was a frail little wiry guy, about five foot eight, in tremendous shape and very alert and aware of everybody and every thing.

Claudie Massop was about six foot four, a great big hunk of a man. He was much older, about thirty-five, and had many dependents. He was ruthless and very smart, very calculating and very well connected.

Knowing that these guys with you were ruthless gunmen there was some trepidation, but at least I was on home turf. I knew they hadn't traveled much in their lives. They couldn't believe that, suddenly, they had landed in Canada. By the time they got their tickets sorted out, many weeks had passed since the concert. This was in the summertime. They arrived with the undeveloped film rolls in their baggage. I met them at the airport and took them to various places. Eventually we got the film to the lab. It was all straightforward. The only thing we had to do was sort out who claimed the film when it came through, as cargo. The guy asked me who it was for, I told him it was for me and them, so I put their two names on too. Once it hit the lab it was never under their names. It became my property as far as documentation was concerned because it was up to me to get it processed, then to show it to them and discuss with them what to do with it. Long negotiations followed.

I had them staying at their own place. Eventually they were taken care of by followers of their own factions, expatriates. I acted as their driver while they were here, taking them to their various meetings. I was very cooperative. Eventually, after receiving a phone call, Claudie told me that he'd got to go back home because there was trouble brewing there. By then we finished all the negotiations. We had to deal with the Marley aspect of it. His people had told me to go ahead and film the show. He had basically put the show on and paid for it out of his own pocket.

Two days after they left, this other guy appeared. He was sent up here to make sure they didn't rip me off! He was a very intellectual guy, named Trevor. Each one knew that the other was incredibly dangerous, but they knew they needed each other. They were nothing without the other one. They were scared to death of each other and yet they needed each other. I also felt that they knew their days were numbered. These people saw life from the point of view that in twenty minutes it could end. I lived life through their eyes while chaperoning them. Very strange. Bucky Marshall was about twenty-four years old when he died in a shootout in New York. He had never known anything but gang warfare from when he was twelve years old.

Bob Marley and I talked on the phone about the making of the movie, but not really in any detail. I also talked to other relatives and Mrs. Booker. I was just so busy working on the film, but Billy Mitchell had many reasonings with him. But we just talked on the phone and when people talk on the phone it is different than in person. I would generally tell him where I was at, how things were progressing, and I tried to get across to him that I was somebody who knew the runnings a little bit so he didn't have to worry, and that he should just cut me some slack until I got the film done, then he could see it. He sensed that, and he was smart enough to know that he was dealing with good people. So there was never any friction, and I guess Don Taylor had said that we were determined to do a good job. Film doesn't lie, especially this kind of *vérité* shooting. You can't manipulate it, it can only tell the truth. If it's got something to say, it's gonna say it.

My last conversation with Bob was in a restaurant. I remember he was very positive, saying words like "forward," all positive stuff. Bob got sick during the period I was working on the production of the film, so it became a matter of dealing with that and living up to my obligations that I made with him.

So I did see the project through, but what choice did I have? Any man would have. It was just a compulsion. This project got much bigger than I expected it to in terms of endearing itself to me. I'm still in touch with Mrs. Marley. They administrate the video; we made it direct to the Estate. And, of course, the Peace Council disintegrated, which didn't surprise me. I don't think it was formed for the right reasons. I think it was hastily founded out of despair, the wrong kind of despair. It didn't really have a lot of chance. Trevor was very intelligent but not a lot of the others were. Peace is such a fragile thing.

GILLY GILBERT: If they had meant it, it would have been a better Jamaica right now. I mean, with ghetto people, even when Bob died, they should have taken that as very important significance. So the peace truce was really like a drop in the pan, it wasn't really authentic. It was just a One Love Peace show. He tried to get everybody together for that one night and figured that it was going to continue, and we all strengthen it, the ghetto people, people from all walks of life within the Jamaican community. 'Cause it was a good gathering. We trying to get away from the evil and the bad, and work for the good, and the betterment of human life and environment. When it failed I felt bad and I know Bob must feel cut up about it also. I just never love what gwan.

JUNIOR MARVIN: Some say the peace didn't hold. But I say the peace did hold. Up until now. Because you see, what you have to understand is that, without that move, a lot of people would be dead now. A lot of people would have died innocently. A lot of people wouldn't have even thought before they picked up a gun. But that instigated a lot of thought in a lot of people. That is, a whole generation of people from that time think differently today, because of that concert. I feel it was a success. Yeah. The battle was won. In life, you have to deal with the positive. Now, what did we achieve from that? And even then you have to look at the positive. Because you know, you're never gonna say, "Well, we won everyone." There's still a lot of people who are hopeless sinners. As it says in "One Love," "Is there a place for the hopeless sinner who has hurt all mankind just to save his own?" The lucky thing is that God always forgives. So therefore, you realize that we won 90 percent of those sinners. So you can't say that you lost.

ROGER STEFFENS: A year and a half later, in November 1979, Hank Holmes (my founding partner on our *Reggae Beat* show on KCRW in L.A.) and I would ask Bob about his decision to return, and how he helped bring the two warring political leaders in Jamaica together on one stage in the National Stadium. At the time we were on the road with the group in San Diego. His exhaustion was apparent, and he rebuffed nearly all attempts at one-on-one interviews. On November 24 he held a pre-show press conference in a Sports Arena dressing room, seated next to his friend and bandleader Family Man Barrett, with keyboardist Tyrone Downie and several Twelve Tribes associates nearby.

BOB MARLEY: Dem never want come. Is we send go tell they have to come. We send go tell them, the man from both sides, go up, go tell

Bob Marley during a press conference backstage at the San Diego Sports Arena, November 24, 1979. This picture became the cover of the posthumous album *Soul Almighty,* which spent fifty-six weeks on the *Billboard* reggae chart.

them say well, the man say they want you 'pon stage to show the people oonoo live and can hold hand together, so the war, the war have to be out between—'cause people every day see dem things. . . . People could say, if Michael Manley and Seaga sit face to face they will fight. And we know say dem will never fight. So why is the people a fight 'gainst one another if the leader dem wouldn't fight themselves? So we bring dem together and show dem the truth in themselves, a fuckery a gwan!

ROGER STEFFENS: As Bob became more and more aware of the liberation politics in Africa, his music would take a turn toward their struggles for independence, with songs like "Africa Unite" and "Zimbabwe." He was keenly aware that without justice there could be no peace, and that it was only united youth in revolutionary movements who would succeed in the coming battles. In Jamaica, the newly invigorated Rastafari philosophy was leading the way.

Africa was riven by proxy wars underwritten by the Soviet Union and the U.S. in their attempts to gain control of the rich natural resources of newly independent countries and those fighting for freedom from colonial control. It was Peter Tosh who sang that he didn't want peace, he wanted equal rights and justice.

BOB MARLEY: When Tosh say no peace, Tosh must know who him a talk no peace for. I say peace for the youth who live in the ghetto who is warring against one another. And I say that again and fight for that and defend that anywhere. No peace with the Devil now. We ourselves have to have peace, then we can have unity, then we can demand justice. Because unity is strength. If we a war, which strength we gonna have? Is we a war against [there's a war against us]—we need the strength. Yet we a war against one another. You see what I mean? That is foolishness, man.

TYRONE DOWNIE: What Peter mean by when Peter say we don't want peace we want equal rights, I think what him mean is, them want peace, but before you say peace you have to show some justice. Then automatically you get peace.

BOB MARLEY: A man who stand up out there and look 'pon it different from a man who involved in it. A man who's there 'pon the outside and just a skate round it, different from a man who inna it. Yeah, mon, a inna it we deh. When peace a make a way inna England de whole a man dem come when a war, say peace, which part we a deh in England? A deh so we get the whole, full overstanding of what we a deal with. 'Cause some people never know nothin' 'bout the peace, dem only hear say like peace and t'ing, dem no know where it a come from, dem no know wha'ppen 'bout it.

ROGER STEFFENS: Marley's remarks were often misinterpreted by journalists. Dr. Matthew Smith, a professor at the University of the West Indies in Kingston, helps to "penetrate the patois."

DR. MATTHEW SMITH: Bob is referencing the One Love Peace Concert. What he is saying essentially is, "When we decided on the peace treaty we were in England [1978] and all the big players [political enforcers] came up to meet with us in England at a time of war [in Jamaica] to discuss peace. That was where we got the full understanding of the power of our influence." [By which he means his influence, though he speaks in the plural we—"oonoo"—on political events in Jamaica: that they sought his counsel and intervention in an attempt to end the bloody political warfare in the island.]

TYRONE DOWNIE: That's the only way Bob would have returned down there. 'Cause there was peace. But if like the war was going to continue bitterly like that, then that's a piracy peace.

BOB MARLEY: Which piracy peace? [He said this to Tyrone, who first used the term—perhaps a reference to how the peace was stolen after the One Love concert.] Now watch me! Society set up themselves that the youth and youth must get a thing that you call frustrated and fight 'gainst one another. Now we say, we will fight with the youth, to make the youth come together, so you a go always have a force what try make them fight, because if them come together then them will know themselves and then them might go on like Ayatollah.

TYRONE DOWNIE: We take them right up to the door of peace.

BOB MARLEY: Because everyone guilty now. Now that peace come, everyone see what the guy was doing.

TYRONE DOWNIE: What this man was saying, it is a false peace.

BOB MARLEY: If the guy hide and do it, it can't false. And a Revelation time now. One aim, one God, one destiny, is that overcome all things. Music is a part of the whole struggle right? Music.

ROGER STEFFENS: In Bob's most militant songs, such as "Burnin' And Lootin'," are lyrics that many critics felt incited a violent response to oppression.

TYRONE DOWNIE: If push comes to shove, I mean, Zimbabwe–Rhodesia don't really want an armed struggle. Nkrumah don't want an armed struggle [in Ghana]. They've lost enough people, but if Smith and Vorster [in Rhodesia and South Africa] and all a them don't want to give up the land they'll just have to fight for it. Nobody wants to fight.

BOB MARLEY: Me personally, you see from dem man deal with Rastafari, me no see the solution. 'Cause anything them want deal with, if them no deal with the right thing then you must a go have a next revolution again. I'm not going to say the peace won't last because you know I no inna that. I just a say, dem have a right to defend Rastafari. That is what can make the peace, the justice and everything. You have two world powers, all right, according to them, Russia and America. Right? That mean we no see where Russia and America no deal with my life forever, seen. Them no inna that. All dem a do is create I and say live forever, who Him name Rastafari. If when man come, you see and talk, the people don't understand, then God going to talk. And God no talk, Him take action. So you see if America want something to bring the people closer to God dem might get it, you know? So is the word come first. 'Cause remember the action is coming.

GILLY GILBERT: When Bob spoke about Africa in 1977, that was the time he said he wanted to go to Africa, after he went through all that changes in the politics, the shooting. He was on that trek when he said "Movements of Jah people, Exodus." At that time he had planned to go live in Africa and set up in Africa. But come 1978 they had this peace treaty thing in Jamaica and they got Bob involved and I would say they persuaded him, or convinced him to come back to Jamaica, which I myself, I don't think he should have done that. We don't make no war with nobody. We come here in peace, love and harmony, and Bob preach about unity, sing about unity.

ROGER STEFFENS: In September 1979, with the Peace Concert of April 1978 and a near-fatal beating by the police three months later still fresh in his memory, Peter Tosh had this to say about the concert.

PETER TOSH: Legendary Peace Concert, so-called. Anything change? Yes. More people dead. Yes, man. Peace? Then what you think peace is? Peace is death. Your passport to heaven. Most people don't know that.

CHAPTER 28

Babylon by Bus from the U.N. to Ethiopia

ROGER STEFFENS: In June 1978, two months after the Peace Concert and in the midst of an international tour, Bob was invited to New York to receive the United Nations Peace Medal of the Third World. It was given to him at the Waldorf-Astoria Hotel by an ebullient diplomat from Senegal named Mohmmadu "Johnny" Seka. As the youth ambassador from that country to the U.N. he had lobbied for several years to get the medal for Marley. (He would later die of melanoma at the age of thirty-six—just as Bob did.)

At the ceremony and the press conference after, Bob was presented with the medal and a painting titled *Jamma*, done by a Mandingo artist. It is now on display at the Marley Museum in Kingston. As he handed it to Bob, Ambassador Seka pointed to his peacemaking initiative at the One Love concert, declaring, "On April 22, in Jamaica, all the artists, Jamaicans, unify, singing and getting together. Because they think we can't unify by ourselves. That's good initiative." He regretted that Bob had not yet come to perform in Africa where "we buy the records of Bob Marley and Stevie Wonder for $20!" [This was about four times the price paid in America at the time.]

Asked by a reporter how it felt to be a hero, Bob modestly denied the proposition, pointing instead to Selassie. "This is the generation that see God," he said, "and Rastafari is the Almighty God. This is where the interest is . . . the Rastafari message. . . . You can't subdue the message." In one of his first public statements acknowledging his awareness that he was channeling a divine source he said, "You open your mouth and God speak out of you and you can't control that. I remember when Jah send Moses to talk and him say him can't talk and Jah tell him open your mouth and Him talk out of it. . . . This is why Jah use music because you can't control it. . . . Music is the biggest gun." Because the oppressed cannot afford weapons, he explained, it's no use fighting that way because they are outgunned on every level. So love is the answer, and it would be a theme of his 1979 album *Survival*.

Bob's 1977 *Exodus* North American tour had been canceled when the melanoma was discovered in his toe, so it wasn't until the following year that he returned, in support of his new LP *Kaya*. Critics were decrying its alleged "softness," saying Bob had taken refuge in ganja-induced oblivion following the assassination attempt on his life in December 1976, and contrasting it with the seemingly more militant *Exodus*, not realizing that all the songs had been cut at the same time in the early part of his UK exile.

A skin graft onto his infected toe led Bob to believe he had been healed, so he scheduled a demanding tour of Europe and North America from May through July 1978, more than fifty concerts from Scandinavia to San Diego. Recordings from the tour ended up on his second live album, a two-disc set called *Babylon by Bus*. Several of those dates would be in California, which is where my path crossed with him for the first time. I had seen Bob at the Paramount Theater in Oakland, California, in 1975, but now I would become familiar with the band members and subsequently with Bob himself, learning what a tightly-knit group he had assembled.

JUNIOR MARVIN: In 1978, at the time, we were touring quite a lot. And the band were really in tune with one another. We were listening to one another, giving each other the right space, appreciating all the points that were brought up by one another about each other. Everyone was totally positive about their criticism. And it helped us a lot, because we were really trying to think positive and make the band as good as possible. At that particular tour everyone was very happy and the vibes, the responses from the audience, were really good. Everyone was singing the vocals along with Bob at the concert, everyone knew the words, and it was very inspiring for all of us. Al Anderson and myself were trading a lot of licks. We were really pushing each other to do better. If you listen to the live album, you will hear both of us playing really well. And Bob feeling very happy about it.

ROGER STEFFENS: The *Kaya* studio LP was different in style and content. Award-winning photographer Kate Simon took the iconic cover image, which was later chosen for the Taschen book *The Photos of the Century: 100 Historic Moments.* In her book *Rebel Music,* she described the day she took the photo of Bob with that beatific smile on his face.

KATE SIMON: I was down in Kingston in '76 shooting Bunny for his album *Blackheart Man.* One day I was racing Chris Blackwell at the breaststroke in the Sheraton pool. Chris gave me a little bit of a head start but I'd been a junior Olympic swimmer so I was pretty good. But

Photographer Kate Simon, double-exposed with her cover photo for *Kaya.* New York, February 2002.

we swam, Chris won, I got out of the pool and there was Bob Marley sitting at one of those tables with tin umbrellas. And that's when I took the *Kaya* portrait. It wasn't a formal photo session or anything. I was wearing a swimsuit, that's how informal it was. The photograph to me is a very special one: Bob's face is so open, his smile is so big, his gaze is so sharp, that the photograph seems to give off light.

NEVILLE GARRICK: On the back cover of *Kaya* there was a drawing I did of Bob between two mountains with like sunset coming up, which they later drew into a poster, somebody redrew. And then Bob looked at it and say, "It cool, but too much of me. Why I am on the back and on the front?" And they needed to get this album out right away. Now I'd gotten this other image [of ganja leaves and a huge burning spliff] from Paul Smykle to make a backdrop from 'cause I liked it so much. So Island had this holding for me, so I just called and said, "Hey, we're gonna change the back of the cover. Let's use Smykle's drawing and put the type over it." So we designed it on the telephone.

ROGER STEFFENS: Marley and the Wailers' second live album, released in 1978, was a creatively designed double LP package recorded at several different venues.

NEVILLE GARRICK: On *Babylon by Bus,* this one Blackwell collaborated with me a little bit on. There was a group he had there that did real well for him before called Traffic. There was a live album this man had submitted, and he did like the back of a truck, like one of those tour forty-foot trailers, and the group like was coming out of there. I think 10cc did something similar later on. And Chris said something like showing them on tour and moving, and I started to work around that kind of idea: some moving him through a bus or an aircraft or something like that. And the bus idea kind of fit the squareness of a jacket. So the title of the album came from the design concept then, rather than the other way around.

ROGER STEFFENS: Marley fans from California have always been puzzled by the idiosyncratic map of their state in the liner notes.

NEVILLE GARRICK: Somehow Santa Cruz, which is about ninety miles southwest of Berkeley, ended up about four hundred miles north of Berkeley! And imagine, California is where I lived and that's the only place I mixed up. Well, you have so much earthquake down there, probably sometime it move.

ROGER STEFFENS: According to several of his closest associates, Marley's favorite concert in North America took place on Haile Selassie's birthday, July 23, 1978, at the Santa Barbara Bowl. Reggae historian Dr. Steve Heilig was there.

DR. STEVE HEILIG: We in Santa Barbara were stoked to have Marley and the Wailers coming through again for an afternoon show, especially as Bob had just been quoted as saying our open-air bowl was his favorite place to play in America. The Rolling Stones, hot on a comeback with the *Some Girls* LP, were playing a couple hours south in L.A. at the same time. Marley and the Wailers put on a legendary, smoking show, with encores stretching into the evening. Towards the end, I was standing on the side of the stage and sensed a presence next to me: Mick Jagger. Now wait a minute, I think. Mick's supposed to be singing right now! As Bob and the boys, drenched in sweat, leave the stage at last, I see Mick bolt for a helicopter waiting in the lot below. Damn, he's gonna be late, I think, and sure enough, he kept over fifty thousand of his fans waiting a couple extra hours so he could catch the Marley show.

ROGER STEFFENS: The herbal-grounding that had softened the *Kaya* record and brought him to California was numbingly evident when I met him for the first time, backstage at the Santa Cruz Civic Auditorium in July 1978. My wife Mary and I had been living that summer in Big Sur, and when we heard Bob was coming, we bought tickets to both his scheduled shows. We were among the first in the auditorium early that evening. The soundboard was right in the middle of the floor, and there was a tall man I didn't recognize standing by it, curling his nascent dreads around his fingertips. I figured he had to be with the band, so I approached and asked him if they were going to play "Waiting In Vain" that evening. "Why?" he asked. "Well," I said with excitement, "that's my very favorite Wailers song, especially that incredible lead guitar solo that Junior Marvin plays in the middle of it."

"You want to meet Bob," the dread said, catching us completely off guard. Without hesitation, of course, we both blurted "Yes!" and he began leading us backstage down a long corridor. "What's your names?" he asked us. I told him and asked his. "I'm Junior Marvin," he laughed. Boy, I thought, did we say the right thing to the right man at the right time! Junior ushered us into a large back room, where four huge cafeteria-style tables had been pushed together to make a giant table around which the Wailers were seated at great distances from one another. The room was virtually soundless; it looked like a convention of zombies. No one was saying anything to anyone. And each had a tall green anthill of herb piled in front of him with his own individual pack of rolling papers.

I had a poster promoting the Greek Theater show coming up three days later in Berkeley, which had been given out to people waiting in line. Junior said, "Why don't you ask Bob to sign it?" "Oh, yeah, sure!" I stammered. Junior graciously introduced us, but Bob was definitely "inna de ites" and well red by this time. He signed the poster for me, as did all the other band members in turn, and we left to find seats, speechless and freaked to the max. I still have the poster, and since then, nearly everyone of major import in Bob's life—forty-one people, saints and sinners alike—has signed it for me, too. When I loaned it to the Grammy Museum in 2011 they insured it for $75,000.

In Santa Cruz that night Bob did two twenty-one-song shows, identical in content (which was rare for him) and both, of course, sold out. He didn't make any small talk or patter during the sets, preferring that the words of his songs speak for him. Or perhaps it was just a tribute to the gift that a young couple we saw backstage had given him. Dressed all in white, barefoot, and both very blond, the couple had presented Bob with an enormous bud about eighteen inches long. He just smiled, smelled it admiringly, and began building a cricket-bat spliff. A-woah!

We drove down to L.A. the following weekend to catch Bob at the Starlight Bowl in Burbank. It was a nightmare getting inside, because there was only one entrance and they were searching everyone. We missed the Imperials' opening act, but found our seats just as Bob was introduced. The show was similar to that in Santa Cruz, at least until the encores. Later we learned that stars like Mick Jagger and Diana Ross had been milling about backstage, trying to wangle an invitation to come on stage with Bob, but he was having none of it. So imagine our shock when, as Bob began to sing his final encore of "Get Up Stand Up," Peter Tosh appeared, loping across the stage with massive strides, just at the part of the song where he comes in on the record. As he reached for the microphone, Bob suddenly caught sight of him and broke into a broad, ecstatic smile. Peter never missed a beat, and the two hugged each other and acted as if they'd never been separated. It was the only time they would ever appear together outside Jamaica after the breakup of the group—a piece of history that, sadly, most people in the audience didn't realize was happening, as few of them recognized Peter.

Afterward, I encountered Peter walking through the crowd. The next day he would be opening for the Rolling Stones in the Anaheim Stadium, and I eagerly assured him that we, like many others, would be there basically just to see him, and that he had lots of fans in L.A.

A few years later, just after Bob passed, I interviewed Peter for *L.A. Reggae*, a cable TV show that Chili Charles and I had just started, and asked him whether Bob had known he was going to come out on stage that evening. "No," he said, indicating that it was the Spirit that had moved him spontaneously and "whatsoever the Spirit tell me to do, I do." What else did he remember of that night? "Well," he drawled, thick smoke pouring from his nostrils, "I remember we go backstage and

Bob clapped my hand and say, 'Bwoi, the Pope feel that one!' " Then, laughing, he announced, "And three days later, the Pope *die!*"

ROGER STEFFENS: In 1978 Bob flew to Africa for the first time, landing in Kenya with a couple of friends in an attempt to visit Ethiopia. His efforts were rebuffed until one day, as he walked down a street in Nairobi, a man recognized him and asked him what he was doing in Africa. When Bob told him he was trying to gain entrance into Ethiopia, the man identified himself as an Ethiopian consular official and wrote him a visa.

The short trip opened his eyes to the reality of the situation in Ethiopia following the coup that had ousted Haile Selassie in 1974. All images of His Majesty were forbidden. He was shocked that there was no evidence of the Rastafarian faith, except for the area around Shashamane in the Oromia region of the country. There, land had been given to repatriating Rastafari, mostly from Jamaica and England, who were forming a homeland for their coreligionists. Bob's idea that he should move to Ethiopia as soon as he had the opportunity was put on hold.

NEVILLE GARRICK: Bob was in Ethiopia for maybe three or four days. Bob was probably in Kenya longer than Ethiopia, trying to get in there. I think he spent most of the time in Shashamane, and maybe a day and a half in Addis, and I think Skill come for him, and then to Shashamane, and spend a few days there and then gone!

There's a Polaroid picture of Bob under the sycamore tree in Shashamane. Bob's friend Malachi is on the left and the man called Lips in the middle.

ROGER STEFFENS: The lack of respect for Selassie was deeply disturbing to Marley.

NEVILLE GARRICK: What I think was his most disappointment was seeing all the Marxist or Communist trappings all over Ethiopia. Statues of Marx and Lenin and not seeing His Majesty and Menelik*

---

* Menelik II reigned as Emperor of Ethiopia from 1889 to 1913.

Prince Malachi, Marley's bodyguard "Lips" and Marley photographed
under the sycamore tree in Shashamane, Ethiopia. 1978.
(Courtesy of Roger Steffens' Reggae Archives)

although some of those statues are still there, but they made those new
ones bigger and grander to mark the change. And knowing that you're
being watched, because Bob's fame had spread enough that everybody
know, and you're defending the monarchy in a Communist state.

ROGER STEFFENS: Over the years, there have been several rumors
that Bob did not actually write "Zimbabwe," but rather bought it from
someone when he visited Ethiopia.

NEVILLE GARRICK: In Shashamane you had Flippins, one of the first
Twelve Tribes members who went there. In the reasoning during that
time, I think ideas for Bob's song "Zimbabwe" came about. Because
at that same time when those lyrics came about was when they were
trying to sort it out in that Lancaster House Agreement in England, so
it was topical in the news. And knowing Flippins and Skill and their

liking and awareness of world affairs, I can imagine the situation that led to that song.

ROGER STEFFENS: Skill Cole has confirmed privately that Flippins was, in fact, the writer of the song and Bob paid him for the lyrics. Its specificity was unique in Bob's catalog, pointing out a nation in upheaval and the answer to its problems. "Every man got a right to decide his own destiny," the song declares, approving the fight with arms (a defensive move, from his point of view, in accordance with the Rasta edict that you should harm no one but not let anyone harm you). The song would become the centerpiece of his new album, *Survival*, and, in one of the crowning achievements of his storied career, Bob would go on to sing it at Zimbabwe's independence celebrations a few months later.

CHAPTER 29

Charity and Survival

ROGER STEFFENS: The original Wailers' longtime dream of having a home studio was finally realized by Marley in 1978, when he completed one at 56 Hope Road. *Survival* would be his first album recorded there. His empire was growing nicely, with a pressing plant, distribution company and plans to expand the label to include other artists as well. The studio and label were both called Tuff Gong. Berry Gordy's success with Motown, a completely black-owned corporation, was Bob's inspiration and he had broadly ambitious ideas for the future.

COLIN LESLIE: I knew Bob as far back as the 1960s. At that phase he had moved back to the country. He was a farmer in Saint Ann and he would come into Kingston. I played in a school band at that time, and there's a girls high school called St. Andrew's that invited the Wailers to play for a school concert. I was the bass player with the band and I actually backed Bob on that show. In those days a lot of artists did concerts for high schools. This one was very special. This was somewhere around 1968.

I became involved with Bob after I worked with Third World, for their production company, and when I left Don Taylor approached me to come on board and help with the formation of what was to become the Tuff Gong group of companies. At that time there was the recording studio, pressing plant and the distribution company. This was around the time of the Peace Concert. He had just started setting up the studio.

When I actually came on board, the studio was actually being built at Hope Road. I was brought in to assist. They wanted systems set up to run the studio. I was the one who designed the job cards and that sort of thing, detailed and mundane stuff.

The hardest part of the job was to make sure that the money that was on the road came in on time. Bob was very peculiar with his money. He didn't want to know about expense vouchers and bills. He wanted to see the money in the bank. He was very clear on that. I had to stay on top of Randy's account [Randy's was a major record distributor], which was the big account then; I would go and deal with these people and get the checks in. And the studio: we had to collect the money from different producers. The biggest challenge was making sure the money was flowing in, and there was a positive cashflow.

In the midst of all that Bob was very focused, very organized. He knew what he wanted to do. Because of his own personality, coupled with the fact that he had spent time in America, in Delaware, and he was exposed to industry and the corporate world, he came back to Jamaica with a sort of sense how things should be ordered in business. So he brought that to bear. He had a structure in his mind how he wanted it. Tommy Cowan was in charge of international distribution, based at Hope Road. Bob was getting ready to export his records, because prior to then he would just sell them around Jamaica. We bought this pressing plant from Mr. Pottinger, Doubletone. We renamed it Addis Ab, Bob took it over. Delroy Wilson's wife, Cecelia, was actually employed to Mr. Pottinger at the pressing plant and Bob retained her and made her the manager of Addis Ab. And there's another young lady by the name of Diane Ellis, who was hired to run the studio; she was studio manager. So there were three different heads of different operations. That was the structure. He had people like Sangie Davis in the studio, staff producer. He was the full-time producer.

ROGER STEFFENS: The first album to be cut in the new Tuff Gong studio at Hope Road was *Black Woman* by Judy Mowatt, still considered by many to be the finest female vocal album ever made in Jamaica. It was filled with classic tracks, many of them penned by her companion at the time, Freddie McGregor.

JUDY MOWATT: When I first met Bob I always said to him, I want you to write a song for me, 'cause I never thought I had the ability to write a song for myself. And he always promise, "Yes, mon, I-man have a whole heap o' song, you know, you must just come down a the gates and come check out the song what I-man have down there." And Rita and myself used to rehearse together before we work together as the I Three. Every night I used to look forward to finishing my work and go down to Trench Town to sit with Rita and when Bob comes in he would work us out. Just for exercise purpose, not as a singing group. Just for voice exercise. But we used to just sing, just jam, he and his guitar. Because from I know Bob, Bob was never without his guitar. He's always singing. And then we'd go down there at nights and join in with him and the folks from the area would sing along. It was very beautiful, and I used to look forward to it.

So Rita and myself used to rehearse this song every night, "Down In The Valley," and is a song that stand out in my mind, I always loved it. And I say if I ever get the chance to do an album, I would put that song on the album. And it was the first song I thought of when I thought of doing the *Black Woman* album. And I wrote "Joseph" for him.

ROGER STEFFENS: In the notes on the *Rastaman Vibration* album Bob identified himself as a reincarnation of the biblical Joseph, who fed the children of Israel during their seven-year exile from Egypt. Bob's international touring, Judy has pointed out, was also seven years, giving spiritual sustenance to his audience.

JUDY MOWATT: As an Israelite, and as a member of the Twelve Tribes of Israel, Joseph, we would recognize him. The other people out there would not recognize him as Joseph, but Bob knew who he is, or who he was. And Bob related it to us that he knew he was Joseph that fed the children of Israel with corn in the time of famine. And not only the children of Israel, but the Egyptians in that time, before Christ; you read about it in the Bible. We see the work that Bob come back to do now, that he has regathered his people, and he's feeding the people with a more spiritual corn in this time.

'Cause the Bible tell us that in this time there's going to be a huge famine, and it's going to be famine for the word of God. Well Bob was the one now who came with that spiritual corn for the word of God, to spread it worldwide, to transport it to the four corners of the earth so everyone could be filled, those who wanted to take a piece of it and enjoy the potency of that food. And I recognized this, and I really wanted to show my appreciation because Bob had really inspired me a lot. As I say, we used to rehearse with him, and knowing who he is, I couldn't go to him and say, "Well, Bob . . ." Words—I couldn't find words to express how I really appreciated him, for being so close to me. I am really impressed knowing that I—God really chose me to be working with such a great man, you know, I'm really honored. And I couldn't really talk to him and tell him that, so I decided to jot it down in a song and sing it to him. He loved it, but he was sort of shy like when he heard it at first. But he really enjoyed it, he said it's a good song, and he's not going to tell you how much he loves it, he's not that type of person. But you can watch him enjoying it, and I have watched him enjoying it, you know, while he was with us in the flesh.

ROGER STEFFENS: Others were also aware of Bob's belief that he was a representative of his people. Many of those closest to him recall his unparalleled generosity. Business manager Colin Leslie was in charge of writing the checks.

COLIN LESLIE: Whenever Bob was in Jamaica the yard would be filled up with people. It would be overflowing into the streets, down the sidewalks. We would go up into the late hours of the night. He would literally have people lined up and he would be interviewing them. Find out what were their particular needs. And there were all kinds of stories, all kinds of people. Women who had lost their baby father through political violence. People who wanted to set up various ventures.

I give you a little joke. Somebody came to him one day with an idea to set up, to produce and manufacture coconut oil. And Bob found it very funny, he would laugh and say, "I always wanted to be in the oil business." So he financed this guy!

People wanted to buy and sell, and he would interview them, literally interview them, and then he would send them to me and say, "Give them X amount of money." And I would write the checks. This would go up till nine, ten, eleven, twelve at night. And I would just be writing checks, to give these people.

There were people who would be on a regular thing. They come every month, in the understanding they were getting the money. And it would go on and on. And it's amazing the great lines. The minute he landed in Jamaica, the yard would be filled with all these people. And he would say, "Speak to the manager," that was of course me. So it was fun. I had to make sure there was a float of funds to make sure that people would be fed. There were those who depended on hot meals from Bob. And I always had to make sure that there was money there to make sure that these people got something to eat. And to this day a lot of them come and remind me about this. Names who you would probably know. They say, because of you and Bob I used to have a hot meal in those days. This was Bob.

Blackwell said in a video that Bob was responsible for the support of four thousand people, but I think it was probably even more. Bob, for example, bought the buildings, the Twelve Tribes of Israel headquarters on Hope Road. He supported those people.

ROGER STEFFENS: Bob's old friend and personal assistant agrees.

DESSIE SMITH: Bob tell me that people would line up out into the street to ask favors from him. He actually say that. "Dessie, Hope Road people, and from country! And them carry them entire family!" Like

Dessie Smith, Marley's personal assistant during his final years,
Los Angeles, February 1992.

a woman might carry her four children, and them drive from miles. Him tell me in personal talk, like late at night, three, four o'clock in the morning. Him have long lines every day; and not only people in the vicinity but people from far. And he'd help all of them. And not too many of them ever speak about it.

ALLAN "SKILL" COLE: The people come from all about. It was like, I don't want to say it was the Salvation Army, I'm trying to find the right word, but it was—you wouldn't believe it, you would have to be there. There were lines, people were coming in and going out. There are people right now out there that have a lot of money because of Bob. And only I alone know the person. I don't even know that they know that I know, but I know.

GILLY GILBERT: People come, hungry, and him try fe help hungry people and poor people. Some him help no appreciate it. Some appreciate, some him give no satisfied, some satisfied. He try to help everyone, he try to please everyone. He gave donations to the Ethiopia Orthodox Church, to the Twelve Tribes Foundation, Theocratic Government, everyone as far as I can recall.

COLIN LESLIE: He always had Rasta elders around him, close by at hand, to advise him. Bob would pull me aside all the time and preach to me about Rasta. In those days I had a heavier beard and I used to wear a lot of tams. And, you know, once a year Bob would fund a Nyabinghi, these gatherings of Rasta elders. He would facilitate these spiritual gatherings. And there at Hope Road there were meetings all the time. This was the political Bob now, unity among them. Bob spent a lot of time trying to do a reconciliation of the various sects, because he was all about unity. He spoke about it all the time and he lived it. Not just words, actions.

CINDY BREAKSPEARE: People begged him things every day. Every day! Whether it was money or whatever. And he gave whatever to whoever. He didn't prize material things, you know. And he didn't prize money. And he would always just say it was just passing through, so it really wasn't that important. I mean, you know Bob well enough to know that he always dressed in a way that looked like he didn't have two cents to rub together. He loved his jeans. They were the only thing he cared about. One shoe laced up, the other one open. One tongue hanging out. One sock up, one down. Rude boy! And that was really, too, part of the essence of Bob, that he was so unaffected. I mean, people would give him gold chains, he'd have them on. Somebody would pop them off his neck in a football match, he didn't even know when it left his neck.

Two days later he'd be looking in the mirror, he'd say, "Rahtid, where me chain?" He really didn't care for what money could buy.

He gave a lot of money away. I mean, he had money still when it was all over, but he gave a lot of money away. He gave his dinner away. He gave whatever, whatever it was that people required of him, he gave it, 'cause I think he felt that that was part of his role in life, was to do for others and to give to others, and I think he felt very blessed because of the level of inspiration and the work that he had been called to do, and I think he just knew that selfishness just wasn't his way. He allowed people to take full advantage of him. Full advantage.

ROGER STEFFENS: Following the mixed reviews that *Kaya* received in 1978, many saying Bob had "gone soft," Marley set out to make his most militant album ever, *Survival*, the only one until then with all-new songs. It was a profound statement of his mature philosophy, turning away from the meet-fire-with-fire urgings of *Natty Dread* to a realization that if the world were going to change, that change must begin with the individual, and the only way to do that was through the healing power of Love, One Love, I and I.

To mix the album, he called upon Errol Brown, one of Jamaica's unsung heroes of the mixing board. Brown had experimented with dub instrumental effects around the same time of King Tubby's early efforts. His career began with his uncle, Duke Reid, founder of major local label Treasure Isle. He went on to work with producer Sonia Pottinger and others, recording a veritable Who's Who of Jamaican musical giants. He joined Bob Marley in 1979 as he was recording his *Survival* masterpiece.

ERROL BROWN: In 1979 I got a call from Marcia Griffiths. She had told me, "Errol, anywhere you go, I'm coming there with you. Nobody can record me like you." Marcia said that Bob Marley wanted to meet me, and to meet him at 56 Hope Road at Tuff Gong. And I go there and I walk in the record shop and while Marcia and I were talking, Bob walks in and asks, "Marcia, who is this brother?" And Marcia say, "Bob, you know the engineer what I talked about, my engineer, this is him, Errol Brown from Treasure Isle." And Bob, with a cheeky smile, said, "Yeah? Nice, nice to meet you," and he shake my hand. Next he said he have a new console in his studio and have an engineer in the hotel waiting because the sound not right in there. That is Alex Sadkin, he was there to work on this new album and can't start 'cause there's no bass in the room. So I went in and lift up the cover off the console. I was frightened! That was the challenge I had to go through. Anyway, I told him I had some two-track tapes that I mixed some songs on at Treasure Isle. I drove out, went for the tapes, played them and definitely didn't hear no bass—and trust me, any song I mix have bass. Something definitely wrong. I said to Bob, "Let's try some JBL woofers. By the next morning, new speakers came. The studio engineer, Chaio, replaced the woofers with the new ones—still no bass. The speakers looked perfect flush in the wall, that's how the studio was built, so I suggested to Bob, nervously of course, "You know something, I think we should take these speakers out of the wall and try to build something up, make them face me, make them come over the console toward me." To my surprise, he call a carpenter from out in the back with some two-by-two and make some stands right across up there above the glass. Thank God it worked. What happened, they designed the control room with no riser. Chaio build a platform after, so the bass was going behind the console. I guess from that day Bob had confidence in me. As they say, the first impression is the best.

So I became the assistant engineer to Alex Sadkin on the *Survival* album. Alex was hired by Chris Blackwell to do the *Survival* album. So though I was the engineer for the studio, I was the assistant to him.

COLIN LESLIE: Between Bob and Chris Blackwell now there was very, very positive mutual respect. Bob would always listen carefully to what Chris had in terms of ideas, and vice versa. It was reciprocal. I remember once there was a meeting scheduled in Miami, where Bob was at the time. Chris was flying from his base in Nassau to meet Bob. Chris missed his flight and he got a later flight. When he got to Miami, Bob was at the airport, still waiting for him. So that would give you an idea of what mutual respect they had for each other.

ROGER STEFFENS: *Survival* featured a song written by Sangie Davis called "Wake Up And Live." In late summer of 2006, Sangie and reggae great Joseph "Culture" Hill visited the Reggae Archives. Davis, who had been a staff producer at Tuff Gong, revealed that he was the composer of the unreleased gems "Babylon Feel This One," a dub-plate commissioned for the Twelve Tribes Sound System, and "She Used To Call Me Da Da." For years, as part of my "Life of Bob Marley" multimedia presentations, I had been telling people that "Da Da" was written by Bob about Cindy Breakspeare. This was the story told me by a Wailers band member who had given me the tape in 1988, but, said Sangie, "It isn't about anybody at all. It's just something I made up."

Sangie was given credit on the original *Survival* cover for cowriting "Wake Up and Live." He received a small payment upon the album's release in 1979, but nothing since. His name has been removed from the credits on all subsequent pressings.

During our rollicking afternoon together, Sangie and Joe reminisced about their early days in Kingston, keeping us in stitches. The most surprising revelation was that one of Bob's most militant songs was inspired by a popular Jamaican morning-after remedy. Sangie recounted how, at the end of February 1978, a few days after Bob's return from his fourteen-month exile, his wife woke him from a deep slumber. "Sangie!" she called. "There's somebody outside who keeps shouting your name." Clad in his pajamas, Sangie opened the gate, to discover Bob Marley standing there beside a yellow VW bus. "Ras-tafari!" Sangie yelled, and embraced his friend. "You get your taxi license yet, Sangie?" asked Bob. "Yeah, mon, just two days ago." "Mek you come and drive me nuh." And the two roared off down the road, heading to Nine Mile despite Sangie's casual ensemble.

"So, wha' you a write?" Bob wanted to know. "Well, brother" said

Sangie, "me have this lickle tune but me not have no chorus yet." So he began to sing a song about how life is one big road with lots of signs, and not to complicate your mind and put your vision to reality. "But I don't have a hook for it yet." After repeating the verse five or six times, they found themselves passing the factory of Andrews Liver Salts, which was dominated by a giant billboard for their product. "What's that?" I asked. Culture laughed and said, "That's for when you stay out all night and, you know, get over hang." "Him mean hangover," laughed Sangie.

"And up there," Sangie continued, "on the top of the sign, with a drunk guy on the left and the guy 'cured' on the right, were huge letters saying, 'Wake Up and Live!'"

"And they had this commercial," said Joseph, as Sangie started to sing it, sounding tired and tipsy. "Bwoi me party haaaaaahd last night!" And, in another voice, "What you tek?" And the hungover fellow says, "Andrews Liver Salts." And then, all languid and syrupy, Joseph drawls their slogan, "Nooooo spooooooon neeeee-ded."

The song itself was destined to be one of Bob's final anthems, designed for show- or set-ending crowd-skanking sing-alongs, especially in its extended admonishment to "RISE!! Ye mighty people!"

When the recordings were completed, Neville Garrick took on the job of designing the cover.

NEVILLE GARRICK: *Survival* was the one I liked the most, and that was the one they promoted the least. It was originally called *Black Survival*. The decision to remove "Black" from the title, I think it really came from all of us for commercial reasons in one way—that *Black Survival* might alienate people, saying that, "Well then, it's a record only for black people so we're not gonna buy it." OK? So, it was for me, now, to still say "Black Survival" without writing the words. That was my concept of saying "Africa Unite" by using all the independent flags of Africa on the cover. Then I said, "How do I represent Jamaica, and Trinidad, and the black people in America and Brazil? Which flags do you use for that?" Then I said, "But we all left through slavery." So the slave ships represent the blacks outside of Africa.

On the back cover we have the Wailers cooking over a rock fire. This was survival—some people cooking and getting ready in army fatigues really. Yeah, this is more than aircraft mechanics or army fatigues. Fancy themselves probably as parachutists, and they were cooking. Basically they were saying a survival scene. They're getting some food, and then they're going out to fight.

The object that looks like a beehive is not a beehive. This is the ruins—this is what is called Zimbabwe. This is the original town of Zimbabwe. Many people who go to Africa say black people couldn't build things like this, it was too intricate. The Romans, the Phoenicians passed through and taught them, or something like that. There is one of the wonders of Zimbabwe. You have to see this when you go down. So this is the Zimbabwe ruins. And beneath, there is a Masai warrior and his wife, and actually this is from the first painting that I ever really sold in California, to the director of the Afro-American Studies Center, Arthur Simms. It was from this. It was for me like pulling it from the past and dropping it there. And the next image was His Majesty during the Italian invasion in Ethiopia—His Majesty behind the machine gun really showing resistance. And on the top is the symbol of the OAU—Africa Unite. And the next is a shot of Bob Marley from the *Rastaman Vibration* campaign.

JUDY MOWATT: The *Survival* album is precious to me because if you listen to the lyrical contents on that title song it tells you everything that is happening in the world, the system that we're up against. It expresses everything that is happening, and how we should be guided. Like, Bob declares in the song, "In this world that hold lifelong insecurity, nuclear misenergy." And it's a world that forces lifelong insecurity. And then you can really see why the people are on so much drugs, why some people just decide to kill, because they are insecure. Is a world that forces lifelong insecurity, and then he goes along to tell you the detours from that type of life, and shows you where you can find peace and where you can find your outlet for your everlasting freedom.

ROGER STEFFENS: With the album completed, the group embarked on an ambitious thirty-two-show late autumn tour of North America. This included a four-night stand at Harlem's legendary Apollo Theater, upon whose stage Marcus Garvey had once preached, making it a very special event for Marley personally. The tour ended on December 15 in Nassau, Bahamas, with the Year of the Rasta Child concert.

At the end of 1979, my new partner Hank Holmes and I had just begun the *Reggae Beat* show on KCRW, and Bob Marley was our first musical guest. [Jeff Walker, his former publicist, had been our first industry guest a few weeks before.] We had been on the air a mere six weeks and were then the only reggae show in L.A., so Bob's publicity people asked if Hank and I would "mind going on the road with Bob" for two weeks. I was beside myself with excitement.

The first show turned out to be a disappointment. Stuck in the upper tiers of the cavernous, echoing Pauley Pavilion, UCLA's cavernous basketball arena, we couldn't even make out the songs that Bob was playing, so distorted was the sound. He still had the presence, though, that was obvious—especially when a huge, burly man jumped onstage from the audience and fell on his belly, holding tightly to Bob's legs. For what seemed the longest time, no one did anything, until finally security guards pulled the man off and hustled him outside.

The next show was in San Diego, and Hank and I rode down the coast on the bus through Babylon with Bob. Don Taylor, Marley's manager (with whom he seemed to be in constant argument), told all the reporters present not to talk to Bob because "he needs to rest." Imagine the mix of feelings when Bob came toward us and sat opposite, one aisle back.

As we drove out of L.A. some kind of dispute broke out between Bob and Taylor. "Drive your Benz, Taylor," Bob spat. Down the aisle came Taylor, leaning into him: "Bob, don't embarrass me in front of the press." Bob sneered and repeated, "Drive your Benz!" Bob was mocking Taylor's flaunting of the wealth he had gained through managing Bob.

The pressures upon Bob were readily apparent, and you can see the stress on his face in many of Bruce Talamon's pictures in our book *Spirit Dancer*. The cancer was coursing unchecked through his bloodstream, eventually finding new homes in his lungs and brain, and he seemed a shell of the man we had met the year before. I remember we drove by San Clemente, and I pointed out Nixon's house, on a bluff surrounded by enormous signal towers and a shabby helipad. Bob's only comment was, "What year him president?"

That evening's venue proved to be another disappointment, as the bass bounced off the boards of the San Diego Sports Arena, and I despaired of ever hearing Bob in decent surroundings. It was the problem of his becoming so big: small clubs were mostly out of the question now. But the audience seemed pleased with the show. On the way home, the band jammed in the back of the bus, guitarist Al Anderson beating time with drumsticks on the bathroom door. I remember writing an article for the new L.A. *Weekly* about the trip, and commenting that the band members and touring party seemed a surprisingly healthy lot by rock and roll standards, eating only ital food and pausing often, mid-puff, to give thanks and praises to Selassie I. When we got back to L.A. the straight-looking middle-aged bus driver told me that he loved driving Marley "because every time the band gets off the bus, I get to sweep up, and they leave behind about a half a pound of roaches!"

A few days later Bob played what would prove to be his final show in L.A., a benefit for the Sugar Ray Robinson Foundation at the Roxy. We were invited along for the sound check, and Hank and I and our wives sat virtually alone in the club for three hours while Bob played all the instruments and Family Man Barrett went up into the little sound booth just above the stage and balanced everything. I was impressed by a new tune that he was working on, something about redemption, which he sang over and over and over again that day. Think of it: five months into a world tour, assuredly a superstar, Bob still managed the sound check almost all by himself, painstakingly ensuring that everything would be perfect for this important audience of music business and Hollywood heavies. It would be the last time I ever saw him.

CHAPTER 30

From the Apollo to Gabon

ROGER STEFFENS: *Survival* was released in late 1979 to mixed reviews. A New York reviewer called it "the album of the year," another pronounced it "a triumph, with Bob's best material in years." Yet many British reviewers were fierce in their denunciation, using words like "undynamic" and "lethargic." Another said that Marley had "become another ageing rock star living off an illustrious past." Bob himself told a Philadelphia writer that it was the album he liked best, because its message was "more forceful." One of the album's biggest fans was John Lennon. Photographer Bob Gruen revealed that *Survival* was one of the only records the ex-Beatle played during his five-year house-husband exile in the Dakota building in New York. "Babylon system is the vampire," Bob sang with renewed vehemence, words far from the dismal pop of the end-of-decade rock world. Yet despite its brilliance, Island gave the record scant promotion, and its sales were not impressive.

To support the album, a tour was arranged, with the band expanding to nine members, now including a horn section, to broaden the sound for the larger venues the group was increasingly booking. The massive touring party provided an opportunity for some unscrupulous dealings among its members, particularly manager Don Taylor, who created a travel agency just so he could take an extra slice from the Wailers' airline tickets and other expenses.

Close observers on the 1979 tour noticed that Bob's energy seemed diminished; the strain of a life of constant motion, little sleep, and myriad pressures was evident. Meanwhile, the threat of cancer lurked in the shadows, unknown to all but his closest confidants.

Bob's tour-mate on *Survival*'s American dates was not a reggae artist. At the age of sixteen, American R & B child star Betty Wright had played in Jamaica with Byron Lee, King Stitt and Judy Mowatt. Nine years later, following her massive 1978 hit "Clean Up Woman," the Miami-born soul singer was chosen to open for Bob, who hoped she could draw a blacker audience to his shows. The fact that Don Taylor was her manager, taking a percentage of her fee each night, helped cement the gig for her.

BETTY WRIGHT: I was very familiar with Bob by the time I had heard his music. As a matter of fact, I was drenched with Bob Marley music because Noel Williams, who was a dear friend of mine at the time, who we call King Sporty, was a childhood friend of Bob's. And not only a comrade, but musician, friend, like a brother. And he always would re-record Bob's music. In those days, because there wasn't a real market in America for roots reggae, Sporty would put just a little bit of something else into the music and unlike playing straight-out reggae, he had reggae, but he had something different. I never really have been able to explain it in words. But when you compare songs, you hear Bob's and you hear Sporty's, but you know that Sporty's was geared to an American audience. And he'd cut the same records: "Concrete Jungle" and different ones. But it would always be a Bob Marley song.

Regarding my going on the road with Bob, let me say first of all that at the time I was very bronchial, as far as the smoke. So in order to get to my dressing room at the Apollo, what I used to do, I used to wet two towels and wrap them around my entire face and just try to breath through the towels to get upstairs. Because you know when you're at the Apollo and you're like the opening act, you're like on the hundredth floor. No, I mean, you're like the fifth floor! It's way up. And I had to pass through to get there. And smoke rises! And it came right up to

"Buffalo Soldier" composer and producer King Sporty at
his studio in Miami, February 1995.

me! So, I mean, I would be red-eyed and I'd be praying, I said, "Lord,
I can't breathe, and I need to sing," and I'd be choking. Eventually, one
night I prayed and I was like, "I'm gonna overcome this." And I just
prayed, I said, "Whatever the offense is in it, I gotta be around it. I'm
working, I'm gigging. Thanks be to God I have a job, and I'm gonna
learn to walk through this." And it didn't bother me anymore. It was

like I tuned it out. 'Cause it was more like I knew it was coming. It's like, you see smoke, it's like, "Here it comes." A cloud!

The band, they all were so friendly and so helpful to me, and the I Three—at the time Marcia I think was pregnant. But Rita and Judy, and everybody was just really getting along. And that's what I really loved about that tour. We had none of the bitter strife and envying that goes on on a lot of tours. But they were very, very kind, and I always believe that you get love and give love and some people don't have the capacity to give as much love as you. But I say we got love for love. And Bob began to open up more.

ROGER STEFFENS: The Apollo gigs ran over four nights in October 1979. Eight shows were scheduled, but only one was held on the opening night because of the chaos in the surrounding streets, with throngs seeking tickets.

BETTY WRIGHT: Bob was drawing an audience that I wanted to get to, and I was drawing an audience that he wanted to get to. And one of the places, the people cheered so loud the windows broke! Maple Leaf Garden in Toronto, a hockey rink, it was incredible.

The good part was, everyone was getting along, and Bob was really nice. You know, we'd sit down and he wanted to talk about him and Sporty when they were kids. And he began to tell me, "Talk to me about your man." And I thought he meant, talk to him about my husband at the time. And Bob said, "No, no, no, *your* man. Sporty is your man!" I said, "No-ooo-ooo. No! That's my friend! That's my friend." But what was happening, he was prophesying. Because he said that to me in '79. And then 1984, I began to date Sporty. And in '85 we were united. So, it was the most incredible prophecy.

After my set I'd stand by the speakers. I had never seen this before. To be on tour with Teddy Pendergrass was like watching women faint from the sexuality aspect. But I had never seen the power of a prophet mystify people and make them pass out. I stood by the speaker and he would point some kind of way with his finger and throw his head back and folks would faint! They would just be caught up, mystified. I'd look at the audience, and you find yourself getting caught up. I was trying not to watch Bob, I was trying to watch them. And if I ever looked at him, I could never look back at the audience, so I would purposely walk to the side of the speaker and begin to look at the audience. 'Cause once you looked, you're hooked. And he was so unrehearsed, almost want to say sloppy. Just fall out there, just mash up people. And I said this man is so bad, he is just tough, he just walk out there in that little fatigue, no flash, no jewelry, one little ring I think he wore on the middle finger. You know, nothin', man! No bombs bursting in air, no pigeons flying, people swinging from trees, just pure little music man. Music man! Jamming with his guitar, singing Zion song.

Bob lived to be a king. From very shabby, humble beginnings, but to be able to go and sing his songs all over the world. And I remember his energy. That dance! Oh!

ROGER STEFFENS: One inspiration for that boundless energy was discovered during the Apollo shows by hornsman Dave Madden. In his forthcoming memoir, fellow saxophonist Glen DaCosta described the devastating effects of Marley's private elixir.

GLEN DACOSTA: And then there was the matter of "Bob's special jug," which remains mysterious to me to this day. David Madden and myself, as hornsmen, we're always close buddies, and we'd share whatever we could whenever—food, whatever—and we got in late for a show and decided to raid the Wailers' fridge. So I had some orange juice (I think) but David went for the more, shall we say, "exciting" drink. It was Bob's jug of—whatever it was, I don't know. Something he took to get onstage, a blended drink especially prepared for Bob.

David had a glass full of Bob's drink and immediately realized it had a very negative effect on him. Onstage, David is always the most responsible and focused musician all the time. He's very thorough and he does a good job so when he was feeling the effects of the drink and told me, "Glen, if I'm making any mistakes tell me," I was truly shocked. I couldn't believe what was happening.

Then as we were playing, I realized that he was leaning on me. Apparently he couldn't stand on his own feet then and then I had to switch parts right there because he was playing very mildly instead. The boldness had gone out from his instrument.

After the show—that was at one of the early shows at the legendary Apollo Theater in Harlem, we had two shows that day—we would normally take like a half-hour break and come back to do the next show. That day we had to stay for over two hours because we had to lift David off the stage and we had to revive him with some very sweet sugar water. He laid flat on his back like a boxer that had just been knocked out, I'll never forget it. It's always a laugh when we remember it.

David learned his lesson and never touched Bob's juice again. For Bob it was OK, he could take it. I don't know what was in that jug, but I'm sure that some powerful ganja was there, or maybe some other mixture of some other drugs. I'm not into the drugs so I wouldn't know. But for it to have that kind of effect on David, it must have been some really special stuff.

ROGER STEFFENS: Sound mixer Karl Pitterson was impressed by Bob's keen control of his audiences while withstanding intense pain.

KARL PITTERSON: In 1979 I think Bob was going through a lot of unannounced suffering that he privately kept inside to himself. But I knew that something was going to happen, a year before Bob's collapse while we were on tour. I said it to Al Anderson, the guitar player, that hey, something is wrong, really wrong, because I could hear it in his voice. Like he would try to get to a certain note. It was one of the hardest things. But to the public they never realized it. Even though, when he would try and before it was really executed he would realize it and—whoops, don't think I'm going to make that note, so he would change. And I would notice that. That was just a telltale sign. That was a flag that was really waving that I saw, especially in that last year. I think he went through a lot of discomfort. A lot.

He was hyper and he was a very, very good singer. He knew stuff that certain artists keep secret, the way to deal with a crowd, like Michael Jackson.

ROGER STEFFENS: A month later, Betty Wright would be the conduit for an intriguing invitation that would bring Bob Marley and the Wailers to Africa.

BETTY WRIGHT: The story is, I, when I was about fifteen, I went on tour with James Brown. And I was introduced to Brown's business associate Charles Bobbitt about two years earlier. When we got to L.A. in '79, Bobbitt showed up and he says, "You know, I'm living in Africa now, I'm working for Omar Bongo. And he's the president of Gabon, Libreville," and telling me all about what he's doing. And I'm going, "What? What? When did you leave America?" And he says, "This is Pascaline and Albertine Bongo. They're real Bob Marley fans. They want to meet him." So we got them some passes to go in and meet Bob. They ended up being the best of friends. Their father had bought them a house I think on Foothill Road in Beverly Hills. And we had a massive party there, and they just rolled out the red carpet.

One of them had a birthday coming up. So they said, "Wonder if you guys would be available, 'cause we may ask my father to have you guys come over." And I thought, "Oh yeah, right, all of us, right?" Don't you know, they brought us to Gabon that January of 1980.

GILLY GILBERT: It was the daughters of President Bongo. They were acknowledging his work over the years. They were fascinated by Bob, and involved with his music, so they invited him over. We were there about a week. We stayed at a hotel named after a palace. Nice hotel.

BETTY WRIGHT: We did two nights, and all I can tell you is, it was the time of my life! Everything was just first-class. They rolled out tables of food. We were all in the palace. Everything, games, shopping, anything we wanted to do, Bob looked out for us. So this particular night they say, "You know, we own a disco." And I thought, whoa, what kind of disco in Africa, what is this gonna look like, 'cause some of the town was very, very rural. Baby, it was like they took it out of the heart of France, the whole decor was so nice. I haven't seen anything like it since. But we got up and started dancing to these songs, and Bob got up with his, you know, hitting the back of his heel and stuff, doing these dances. We danced all night, he had so much energy! We danced to all kinds of music! They had everything from America, they had African music, they had Bob's music. We were dancing to his songs at the time, like "Jamming"—we had fun!

GILLY GILBERT: I can remember traveling to the marketplace and mingling with the people. It seems to me that the folks treated us like royalty. They followed us everywhere we go; every step we took, they were right behind us. During that time we took on the road with us tapes, records, posters, and they went like hot bread. We were giving some away and selling some, just trying to pick up a vibe. People that was coming to the market just buy stuff off us. We bought collard greens, cabbages of various kinds. They cooked for us also at the hotel, African style.

ROGER STEFFENS: One afternoon they met with President Bongo in the royal palace, a scene described by Bruce Talamon, the photographer whom Bob had summoned to accompany him on the trip, as "looking like something straight out of the opening scenes of the Eddie Murphy movie *Coming to America.*" Gilly accompanied Bob and remembers two enormous doors opening to reveal Bongo on his throne.

GILLY GILBERT: We met him at his palace. He was attired in his robe and his ornaments. He talked to Bob about his music and his life, his country and his people. The trip was really for his kids, they were really the main focus of the trip—the Bongo sisters.

ROGER STEFFENS: Bob was most comfortable in spots like the marketplaces and the beach in front of the hotel. He welcomed all comers to his hotel room, and mingled freely with other early risers who strolled along the lapping waters of the Gabon estuary.

GILLY GILBERT: In the mornings we would walk on the beach. A lot of people came to see Bob and was around us. Mostly a lot of kids. They were waiting on us as we stepped out of the hotel. They were fascinated over our lifestyle and our music and Bob himself. They looked upon Bob as a king. They knew Bob's music, it was amazing, people so far off. Bob was so happy to be with his people and be spreading the word through his music and through his image of Rasta livity.

BRUCE TALAMON: One morning Bob was walking along the beach and this young man came up to him and challenged him: "What's this Rasta stuff? What do you mean coming to Africa, telling *us* about Africa?" The kid wanted him to tell them more. Bob took his time and explained to them about his excitement being there and also about the black diaspora, you and me are the same, I'm a black man from Jamaica, you're from Africa, we all come from Africa. Then he posed for some pictures with him, gathering soccer style like they were on a team together. I was so impressed by the symbolism of Bob standing there on the roots of a huge tree and being the teacher.

BETTY WRIGHT: Once we went market shopping with him. And I think we went looking for some fabric for the I Three. But most of the time when I was with Bob, like I would just watch him play what they call football, what we call soccer. Just out in the street, anywhere, 'cause Bob would take the ball out and play anywhere. So basically, he didn't do a lot of excursion kind of things. We did interviews, but they had events for us. Like at night they'd close a restaurant and we'd eat in there.

JUDY MOWATT: It was my very first time in Africa. I was expecting to see African people speaking in their own tongue, but then Gabon was a French territory, so they spoke French. I was hoping to see African people ruling their own destiny there, I wasn't expecting to see people—not that they are colonized, but they weren't free. There were people that were unemployed and there were people that were employed who were menially paid. Their wages were very, very low. And when I went to the marketplace, I saw the people, they didn't have refrigeration for their meat. And I saw their meat turn blue, and they were still selling it.

I think Bob stayed extra time, because going that far he would need to see what the country is like. I mean, you have seen one side of it, you need to see the other part of it, you need to interact with your own people. The streets. The people were so happy to see him. Bob is always communicating, and he's always giving them fatherly advice. He's always asking them questions, so he was able to say a lot with the street people. He had young people with him who spoke English.

Gabon was beautiful, yes. But we never got to play in a large stadium where all the people could come out and see us. We performed for the King and the King's daughters in a small stadium and all the elites were there. And it disturbed us because our people, who we are really appealing to, they weren't able to come and see us.

ROGER STEFFENS: Danny Sims's brother Eddie, a prominent record executive, was also a member of Bob's party.

EDDIE SIMS: We were there for their holidays, about ten days. The president was running for office again, and he was the only one running. It was really strange. Otherwise, it was an interesting country. I got a chance to run around the markets and the ocean where the slaves used to be sent to here. Rich country—poor, but rich, with timber and all that stuff. We went to the nightclub at night and had a good time. They played mostly American music, and Bob Marley music. But what really stressed me, though, I was in the club and ordered a Coca-Cola and Coca-Cola was seven dollars American money. We said, wait a minute, how do these people afford this, especially these people who live there who have very little money. Most of the money in the country is from the people who got these jobs, who's running the government and who's running the big companies and who's running the industries. Which is cool. They put us in a five-star hotel, guards around us every night with shotguns and AK-47s, guarding the hotels.

We played in the state soccer field, and I was jogging around the compound and came around the corner of these buildings and I saw these kids lying on the ground. Police officers and soldiers had a long stick with a big round ball on the end of it, hard like a knot from a tree, and they take like a little whip and they was popping these kids upside the head, sounded like a watermelon being crushed. So I said boy, let me get out of here. I shot back up to the stage and I said, don't you guys go over to that corner there. That's not nice. The kids was jumping over the fence, they had no money. It's like anywhere else, people try to get in for free.

ROGER STEFFENS: It was during the Gabon trip that Bob discovered irregularities that led to Don Taylor's dismissal as his manager.

BETTY WRIGHT: I would always say, what is done in the dark always comes to the light. What happened with that situation was, we had received a phone call from Mr. Bobbitt [her friend who had worked with James Brown] in America and he came to take care of whatever business was to be taken care of. And we met him—myself, Don Taylor's wife, I think her name was April—to pick up said monies for the job. And like any other job, you get to have your money up front, and then you go. But, unknown to Bob, there was a situation of some airplane tickets. The story has it that the travel agency was even owned by the same set of people [Taylor]. And the prices were real different from what they were supposed to be. Everything was like kicked right back into the same hand. So there was a statement made, in just like casual talking where somebody was saying, "God, Bob has almost three times as many people as Betty, but she's making almost as much money as Bob!" I said, "No, I'm not. He's making three times what I'm making." You know, without giving figures. I knew that! Because I know I picked up my half, and they picked up their half. But it was told to Bob that there was no other half. That it was just what he was picking up. So I don't know who the exact culprits were, but on the nice side I tried to get it dispelled with. My allegiance was to Mr. Bobbitt who I knew all my life. And I said, "I can't allow this to go forward like it's going when I know the truth! If they ask me, I'm not going to stand up there and lie. And I don't have no fear. What are they going to do, beat me up, you know what I'm saying? No, you got that money. I was standing there. Your wife, you signed, you got it." And Mr. Bobbitt was explaining to me that they were trying to make it look like he was not taking care of his end of the business. I went to who I thought could get the message to Bob. Eventually, I just had to go direct. And when they checked it out, they found out I was telling the truth. Because I'm an entertainer, and we work hard, and how dare someone try to take it. They called me, I was like the third confirmation, because different people knew the story. But what they wanted to know was, who was in America at that time that knew. Someone had already, you know how beans spill. But I could not lie.

So Bob asked me. He knew that this was my friend, he knew how he had met the girls, Pascaline and Albertine; he knew the whole situation. And he knew that if anybody's going to tell the truth, it's going to be Betty. He knew that I was a minister, he knew that my first allegiance is to God Almighty.

ROGER STEFFENS: Betty had uncovered a plot to rob Marley of his proper fee. Soon rumors began that Don had been roughed up by members of Bob's entourage, and actually hung out a window in an attempt to get him to confess his perfidy.

BETTY WRIGHT: I heard that Taylor got a beating. I heard that there was a gallon of milk poured over his head or something. I wasn't up there. I was in the hotel, but I didn't go on the floor, because I heard it was a ruckus. And I knew that certain things had transpired, but see, that was like the fuse was already lit. That was just like, hey! It was inevitable.

Taylor did fly back with us. I just have to compare it. Going over he was like real catty and stuff, but going back he was real quiet. He was very demoted. I heard about the fight while we had a layover at this hotel, the Novotel in France. They were talking about it. They just said that nobody's going to steal anything from Bob. How hard Bob works. And that Taylor should have come clean. You know, just basically the same thing that I thought. They kept saying he got what was coming to him.

Since then, I've talked to Don. You know, we kick it. I don't know if he ever came to grips with that, but that's what really happened.

ROGER STEFFENS: I interviewed Don Taylor at the Reggae Archives in 1988. He offered a revealing comment about Bob's character that indirectly reflects on the controversy.

DON TAYLOR: Bob is a man that sifted out people. For instance, Bob would have one girl, and he would try to get all her friends in line. But the thing is that the minute they allow themselves to be manipulated he lost respect for them. There's nothing else there. That's how he'd work. Bob was always trying to be. And you see, Bob was the kind of guy who played stupid, but was one of the most intelligent, wisest persons that I ever dealt with. He's the only artist that takes three days to count tour receipts after you give it to him.

ROGER STEFFENS: Taylor's alleged machinations weren't what ended the trip, however.

EDDIE SIMS: We had a nice time and we were enjoying ourselves up to a certain point. And that was the point we had a little altercation and we had to leave.

ROGER STEFFENS: Donnice Sims is Danny Sims's sister. She was a member of the party that went to Gabon with Bob, doing wardrobe, mostly for Betty Wright.

DONNICE SIMS: I remember being evicted from the country over herb. It wasn't everybody; it was one particular guy, who was our guide. One day we said, come on, let's get a bus. And we all went out in the wild and drove through and stopped. All the Rastas, Bob, everybody went. And the way the Rastas smoke those big things—the guide wasn't trying to be a smoker. You can't even see in front of you because of the smoke. So I'm sure he had that. Then he had some kind of stuff that we pulled off at the side and the smoke was coming off the bottle. They were making it, and Bob and them loved it. And they were so happy, they got off the bus and the people welcomed all the Rastas and Bob. It was a big thing. And the guide had some of that, whatever that was. I know he smoked, 'cause when he got back he was going up and down, the music was going, he went from being introverted and dignified to a "Yes! Whoop! Ras-ta-mon!!" And he got into an altercation with the police and he hit them and they asked him if he'd been smoking. And the next thing we know, there's heavy knocking on the door. "Get out! Get out! Get out!" We were like, "What? What?" I don't know if it was early morning or late at night, we had to get out. "But we have to do a concert," we said. We couldn't do the concert. They threw us out, because they don't allow any kind of drugs. That's not something that they do. They had a bus and they drove us to the airport right up to the plane and made all these schoolgirls, I think they were going back to Sweden or London or somewhere, but they made them get off and made us get on. I don't know if all of us got totally into the plane. But the next thing I know is that they told us we had to come back because they were having a riot because Bob wasn't going to be there and there were all these people at the stadium waiting for Bob. But they had to set an example and said we don't have none of this smoking and stuff around here. But to Bob and them, that wasn't a crime, that was part of their religious culture.

And so then we got back on the bus. And we drove into a crowd of zillions of people. I had never seen anything like it. And they were cheering and everything. So when the bus came in we run into a mob—all I know is that we had one of those huge school buses, and the crowd was banging, "Bob Marley! Bob Marley!" And the bus was rocking, we went all the way down and then all the way back. It was all those people pounding, you know how they could turn over something with the force of people? Next thing I know he was up on the stage.

Everybody came back. It was night by the time we got back. And all of these people were looking through the windows. It was a frightening experience. But they were trying to show their gratitude and their love. But you know how people get happy after soccer games and they start riots? It was near a frenzy. And Bob was just calm, smiling away. It's amazing, because what are you going to do? I mean, it's a good lesson. I try to practice that. It doesn't work too much, but I do. Because what can you do?

In Gabon Bob was very, very happy to be there. I would see him early in the morning, because he could get up very early. And he was very, very kind. We were in a five-star hotel, the best that they had, and the people that were there were just very, very, very poor. And many of them had never seen an inside toilet. And they [their hosts] were ready to see us go because Bob would bring them up. [Mimicking Bob:] "They're with me! They're with me! C'mon, c'mon." So we'd be marching through this beautiful lobby with people with no shoes, dirty feet. And they'd bring them into the room and give them clothes. I don't think we left with too much of anything, because we gave so much out. I remember having breakfast with Bob a lot in the morning. We'd just sit there and look at each other and smile. He'd always have a big thing of fruit.

But he didn't look at them as having so much poverty, because they had so much wealth in the natural resources. Even with all of the property that was there, the people did not usually come to that area where we were. They heard Bob Marley was there. But they wouldn't dare come near that hotel and hang around that type of hotel. That would not be their stomping grounds. But thanks to Bob they came into the hotel, and they'd look around with their eyes wide, looking at everything. It was like he was giving them a tour of the hotel. And they would rub his hair.

ROGER STEFFENS: Marley was disappointed that he was playing mainly for President Bongo's cronies, the special people who had the pull to get into his concerts. What he really wanted was to get out to the people at large.

DONNICE SIMS: Oh absolutely, because those were the people that were out there, banging on that bus. That's what he wanted to do. And that was when Don Taylor got hung out the window. Because Bob, that was the last thing on his mind is to take some money. And if that were the case, I know, I'm sure his mind was saying, "If that's the case, I would have done it for the people. I would have done it for free." He wouldn't have to get paid.

CHAPTER 31

Natty Mash It inna Zimbabwe

ROGER STEFFENS: Marley's trip to Gabon had been instructive, if unsettling, but his most triumphant return to the motherland was yet to come.

Bob's three excursions to Africa—to Kenya and Ethiopia in 1978, to Gabon in 1980 and to Zimbabwe the same year—gave him a much clearer picture of the fabled continent. His determination to move to Africa grew. Privately he told Dessie Smith and Yvette Anderson, "Our duty is to build a blood-claat studio inna Africa, have hit after blood-claat hit, then we number one, then we laugh!"

During this period Dr. Gayle McGarrity continued to give him insight into the wave of political insurrection happening in the 1970s throughout Africa.

GAYLE McGARRITY: By the time I went to Cuba it was already known, the role of the Cuban military in supporting the Ethiopian military. So I remember Bob saying that he used to think that Cuba was really a great place, and that they had eliminated capitalism, and blah blah blah, but they clearly were doing the Devil's work now, because they had this role in Ethiopia. And thus a kind of struggle began between Bob and me, with me trying to tell him the positive things of socialism and him being more and more convinced of the negative. And also the fact that he saw Communism as godless and that it was an "ism"—you know, his whole thing about Rasta don't deal with ism. So that whole thing of Marxism and socialism he was very against. So I would continue to try and talk to him.

I also introduced him to someone who he became very close to. I had dated a Rhodesian guy in England called Joe Steblecki. We dated for a long time. His father was a Polish aristocrat and his mother was a colored woman from Rhodesia. And I met him in London in '72. Joey was madly in love with me and I remember when I said goodbye to him in London, I gave him my address and phone number and the next thing I knew, I had been in Jamaica a week and he called me from the airport, he was in Jamaica. I wasn't particularly interested in him anymore and I didn't know quite what to do with him, but I remember taking him over to Bob and them instantly getting to be very close, and Joe teaching Bob a whole lot of stuff about the realities of southern Africa. Because at that time Bob was very interested in South Africa and the anti-apartheid movement and Africans liberating Zimbabwe. I think that came out in "Africa Unite"—that's definitely after he met Joe, because he talked to Joe a whole lot and I remember long reasonings when we'd go over there. I would be present and, as I say, as long as it didn't get into the Cuban role in things, Bob was all in favor of it. But whenever it came up that the Cubans were helping the black South Africans or the Zimbabweans, he would get very upset and say that couldn't be because of what they'd done in Ethiopia.

ROGER STEFFENS: One of the greatest moments in Bob's career came when he was invited to headline the independence celebrations in Zimbabwe in April 1980. Known as Southern Rhodesia when under the colonial control of Britain, the country, under a white-minority government, declared itself independent in 1965 as Rhodesia. A lengthy civil war continued until 1980, when the independent nation of Zimbabwe was declared. Robert Mugabe's faction invited Marley to headline the formal turnover of control on April 18. Marley's song "Zimbabwe," though banned, had become a rallying cry among the freedom fighters. Bob paid the way for his troupe and for the costs of a stage, lighting and sound, but stayed busy on his new album right up to the last minute before departure.

ERROL BROWN: I can remember in Jamaica working on "Could You Be Loved" right to daylight, went home and packed and head to the airport. We had to go to England and from England we go to Zimbabwe.

NEVILLE GARRICK: I think Bob's financing the whole trip to Zimbabwe is one of the biggest things he ever showed in his commitment money-wise, that a lot of people still don't really talk about it all the time, 'cause it was kind of amazing to me. It's not like at that time he was no millionaire or anything, but I think he felt a commitment that—I think basically him said to me, like, my baby gonna be born and I haffe be there, can't cause no stillbirth or nothing like that. Because we were invited but what they sent us was like an invitation for two people. They said that's what they could afford, because of what these independence celebrations cost in bringing people in from all over the world. Some people say Bob spent $250,000 to go there, but it was more like $90,000 if I remember correctly. We didn't bring the stage, we built the stage there. What Bob basically said is that, when we checked out what they had, Bob say him want to perform like he was performing at Madison Square Garden, so we rented lights and sound and all that was on one plane. That was how we were able to do the second free concert the next day, because we had all the equipment there, we're paying for it, we're paying for the plane on the tarmac. He didn't donate that to Zimbabwe. That's a rental! That would have been a quarter of a million dollars right there, all that rigging. No, he just wanted to perform on the same kind of level that he performed in Europe and America. He didn't want to give Africa a show like under a streetlight with some floodlights!

ROGER STEFFENS: The person who shepherded Bob throughout his stay in Zimbabwe was Dera Tompkins, a fiery, dreadlocked American Rasta woman who had met the Wailers in the mid-1970s during her research into Jamaican religion, culture and music. But it wasn't until 1979, at the Black Music Association convention in Philadelphia, that she and Bob began to reason heavily. A medical librarian at a national institute, she was an adviser to Bob's cancer team and an unofficial host of his Zimbabwe entourage. Her father had been active in the movement to free the country, and he invited her to join him at the independence celebrations. Her testimony here is adapted from an interview we did at her home in Washington, D.C., in 1988 for *The Beat*, in which she tells the most complete story of events.

DERA TOMPKINS: I was in different places with the Wailers and I was invited to come tour. Sometimes I would come meet them in New York, and I would move with them. I was there for the four days in Harlem at the Apollo, the International Year of the Rasta Child show in Kingston, Reggae Sunsplash '79 in Montego Bay, Madison Square Garden. And of course Zimbabwe.

Historian and activist Dera Tompkins in Washington, D.C., with a banner from Zimbabwe's 1980 independence celebrations.

My story has its roots in an uptown church in Roxbury, Massachu-setts, my hometown. It was called St. Mark's and there was a council that sends ministers to different congregations. Many people were fair-skinned in our church. They sent us a brother from home. The people in church were not pleased. He was dark-skinned and he was from a place they probably never heard of, Rhodesia.

My father was a radical. He looked white at a distance, but he was not white at all. He was very black, and my father was my political guide, how I got where I am. He was a pan-Africanist socialist, very progres-sive throughout his life. The African minister, the Reverend Mazobere, and my father struck up a strong friendship, visiting prisons, attending the sick. But three years before Rhodesia's transformation into Zimba-bwe, the Reverend Mazobere returned home to contribute to the final struggle. My dad took out his first adult passport and prepared to join him. But I convinced him to wait until the war was over. When, in January 1980, it was announced that independence celebrations would take place on April 18, my father called and said, "Dera, do you want to go home?" And I said, "Yes! You kidding? We're going to go to Africa!"

ROGER STEFFENS: When they arrived, the week before the festivities, Dera found Reverend Mazobere to be a staunch supporter of Joshua Nkomo, whose ally in the civil war, Robert Mugabe, was now his politi-cal rival and was to be the nation's first prime minister. So the good reverend decided he'd boycott the festivities, opting to watch them on a little black-and-white TV. Dera gathered her robes around her and high-tailed it to downtown Harare (actually still called Salisbury, for a few more days), where her dreadlocks caused her to be mistaken for Rita Marley. She had brought ten copies of Bob's African liberation album, *Survival,* with her as gifts, thinking that it would be new to everyone.

DERA TOMPKINS: Instead, when I got off the plane, very soon I found out that *Survival* was the number one album in the country. And number two was Eddy Grant's—he had a revolutionary song, "Living On The Front Line." Those two songs were the unofficial anthems of independent Zimbabwe! So they did know about the albums and the music, but nobody knew about Rasta, really. The energy on the streets and in the homes was electric, like a thousand Christmases celebrated at one time. We had flags! The red, black, green and yellow flags of the new nation of Zimbabwe were everywhere. It was Zimbabwe and that sounded and felt just right. We had won a seven-year war and endured many more years of wicked colonial oppression. Now we were going to have the biggest African Liberation party we could have. We won in Zimbabwe! Their guns were greater but our cause was greater than their guns. We chased those crazy baldheads out of town!

When I say it was like Christmas, I mean that there was just pure excitement all day everywhere. The people of Zimbabwe chant. They sing beautiful a cappella songs wherever they may be gathered. The streets were always full of music. Every day there were bands playing in the city center and the schoolchildren would come to town after school in their uniforms to join the daily celebrations. Their parents were busy shopping for new clothes, food, fabric and decorations—hats, posters and flags, banners that were fluttering everywhere in the city that said "Welcome to Zimbabwe" with pictures of Mugabe hand-painted. But the flag was the more important, representing to us that we had our country and our land back in the hands of our people. It was "Viva Zimbabwe! Long Live Zimbabwe!"

When I learned that Bob was coming, it was just too fantastic to be believed. At the invitation of ZANU, Mugabe's party! It was as if Jah had interceded to place his son just where he was supposed to be on this great African Liberation day. The street excitement grew into a wild and joyful frenzy.

I was at the airport when Bob arrived on April 16, at the same time Prince Charles's plane landed. Some officials were there, but most of the top officials were present to greet Prince Charles. There were not many members of the public there to meet Bob because Bob's arrival time was not publicly announced.

AL ANDERSON: Prince Charles and Bob met briefly in a transit lounge. The Prince wanted to know where Bob got his sneakers.

GILLY GILBERT: The entire revolutionary cabinet met us at the airport in Harare. When we stepped off the plane, they said, "Welcome home, brother!" They took Bob in a jeep and paraded him all over and the people yelled "Viva Bob Marley! Viva Mugabe!"

DERA TOMPKINS: The Wailers were a bit suspicious at my unexpected appearance far from home. I'm certain that everyone wondered if I was really an agent. This was, of course, an incredible coincidence for all of us. During the bus ride from the airport, I was able to tell my story and all fears were calmed.

The entourage included the band: Bob, Tyrone, Wya, Family Man, Carly, Al, Junior, Seeco, the soundman Dennis Thompson, Judy, Rita, Marcia, sons Stephen, about to turn eight, and ten-year-old Ziggy, Tommy Cowan, lighting director Neville Garrick, Jamaican lawyer Donna McIntosh and Island Records' Denise Mills. First we were taken to Rufaro Stadium, because Bob wanted to see the stage. That was in the afternoon. While we all stood on the slope of a hill inside of the stadium beside the stage, we heard beautiful chanting and the sound of people marching coming from the outside of the stadium to the right. It sounded like an African choir. At first, we could only hear the voices because the stadium bleachers blocked our view. The voices drew closer and closer and soon the entire group rounded the corner. All eyes were watching. The officials at the stadium told us that they were the ZANU freedom fighters arriving at the stadium for practice. They were singing *chimurenga* songs, songs of the revolutionary war. There was one soldier out front who led the chanting. The marching was strictly African, rhythm and style.

They were at least three hundred strong, brothers and sisters. It is important to note that the women of Zimbabwe have the maximum respect of the people because they fought the guerrilla war in the bush side by side with their brothers for all the years of the revolution. They all wore green army fatigue pants with different solid-color shirts in the colors of the new flag: red, green, yellow and black. And when you heard them chant, you know that it was songs of freedom! And we all collectively felt so unbelievably proud. These are the brothers and sisters who put their life on the line for all of us. Frontline soldiers. They were the reason we all could be standing there today. We owed everything to them.

I turned to look at Bob, who was standing beside me, and he was staring directly at the soldiers and he had tears in his eyes. I knew exactly how he felt. These were tears of the deepest and highest respect from one committed freedom fighter to another. This moment touched my soul. I cried too. I don't know if you understand in Rasta how much we look up to our freedom fighters. There's just an overwhelming sense of pride and respect. We all had that. But I saw him cry, and it was because he loved revolution and he loved revolutionaries. Because he was really like them, he identified with them, he's one of them, and he just felt it. He was captivated by the presence of an African army. It was the first time he had seen a revolutionary African army: the ZANU Patriotic Front. These were the people who fought and won this war for us. So you could really see that in him. He was very proud. I will always keep that moment in my mind and heart.

After that we were taken to a hotel that was twelve miles outside of the city, the only available hotel space for the number of rooms required. The accommodations were substandard. Everyone was disappointed and soon we were rerouted back to the city.

ERROL BROWN: When we got there from England they took us to some village, lot of people running up and down there. There was no safety in that place, outside bathroom. So the group say we can't stay here, and that's when they took us to an international hotel with nuff security.

DERA TOMPKINS: From there, everyone got taken to a nightclub owned by an entrepreneur named Job. They took us there to eat—and they served pork! Our hosts did not know the dietary restrictions for Rasta against pork, and took the appetizers off the table immediately. When Job learned that the hotel situation had failed, he offered his own home complete with pool and house help, while he stayed in the city. The only thing was, his phone had been disconnected. It appeared that Job was in the black upper class. And this is where everyone had to stay until hotel rooms were available. But it was a really strange situation for the Wailers to be in. I mean, this is Bob Marley! We are in a home where no one knew the address, with no phone, and no one attending the group other than the house help.

Now I became a vital link to the group—this is my special story—because when they arrived, they were taken from place to place so nobody had time to change their money to Rhodesian dollars. They didn't even know what the exchange rate was. I had Rhodesian dollars because I had been there a week.

There was invariably a Jamaican posse in each of the cities that Bob played, to give him a back-home vibe, but in Harare there was only one Jamaican, Joe Steblecki, who was living there. Horace Campbell, who wrote *Rasta and Resistance,* was there. And me. That was the whole "team." They took some of the Wailers to another house that was vacant in the same neighborhood. The I Three and Bob, Tommy, Denise and Neville and a few others stayed at Job's. The I Three only stayed two days. They had promised to be at a Twelve Tribes performance back in Jamaica, so they stayed for independence and left.

ERROL BROWN: It was the first time I mixed Bob live. That experience was great. You know, all of that equipment is Bob Marley carried them. He paid everything, shipping, everything. When we arrived to the stadium there was no stage. Bob freak out, after he went through all of these things—everything is Bob Marley, his contribution—lights, sound, plane tickets. Next thing we know, stage come and everything start late but we get through. Finally they built the stage and we did it.

DERA TOMPKINS: On Independence Day, from six o'clock that night up until about eleven, on the field there were performances by mostly local African traditional dancers and drummers, Indian religious groups and Christian choirs. Then, in a flash, Marley took stage at the far end of the field, declaring, "Greetings brothers and sisters of Zimbabwe. Bob Marley and the Wailers give thanks for the invitation to your independence celebration. One Love. Rastafari. Yeah, Rastafari live! Viva Zimbabwe! Viva Zimbabwe! Viva Zimbabwe!"

As he broke into "Positive Vibration," the crowd began to sway to the groove, swaying joyfully into "Them Belly Full" and "Roots Rock Reggae." Suddenly, halfway through "I Shot The Sheriff," the stench of tear gas filled the air. I had come down front to take pictures of Bob's performance. I was on the field when the tear gas hit. I was crying because I thought it was all over. I thought there was going to be a riot. Here we're coming to celebrate independence, and now it seemed that the whole event would be spoiled. I remember I ran all the way to the back, and that's where I grabbed the cloth banner that said "Welcome to Zimbabwe" from the rear wall of the stadium. My eyes were burning badly and I needed something to protect my face from the tear gas.

ERROL BROWN: I can remember after the concert started, I felt something burning my eye and when I saw everyone leaving the stage I say, "Something wrong." And then the engineer that came with the sound system, the P.A., told me that's tear gas. Freedom fighters threw tear gas over the gate because they didn't want to give them entrance to the stadium. That was so horrible; the men fought for their independence and you don't want to let them into the park to celebrate? They should be the first in the park! I don't blame them. The tear gas was fired by the freedom fighters themselves. After it cooled off, everybody came back and finished the concert and do all the songs they were supposed to.

DERA TOMPKINS: Soon everything calmed down. People calmed, the air cleared, and finally activity resumed on stage. But somebody took Judy, Marcia and Rita back to the house, along with Stevie and Ziggy.

What it was, was some people who were just anxious to get inside the stadium. The crowd got more excited when they heard Bob Marley playing and they pushed their way in through the barricades, so the police shot tear gas and it floated into the stadium. It was not a riot at all! No one got hurt, maybe just small bruises. Nothing really happened.

Bob resumed with "War," the audience pressed forward for the sixth and final song, the one they had raised their battle standards to, the anthem "Zimbabwe." Before walking offstage, Bob saluted the crowd: "A Luta Continua! Viva Zimbabwe! Pamberi Zimbabwe!"

ROGER STEFFENS: Standing together on the stage, Dera and the Wailers' entourage and dozens of others watched as a decidedly discomfited Prince Charles saluted while the despised colonial symbol of the British flag was lowered in Africa for the final time. An orgasmic cheer split the air as the wind whipped the Zimbabwe flag hoisted in its place.

DERA TOMPKINS: We all cried and cheered, and Bob saw me cry again, and he remembered that. I mean, people screamed, yelled, shouted, just vocalized for thirty minutes straight. Ahhhhh, all the suffering of ninety years of white minority rule were drowned by the cheers of the people. You know, people just shouted it out. That was like Glory Day. That was one of those hallelujah times, like Bunny Wailer said, "Hallelujah time, when the people will be singing." It was like, we won, we won, Zimbabwe is ours again! It was much, much more than any football game. And we just couldn't believe it. And the cannons are right near us, so we felt them, twenty-one! And that was it. And that was the highest moment, the highest I've ever been.

ROGER STEFFENS: Other witnesses to the so-called riot on Independence night were sound engineer Dennis Thompson, Junior Marvin and Judy Mowatt.

DENNIS THOMPSON: I was on stage and they fired. I think people wanted to come in and the security guards fired the tear gas, and the wind shifted and blow the whole tear gas into the stadium. Here comes Prince Charles and all these heads of state and they get flat! I say what's going on, and then it hit us. So I picked up Steve and run off the stage for about ten to fifteen minutes. It was funny. We thought something happen, but it was just tear gas.

JUNIOR MARVIN: We were tear-gassed on the first night. The flag had just gone up, the Prince of Wales had just taken down the British flag, the airplanes had just flown over, and we thought we were in space, because they were so close and the sound was like you were on another planet. Five minutes after the flag came down, the Wailers started off with "Natural Mystic." Apparently there were freedom fighters outside. There were thousands of people outside. Hundreds of thousands. There were more people outside than there were inside. And, of course, all of the gates were locked. The freedom fighters wanted to come in, and they were refused entry. So they said, "Well, listen, Bob Marley is here, and 'Zimbabwe' was the song that carried us right through this war. 'Natty mash it inna Zimbabwe.'" And they decided to just blow the gate down. So they blew the gate down; they hand-grenaded the gate down! And when the gate came down, everyone just came in. All the soldiers came in, all the freedom fighters came in. So the authorities saw the people running, and thought there was a big panic and the war was all ready to start all over again. The people who were on guard at the security panicked and started to use tear gas to control the people. And of course, tear gas drifted onto the stage. At the time, Ziggy and Stevie Marley stayed with us. All of us had to hit the deck. And I think it was in the middle of "I Shot The Sheriff"! We hit the deck, and our eyes were running with tears, and it affected Ziggy and Stevie the most, and the I Three. The I Three ran offstage, and the band were all onstage—we never left the stage.

I think Bob was the last person standing. And then he also hit the deck. Eventually the tear gas cleared, and we got some water for Ziggy and Stephen, and everyone wiped their eyes with towels, the freedom fighters came in and everyone cooled out, and everyone started to relax again. The people didn't panic. For some unknown reason, everyone just cooled out. The freedom fighters were allowed to come in, the gates were left open, the place just got rammed and then we started playing again. We had stopped for about twenty, twenty-five minutes, and when we started again it was like the place went up in a roar. It was like the biggest roar I ever heard. For a long time.

JUDY MOWATT: In Zimbabwe the night of the Independence celebrations it was a very good, it was a irie inspiration for us, but it was kind of frightening too, because while we were there, Prince Charles was there, and all these tankers and soldiers and machine guns that I'd never seen in my life before were there, and then these freedom fighters who made it possible, the independence possible, they were not invited to the celebration. So while we were onstage, we were about doing the third song when we smell something strange. And I look at Marcia and I see like she coughing, and I see Rita coughing, and I look at everybody—is like everybody knock out. So I left the mic, and everybody left the mic and ran from the stage. And I see little children fell on the ground, and you know I'm a mother and I couldn't stop to help them because I began to run.

And when we get to find out that it was these freedom fighters heard the music thumping, and they followed the music like they were invoked by the music. And they came barging into the gate, but they were not allowed inside, so they put up a fight to come in, and the soldiers and the police who were there, they tear-gassed the area, and that was what affected us. So we thought it was war! Because, you know, Zimbabwe is a war zone, so everybody run. So we wanted to get out of the place and is a brother from Zimbabwe now was taking us to the place where we're staying. And everywhere we go, we were blocked by soldiers with machine guns so he himself say, "We going dead now." And everybody is running for their own life, because even Bob himself, he was the last one to come offstage, because you know when Bob is singing, he is gone in a trance, and when he really came down to earth and really realized what was happening, he had come off. I don't know if anybody helped him off, because everybody ran and left him onstage. So we run into this trailer now, and lock the door but in there was still stuffy. So we got a ride from this brother trying to find the house where we are supposed to be staying. When we finally got there, we was watching it on television that the crowd had dispersed and everything. And we saw the Union Jack came down, the Zimbabwe flag went up, but we weren't there to witness it, eye to eye.

Rita now, she went back. She went back in the car, say she going to see what happened to Bob. She say when she reached back, she met Bob, and Bob say, "Mmm-hmm. Now I know who is the true revolutionaries." Because we're supposed to be some freedom fighters and we ran! But Bob went back, he did "No Woman No Cry," Bob did "Zimbabwe" with the band. Because he never got the chance to do those songs, because we just began the show. It was just the I Three broke away and ran out!

DERA TOMPKINS: Following the independence celebration, all the balls began for all the diplomats and invited guests. Job and our other hosts all left Rufaro Stadium to attend the balls. The I Three had taken a vehicle and a driver to return to the house following the tear gas episode. The rest of us were left with a truck and a driver who could not drive a manual transmission vehicle. So everybody who could help had abandoned the Wailers! To make matters worse, we didn't know where we lived! We didn't know which street Job lived on and we did not know what section of the city. Nobody knew a thing. And there was nobody to ask. A couple of times we all just stood there and looked at each other. This was unbelievable. Bob Marley had just finished the most important performance of his career and we had no way home.

It was early in the morning and everyone was tired. The truck was there but no driver, and nobody in our group could drive the truck either. So finally we get a driver, but then we still don't know where we are going. So we literally drove around for hours! 'Cause you figure you're driving, you're going to run up on it somewhere, right, somehow, eventually, maybe. But we don't even have a map of the city and we drove around till daylight.

That night, Bob played a second, unplanned show. The equipment was there, the stage was there. I don't think that anybody knew that the celebration was just going to be diplomats. So he said he wanted to play for the people. Now, it was originally going to be a paid show, but what happened is that we couldn't figure out how to set that up. We didn't really know the value of their money, and what was fair to charge. So luckily they abandoned that idea and decided to just do a free concert.

But Zimbabwean audiences were just not used to performances. So Bob did a show, and it was as strong as the night before, because he probably felt more like he's singing for the people tonight. So it was a powerful show. The first night there were forty thousand people, but not nearly as many the second night. It was unannounced, the lights weren't as bright, they didn't use the bleachers. The people were standing on the field. And when he sang "Zimbabwe" it was unbelievable the energy that he felt, and the people too. The crowd just stood and just cheered.

So Bob did his set, and as you know Bob would do a set and go offstage, and at an appropriate moment, with enough applause, he would come back out and do an encore. And he's been known to do as many as three encores. And I'm sure that Bob had mentally planned to do the show that way, with encores. He probably would have done five encores if people called for more. But what happened was Bob ended his last number, and everybody turned around and filed out of the stadium. Because they didn't know that if they applauded that he would come back to perform more songs. They really just didn't know. So they left! And everybody in Bob's entourage was shocked! It's a culture that didn't understand the concept of an encore—that's an acquired habit. They walked out, and we wanted to say, "Come back!'" His final number was "Exodus." "Yeah," the people said, "exodus?" And they did. It was really kind of funny, and it was kind of innocent. Because anywhere else, people would be begging, hammering and clamoring for more, and they just politely said, "Thank you, Bob Marley. OK, it's over. Bye."

Next it was important to secure a supply of herb. I was taken to meet a man who said he was a prince from New Zealand. He really checked for Bob and he gave me a large portion, and said take it back to him. So I took it to Bob and Bob was most grateful. By this time they had moved the whole family to a hotel, the St. James in downtown Harare, nice hotel.

Now, one thing to really comment on that reflects Bob's whole personality and style—the door to his room was open, all day, and maybe all night. He wanted people to come. It was Bob's spirit to have his door open. And one of the most important outings was when the ZANU soldiers came to pick him up at the hotel to take him to the bush. I heard that they gave him a uniform. Those were important things to Bob Marley. He wanted to identify with the soldiers and the bush. He wanted to go looking for lions, he wanted to go and see lions. They took him to the zoo!

The day before he was to leave Zimbabwe, he called me to his room and put a hundred dollars in my hand. He told me to go shopping and to get something for myself. It was his way of thanking me for being there. I was so humbled. I was the only one to see them off the next day. A couple of limos were sent, and Bob asked me to ride with him to the airport. He sat by the window on the right-hand side and I sat beside him. It was a revolutionary dream come true. The people were victorious.

JUDY MOWATT: Now when I think of Zimbabwe, I think of Bob's message to Africans. I remember, even in Zimbabwe, he said to some of the soldiers, "Where you get them weapon there from?" And I think they said Israel. So him say to them, "With all the uranium and all the minerals and things that you have, why don't you make your own?" I don't remember who he spoke to, if it was the Minister of Communications or whatever, but he was a little astonished to see this man coming all the way from Jamaica and asking them why they have to be importing weapons from another country when they have materials there that they could do it themselves.

DENNIS THOMPSON: The people in Zimbabwe were familiar with Bob's music, oh yes. They wish he had stayed there. They wanted him to make it his home. That's the first thing they said when we came off the plane: "Welcome home, you're home, don't leave." But we had just started doing production for *Uprising* and we had a lot of commitments. So they say, finish those projects and come back.

CHAPTER 32

Uprising

ROGER STEFFENS: Bob's Zimbabwe experience interrupted the work he had been doing since early 1980 for what would be his final album, the melancholy *Uprising*. It was filled with intimations of mortality, with songs like "Coming In From The Cold," "Real Situation" ("seems like total destruction the only solution"), "We And Dem" ("we no know how we and dem a go work things out," which some heard as a reference to the cancer cells coursing through his body), "Zion Train"—headed his way to take him to Zion, and "Work," in which he counts off his final days. The album's emotional closer remains one of his best-loved songs, the acoustic "Redemption Song," in which he insists that "none a them can stop the time." A thirty-three-date European tour with stops in several massive stadiums was booked from May 30 to July 13.

ERROL BROWN: After *Survival* I started to record Rita Marley's album *Who Feels It*. I realized now and again Bob would come into the room and listen and said, "How I no hear that sound when I do my stuff?" and smile and walk out back. Shortly after, he went off on the *Survival* tour. When they came back Junior Marvin said, "Errol, Bob and us had a talk and decided we want you to do the next album," saying they paid Alex Sadkin all this whole heap of money when they could give that to me as one of them, as one of us. So I did the next album, *Uprising*.

You see, on the *Uprising* album every single vocal is live. He tried to redo the vocals, but they all would be different, so much thoughts and ideas in his brain, it's unbelievable. So I used all the vocals tracks he did when recording with the band; the band vibes off that vocal, so in reality it's the best vocals. So all of those vocals was with the band. We never redo. Listen to "Zion Train" when he said, "To the bridge." It's Bob telling the band to go to the bridge. You know something, it was Chris Blackwell was the one who told Bob the live vocals are the best thing to use.

"Redemption Song"? Bob was burning out trying to get it right with the band, playing over and over, and Chris Blackwell just walk in the studio and listen to the band play it. And he said, "Bob, you see this song, I just see this song with you and your acoustic guitar." And Bob say, "Yeah?" and laugh. Said, "All right guys, I'm going to try it with acoustic." And it's a classic. Although people always cussing out Chris Blackwell, Chris Blackwell did his part too. I was there mixing, he's there in that seat beside me. He will be there touching buttons, mixing, night and day. Chris did his part where the reggae music is concerned.

ROGER STEFFENS: Some of the songs on the album were written while Bob was living in Miami, where he had ensconced his mother and sister Pearl in a big house on Vista Lane. With him was Dessie Smith, a friend from Trench Town, who was his personal assistant on the road and often helped Bob compose songs.

DESSIE SMITH: On a typical day in Miami for us, Bob would get up around ten, eleven. He used to go to bed real late. Then he'd wake up, get some mint tea. He might burn a spliff. He might reason, and within that time now, him read up the Bible, read a psalm out loud and discuss it with us, like a teacher discussing the meaning of the psalm, how it's relevant to everyday life, what it's saying. And after that, he takes the guitar and might come up, depending on the vibes him get, we might or might not get a song. A spliff, the Bible and music, that's the best, that's how the day run! Might just play some ball after that, the guitar, eat, back to the guitar. We played ball outdoors and some-times play indoors, inside the kitchen area, Bob used to play scrimmage in there. Mrs. Booker was crying out, "Why you mosh up the things? Play ball outside!"

And then we had boxing matches there, 'cause me and him bought two pair of boxing gloves. We always sparred. He tries to hurt me but I always hold back. And he has everybody in his corner, like him say, "We haffe fight now." I can't even get one of the ten people there. Everybody's his cornermen! We spar all the time, even before his shows, 'cause he likes to warm up before a show. So by the time he goes on the stage, he's wet already. He warms up just like he's gonna play a football game or a track.

We would play football, then we'd play bigger football. We used to play in the backyard, over by the jeep: Seeco, Gilly, Neville Garrick is usually there. We played before dinner, then we'd eat and then go around the back and have music again, guitar vibe. You'd have a lot of people there who would join in the singing, when we were making them songs. And we'd call them to come in and sing the chorus. The back room, it had sliding-glass doors. I used to sleep out there. Bob used to sing to us at night, and we would end up sleeping on the couch, cowboy style. Most of the time! Boots, shoes. Bob was just like that.

And most of the time there was a tape running, but not all the time. Sometime him haffe just get jamming. You have another time when him jammin' just like that and him say, "All right, get the tape player." Him figure that very effective.

Many of those are unfinished, like the first three or four lines. We had one called "Drastic Step," we just got that line three times and then we left that. Same time we start one small little one, four lines:

Come down, come down from your high riding wall
Can't you see you're riding in the past?
False pride cometh before a fall
So when you drop don't bother bawl
Can't say me never warn you

Before we spurn you
Some just a show off naturally
Fighting battles and personality
Then come the bounce-back my friend
Some call it reaction again
Come down from your high riding walls
Can't you see you're riding in the past?

I remember "We And Dem" was definitely made around '78. I remember when me and him sit down and I told him that in that song, we had actually written, "We no have no friend / in the House of Parliament." And even I said, "That too direct." 'Cause we usually try to word it that you can hear something and feel that it deal with you, but you can't be sure, you can only assume. So I figure at that time that was too direct towards the politicians. And he must have been thinking the same thing. He went to Jamaica to record and when he came back he had pulled that out. He must have seen that that was too direct. [It was changed to "we no have no friends inna high society."]

I used to write a lot because my top subject in school was English literature. Used to do a lot of Shakespeare, and from we start jamming, sometime he just come and hum, and I get a vibes. Don't get the word but get the melody. Either write the song by getting the lyrics first or the melody. He might play the guitar and find a good melody on it. Like me and him might sit down face to face and him [hums] and wait for me to come up with something. But most of the songs him come up with the lyrics. We worked together that way on the *Survival* and *Uprising*, songs like "Zion Train," "Coming In From The Cold," "Redemption Song," "Real Situation," "Pimper's Paradise." Most of these were Miami songs. "Coming In From The Cold" was written about three or four years before it was released. "Redemption Song" too, from around early '77.

"Pimper's Paradise" was written about some girl in England he had an experience with. I think it was a friend's experience, really. Bob writes from other people's experience too—me and him, we could kick like that. He could take one of the lines, like hum for me to come up with the line, look me in the eyes. If I can't come in, he tries. Like that song, "We Getting The Fight," it took us about a week. We tried but couldn't come up with one line. He was singing "we getting the fight from all direction." I come up with "complexion," and he acknowledge this, he smile, shake his head out.

The songs that I collaborate on that I'm proudest of are "Black Survival" and "Real Situation." But I never think of asking for cowriter's credit; no, we just deal on a different level. We don't deal with that; that never mean anything to us. We just get up and do that stuff. And that's how he is. You don't hear him speak or argue about "Where's money?" Never, never.

ROGER STEFFENS: *Uprising* was released in mid-June, while Bob's record-shattering final tour was in its early stages.

ERROL BROWN: We started the tour in Europe. That was a dream, to see how people went on over reggae music. It's like you are at pop concert, everywhere sold out!

ROGER STEFFENS: Two months after his triumphant performance in Zimbabwe, Bob played to the largest audience of his career in San Siro, a soccer stadium in Milan, on June 27, 1980. Pope John Paul II had appeared there the week before and Bob outdrew the Pope!

JUDY MOWATT: The most indelible show for me was really the one in Milan. It was about 110,000 people. And when I saw the amount of people my mind reflect on the first time we toured together, in 1975, with the *Natty Dread* album, in a little place called Paul's Mall in Boston—you know, it was very small. And we had to work seven nights a week, it was so hard, and even working for seven nights a week we never accumulated that amount of people! Yeah, for one place now, we see this huge mass of people, it was really impressive. All these Italians singing "No Woman No Cry," and they don't speak English. It's the same thing like when we toured Japan, the people don't speak English, but they know every one of Bob Marley's songs, they can sing it for you word for word, but they probably don't know the meaning of it.

ERROL BROWN: Biggest show was in Milan. Oh, God! You can't imagine how big that was. Remember, Italy is all about the Pope and football, and then you see "RASTAMAN BOB MARLEY" on the front page of their biggest newspaper. And it said, "Bob Marley create history in the stadium." Not even football! Football couldn't carry so much people, because we use the field too, obviously. That place was beyond packed. We had a group named Average White Band that was touring with us. Them have to cut their set short when people start throwing eggs onstage and run them offstage, shouting, "Bob Marley! Bob Marley!" It was a joyous experience. To me it's like a concert you see today with the biggest pop artist. Big! To me it was a dream. I didn't want to wake up out of that dream, you know. And right through. That was the biggest one. But I remember Crystal Palace in England, with the big pool in front of the stage full of dirty water. You see, when Bob came onstage, everyone went in that dirty water, just to get close to Bob Marley and the Wailers. The place ram, every show sold out.

At the end of the tour everybody got bonus, more than their salary for the tour. It was my first big tour like that. At the end of the tour everyone stayed back at Bob's request. I just wanted to go home. I remember Bob saw me down in the lobby and asked me where I'm going, I said home, he said, "Hold on, Errol, we have some bonus money coming in." I said, "Bob, you bring it when you coming, I just want to go home." He said, "All right, little more then." But it happened that, unfortunately, Bob never come home. You see, Bob was a good person, he get bonus and shared it among us all. Which other artist would do this?

ROGER STEFFENS: BY 1980, Colin Leslie, Bob's business manager, was setting up Bob's escape mechanism from Island. The release of *Uprising* in 1980 finished the contract, and Bob was considering a change of label. A multimillion-dollar contract was being offered by Polygram.

COLIN LESLIE: For Bob that was a package deal, involving all the Tuff Gong artists. He distributed the Abyssinians, Burning Spear, Freddie McGregor, a lot of products for a lot of people. But it wasn't about escaping necessarily. It was about setting up a sort of organization that would offer an alternative for the Jamaican artist. He wouldn't have to go to New York or London or wherever. They could get signed right here in Kingston and still get international exposure. For want of a better example, a Motown in Kingston. That's what he was trying to set up.

ROGER STEFFENS: But the dream was never to be. As the American leg of the planned world tour began, tragedy struck.

CHAPTER 33

Madison Square Garden
Then Everything Crash

ROGER STEFFENS: Marley was now a huge superstar, filling stadiums, hounded day and night by admirers and charity-seekers. Great strains were altering his relationship with Cindy Breakspeare.

CINDY BREAKSPEARE: Well, Bob was not someone that you could really harness his time or his attention, because his life was so demanding and he was so committed to what he was doing that you really had to find yourself or you would become very insecure, very disillusioned, very distressed. Because the man in your life, as it were, probably could never be there quite as much as you wanted him to be. So you really had to look within, and look for your talent, and he was all for that too. He was very encouraging that way, you know. All things constructive and creative, and he was very instrumental in the formation of my shop, Ital Craft. He brought us our first power tools, he brought us our first materials from London, which he sent someone out to buy for me. So he really was very inspirational in my growth and development as an individual, and as I say, just being secure within yourself, and knowing the things you want to do and going after them and not sitting back and waiting for anybody to make your life feel important or exciting or whatever. You had to get it on yourself.

Our breakup never actually happened until he fell ill. The summer that he fell ill, I moved away from Russell Heights, the home he bought for me in Kingston, Barbican area. I sold it. And to be honest with you, it was never really an official situation where I said, "Look, it's over," or he said, "Look, it's over." It was just more or less a situation where he'd gone up to Miami to prepare to go out on tour, and I decided I wanted to move away from Russell Heights, because it was just too much of a scene, you know. I felt like I needed some space. So I found a small place in the hills that was just big enough for Damian and me and told everybody else they needed to find their own yard. And when he called me and asked me to come up to Miami and spend some time before the tour began, and I sort of said, "Well, what's the scene there?" and he described it to me, and I said, "No, I don't think I can penetrate that scene again. If you want to come back down here and we do something." Some quality time was what I was looking at. But, of course, when I heard the news that something was seriously wrong, you know, you drop everything and you go.

ROGER STEFFENS: Unknown to his intimates, Marley's final act was imminent, made more heartbreaking by the great success of the summer in Europe, where he played to over a million people. The turning point came shortly after the North American leg of the world tour began, following two sold-out shows at Madison Square Garden. By this point, Bob had fired Don Taylor and hooked up again with Danny Sims.

DANNY SIMS: When we came off the European tour in 1980 the New York DJ Frankie Crocker was coming to Jamaica with us trying to get him and Pepe Sutton, the owner of WBLS, to get me to get Bob to come and do the show with the Commodores. They did that tour and I did the American tour. There was a lot of setting up and rearranging from agents and everything from the way Don Taylor had things set up. Bob Marley wanted to do arena soccer in every city. That wasn't an easy setup, to get in touch with everyone so they could play indoor soccer. He wanted to play all the indoor arenas on every concert, he wanted to play in them during the day. And that took a long time to set up.

ROGER STEFFENS: The idea for the tour was to go on the road with black artists like the Commodores in an outreach to the African-American audience. Bob wanted Sims to help him because he had access to that audience and to stations that could break him in a black market. He was talking to Stevie Wonder about doing a number of shows with him. (The 1980 world tour had been originally planned with Bob co-headlining with Jacob Miller and Inner Circle, but Miller had been killed in an automobile accident in the spring.)

DANNY SIMS: Yes, yes. That's what he wanted to do. And that's how the WBLS show came about. Because for Bob Marley to open at this time in his career for the Commodores was nearly an insult. And I'm not putting the Commodores down, because they were a huge act. But the difference was that WBLS was having trouble, 'cause it was their show and they had put a lot of money in it, and the tickets weren't selling, even to the black market it wasn't selling. So they agreed to play Bob Marley's "Could You Be Loved" every hour on the hour for three months. For how much? For nothing! To play Madison Square Garden and open the show for the Commodores, that's for how much.

And I remember my being on the bus and my introducing it to Bob. I remember Bob had met Frankie Crocker, WBLS's top DJ, and he liked Frankie Crocker. He was animated and a big-time name, and this was right down Bob Marley's alley, he wanted the black market. And Frankie Crocker went back to New York, they called me in and said, "Danny, can you get him to do it?" I said, "Well, I'll talk to him." And I went and had a talk with Skill and Bob and I said, "The Commodores are going to have a lot of trouble and are you afraid to open the show for the Commodores?" He said, "No." And I said, "Frankie Crocker and Pepe Sutton have been playing your record but they're getting no response from the black market." No acceptance, nobody went out to the stores to buy it. And I think Chris Blackwell was very disappointed 'cause he was anxious to break that market, it would just expand Bob. And we put that record on nearly every major black station, major play, "Could You Be Loved," even in Los Angeles on

KJLH. They played the record every hour on the hour pretty much. That was for money.

ROGER STEFFENS: Marley gave Danny Sims $80,000 to promote it by buying airtime on black stations in America.

ERROL BROWN: Bob Marley wasn't big in the U.S. until "Could You Be Loved" was released. That's the song broke Bob Marley in the U.S. 'cause it was a disco-reggae song, it was a crossover. U.S. never really accept reggae before, it was a hard market.

DANNY SIMS: Then I started to hear complaints. How could Bob open for the Commodores? Just a lot of rhetoric. And I told Bob, I said, "Bob, that's gonna happen." They said they'd only give us an hour. And, shit, how could Bob Marley do a show for an hour, when he's used to doing an hour and a half or two hours and overtime? I think the Commodores underestimated Bob. Now, Bob had been touring and his shit was on the spot. I remember my saying to Bob, we only got an hour, so you have to cut your show. Bob wanted to do that show—it wasn't me encouraging him, which I was accused of.

ROGER STEFFENS: Marley was seen in New York with Vivian Blake, who ran the notoriously violent Shower Posse gang, responsible for over 1,400 murders. A frightening picture of them together, in which Bob appears gaunt and ghostly, was published years later in *Shower Posse*, a book by Blake's son Duane.

DANNY SIMS: I remember that Bob said that he was a little bit afraid for his life. And Allan said that he thought that the posse or whatever it was wanted to assassinate him. But here's what I'm saying: he felt threatened either because he got shot in Jamaica or there was something looming from that.

ROGER STEFFENS: To ensure that Bob would feel safe for the show at Madison Square Garden, Danny Sims took some unusual measures.

DANNY SIMS: I took him to see a guy named Joe Armone, the head of the Gambino [Mafia] organization. Joe Armone was my partner for forty years before he died. And at the same restaurant that Castellano got killed, I took Bob and Allan to that restaurant to meet with Joey Armone. And Allan told Joey that they wanted protection for the Madison Square Garden. And you remember one of the members of Bob's band, Wya Lindo, came late for the show, and wound up in the audience. That was one of the Gambino guys who had him out in the audience. Because he came late they didn't know who he was. They thought he was coming to do something wrong. So when he came in, they shifted him right into the audience. So he had that place surrounded. And the whole country would have been the same thing, because the Gambino organization was the biggest in America. They would have been the security people for the rest of that tour because of the death threats. It wasn't just for New York; the Jamaicans were in the whole country. And then, the Jamaican government's hit squads, they can go anywhere.

And I don't think he knew where the threat was coming from. Because although you had the Jamaican posse, there was another outfit of bad guys. Then you had another crew of Jamaican government bad guys. So I think he was a little leery after being shot and he wanted security and he got it.

ERROL BROWN: I hear Danny Sims say there were death threats against Bob but no, that's not true—not Bob Marley, it was Skill Cole. He was with us, I don't know about the politics of that part, but I know security was doubled up. 'Cause New York is New York; whole heap of bad men there. But it was cool, nothing no go on at all. It was smooth.

ROGER STEFFENS: Gilly Gilbert could sense the change in mood, however.

GILLY GILBERT: That fall '80 tour, the opening was just fucked up. The whole scene was just fucked up. The whole vibe with the people— something was wrong. They separated Bob from us, put him in the Essex House and we were staying at the Gramercy. The first tour we been on where Bob stayed at a different hotel than us, it was just weird.

ROGER STEFFENS: Meantime, the addition of Marley to the Garden show changed the whole dynamic of the event, as Sims had predicted.

DANNY SIMS: So just what I told Bob was going to happen, I said, "Bob, the Commodores are not drawing, and when they draw they only draw black people." As soon as the tickets went on sale, the tickets sold out that day. Now isn't that amazing, that now Bob Marley was added to the show and the tickets sold out? So guess who bought the tickets? White people.

GILLY GILBERT: At Madison Square Garden, Bob just hit them with his music and them feel no pain. It seemed to me that the American people were ready now for reggae music. Something is on its way: something good is going to happen for reggae and for reggae people. But there was something wrong during those times. Some weird vibes. But they were dynamite shows both nights.

DANNY SIMS: During the shows I was backstage part of the time, I was patrolling. I wasn't worried as much as Bob was, but I don't see how anyone would have been able to get to him, because we had the security there. And it wasn't hard to get the guys, everybody lived in New York. So to come to the show and to be backstage, if you were a gangster, that's great. You're having fun, everybody's sniffing cocaine and smoking marijuana, the place was full. So I think that that was incredible.

ROGER STEFFENS: His performances were ferociously received, but intimidating to his costars.

DANNY SIMS: When Bob Marley did that hour the black people in the audience got a chance to see him; there were a lot of Jamaicans there. So what happened was, by the time Bob Marley started to go off with the show, the audience was hypnotized, they just went crazy. And by the time he got to the last song—I think it was "Get Up Stand Up," that was always a great closer—by the time he got to that last song, Bob Marley took the audience into a hypnotic state. And I felt bad for the Commodores. They came on to do three hours, and the audience walked out. Only their die-hard fans, the black people, stayed. You know the Jamaicans aren't going to stay for an R & B show, and the white people certainly they were not going to stay there, because they wanted to hear some rock and roll. More than half the audience left.

ERROL BROWN: The two shows we opened for the Commodores at Madison Square Garden, the first show Bob Marley and the Wailers had the audience on their heels and time was running out. The Commodores' manager look at Vivian Phillips (Bob's tour manager) and say, "Cut. Cut!" And Vivian told Bob he had to come off the stage, so he did, not doing "Could You Be Loved." Pure noise. Pure screaming, they were forced to put Bob Marley and the Wailers back onstage, so Junior Marvin started that guitar intro. I could not hear the P.A., the audience was so loud, you can't imagine. Madison Square Garden tore down! And when the Commodores came on with all their laser beams effects and explosions in the center of the stage, they just couldn't move the audience, they were burnt out by Bob Marley and the Wailers, all the lasers and explosions in the center of the stage couldn't wake them up. Lionel Richie asking them to "Get up! Get up! Let's dance! Let's party!" But they all sat down burnt out, burnt out by Bob Marley and the Wailers. It was something else. I could see people leaving too.

ALVIN "SEECO" PATTERSON: I remember when Bob finish, everybody walked out, nobody was even watching, just a couple of people.

JUNIOR MARVIN: I think a lot of people came expecting it to be just the Wailers. And when we performed, we played first. They thought the show was over.

DANNY SIMS: Bob opened the second night too. The Commodores' ego—the headline in the *New York Times* was that it looked like a ghost town after Bob left the stage. The smartest thing that we did, for me to get Bob to agree, that if the lineup for the show was right the Commodores couldn't follow him. And Bob knew that. So I think Bob played on that a little bit too. But the radio station didn't know that. They just wanted to sell out the tickets and Commodores is their act. I don't think that anybody other than Bob and me knew what was going to happen. But we didn't know it was going to turn out as good as it did.

ROGER STEFFENS: Marley got the headlines and rumors abounded that there was much bad blood backstage because Marley had blown away the Commodores. Junior Marvin disagrees.

JUNIOR MARVIN: A lot of rumors go around about the vibes between us and the Commodores. We had a great time with them and they respected our music and we respected them. Timewise, it was difficult to get a sound check, but it was a great performance, everyone had a great time.

SEGREE WESLEY: I went both nights. I remember the Friday night when I went, paid for my wife and my daughter 'cause they wanted to go. I said once I get in I know I would just go down where the artists were. I didn't get a good seat. I remember I said to my ex-wife, I'm gonna go around the back. And I walk out there and I saw Seeco and he says, "Segree, what you doing here?" He says, "Man, we've been looking for you." So, then I went around the back and then, as a matter of fact, the duration of the show I was in the back with the group and Family Man and the rest. Well, that night he did me proud, you know? Because he stole the show from the featured artist, which was Lionel Richie and the Commodores. And when they were through, more than half of the audience walked. Both nights. The only difference, I would say the Saturday night had more of a mixed crowd than the first night. The first night was mostly whites. The second night was more mixed. But the first night, why it will always be embedded in the back of my head is that he was singing and he had the Garden, people in the Garden, standing up in unison. I mean, one section after another without, I mean like a rehearsal or such. He had them standing up before he even went into the song, which was "Get Up Stand Up." And when he was through with it, I mean, they stood for a while before he even finished the next song. He doing the wo-yo-yo chant? And his jeans, as usual. I even teased him, I says, boy you love them jeans.

SEECO PATTERSON: That was a special one in Madison Square Garden, the last one, that was great, man, that was the best. I'm telling you bwoi, that was good. The performance, people appreciate it.

ROGER STEFFENS: The Garden shows represent Marley's penultimate triumphs. With a series of shows with Stevie Wonder coming up, Bob seemed to be at the height of his powers. But fate had other plans.

DESSIE SMITH: After the show in Providence, prior to the Garden shows, there were no signs that Bob was sick. We were running around. The night before we went and got ice cream, just as usual. He was so happy. I remember I run a little joke with him because we used to stay in the same suite, so I said to him, "Bob, your friends stay up too late. You stay up all night. I need to get some rest. I need my own place." And he lift up him sneakers and I say, "Bob, where you going?" Say him going upstairs. He went in the closet, he was moving. I say, "I move! Change me apartment." So I got a big suite to myself! That's how we are, like we love each other. But no, he showed no sign of sickness then.

Sunday, after the Garden shows, there were four or five guys there, Danny Sims and some of his friends. Shorts, sneakers. They were going across the road to jog in Central Park. Everybody went: Skill Cole, Biggs. When he's in New York, Biggs take care of Bob, bring him Jamaican kind of food stuff. But l had to stay in the hotel to monitor the phone. So where I was in the Essex House, I could see them going over the park. And when he came back he was with that kind of bad-man type of walk. He walks like a hot stepper! And he walked back. So when he came in the room I could tell that there was like a frightened look on his face. He didn't say anything, he keep pacing back and forth, spinning round and round. Then he said, "Dessie, you hear what happened?" I said, "No." Then he told me that him hook up [became paralyzed]. Then Skill tell me that he had fallen back and hooked up.

DANNY SIMS: You see, the tragedy next day, what happened, my brother Eddie was with us and every day we went to Central Park to play soccer. Although I don't play soccer, I would exercise by running around the park, and my brother didn't play either, but we were there in the park with him. Eddie was working for Sony at that time working on promotion. We were in the park now with Bob. Allan "Skill" Cole and Bob's band formed his team. We were jogging to the soccer field, and as we approached it and started to play, all of a sudden Bob Marley had an epileptic-type fit, foaming at the mouth, and he said, "Allan, Allan." He was like delirious, and the only thing he could say was, "Allan, Allan." Allan took him in his arms and we walked him to Mount Sinai hospital next to where I lived and where he was staying with me.

DESSIE SMITH: When Bob told me, like, he had a seizure, that's what he said. Anyhow, they decided to take him to the doctor to check him out because it was so serious. And when he came back, he was just like out of it. That's the thing that surprised me really, he was just like limp. He wasn't saying nothing. You could feel like something was wrong. There was this look on his face, you could tell that something serious, and him didn't even tell me at the time. But Skill Cole came to me and told me don't give Bob no weed to smoke. I still didn't query anything further. Well, I know something is wrong, putting one and one together.

GILLY GILBERT: Seeco called me on Sunday and said, "Gilly, come to the hotel fast because trouble, boss." So he started explaining to me that Bob went over to Central Park with some of the guys and he was jogging and while jogging he had like a relapse, he just collapse, had like a seizure, like when someone had epilepsy type of fits. Seeco told me that they tried to render help and stretch him out and let him deep breathe and he come around. Immediately they took him to the hospital for observation and they had him there for quite a while.

DANNY SIMS: Dr. Rothman then made an appointment at Sloan

Kettering, the number one cancer hospital in the world. We saw the most renowned cancer doctor on the planet. They took Bob in and told us to come back: Milton Rothman my lawyer, Dr. Rothman's brother, Allan "Skill" Cole and me and Bob Marley. They did a scan on him. But the doctor called us in another room to talk to the lawyer, Allan and myself. Now this is the first time I found out about the cancer; he said, "Bob Marley is probably the strongest man I've ever seen. I could see how he played soccer, and you're getting ready for this soccer tour." And he said, "But Bob Marley has more cancer in him than I've seen with a live human being." He said his head was full of cancer, melanoma. And he knew Bob's father had white origins. And he said that he had found out about the toe. He said that if Bob Marley had followed the instruction after he found out he had the cancer and cut off half of his toe, he'd live longer than all of us. He said, "Who's going to tell him, Allan, you?" Allan said, "I can't tell him." He said, "You, Danny, or you, Milton?" So Bob was waiting for us to give him the results. And I don't remember which one of us told him, but it wasn't Allan. I think it was me. He said nothing. He held his head down, and I never saw him raise his head up again.

SEGREE WESLEY: I was in his hotel, I was by the hotel room on Monday. I remember I was there and he says to me he was going to Pittsburgh. He said he was going on tour and the bus was outside, you know? And I didn't go to work that day. Then he was telling me he was having some problem with the keyboardist, Wya Lindo, 'cause he says he brought this girl from wherever, she was an American. And he says, well, it's like they fighting and he told him that he's either gonna have to get rid of the girl or he's not gonna finish up the tour with them. But he never mentioned collapsing the day before in Central Park. He looked smaller, like he lost a lot of weight, 'cause I even said to myself, man Rasta, how you so maga [scrawny, sickly]—in Jamaican terms, it's maga. He says to me, "Man, I'm not like you no more, you know, I man just eat fish and vegetables." I said, "But Rasta, you look maga."

He said, "No, I'm all right. It's only this toe." Bob says it was only this toe give him some problems. Another thing we talk about is, he asked me which was the best song he ever sing? I said to him, "War." He shook my hand and says, "Rasta, only you can know that 'cause I tell anybody out there, that is the best song, I don't care what nobody say, you know. It's that song." But, I mean, he's dead and gone but today I would say the best song now is "Redemption Song." 'Cause the words are great. That's my favorite song of Bob's, yeah, "Redemption Song."

GILLY GILBERT: Everything was kind of hushed, they tried to keep it down, keep things cool until they get the final results of the tests. We didn't know anything until he flew into Pittsburgh. We had a meeting before the show. He told us everything that went down. We all knew that this was going to be the final show.

DESSIE SMITH: We didn't know how sick he was until Pittsburgh. 'Cause I was in the changing room before the show and he was in the chair, out of it. I was there, cleaning off his shoe, and he was leaning all the way back in his chair. So him say, "Give me a little spliff." And I give it to him. And you know what he did? Like he hide and did it. He took it and he finished it in the bathroom, he didn't want nobody to see him. So it was showtime now and I walk to the side of the stage first, and he came up behind me and he said, "Dessie, keep an eye on me." When he start playing, Skill Cole came up behind me, and I remember distinctly he said, "Dessie, this might be the last show Bob doing." So I say, "Why?" And Skill say, "The doctor say he's filled with cancer." When I heard that, me knee just buckle. 'Cause I know something was wrong. I never seen Bob how he took it that hard. He had realized the reality of it, to really take it like that. 'Cause he was out from that day, saying nothing to me or to Neville. So it's really after that show they decided to end the tour.

DENNIS THOMPSON: The final sound check in Pittsburgh lasted about an hour. I remember him singing "Another One Bites The Dust," song by Queen. He just start the sound check with it, and I said to him,

"Why you keep singing this song?" I say, "Is this your song?" And him say, "No." I never heard Queen songs. I never know Queen. But Bob went to a concert by Queen at Madison Square Garden, and he said to me to come to the Garden and me say no. He went and that's where he must have heard it. He kept singing this song, "Another One Bites The Dust," and he laugh. At the time I didn't even know about the incident in Central Park. I knew nothing about it. Even if the band knew, I wasn't looking at them for that. For me it was business, getting my things right. If there was a problem before, I didn't even know about it. I didn't notice any sign of strain in his performance.

JUNIOR MARVIN: I think Bob went to Pittsburgh instead of going right into the hospital because Bob had a lot of determination. And he had a lot of faith in what he was doing. If he could have done a dozen more shows after that, he would have done it. If it was up to him, he would have kept on going. The reason why we stopped in Pittsburgh was because everyone was saying to him, "Bob, let's go check out a doctor. Cut the tour." I think Allan Cole convinced him that he should stop the tour. And because physically he was sorta run down, he accepted the idea.

Yet at that show in Pittsburgh you would never have known that he was sick. At the sound check that afternoon I remember he did "(Lord, I Gotta) Keep On Moving," but I think he did others as well. I remember that we had an intense sound check, because every sound check we do is always intense. We try to make sure that everything works properly, that everything is fitted right, that all the sound is balanced properly, and that we're gonna give the best show we can give. And we went through the sound check just like any other sound check. There was no negative vibe about Bob or anything, you know? What happened after the sound check was that Allan Cole came to us and said, "We gonna cut this tour. We gonna finish this tour. This is the last concert for Bob Marley and the Wailers." So we knew that this was the final show that we were about to play.

All I can remember is that I prayed, and I said to God, "If this is the show that You want us to go out with Bob with, please help me to do the best I could ever possibly do." And I think every member of the band felt the same way. Let's just do the best we could ever do, and let's hope that it's not the last show. To tell you the truth, during the show, the thought that this was the last show never crossed my mind once. Bob never made any kind of movement that would make you think that. He sang every song great. Every song was sung perfect. It was like any other show—he gave 110 percent. The show went flawless. Everyone tried not to make any mistakes at all. Not even half a note! And we were all totally behind Bob, totally in tune with Bob, it was just like magic, the audience went wild. In fact, I don't even think that Bob believed that anything was really wrong with him. It was like he was trying to prove that, hey, nothing's really wrong with me! And it was a great show. He did a perfect show.

In my recollection, "Work" was the final song [actually performed in a medley with "Get Up Stand Up"]. And if that was the last song, then it's perfect, because we got a lotta work to do. And you know, the work continues.

DENNIS THOMPSON: After the show I got the call, go to the hotel immediately. I was packing up all the stuff and I had to go now. So I go directly to the hotel. Bob was in his room, everybody is long-faced. I say, "What's going on?" Tell me the results came. I said, "What results?" Say Bob collapse in the park, Sunday. Result came and he got cancer. You could just tip me with a feather. Then the whole thing came to me about "Another One Bites The Dust." Some people say he also sang "Keep On Moving," but I never remember that.

ERROL BROWN: It was the first time I heard Bob Marley crack on a high note. Dennis Thompson and I switch position for that show, Dennis was mixing the front of the house, I was doing the stage monitors. And the first time when I look upon Bob's face he never look happy. Performance was normal, but I could see something was bothering him. There was meeting after the show, then I heard that the tour was canceled. It was either at the hotel or in the dressing room. Rita said Bob's sick, he collapsed in Central Park, then I realized that's what was bothering him.

Then we got on a bus and drove to Florida. We were in a hotel for a week while Bob went into a hospital. When Bob came out he looked so fresh I actually said to him, "Bob, you look fitter than any of us right now, probably it's just rest you wanted." He said, "Yeah, don't feel sick. But I still want to check out what they are saying." So that was it. And next time I see Bob he was in a casket. No turning back.

DESSIE SMITH: After Pittsburgh we decided to leave the next morning for Miami. Couldn't catch a flight to Miami, so we had to take one to West Palm Beach and then drive by limo, 'cause him want to get back to Miami fast. Because after what this doctor tell him, he had to get a second opinion from this doctor in Miami. And then the doctor gave him the same kind of report. On the plane all the way back I was all tears, I can't believe that he was right there on the other side of the aisle of the passenger plane. Was just me and Rita, Danny Sims, Skill Cole, like five of us. We left the band there, they came later. I was just crying. Tears, tears, tears. Right beside him too. I don't really believe in all them things people said about "them poison him, them kill him" and all of that. I don't believe that. Just nature. It's a reality. I don't know why. Probably God feel he done enough already, although Bob might not have felt so. I figure he was probably bearing too much burden, 'cause when he died, he really know how much thing he was dragging around. See what happened? Everything collapsed. And he might not have shown it but he felt it.

ERROL BROWN: Bob had a load, too much load on him. But he never complained, never said no. Bob left back a great legacy. His music, up to today any Bob Marley music you put on and play now, it's like today's lyrics and music.

BUNNY WAILER: Bob Marley's only flaw, in my opinion, was that he could never say no to anyone.

GILLY GILBERT: The final meeting was in Miami with the whole band. He told us that the doctors said he had cancer and one doctor said he had three months to live and another say he had six months, nine months. Then everybody went their separate ways. I went back to Jamaica. Then I was there in New York cooking for him. I was so cut up about it. I was in Miami when I heard they decided to go to the Alps in Germany in winter. New York was the last I saw of Bob.

CHAPTER 34

Dr. Issels and the Final Days

ROGER STEFFENS: Bob underwent medical tests in Miami and New York. They quickly confirmed that he was fatally ill, the cancer that had first been detected in his big toe having spread to his lungs and brain. Chemo began in Miami and continued at Sloan Kettering in New York, and his locks were shorn. He was about to separate from Chris Blackwell and Island Records, saying all they could do was to bring white college kids to him. Blackwell was losing his biggest money-maker.

Rita Marley has said that throughout their touring years she was more like Bob's mother, taking care of him while having love affairs of her own. She had her own agenda, especially because Bob refused to make a will. Still legally his wife, she stood to inherit the estate. (This would lead to more than a dozen years of lawsuits.) Don Taylor knew where all the bank accounts were, so he was still kept around on the periphery of things, though under heavy manners [i.e., under strict discipline]. Each had their own pecuniary interests.

Ironically, Danny Sims regained a primary role in Bob's last days. He was negotiating a new label deal for Marley with two major companies and huge advances. Now, with that an obvious impossibility, an irredeemable sadness set in.

DANNY SIMS: When Bob collapsed in New York in 1980 the doctors told him he had six weeks left to live and he might as well go back out on the road and die there. After Bob got this news I never saw him smile again. His smile dropped and he went silent and became so sad.

GILLY GILBERT: Bob had a complete physical just before the fall 1980 U.S. leg of the *Uprising* tour. He passed it. To this day I just can't understand. Bob played soccer in Australia, Zimbabwe, everywhere we go. And he was playing like a champion. Even before we went on the U.S. tour in '80 we had a send-off game in southwest Miami here against a Haitian team with my team, America Jamaica United. He was running well, like anybody else. He was kicking the ball like a bullet. If Bob was feeling pain I would have seen it while he was playing.

DANNY SIMS: I canceled the tour when we found out he had cancer. I also canceled the negotiation. We were getting ready to sign a record deal. We had choices of Sony and Polygram. We then were on to a five-album deal, an album a year, for ten million an album, and we could have got it with anybody. For a record company to make fifty million dollars back off of an album is nothing with a Bob Marley. Your insurance is there. How much do you have to sell? You are the record company, you are the distributor, so every sale you get all the money. You own your own pressing plant. If you're a record company guy like me you understand that, when you talk about a big advance an artist gets. I don't think anybody else would have known how to negotiate a deal like that. But I think that we were close to closing a deal. But I told everybody that Bob Marley had cancer.

I saw him on stage at his last show in Pittsburgh. I watched every show. And let me tell you something, it was just as dynamic. You know what the Sloan Kettering doctor said? "Bob Marley is stronger than an ox. He's going to walk out onstage one day and he's going to drop dead. Just like the times he collapsed, one time he's not going to wake up. If I were you"—this is the time we were deciding whether to tell him or not tell him—"I wouldn't tell him anything. I'd let him die happy, because he's not going to know when he's going to die. He is dead, he's a dead man walking." He thought he could die immediately, but within six months he was going to be dead. And in six months he was dead. The doctor's prediction was right on time. What he told us to do was what we should have done.

During the Sloan Kettering treatment I had Bob live with me in a penthouse with nine rooms. It was all white in the building, and then there were Rastas up and down all day. They stole the seat out of the elevator, they were smoking everywhere. Rita served Bob and Cindy breakfast in bed together. Rita hadn't seen Bob naked in ten years.

ROGER STEFFENS: It was around the middle of October in New York City when Bob's locks were trimmed. Cindy Breakspeare, Rita Marley, a woman named Jennifer and Yvette Anderson were there to care for him while he lived at Danny Sims's apartment.

CINDY BREAKSPEARE: I think Bob was trying to be strong for all of us. But I think he probably realized that it was the beginning of the end. He tried to maintain his sense of humor. I think it was really hard at that time. He didn't rest well at night. I don't think he was in any great amount of pain. I think it was the mental anxiety, what to do, where to go, who to turn to, what's the road to take.

ROGER STEFFENS: Danny Sims has very strong feelings that Bob's care was mismanaged.

DANNY SIMS: When Bob got sick in Central Park Allan Cole was staying at my house and Pee Wee Fraser was staying with friends in New York but was at my house every day. And I was very, very upset that they had kept it away from me. And people don't realize that a publisher for an artist is very important to you. And nobody told me.

DR. PEE WEE FRASER: I think where any individual could be said to be blamed or fell short is that there was no actual follow-up. We could go into some more detail, because by the time we had reoccurrences and showed metastasis the doctor, who I think Danny Sims had recommended, a female doctor in Florida, she had obviously overlooked a coin lesion in his lung.

ROGER STEFFENS: Bob and Pee Wee were both members of the Twelve

Tribes, and Bob often sought his advice and sometimes unorthodox treatments. He and Sims locked horns over Dr. Herman's advice.

DANNY SIMS: I found out that they gave him chemotherapy in Miami a little bit. Pee Wee Fraser told Bob Marley—and when I found out I put Pee Wee Fraser out of my house, never spoke to him ever again—because how could he tell Bob Marley that cancer couldn't live in a Rastafarian? That's the biggest bullshit I ever heard, that's like a Christian telling a Christian, "You're a Christian, cancer can't hurt you." I said to Pee Wee Fraser, "How could you say that? You're a medical guy, how could you say that to a person? How could you stop him from taking chemotherapy?"

DR. PEE WEE FRASER: I never said anything like that because I'm the one who explained to Bob what melanoma is. He had third-stage and the doctors at Sloan Kettering said that he would die by Christmas. I told them they couldn't say he's going to die at a certain time and I'm not going to tell Bob that.

DANNY SIMS: Certainly chemo is a poison, but if you got a chance you give it to a person. You don't say stop taking chemotherapy, it's poison. You hear that from a lot of people that they take chemo, their hair falls out. They said he's going to lose his dreadlocks if you take chemo, because he's an artist and all the crazy things. He can't dance on stage. What's better than life? The man had all these kids and grandkids coming, he had so much to live for. Even if he didn't do another concert in his life or record another song in his life, if he was alive he could enjoy his kids and his grandchildren. So I just think that Bob was unfortunate. I was just pissed off.

It seemed to me that Chris Blackwell, who knew the difference, should have, if he was in position to send him to a doctor [should have done so]. Maybe he wasn't, because when Bob came back to me he had nothing to do with Chris Blackwell. I think the only person who was dealing with Chris Blackwell was Don Taylor and he wasn't there anymore.

ROGER STEFFENS: After the doctors at Sloan Kettering told Bob there was no hope for a recovery, Marley's circle began looking for a successful alternative treatment. Roots Rasta claimed that traditional healers in the hills could cure him and urged him to return to Jamaica; the more scientifically minded among his entourage urged aggressive chemotherapy; naturopaths were consulted; Rita, Danny and Cindy were in favor of a Mexican clinic where Hollywood actor Steve McQueen was reportedly recovering from cancer.

DANNY SIMS: I told Bob that I was going to put him down in Mexico at the hospital where Steve McQueen was. I paid the money out of Bob's royalties from Cayman Music. Then Bob said he didn't want to go to Mexico because Steve McQueen had died and that was his favorite movie star. Bob wanted to go where he thought he had a fighting chance. His hair was gone because of the chemo. The pain was really starting to come.

Then he chose to go with my second choice, Dr. Issels. So Allan and them decided to have me call Dr. Issels and set him up to go there. I knew of him through his interest in alternative medicine.

ROGER STEFFENS: Dr. Josef Issels was an ex-Nazi doctor who had a clinic in the German Alps, using alternative treatments.

CINDY BREAKSPEARE: Rita and I personally felt that Mexico would have been a better place, because we felt the climate and the culture, he just would have been more comfortable there. I mean, in Germany you couldn't even walk outside without boots up to your knees. Snow and cold, and you know we are tropical people. All those things affect you. They affect your whole headspace. So we really would have preferred that. And if it was left to me and me alone, I would have said Saint Ann in Jamaica. With lots of organically grown vegetables, tea, a good rest, and just deal with a different way. I wouldn't really have added to the stress by placing him in a strange place in a climate he hated, surrounded by people he didn't know. I never agreed with that decision and I know Rita didn't either.

I don't know who forced him to do that because we didn't have much say. We were merely women. And the brethren seemed to think that that was the best place. There was a doctor in the camp, Pee Wee, who I guess weighed up the various track records of the two clinics that were being considered and decided that Dr. Issels was the better place go. I don't know how he really arrived at his decision, but I always felt that it was a very miserable time for Bob, those seven months he spent in Germany. It just broke my heart to see him like that. I was there for three weeks with him.

DR. PEE WEE FRASER: Consultation in Germany was quite by accident. We were in Bob's hospital room after Dr. Rittenhouse of the department of neurology at Sloan Kettering had told me that Bob's chances of surviving beyond Christmas '80 were very unlikely and I should inform Bob. I had told him no one knows when anyone would die—we lived by faith. I wouldn't tell Bob he would die by Christmas but I would re-emphasize how much we would have to fight to overcome his illness.

After this conversation, I had returned to Bob's room. We had just prayed with the Ethiopian priest. Allan "Skill" Cole, Bob and myself were in the room. The priest and his assistant had left. It was almost as if the last rites had been accomplished—the doctors sounding the death knell and the priest giving the familiar final entreaty. Everyone seemed preoccupied with their own thoughts. Then I noticed this newsletter on the ground that was partially dried out after covering some water that had spilled. The newsletter announced the Omega Conference at the American Institute of Science. The guest speaker: Dr. Josef Issels.

We didn't meet Issels until we had clandestinely entered his hotel. Myself and Allan spoke first with his wife while Issels was at the conference. And we interviewed the doctor in charge of the clinic in Mexico, the same clinic Steve McQueen attended. The consensus was that Dr. Issels was not only the best holistic/alternative practitioner of the time, but he had the highest cure rate of terminal illnesses, viz. cancers, and he had a documented cure of a previous case of melanoma. Probably not as serious as Bob's, but his track record was genuine since everything had clinical documentation to support his claims, viz. radiographs, all the usual clinical investigations, serum studies, etc. Thus we went to Rottach-Egern, Munich, in what was then West Germany, where they had the program. This was done despite the threats from personnel at Sloan saying not to go.

ROGER STEFFENS: As Dr. Fraser attests, Archbishop Abuna Yesehaq of the Ethiopian Orthodox Church baptized Bob in the presence of his wife, Rita, and other members of his family before he left for Germany. In an interview with Barbara Blake Hannah in the *Jamaica Sunday Gleaner*, he recalled the events of that day.

ARCHBISHOP ABUNA YESEHAQ: Bob was really a good brother, a child of God, regardless of how people look at him. He had a desire to be baptized long ago, but there were people close to him who controlled him and who were aligned to a different aspect of Rastafari. But he came to church regularly. I remember once while I was conducting the Mass, I looked at Bob and tears were streaming down his face.

When he toured Los Angeles and New York and England, he preached the Orthodox faith, and many members in those cities came to the church because of Bob. Many people think he was baptized because he knew he was dying, but that is not so. He did it when there was no longer any pressure on him, and when he was baptized he hugged his family and wept, they all wept together for about half an hour.

ROGER STEFFENS: Much controversy remains because of this. Did Bob in fact accept Jesus as his personal savior and reject Rastafari? In December of 2013 I posed this question to Neville Garrick.

NEVILLE GARRICK: No, I've never seen it that way. I couldn't say that Bob embraced Jesus Christ at the end of his life.

ROGER STEFFENS: The choice of Dr. Issels to treat Bob was highly controversial. He only took patients who had been given up as hopeless by other doctors. He had been called a quack, and rumors abounded of his unorthodox treatments and his rate of actual cures. It was also alleged that he had been in the SS during World War II.

His true history is much more complex. He received his MD in 1932 and went to work for a Catholic hospital, which demanded he become a member of the Nazi Party and suggested he join the SS to advance his career. Though he described himself as "politically uninterested," he resigned from the SS in 1938 when he was ordered to stop treating Jewish patients. He subsequently spent time as a prisoner of war in Russia.

The German medical establishment sought to shut down his clinic in 1960, and he spent three months in prison before being acquitted of all charges in 1964. The outcome of the trial paved the way for immunobiologic treatments to be allowed in Germany. According to his wife, the Issels cancer treatment achieved complete long-term tumor remissions of advanced standard therapy-resistant cancers, and patients led cancer-free lives for many years. In 2000 the Italian reggae writer Marco Virgona interviewed Ilse Marie Issels.

ILSE MARIE ISSELS: In the first months of treatment Bob Marley improved considerably and was again able to play football for fun. This helped, of course, to be optimistic and he also saw other seriously ill patients getting better. He took long hikes in our beautiful mountains and seemed to have fun, in spite of the disease and its treatment. His private physician/friend was always present and Bob Marley was during all the time surrounded by family and friends. Everybody adored him. The inhabitants of our town were proud to have Bob Marley staying with us.

Dr. Issels knew about the tremendous importance of the mind and soul in the development and in the cure of disease—any disease. He tried to teach his patients forgiveness—the first step towards healing. Cleansing the mind and the body, to give the inner physician a chance. Medical doctors and medications are only tools to help the body help itself. These convictions he talked to his patients about and he did the same with Bob Marley. I know one thing: that it was a relationship of respect and trust. Dr. Issels respected highly Bob Marley as a person, his convictions, for what he stood in life, his purpose in life for which he fought. They had many long talks not only about medical subjects, but about life, religion, his music and art.

DANNY SIMS: The problem with Dr. Issels's Bavarian clinic is that it's so cold there. I was in the army for two years in Germany. I can tell you that I come out of Chicago where it's really cold, but Germany and Austria was colder than that for a long time. And they didn't have sufficient heating. And Allan went with Bob. I had to work, I was busy during that period, I couldn't go there to stay with him. I never went there.

CINDY BREAKSPEARE: I was there for three weeks in the early part of the year that he died. It was heartbreaking, you know. But some of the brethren were there. Skill was there. Pee Wee was there. But it wasn't a happy time, and I don't think anybody really wanted to be there. Well, naturally not, least of all poor Bob. And by then it had begun to affect the side of his face, and the use of his arm, and what have you. And I mean, when you see someone that you love, who has been so vital and so incredibly healthy and physical, physically fit and loving, to be that way, I mean somebody who believes in exercising every day whether it was running, football, some light weights, just love to be fit. And when you see pictures of Bob without his shirt you can see how fit he was. There's not an ounce of fat anywhere. It was just dreadful to watch him deteriorate like that. And I mean, it wasn't only hard for me alone. I'm sure it was hard for everyone who knew him and cared for him.

ROGER STEFFENS: Bob had played frequently in Germany. His final concert there, in Dortmund, was indoors in front of a sold-out crowd of sixteen thousand, whose minute-long chant of "Mar-ley, Mar-ley" shook the walls of the building at the end of his opening set. Stefan Paul had filmed that concert, and his appearance at Sunsplash in 1979.

STEFAN PAUL: Bob had learned of this German doctor in New York,

Josef Issels. We knew Issels's son in Germany, his son studied with my producer's son. So we organized that Bob could come to Bavaria. Every second weekend we would come to see him and bring 16mm film cans filled with herb. He arrived in late October looking completely weak and sick. I remember a period of time in February of '81 when there was tons of snow. They hated the snow. He had sort of recovered and was playing soccer in the snow, and they were talking about touring in March and April, so it was somehow healing. He did fine for two weeks despite his loss of dreadlocks.

We showed him Sunsplash '79 in a theater, and he was covered in rugs. He hadn't seen his kids in quite a while. He laughed a lot at the film. He couldn't believe how he danced on stage. We had almost no lights to shoot by, so we had focused on him and Rita. We had the chance to talk to Bob more, but out of respect we never filmed him in Bavaria. We had been glad to come along as friends, and this was such an exorbitant time.

ROGER STEFFENS: American reggae singer Zema, a longtime resident of Los Angeles, found herself in the Bavarian clinic where Bob was being treated at the start of his stay there. She spoke about that experience in 1998.

ZEMA: As Jah would destine, back in November 1980, my mother was receiving cancer treatments at the Issels clinic in the mountain resort town of Rotach-Egern, Germany, when Bob Marley arrived there. She knew I liked Bob's music and sent me an article on him from a German newspaper that basically said he was the "Rock Superstar of the Third World" who in June had performed to tens of thousands of people in Germany, playing guitar and singing for freedom for people of color. The article stated he was critically ill with metastasized lung cancer to be treated by Dr. Issels when cancer specialists in the U.S. couldn't help him.

In February 1981, I went for ten days to visit my mom and be on Issels's anti-cancer program. As with most alternative medicine, Issels's program was no picnic. By the time most people came to this clinic they had failed treatment elsewhere and were thin and weak from the ravages of chemotherapy, radiation and their disease. Unfortunately, Bob was quite ill and really only spoke when he was spoken to.

The first time I saw him was when he came into the clinic towards the waiting room. He had just gotten his tonsils out, which was part of the program. He was weak from that and was just kind of bouncing off the wall. He had lost his locks and had a knit cap half on in typical roots style. He wasn't there long before he was called to see the doctor.

The clinic was nearly always full. It was hard to get scheduled for these ultraviolet light treatments, where light was focused to part of your body for about forty-five minutes. One night when there was hardly anyone in the clinic, Bob's Jamaican doctor had made arrangements to administer these light treatments to Bob and two other patients. On the third floor, there were three beds in the treatment room with half-dividers between so you could see the head of the person next to you. I was next to Bob and asked him how he was coping with everything, since Dr. Issels emphatically told me, "No marijuana! No marijuana!" It's been so long now and I don't remember his exact words, but he said he remembered Jamaica. It was almost like he was in a trance. He spoke slow and pensive and described the beauty of Jamaica—the white sand beaches, the warm sun. He spoke with such feeling and love for Jamaica, he made you feel like you were right there in Jamaica even though there was three feet of snow outside.

It was Bob's birthday, February 6, during that time and they invited people at the clinic to a birthday party at their apartment. Before a lot of people arrived, he came into the room and we started to talk a little. My mom had told him I was a musician and when that came up, he told Mrs. Booker to bring out guitars. She hurried off and brought two guitars. He started to play one and I picked up the other. Bob didn't play very long or very loud, maybe a half hour, just jamming. Everyone seemed really glad that he was playing the guitar and I got the impression he wasn't doing much of that anymore. Also present that evening were Rita, Tyrone Downie, Bob's friend Bird, as well as the ever-present yardies. They had a cake that said "Happy Birthday Reggae King," but I remember they spelled "reggae" wrong. Unfortunately a lot of the time he was in bed in the next room. It wasn't long after that when Jah took Bob home. He had a presence even then, when the illness had reduced him to a fraction of what he had been. He seemed so vulnerable and out of his element.

ROGER STEFFENS: In late April 1981, Edward Seaga, newly elected prime minister of Jamaica, called Bob in Germany to inform him that he was going to award him the Order of Merit, Jamaica's highest civilian honor. Bob's only reaction was, "Big man, if you can do it, do it." It was a reflection of his disdain for anything originated by what he termed Babylon. "Babylon," Bob often said, "have no fruits."

By the beginning of May, Dr. Issels said there was nothing further he could do to help Bob. A plane was chartered to fly him back to Florida, into the bosom of his family.

CINDY BREAKSPEARE: When he was carried back to Miami in May I was able to see him on May 10th, the day before he passed. And I took Damian with me, so he saw me. And we went into intensive care and he recognized me and say, "Hmmmph, think you never did a come." Which is to say he thought I wasn't going to come. So I said, "No, man. I must have to come." He said, "No you don't must." So I said, "Yes, I must." But by then he looked quite different. Unrecognizable really. Almost like a little boy. And he just touch Damian's hand.

STEPHEN MARLEY: His last words to me were "Money can't buy life." Just that him say. "Just sing that song there, money can't buy life," and say, "You fe deal with it." Yeah, He will do the rest.

ZIGGY MARLEY: His last words to me were "On the way up bring me up, and on the way down, don't let me down."

ROGER STEFFENS: During Marley's final months, his original partner

Junior Braithwaite surfaced in Kingston. (Tragically, Junior would die by gunshot in 1999.)

JUNIOR BRAITHWAITE: At times I considered going back to Jamaica to join the group again. Even Bob Marley expressed that. But the time wasn't right. I was at Tuff Gong when Bob died. Because Bob had talked about us coming together again and singing, right? And it so happened that I was there at Tuff Gong awaiting his arrival, I was waiting for him to come home. And he used to call there sometimes from Germany and I personally would talk to him. I was just waiting and anticipating his arrival, but he just never came home. I spent a week at Tuff Gong. I just hang around Tuff Gong and slept in a room, hoping that Bob would come home.

ROGER STEFFENS: Edward Seaga, the man whose forces had come to kill Bob Marley in 1976 (although it must be noted there is no evidence that Seaga had advance knowledge of the plot), delivered the eulogy at Bob's funeral. It was the largest such gathering in Caribbean history, with more than a million mourners, half the island's population, lining the route from Kingston all the way to his burial place in Nine Mile. That day there were seven rainbows over the city of Kingston, on a bright morning when Bob's work was over and he flew away home to Zion.

CHAPTER 35

Marley's Legacy and the Wailers' Favorite Songs

ROGER STEFFENS: In the summer of 1969, when he was twenty-four, Bob Marley was living in Delaware at his mother's home. There he befriended Ibis Pitts, who had a small jewelry-making business and gallery nearby, in which he sold African art. Bob told Ibis and his friend Dion Wilson that he was going to die at age thirty-six.

IBIS PITTS: Dion is my buddy. He used to work with me at the shop. And he got to meet Nesta [Bob] too. He was around us a lot. And Nesta told us about him not being on this earth many more years than Jesus Christ was. And I just kind of passed it off, but Dion remembered the details. And when he heard the news about Nesta passing, he said, "Nesta said he was going to be leaving at thirty-six. And he was thirty-six years old when he died in 1981." And I said, "Wow, yeah, Dion."

ROGER STEFFENS: Bob's mother, Cedella Booker, confirmed that both Ibis and Dion mentioned this story to her in the 1960s. Following Bob's passing, others were eager to speak of his humility and generosity.

COLIN LESLIE: Bob bought many homes, but not for himself. He slept on a little cot upstairs, right above the garage at 56 Hope Road. It was very, very late in his career when some of the ladies in his life decided that it was very bad. We need to get a proper bedroom set up for him and they went up and got this custom-made furniture made for him. Beds and carpets.

Bob never thought about going off and making a nice comfortable life for himself, because that's not Bob, he never wanted that. He always wanted to help. He used to think that part of his job was to share whatever he had. He was a channel, if you like, from God, and it was his job to do what he could to help people. It was more a private thing.

Bob never wanted to go off somewhere and live like a rock star. Bob wanted to be with his people; man, he loved the people. And he wanted to stay with his people. He 's not a person who's going to leave his roots. He's going to be there. Regardless of how big Bob Marley got, he's not going to leave the people.

ROGER STEFFENS: Yet despite the constant stream of people, he always seemed alone.

GAYLE McGARRITY: With Bob, I don't remember too much small talk at all. Sometimes he would get kind of lighthearted and childlike, be in a really good mood, and be really happy, flashing his radiant smile. Bob and I became quite close for a while. I'm trying to remember exactly when; I think it was during the period right before some of his brethren apparently started telling him that he should not trust me, because I might be a spy. However, I have wonderful memories of us going to the beach together, and of us tearing up the dance floor at a roots dance together in Rae Town. He used to tell me that one of the reasons he liked being with me is because I looked like him. He was getting ready to go on tour once, and he really wanted me to come to the airport to see him off. When I told him that I didn't think I could, I remember him saying, "You think I have so many women and I have so many people I care about, but really I'm very lonely." It was a very sad kind of thing—the fact, despite all of those people around him, all of the hangers-on from Trench Town and Twelve Tribes, the Bull Bay contingent and the women, along with those who I'm sure genuinely did love and respect him—still the great Gong often felt very alone. Loneliness and being alone are two different things. He was never alone but sometimes with all the people there, he would just go up to his room and sit alone, in silence. That's when he would pick up the guitar. People wondered when did Bob actually have time to actually sit down and write his music, as he always had a zillion people around. Sometimes he would just escape from people and be by himself. Deep down inside Bob was kind of insecure, surprisingly, and he was very lonely.

ROGER STEFFENS: In an unreleased documentary called *Bob Marley: Stay with the Rhythm,* director Jonathan Demme interviewed a relative of Marley's in Nine Mile who declared that Bob told him he had nineteen children. Dessie Smith, Bob's personal assistant, spoke with me in Los Angeles in 1996 about Bob's role as a father.

DESSIE SMITH: Their father used to really have a strong hand on his children. Him deal with big men, when them did talk. When he like scold them, he talks to them like grownups, stern and that same kind of mannerism. So they have that toughness and them know right from wrong. He put it forward as forceful as he put it forward to a grownup. So them know, and they've got that type of drive, and the knowledge of what's right and wrong, they have it firmly in them from that time. I can see that in them. They have a strong presence, just like him.

ROGER STEFFENS: In 2012 the long-awaited official documentary film *Marley* was released. Many viewers were shocked by revelations from some of his children about Bob as a parent. Twenty-one years earlier, I had spoken with Rita and Bob's children, Ziggy and Cedella, regarding that subject, especially about the fact that Bob was so absent in their lives.

ZIGGY MARLEY: Biggest lesson we learn from Gong is to be strong still. Though not by any verbal teaching, but just by living life and watching things around. Just to be strong. Even in the face of death, as them would say, you haffe be strong.

CEDELLA MARLEY: We had a lot of good people around us. Our auntie

Ziggy Marley with the rejected cover for the first Melody Makers album.
At the Reggae Archives, Los Angeles, 1991.

was there, and she kind of take up the reins and bring us up certain way. Parents being away, they used to write and so on. We didn't realize they were away until they came back and we didn't have to go to school today because Bob and Mommy coming home. The lesson I learned from Bob was not to go anywhere! We could not go anywhere. It was like: "Don't go anywhere. You don't really need too many friends." And it's true. At that time when you're growing up everybody wants to have thousands of friends, but we weren't allowed to. I did resent that. You're a child, you want to be able to run across the street. We had to sneak across the street when Daddy was gone. And it was like, every time he would get back he would know.

ROGER STEFFENS: I wondered if the story were true that Bob had chased Ziggy one time, beat him, and then bought him ice cream. Ziggy laughed and admitted it was true.

CEDELLA MARLEY: You know, he does things like that. I think it's true, because you can never trust a lot of friends. You know, "Man to man is so unjust—your worst friend," blah blah. So it's true. You can be used and abused by friends, and I think that's what he was trying to let us know from such a long age. So that's one thing I would teach the kids.

ROGER STEFFENS: On Valentine's Day, 1987, the Wailers Band—Al Anderson, Junior Marvin, Seeco Patterson, Earl "Wya" Lindo and Carly and Aston "Family Man" Barrett—came to see the Reggae Archives on Valentine Street in L.A. It was their first look at a massive assembly of their works: films, videos, records, tapes of hundreds of hours of concerts and other unreleased Wailers material, cabinets filled with clippings, photographs and more. The band was on a ten-hour layover in L.A. en route home to Kingston from New Zealand, where they had played to a huge sold-out crowd. Their tour had also included three dates in Israel. The future looked brighter for the band than it had in a long time, with an album deal almost set and a major summer tour in the works. Carly, the enigmatic drummer, was healthy and coherent, belying recent rumors of emotional problems and obesity. Even Wya joined our conversations, albeit somewhat shyly. That evening, we looked at three hours of videos that have been held back from the public. Most of this footage the band had never seen, including historic moments in London in 1973 with Bob Marley and Peter Tosh, the Smile Jamaica concert in 1976, the Amandla benefit in Harvard Stadium in 1979 and the Zimbabwe independence celebration in 1980. As of this writing in 2016, none of these videos has been officially released, although the Marley estate bought the footage of Amandla and Zimbabwe in 2009.

After viewing the tapes, we spoke about each of the musicians' favorite tracks that they recorded with Marley. Excerpts from our conversation were broadcast in two parts in May 1987 on the cable TV show *L.A. Reggae*. The programs marked our final look at Carlton Barrett, the rock-solid heart of the Wailers, together with the men he played with for all those years. He was murdered in April 1987 in Kingston, supposedly by a gunman hired by his wife, although her conviction for conspiracy to commit murder was reversed on appeal. This was his final interview.

JUNIOR MARVIN: My favorite is "War." The words were written by Haile Selassie. And that's the message to mankind right now. That's the best song Bob ever do! Every time Bob sing "War" is like the first time him ever sing it, and the last time. His Majesty said that you must revel in the Bible. And when he said that speech, he didn't say it for anyone in particular, he said it for the whole world. But people don't even realize that yet; they're slowly coming to realize.

CARLTON BARRETT: My favorite is "Forever Loving Jah." Why? Because we have to!

AL ANDERSON: I'd say "Roots." I was around when he was writing it, and I saw how it came about to him. It was in Jamaica. Just as he sings the words, that's how it came about. All the people around him: there were certain people cooking food and motivating certain things, and certain energies were going down. I just hadn't seen anyone work like that, and use all the elements that were in front of him, and put them into songs like that.

FAMILY MAN BARRETT: Well I've got a wide range. What I will do is give you just three! Number one is "So Much Things To Say," and "Guiltiness" ("rest on their conscience every day"), also "Get Up Stand Up" ("for your rights").

EARL "WYA" LINDO: The *Confrontation* album was the heaviest. "Give

Thanks" and "Jump Nyabinghi." I love all of the songs on *Confrontation*. Some very good songs.

ALVIN "SEECO" PATTERSON: Mine is "Natty Dread." I'm a part of it! I think I got a few lines there.

ROGER STEFFENS: It's said that Bob wrote his songs in community, that the band would sit around on the porch or in the studio and people would throw lines at him, and he would incorporate them into a verse; if he found something he liked, he'd work it out a little further.

FAMILY MAN BARRETT: That's how it worked at times. We were all cowriters.

JUNIOR MARVIN: Bob used to give me ideas. But like my solo on "Waiting In Vain," that came to me in a dream. I heard the track, and then I tried it once and I said, "OK, I'll do it tomorrow." I went home; I slept, came back and did it in the first take. While I was sleeping, I dreamt about the song. And that's what came out.

ALVIN "SEECO" PATTERSON: You remember the "Work" song?

ROGER STEFFENS: "Five days to go, four days to go."

ALVIN "SEECO" PATTERSON: It wasn't days! It was miles. I was coming from the country. I start to run a riddim, and sing about the miles. And him say, "Continue that song. Just pick up the miles and put a melody to it." And me just go in the studio go work out on some records, and him say, would I work 'pon that, and me say, "Yeah mon," and me turn the miles into days. And there we go on so.

ROGER STEFFENS: The lyrics counting off the final days of his life became the last song on side one of his farewell album, *Uprising*, and the last song he sang (in a medley with "Get Up Stand Up") at his final concert in Pittsburgh.

Years later Wya and Junior spoke of their favorite concerts.

EARL "WYA" LINDO: I think that Ethiopian celebration in London with Bob was my favorite show with him. It was a charity performance in 1978. What made it so special was the momentum, the buildup, it was like all over London prior to the performance. That night I think he was kinda like more specially originative, like not just another performance. That's when he made an impression, he got over. That was the performance that made him a star.

JUNIOR MARVIN: To me every concert was a high point. They were all a little different. And the way that we looked at things is that every concert is the first and the last we'll ever do. That was something that rubbed off from Bob. We all feel the same way now. His influence has rubbed off on practically all the forerunners in reggae now. That's a foundation for reggae, the spiritual foundation. And you can't go any further than the spiritual foundation. The money and everything else is just part of it. Money can't buy life. But the spiritual foundation is for eternity.

EPILOGUE

ROGER STEFFENS: For a dozen years after Bob's passing, the story of the Marley estate was a sad one. Lawsuits abounded. Rita was accused of having forged and predated certain documents so as to transfer Marley's assets to herself. She admitted to having done so on the advice of Marley's attorney and accountant, who were found guilty of fraud and criminal conspiracy. Charges against her were dismissed, but she was removed as executor and the new Seaga administration in Jamaica took over the running of the estate for several years.* Eventually eleven children, including three who did not bear Bob's blood, were given a million dollars each.

Bob had predicted that reggae would just get bigger and bigger until it reached its rightful people. He might as well have been speaking of himself, as he has become one of the most abiding superstars of the twentieth century.

In 1994 he became the first third world inductee into the Rock and Roll Hall of Fame and Museum. At the millennium, the *New York Times* hailed him as the most influential musical artist of the second half of the twentieth century. A concurrent time capsule, meant to be opened at the dawn of the next millennium, in the year 3000, included

---

* http://www.forbes.com/sites/trialandheirs/2011/12/05/are-bob-marley-heirs-destroying-his-legacy/#5cdf871127d2.

the video of Marley's 1977 Rainbow concert as an example of the finest musical moment of the 1900s.

Time magazine chose *Exodus* as the best album of the century. And the BBC's twenty-four-hour coverage of millennial celebrations around the world opened each hour with local renditions of "One Love," as the millennium's anthem. A Grammy Lifetime Achievement award, a star on Hollywood Boulevard, the inclusion of *Burnin'* in the Library of Congress's historic music registry, are all indications that his work will never be forgotten.

Marley's posthumous greatest hits album, *Legend,* holds the distinction of being the longest-charting album in the history of *Billboard* magazine's catalog album chart, topping it frequently between 1984 and the present day.

In the social media era, Bob Marley has the second highest following of any late celebrity, with his Facebook page attracting more than sixty million followers.

Several of his children and grandchildren have successful recording careers, winning Grammys while touring the world with Bob's material and hits of their own.

Surely Bob Marley, the undisputed King of Reggae, would approve.

ACKNOWLEDGMENTS

First and foremost, I would like to thank every one of those whose words appear in these pages. Each was generous with their time and memories, and understood my desire to preserve their stories for posterity in unfiltered form.

My early comrades in the broadcasting world were the masterful Lance Linares of KUSP in Santa Cruz, California, and the hugely innovative DJ–VJ "Duppy Doug" Wendt, who, beginning in 1974, brought Jah music to several commercial stations in the San Francisco Bay area. These precedent-setting men created an environment in which the best of conscious Jamaican music would influence generations of listeners and musicians who have kept reggae alive and thriving in California. To this day, almost four decades later, we are in almost daily touch.

The "reggae recluse," Hank Holmes, probably taught me more about the music than anyone else ever has. Our seven-and-a-half-year partnership on *Reggae Beat* made it L.A.'s most popular "appointment radio," turning Sunday afternoons into a city-wide grounation. In addition, our one-hour syndicated program, *Reggae Beat International*, was eventually heard on 130 stations around the world including the Voice of America's Africa service, which led to fan letters in Swahili.

The esteemed bluesmaster Leroy Pierson embarked on his reggae studies in 1977. I was one of the first he contacted when he began a mail-order list of rare Jamaican seven-inch records. At great personal risk, he ventured into Kingston's no-man's-lands to unearth tons of vinyl gold. Some of the most cherished parts of my Reggae Archives I owe to him. I love him like a brother for all we have shared together, especially three weeks spent in Bunny Wailer's company as he poured out his soul to us in a Kingston hotel room. We then collaborated on the definitive discography of the Wailers, the prime resource for Wailers' vinyl collectors.

CC Smith and I met at Sunsplash '81 in Montego Bay and became friends and partners immediately. She came to KCRW determined to "straighten out the chaos," doing a weekly calendar of events and cofounding with me a newsletter originally called *Reggae Beat*, after our show. It contained playlists of our programs, Hank's Rastafari reasonings, and a column I called "Ras RoJah's Reggae Ramblings." As interest in world music broadened and I became the National Promotions Director of Reggae and African Music for Island Records (1982–83), its focus broadened and the newsletter became a full-fledged magazine called the *Reggae and African Beat*, which was finally shortened to just *The Beat*. It lasted an impressive and often precarious twenty-eight years, until in 2009 the Internet's toll on print publishing and the music industry led to its demise. CC provided the outlet for me to publish my interviews with reggae's greatest figures, many of which were adapted for this book. I will be eternally grateful to her for her perseverance and tight editorial guidance and counsel, and the great gift of her friendship. She is the prime reason the material for this book exists.

In 1980 I was invited by Trinidadian drummer and videographer Chili Charles, to be the host of his new cable TV show, *L.A. Reggae*. We worked side by side for twenty-three years. He was only a phone call away and ready with camera and lights for our *video vérité* interview sessions with the Wailers en route home from New Zealand, Peter Tosh in a Hollywood hotel, Fela Kuti in his underpants, Bunny Wailer in our backyard, Freddie McGregor at a hundred-year-old piano, Judy Mowatt in MoBay. And hundreds more. Without him, much of this book would not have been possible. And special appreciation to Chris Wilson, Heartbeat Records' longtime collaborator on the reissues of Coxsone's Wailers catalog.

Many writers have come through the Archives to research their books, and have become friends in the process. Among them are learned folks like John Masouri, Garry Steckles, Chris Salewicz and Stephen Davis, the latter a regular and valued contributor to *The Beat* magazine, with whom I have shared a laughter-strewn journey. His gregarious partner, photographer Peter Simon, was a willing co-conspirator in *The Beat* and gave us free some of our most important illustrations. He and I collaborated in 2007 on the award-winning *Reggae Scrapbook*.

I have also learned much from the distinguished poet, actor and author Kwame Dawes, whose insights in *Bob Marley: Lyrical Genius* proved invaluable on my *"Survival* Revival" tour with the Wailers in 2013. Similarly, wise counsel has always been a phone call away from revered broadcaster Dermot Hussey, a cherished friend who is a key voice on the reggae and jazz channels of SiriusXM satellite radio. Impeccable Marley publicist Jeff Walker and his keen-eyed photographer wife, Kim Gottlieb-Walker, have been close friends since the mid-1970s. Jeff was our first guest on the *Reggae Beat* and his eyewitness tales of the assassination attempt's aftermath proved riveting to our early listeners. I was honored when Kim invited me to write text for her excellent book *Bob Marley and the Golden Age of Reggae*. The Walkers introduced me to the esteemed oral historian David Rensin, whose precise instruction in the form helped give me the confidence to reconfigure the original conception of this book.

Kate Simon and Vivien Goldman, vivacious partners in the 1970s covering the emerging Jamaican musical revolution, have given me invaluable advice and warm friendship and freely shared stories of their time with Marley and his mates.

It was Warren Smith, the impresario of the Sierra Nevada World Music Festival, who gave me my first publication as a reggae writer in

his broadsheet, *Reggae News*. That led to my meeting with the flam-
boyant Liverpool Irish publicist for Bob and Peter, Charlie Comer. He
became like a Dutch uncle to me, introducing me to Tosh and treating this neophyte as if I were some bigshot journalist. He spent the
last week of his life with me at the Archives and left me his Diamond
Record award for ten million sales for *Legend*. He is one of the behind-
the-scenes people most responsible for Marley's enormous success.

Over the past twenty years I have had the great honor of being a
part-time member of the Midnight Ravers posse at WBAI, New York
City's estimable Pacifica outlet. The brilliant Terry Wilson, along with
"Sir Henry" Eccleston and their partners, have arranged for some of
the most important interviews of my life, finally corralling original
ska-era Wailers Cherry Green and Beverley Kelso for hours of amazing
conversations about the birth of the group. And thanks to meticulous
label chiefs Randall Grass and Chris Wilson for commissioning many
Wailers liner notes.

Bruno Blum, from Paris, is one of the most awe-inspiring and talented people I've ever encountered. Bruno has been a partner to me on
books and discs and magazines, most especially the fifteen-CD series
The Complete Bob Marley and the Wailers: 1967–1972. He is France's
greatest gift to reggae, and I value his friendship more than tongue can
tell. From Toronto, big-hearted humanitarian Greg Lawson provided
some of the most significant records in the collection.

South African documentarian Jo Menell is one of the Earth's
great characters, whether filming Castro's revolutionary advance into
Havana or running Allende's television network in Chile, or directing
BBC-TV's documentary wing, or seeking the hand of Haile Selassie's
granddaughter at the palace in Addis Ababa, or smuggling reggae tapes
to Nelson Mandela during his imprisonment. Jo was hired to be the
original director of the official Marley documentary, and his ability
to contextualize much of Marley's puzzling relationship with Chris
Blackwell put things into needed perspective for me.

In Jamaica, Marley's business manager and my dear friend, Colin Leslie, has provided guidance on many levels, determined as he is to find a way for my Archives to be institutionalized in his country. At the University of the West Indies I am deeply indebted to Dr. Matthew Smith, a scholar of immense knowledge and keen perception. He vetted my text and corrected my patois, placing things in proper context. His hand, though invisible, is present in much of the 1960s material herein. I am also grateful to scholars at UWI including Doctors Donna Hope, Michael Witter, Omar Davies and Clinton Hutton. Herbie Miller, Tosh's former manager, has been a thirty-year font of information. And I must pay deep thanks to the extraordinary broadcaster and dub poet Mutabaruka for his constant support in my quest to place my archives to Jamaica.

Throughout my reggae career I have been involved in countless projects, writing and otherwise, with my brother-from-another-mother Gary Himmelfarb, better known as Doctor Dread, the founder of RAS Records. He has opened many doors for me and given me many assignments that opened my eyes to new discoveries, and I will always be thankful for the many aspects of his zany creativity. Raggae activists "Native Wayne" Jobson and Amy "Night Nurse" Wachtel have been invaluable friends for decades.

In the present moment, perhaps the most important internet site for the study of the Wailers and their individual legacies is run by the indefatigable Mike Watson at midnightraverblog. With great integrity, he has been a tireless promoter of my work, ensuring that Marley's message will not be forgotten by future generations.

European collectors have shared their knowledge with me, most notably, in the UK, Dr. Sam Dion and Glen Lockley, founder of the Wailers fanzine *Distant Drums*. Expert London-based encyclopedist Dave Katz helped correct several points in my final draft. In Holland, I'm deeply indebted to the omnivorous Mike van der Linde. Erudite magazine editors Gilbert Paytel in France and Peter Lilly and Ellen Kohlings in Germany continue to publish my work in translation.

I would be remiss not to mention the support and tolerance of my loving family. My wife Mary, a beautiful Berkeley grad with a fine eye for style, is the first editor of everything I write and is unafraid to tell me when I am off-base. Daughter Kate and son Devon Marley have witnessed virtually every stage of my evolution from crazed young fan to grizzly elder, and both are writers and photographers of impressive ability. My love for them is boundless as they continue to circulate my photographs worldwide on instagram.com/thefamilyacid.

Linton Kwesi Johnson, author of this book's introduction, is the poet laureate of the reggae movement, an award-winning writer who is the genre's finest voice. We've known each other since 1982, and his acceptance of my invitation to do this still leaves me stunned and humbled.

Others who have helped in a wide variety of ways include Jessica Friedman and Laura Goldin, whose advice was invaluable. At Norton, I am deeply grateful to all who assisted in the design, editing and marketing of this book: Sarah Bolling, Don Rifkin, Elisabeth Kerr, Mary Kate Skehan, Allegra Huston, Ingsu Liu, Eleen Cheung, Louise Mattarelliano, Anna Oler, Kyle Radler, Steve Colca, Meredith McGinnis and Bill Rusin.

Finally, I would like to express my gratitude to one of the finest men I have ever encountered in my life, my original editor and sponsor of this project, W. W. Norton's vice president Jim Mairs. Throughout all the computer crashes and other setbacks he remained constant and encouraging and never let me lose sight of our goal. At the very end, as he neared retirement after a long and distinguished career at America's oldest independent publishing house, he turned the book over to a terrific young senior editor, Tom Mayer. Tom, himself a roots band veteran and deeply knowledgeable about all things reggae, spent the past two years directing the final shaping of this book which, he said proudly, he "was born to edit." My appreciation for both these learned men is beyond words.

Sadly, Jim passed away in 2016, but his spirit and guidance is alive in these pages.

LIST OF INTERVIEWEES

Al Anderson

Esther Anderson

Bob Andy

Carlton Barrett

Aston "Family Man" Barrett

George Barrett

Pablove Black

Chris Blackwell

Cedella Booker

Junior Braithwaite

Cindy Breakspeare

Errol Brown

Carl Colby

Allan "Skill" Cole

Charlie Comer

Cat Coore

Glen DaCosta

Stephen Davis

Coxson Dodd

Tyrone Downie

Alton Ellis

Bobby Ellis

Dr. "Pee Wee" Fraser

Lars Fyledal

Gilly Gilbert

Cherry Green

Norman St. John Hamilton

Dr. Steve Heilig

Joe Higgs

Dermot Hussey

Lee Jaffe

Dickie Jobson

Beverley Kelso

King Sporty

Colin Leslie

Jim Lewis

Earl "Wya" Lindo

Christopher Marley

Bob Marley

Cedella Marley

Rita Marley

Stephen Marley

Ziggy Marley

Junior Marvin

Dr. Gayle McGarrity

Judy Mowatt

Jimmy Norman

John Pareles

Alvin "Seeco" Patterson

Stefan Paul

Karl Pitterson

Ibis Pitts

Mortimo Planno

Bernard Purdie

Ras Michael

Kate Simon

Danny Sims

Donnice Sims

Eddie Sims

Dessie Smith

Matthew Smith

Bruce Talamon

Dr. Lowell Taubman

Don Taylor

Dennis Thompson

Dera Tompkins

Peter Tosh

Joe Venneri

Bunny Wailer

Constantine "Dream"

"Vision" Walker

Jeff Walker

Segree Wesley

Neville Willoughby

Betty Wright

Zema

INDEX

Page numbers in *italics* refer to illustrations.

Abyssinians, 369

Adams, Glen, 117, 119, 127

Africa, xiii, xxv, 21, 165, 202, 206, 223, 257, 266, 278, 303–4, 305, 325, 326, 347, 348, 350, 356
  BM's trips to, 312–14, 336–45, *346*
  liberation movement in, 301

"Africa Unite" (song), 301, 347

Afro-American Studies Center, 326

Alderson, Richard, 100

Ali, Muhammad, 97

Alphonso, Roland, 29, 44

Althea and Donna, 293

Alton and Eddie, 41

Amandla benefit, 403, 404

"Ambush In The Night" (song), 195

America Jamaica United, 387

American Film Institute, xxiii

American Institute of Science, 391

Am-Jam United, 286

Anderson, Al, 195, 203, 204, 207, 258, 268, 270–71, *272–73*, 307, 328, 335, 352, 403, 404

Anderson, Esther, *161*, 165, 180, 190, 192
  BM's relationship with, 159
  in collaboration with BM, 160, 161–62, *163*

Anderson, Gladstone, 115

Anderson, Rita, *see* Marley, Rita Anderson

Anderson, Yvette Morris, 180, 346, 388

"And I Love Her" (song), 47

Andy, Bob, 47, 57–58, *57*, 61, 63, 151

"Another One Bites the Dust" (song), 381–82, *383*

Apollo Theater, 327, 331–33, *334*, 335, 349

Armone, Joe, 373–74

ASCAP, 147

Asfa Wossen, Crown Prince of Ethiopia, 279

Asher, Dick, 140, 141, 145, 147

Aspen, Colo., *6*, 60, *60*

Atlantic Records, 100, 103

Australia, 286, 387

Austria, 394

Average White Band, 368

Babylon by Bus (album), 283, 306, 307, *308–9*

"Babylon Feel This One" (song), 324

Back O' Wall, 10, *18*, *25*, 40

"Bad Card" (song), 190

Bahamas, 254, 264

"Bangarang" (song), 119

Barrett, Aston "Family Man," xxiii, xxv, 117–19, *118*, 127, 128, 138, 142, 145, 151, *156*, 157, 159–60, *163*, 164, 173, 177, *179*, 203, 204, 207, 211, 224, 231, 235, *236*, 238, 243, 248, 250, 251, 268, 272, 273, 300, 328–29, 352, 377, 403, 404, *405*

Barrett, Carlton "Carly," xxv, 117–19, *118*, 128, 138, 142, 145, 152, 159, *179*, 207, 211, 224, 238, 248, 250, 251, 273, 274, 352, 403, 404

Barrett, George, 117, *118*, 129, 130–32

Barretto, Ray, 229

Basing Street Studios, 158, 267

Bass, Charlie, 127–28

Battle of the Giants show, 68–70

BBC, 111, 152

Beat, The, xxiii, 69, 134, 228, 287, 349

Beatles, 47, 56, 87, 113, 157, 168, 274

Beck, Jeff, 270

Before the Legend (Farley), xxv
Belafonte, Harry, 27–28, 100
"Bend Down Low" (song), 81–82, 136–37, 142
Bergman, Ingmar, 134
Berkeley, Calif., 309, 310
Berry, Chuck, 202
Bertram, Arnold, 219
Best of the Wailers (album), 113, 115–16
"Be There When I Come" (song), 25
Beverley's (record label), 16, 22, 108,
    113, 114, 164
*Beverly Johnson Guide to Health and
    Beauty, The*, 286
Bible, 71, 77, 318, 364, 404
Big Youth, 293
Billboard, 300, 408
Bill Graham Presents (Greenfield), xxiv
Birth of a Legend (album), 212–13
Black, Pablove, 195–97, 196, 219–20, 222–24,
    233–34, 239
  on BM assassination attempt, 230
  on BM's decision to do Smile Jamaica con-
    cert, 240, 242
  on motive for BM assassination
    attempt, 257, 258
  on Smile Jamaica concert, 247,
    248, 251, 253
Black, Solomon, 4
"Black Cinderella" (song), 128
Blackheart Man, 2
Blackheart Man (album), 182, 307
Black Man, 204
Black Music, xx
Black Music Association, 349
Black Power movement, 14, 74, 79, 127
"Black Survival" (song), 367
Blackwell, Chris, xv, 81, 109, 126, 138, 139,
    150–51, 152, 155, 159, 160, 185, 189, 199,
    210, 234, 251, 268–69, 274, 307–8, 319,
    372, 386, 389
  Bahamas studio of, 254
  and BM assassination attempt, 225–26,
    230, 231, 236
  BM's contract acquired by, 147–48, 213
  BM's relationship with, 208,
    277–78, 323–24
  BM's toe injury and, 283–84, 286
  and breakup of Wailers, 166–68
  Cliff and, 176, 177
  commercial focus of, 180
  Hope Road sold to BM by, 199, 222
  Marvin and, 268, 270
  piracy charges against, 145–46
  "Redemption Song" and, 364

in royalties disputes with Wailers, 149–50,
    163–64, 269
  as Smile Jamaica film producer, 228–29,
    232, 233, 236, 260–61
Black Woman (album), 316–18
Blake, Duane, 373
Blake, Vivian, 373
"Blood Stain" (song), 60
Blues Busters, 41
Bobbitt, Charles, 336, 340, 341
Bob Marley (Davis), xxv, 128
Bob Marley: Spirit Dancer (Talamon and Stef-
    fens), 328
Bob Marley: Stay with the Rhythm (unreleased
    documentary), 401
Bob Marley and the Wailers, 185–87, 207,
    208–11, 214–15, 216–18, 225, 226, 240,
    242–43, 255, 264, 268, 274, 278, 308,
    326, 348, 363–64, 385
  BM's cancer and, 381
  Gabon trip of, 336–45
  I Three as backup singers for, 184–85
  in London, 270
  Marvin's joining of, 270–73
  1975 tour of, 202–4
  1976 tour of, 210, 214, 221
  1977 tour of, 282–83
  in 1978 world tour, 306–7, 309–12
  in 1979 North American tour, 327–29,
    330–36, 349
  in 1980 tour, 367–68, 371–84
  in One Love Peace Concert, 288–304
  as opener for Commodores, 372,
    373, 375–77
  Pittsburgh (last) show of, 381–82, 387
  in Zimbabwe independence tour,
    347, 351–62
  see also Wailers (original lineup);
    Wailers Band
*Bob Marley and the Wailers: The Definitive Dis-
    cography* (Steffens and Pierson), xxiii
Bob Marley Music, 276
Bongo, Omar, 336, 337, 339, 345
Bongo, Pascaline and Albertine, 336,
    337, 339, 341
Booker, Cedella Malcolm Marley, xvii, xxiv,
    1–2, 3, 4, 5, 7, 8, 10, 11, 17, 67, 68, 106,
    107–8, 198, 214, 266, 274, 280, 287,
    298, 364, 365, 396, 399
Booker, Edward, 68
Book of Exodus, The (Goldman), xxv
Box Tops, 104
Boys Town, 64, 85, 283
Braithwaite, Junior, 12, 13, 17, 21, 25–26, 28, 31,

33, 36, 37, 39, 40–41, 42, 43, 44, 45, 48,
    49, 190, 397–98
Braithwaite, Zebedee, 25
Bramwell, Ermine, *see* Green, Cherry
Brando, Marlon, 160, 165
Brazil, 139, 325
Breakspeare, Cindy, xvii, 98, 192, *199*, 274,
    282–83, 324, 394
    BM's breakup with, 370–71
    on BM's cancer, 285, 388, 390–91
    on BM's generosity, 321–22
    on BM's last day, 397
    BM's love affair with, 198, 200–201,
        206, 220, 221, 264, 265, 266,
        267–68, 279–80
    BM's politics influenced by, 266
    on BM's toe injury, 282–83
    Hope Road apartment of, 198, *199*–200
    as JLP supporter, 265
    as Miss World, 198, *199*, 201, 203, 221, 264,
        265–66, 267
Breakspeare, Stephen "Reds," 165, 192, 199
Brevett, Lloyd, 44
Brief History of Seven Killings, A (James), 259
Broccetti, Fred, 229, 232, 237, 239, 247, *250*
Brown, Dennis, 130
Brown, Errol, 322–23, 348, 363–64
    on final show, 383–84
    on Madison Square Garden shows, 376
    on 1980 tour, 367, 368, 374
    on Zimbabwe tour, 353, 354, 355
Brown, Hux, 115
Brown, James, 127, 336, 340
Brown, Jim, 257
Brown, Phil, 159
Bucknor, Siddy, 37
"Buffalo Soldier" (song), 56, *332*
Bundrick, Johnny "Rabbit," 135, 136
Bunny and Skully, 41
Burbank, Calif., 311
"Burial" (song), 47–48, 90
Burnin' (album), 157, 158–66, *161*, 169, 174,
    180–82, 408
"Burnin' And Lootin'" (song), 163–
    64, 212, 303
Burning Spear, 369
Buster, Prince, 146, 289
Butler, Delroy, 195

California, 210, 306, 308–9, 326
California, University of, at Los Angeles
    (UCLA), 327
calypso, 24
Campbell, Charles, 216, 219

Campbell, Dennis "Ska," 44
Campbell, Horace, 354
Canada, 99, 254, 291, 296, 297
Capitol Records building, 174
Caribbean, 75, 107, 108, 109, 139, 160, 291
Caribbean Preserving, 53
Carib Theatre, 42, 198
Castellano, Paul, 373–74
Catch A Fire (album), xix, 138, 151–52, 155–56,
    157, 158, 159, 170, 175, 185, 198, 250
"Caution" (song), 113, 114
Caymanas Park, 258
Cayman Islands, 94–95
Cayman Music, 94–95, 133, 140, 147, 390
CB Enterprises, 274
CBS Records, *see* Sony Records
Cedars of Lebanon Hospital
    (Miami), 284, 286
Central Park, N.Y., 186, 378, 379, 380,
    382, 384, 388
Chaio (studio engineer), 323
"Chances Are" (song), 104
Charles, Chili, xxii, 311
Charles, Prince of Wales, 351–52, 356, 357, 358
"Cheer Up" (song), 113, 115
Chicago, Ill., 42, 137, 394
Chieftains, 274
Chin, Randy, 96, 99–100, 101
Chosen Few, 130
Christians, 184, 389
CIA (Central Intelligence Agency), xiii, xxv, 73,
    260, 261, 262, 263, 287
    accused of involvement in BM assassination
        attempt, 227–28
Cimarons, 251
Clapton, Eric, 147, 160, 202
Clarendon, Jamaica, 1
Clarke, Sebastian, 167
"Clean Up Woman" (song), 331
Cliff, Jimmy, xx, 145, 148, 159, 175, 176–77
Club 21, 130
Coasters, 101
Cockburn, Alex, 165
Coghile, Leghorn, 177–78
Colby, Carl, 227–30, *228*, 236–39, 247, 248
    accused of involvement in BM assassination
        attempt, 259–63
    BM film interview by, 239, 261
    on BM's strength of character, 262
    on motive for assassination
        attempt, 259–60
    on Smile Jamaica concert, 245–46,
        249–50, 252–53
    on Smile Jamaica film, 232–33, 236–37

Colby, William, 227, 260, 261, 262, 263
Cole, Allan "Skill," xvii, 15, 113–14, 202, 207,
    312, 313, 372, 373, 374
  on BM's adolescence, 14–15
  and BM's cancer, 378–82, 384,
    390, 391, 394
  BM's friendship with, 14, 110–11, 194–
    95, 214, 255
  on BM's generosity, 320–21
  on BM's relationship with Sims and
    Nash, 133–34
  as possible target of assassination
    attempt, 224, 255, 256–57
  on pressure felt by BM, 84–85
  in Twelve Tribes, 214, 219
  as Wailers manager, 107, 111–12, 137–39
Cole, Nat King, 28
Cole, Stranger, 119
Columbia Records, see Sony Records
Comer, Charlie, 274–76, 275, 293
"Coming In From The Cold"
    (song), 363, 366
"Comma Comma" (song), 90, 100
Commodores, 275–77, 371, 372, 373
Communists, Communism, 79, 266,
    312, 313, 346
Compass Point studio, 254
Complete Bob Marley and the Wailers 1967–
    1972 (box set), 102, 139
"Concrete Jungle" (song), 331
Confrontation (album), 404–5
Constantine, Alex, 260, 261
Cooper, Michael "Ibo," 171, 251
Coore, Cat, xvii, 51, 121, 129–30, 131, 170,
    171, 195, 235, 248, 251
  on BM's Smile Jamaica per-
    formance, 250
  on motive for assassination
    attempt, 258–59
  on Smile Jamaica concert, 242–44
copyright law, 176–77
"Could You Be Loved" (song), 348,
    372–73, 376
Count Nick the Champ (sound system), 24
Count Ossie and the Mystic Revelation of
    Rastafari, xix, 17, 120
Cowan, Tommy, 316, 352, 354
Cowsills, 104
"Crazy Baldhead" (song), 208
Criteria Studios, 208, 210
Crocker, Frankie, 371, 372
"Cry Baby" (song), 32
"Crying In The Chapel" (song), 110
Crystal Palace, 368

Cuba, 1, 79, 132, 346, 347
Cuthell, Dick, 268

DaCosta, Glen, 224, 334–35
Daley, Lloyd "Matador," 119
Daley, Richard, 248
"Dancing Shoes" (song), 60
Dark, Frankie, 110
Darlington, Mrs., 23–24
Davis, Clive, 145
Davis, Sangie, 196–97, 316, 324–25
Davis, Stephen, xxv, 128, 216–17, 225, 231,
    239, 254, 256, 257, 258
"Day Dreaming" (song), 103
Dean's (sound system), 24
Dekker, Desmond, 16, 100, 113, 159
de Kooning, Willem, 237
Delaware, BM in, 4, 59, 68–69, 73, 76, 80,
    87, 107, 283, 316, 399
Demme, Jonathan, 401
Desmond Dekker and the Aces, 100, 113
Diddley, Bo, 202
Dion and the Belmonts, 32, 47
Dizzy's (club), 265
Dodd, Clement "Coxson," 23, 29, 30–33,
    32, 37, 40, 45, 48, 49–50, 51, 52, 53,
    61, 67, 68, 77–78, 113, 114, 117, 121,
    132, 141, 152
  on Birth of a Legend album, 212–13
  Higgs and, 46–47
  payment issues and, 46, 81–82,
    108–9, 149–50
  on "Simmer Down" release, 38
  Wailers' break with, 80–82
  on Wailers' first recording session, 31–33
  see also Studio One
"Do It Twice" (song), 113
Domino, Fats, 2
Donahue, Tom, 173
Don and Juan, 61
"Don't Look Back" (song), 74
"Don't Rock My Boat" (song), 94
Doreen (Cherry Green's friend), 53
Dortmund, Germany, 394
"Do the Reggay" (song), 12
Downie, Donald, 127
Downie, Tyrone, 127–28, 231, 235, 248, 250,
    251, 254, 271, 300, 301, 302–3, 352, 397
  on BM assassination attempt, 224–
    25, 255, 256
  in 1975 tour, 202–4
  on Wailers Band as musical co-creators,
    276–77
"Down In The Valley" (song), 317

"Do You Still Love Me" (song), 16
"Drastic Step" (song), 365
Dread, Gabby, 193
Dread Beat an Blood (Johnson), xv
Dream Concert, 194
"Dreamland" (song), 48, 60
Drive-In Cracker Boys (Jiving Crackerballs), 117
Drummond, Don, 44, 82, 115
Dunkley, Errol, 128
Dunrobin school, 61
"Duppy Conqueror" (song), 122, 142, 164
Dylan, Bob, 32, 245
Dynamic Sounds Studio, 111, 115, 125, 129, 149, 151, 218

Echo Squad, 225
Eckstine, Billy, 23
Egypt, 317, 318
"Eleanor Rigby" (song), 87
Eleven Mile, Jamaica, 193
"Eleven Sound" contest, 24
Ellington, Duke, 28
Ellis, Alton, xix, *18*, 55, 130
    on BM's self-confidence and spiritual
        powers, 54–56
Ellis, Bobby, 50–51
Ellis, Diane, 316
Ellis, Hortense, 39
El Tempos, 48
England:
    BM in, 133, 144–45, 201, 264–72, 274–75
    Wailers in, 137–39, 140, 142–43, 156–57, 158–59
    see also London
Epstein, Brian, 274
Equal Rights (album), 182
Essex House, 374, 378
Ethiopia, 74, 206, 233, 257, 279, 347
    BM's trip to, 312–14, 346
    Italian invasion of, 71, 326
Ethiopian Orthodox Church, 321, 392
Europafilm, 135
Exodus (album), xiii, 147, 210, 211, 266–68, 270–71, 274, 277, 278–80, 282, 306, 408
"Exodus" (song), 360

Facebook, 408
Fallout Shelter, 267
Fanny and Alexander (film), 134
Farley, Christopher John, xxv
"Fifteen Minutes" (song), 136
Flack, Roberta, 103, 238, 242
Flippins (Twelve Tribes member), 313–14

Florida, 23, 384, 388, 397
Folks, Jeff, 109
Forbes, xxvi
Ford, Gerald, 261
Ford, Vincent "Tata," 67, 75
"Foreigner" (song), 103
Forest Hills, Jamaica, 201
"Forever Loving Jah" (song), 404
France, 216, 282, 283, 342
Frank, Peter, 226, 228, 230, 232, 237, 249
Franklin, Aretha, 99, 103
Fraser, Carlton "Pee Wee," 233, 247, 283–85, 394
    and BM's cancer, 388–89, 391–92
"Freedom Time" (song), 81
Fyledal, Lars, 134

Gabon, xxv, 346
    BM's trip to, 336–45, 346
Gad, Prophet, 240
Gale, Eric, 99
Gallimore, Neville, 128
Gambino organization, 373, 374
Garnett Mimms and the Enchanters, 32
Garrick, Neville, *11*, 202, 209, 214, 215, 218–19, 253, 254, 291, 309, 312–14, 352, 354, 365, 381, 392
    as BM's art director, 209–12
    on *Exodus* cover, 278–79
    on *Kaya* cover, 308
    lighting effects of, 211–12
    on *Survival* cover, 325–26
    on Zimbabwe trip, 348
Garvey, Marcus, 202, 327
Gaye, Marvin, 175, 176, 187, 198, 209
Gaylads, 54, 56
Gayle, Carl, 204
General Penitentiary, 94
Germany, BM's cancer treatment in, 385, 390–97, 398
"Get Up Stand Up" (song), 72, 160, 182, 311, 375, 377, 383, 404, 405
Ghana, 303
Gifford, Marlene "Precious," 61, 63, 66, 77, 83
Gilbert, Gilly, 182–83, 191–92, 281, 282, 303–4, 321, 336, 352, 379
    on BM's cancer, 385
    on BM's diet and exercise habits, 192–93
    on BM's final show in Pittsburgh, 381
    on BM's Gabon trip, 337–38
    on BM's soccer playing, 285–86, 387
    on Jamaican peace movement, 299
    on Madison Square Garden shows, 375
    on 1980 tour, 374

"Give Thanks" (song), 404–5
Godfrey, Arthur, 137
Goldman, Vivien, xxv
Good, The Bad and the Ugly, The (film), 162
Gopthal, Lee, 139, 145
Gordon Town, Jamaica, 152
Gordy, Berry, 315
"Go Tell It On The Mountain" (song), 113
Gottlieb-Walker, Kim, 217
Gough, Miss, 192, 222
Graham, Bill, 202, 212
Grammy Awards, xxiii, 408
Grammy Lifetime Achievment award, 408
Grammy Museum, 310
Grant, Eddy, 350
Gray, Claude, 16
Gray, Miss, 5
Green, Cherry, 25, 26–29, 27, 31–32, 43, 46
    on BM's adolescence, 28–29
    conflicts between work and Wailers
        gigs of, 53
    on recording sessions, 44
Greenfield, Robert, xxiv
Gregory, Tony, 45, 63
Griffiths, Marcia, 63, 151, 183–84, 183,
    204, 221–22, 223, 322–23, 333,
    352, 355, 358
grounations, 61, 90, 96, 289–90
Gruen, Bob, 330
"Guava Jelly" (song), 100, 147
Guevara, Che, xiii
"Guiltiness" (song), 404

"Habits" (song), 33
Haile Selassie I, Emperor of Ethiopia, 12, 74,
    129, 164–65, 181, 192, 202, 305, 309,
    326, 328, 404
    in Jamaica visit, 71, 72, 75–78, 82
    overthrow of, 279, 312
    as second coming of Christ, 71, 76, 77, 78
Haiti, 160
Halfway Tree, Kingston, 48, 97, 225
Hall, Gary, 110–11
"Hallelujah Time" (song), 182
Hamilton, Norman St. John, 221–22
"Hammer" (song), 94
Hammond, Beres, 293
Hannah, Barbara Blake, 392
Hanson, Junior Kerr Marvin, see
    Marvin, Junior
Hanson (band), 270
Harare, Zimbabwe, 350, 352, 354, 361
Harder They Come, The (film), xix, 97, 175,
    176, 229, 232

Harder They Come, The
    (soundtrack), 176, 252
Harlem, N.Y., 327, 335, 349
Harriott, Derrick, 47, 95
Harris, Richard, 274
Harry J, 151, 158, 184
Hartman, Daniel, 97
Harvard Stadium, 403
Harvey, Touter, 204
Hathaway, Donny, 103
Haynes, "Jah Jerry," 44
Heartbeat Records, 213
Heartland Reggae (film), xxi, 290–91, 291,
    292–93, 294, 296–98
Heilig, Steve, 309
Hendrix, Jimi, 270, 271
Henzell, Perry, xix, 175, 176, 226, 229, 232,
    233, 237, 242, 248–49, 260
Heptones, 54
"Here Comes the Judge" (song), xxii
Hibert, Toots, 270
Higgs, Joe, xvi, 8, 10–13, 11, 14, 17, 24–25,
    30, 32, 39, 41, 45, 150–51, 152,
    163, 176–78
    BM mentored by, 54
    Dodd and, 46–47
    on founding of Wailers, 12–13
    on "Simmer Down" release, 38
    on Tosh, 20
    in Wailers' 1973 U.S. tour, 172–74
    on Wailers' first recording sessions, 33–34
    Wailers mentored by, 15–16, 22, 25, 28
    on writing and performing rights, 47
Higgs, Valerie, 194
Higgs and Wilson, 39, 41, 46
Hill, Joseph "Culture," 293, 324, 325
Hill, Stephen, 175–76
Hippy Boys, 117, 119
Hofler, Walter, 107
Hold Me Tight (album), 99, 107
"Hold Me Tight" (song), 137
Holly, Buddy, 202
Hollywood Sunset Marquis, 236
Holmes, Hank, xx–xxii, 181, 299, 327, 328
Homestead, 173
"Hooligans" (song), 50
Hope Road, as Island Records headquar-
    ters, 150, 156
Hope Road, as Tuff Gong headquarters,
    188, 189–91, 192, 193–94, 195–96,
    205, 208, 209, 215, 216, 220, 222–25,
    230–31, 238, 256, 257, 260, 265,
    288–89, 315, 316, 319, 321, 322–
    23, 398, 399

apartments at, 189, 194, 198, 199–200
film of assassination attempt aftermath
    at, 235–36
recording studio at, 163, 189, 315,
    316–17, 322–23
House of Blues, Cambridge, 153
House of Chen, 184
"How Can I Be Sure" (song), 46
Hurrell, George, 237
"Hurting Inside" (song), 94
Hussey, Dermot, xvi, 152, 153, 178, 182, 187–
    88, 194–95, 206
Hutton, Clinton, 40

I Can See Clearly Now (album), 140, 141
"I Can See Clearly Now" (song), 144
"I Love You, Baby" (song), 66
"I'm Gonna Get You" (song), 140
Imperials, 311
Impressions, 33, 42, 61, 74, 102
"I'm So Proud" (song), 42
"I'm Still Waiting" (song), 69
"I'm the Toughest" (song), 59
Incredible Sounds studio, 100
Industry, Gordon Town, 152
"I Need You" (song), 60
Inner Circle, 129, 170, 293, 372
Institute of Jamaica, 93, 180
Intel-Diplo, 181
International Year of the Rasta
    Child show, 349
Isaiah, Book of, 77
"I Shot the Sheriff" (song), 147, 160–63,
    202, 224, 355, 357
Island House, see Hope Road
Island Records, xv, xix, 109, 145, 146, 147,
    148, 149, 151, 158, 166, 167, 175, 177,
    185, 186, 189, 204, 212, 217, 232, 235,
    238, 261, 267, 269, 274, 277–78, 284,
    308, 330, 352, 368, 386
Isley, Ernie, 271
"isms," Rastafarians' rejection of, xv, 109,
    165, 182, 346–47
Israel, 317–18, 361, 403
"Israelites" (song), 100, 113
Issels, Ilse Marie, 393–94
Issels, Josef, 390, 391–97
"I Stand Predominate" (song), 60, 73
"Is This Love?" (song), 266
Ital Craft, 370
Italy, 71, 368
    Ethiopia invaded by, 71
I Three, 184, 185, 205, 221, 317, 338,
    354, 357, 359

"It Hurts To Be Alone" (song), 25, 31, 33,
    41–42, 48, 57, 69
"It Was Your Love" (song), 25

Jackson, Jackie, 115, 203–4
Jackson, Michael, 39, 336
Jackson Five, 187
Jacksons, 203
JAD Records, 95, 99, 100–101, 102, 107, 108,
    110, 132, 146, 147
    BM's contract with, 103–6, 139, 177
Jaffe, Lee, 160, 162–63, 186–87
Jagger, Bianca, 278
Jagger, Mick, 274, 278, 293, 309, 311
"Jah Live" (song), 296
"Jailhouse" (song), 57
Jamaica:
    anti-violence movement in, 288, 290–91,
        293, 298–99, 304
    BM in 1978 return to, 288–304
    colonial history of, 7, 128
    Haile Selassie's visit to, 71, 72, 75–78, 82
    High Court of, 109
    middle-class exodus from, 179
    music business in, see music busi-
        ness, Jamaican
    nationalistic pride in, 40
    1976 election in, 216–18, 232,
        258–59, 288
    political and gang violence in, 78–79,
        119, 178, 179, 193, 216–17, 219, 258–
        59, 288, 302
    racism in, 7, 220
Jamaica College, 121
Jamaica Daily News, 209
Jamaica House, 219
Jamaica Labour Party (JLP), 28, 40, 119,
    128, 129, 131, 220, 255, 257, 258,
    265, 288, 293
Jamaican Broadcasting Company (JBC), 90,
    93, 110, 194
Jamaica Sunday Gleaner, 392
James, Marlon, 259
Jamma (painting), 305
Jamming (TV show), 291
"Jamming" (song), 272, 276, 337
Japan, 368
Jeff (Rasta cook), 96
Jenkins, Arthur, 95, 96, 99, 101, 102, 148
Jesus Christ, 71, 72, 76, 78, 318, 392
Jiving Crackerballs (Drive-In Cracker
    Boys), 117
Job (entrepreneur), 353, 354, 359
Jobson, Diane, 292

Jobson, Dickie, 150, 151, 152–53, 154–55, 200, 222, 230, 231, 236
John Paul II, Pope, 367
Johnson, Al, 48
Johnson, Linton Kwesi, xiii–xvii, *xiv*
Jones, Tom, 47
Jones Town, Kingston, 27, 29, 34, 53
Joplin, Janis, 202
Jordan, Fred, 135
Joseph (biblical character), 317
"Joseph" (song), 317–18
"Judge Not" (song), 16–17
"Jump Nyabinghi" (song), 405

Katz, David, 125
Kaya (album), 211, 266, 268, 270, 306, 307, *307, 308*, 309, 322
"Kaya" (song), 122
KCRW (radio station), xx–xxi, 128, 299, 327
"Keep On Moving" (song), 74, 142, 143, 382, 383
Kelso, Beverley, xvi, 26, 34–39, *34*, 41, 43–44, 52–54, 68, 72–73, 201–2
    on BM as Wailers' leader, 45
    BM's friendship wtih, 66–67
    on BM's Hope Road headquarters, 190–91, 193–94
    on BM's infidelities, 83
    in break with BM, 201
    in departure from Wailers, 82, 83–84
    in move to U.S., 84
    on recording sessions, 44–46
    Rita Marley and, 61–67, 84
    on "Simmer Down" release, 37–38
    on Wailers' collaborative writing, 49
    on Wailers' first recording sessions, 36–37
    on Wailers' first stage shows, 52–53
Kennedy, John F., Jr., 278
Kenya, 312, 346
Khouri, Paul, 105
King of Reggae tour, 138
King's Theatre, 10
Kingston, Jamaica:
    BM's childhood and adolescence in, 7, 8, 28–29
    see also Hope Road; Trench Town
Kingston, London, 140, 158, 162
Kingston Central, 187
Kingston College, 14, 90, 127
Kingston Legal Aid Clinic, 180
Kinsey, Donald, 210, 224, 225, 243, 250, 251
KJLH (radio station), 373
Kline, Franz, 237
Knibb, Lloyd, 44

Kong, Leslie, 16, 22, 107, 108, 112–16, 132
KSAN (radio station), 173

LaBelle, Patti, 35
Laing, Denzil, 169
Lako, Skipper, 12
Lancaster House Agreements, 313
Langston Road, East Kingston, 117
L.A. Reggae (TV show), xxii, 311, 404
Las Vegas, Nev., 173
L.A. Weekly, xxi, 328
Lazarus, Ken, 176
Lee, Bunny, 119
Lee, Byron, 95, 101, 104, 129, 176, 331
Lee, Carlton, 115, 151
Legalize It (album), 186, 187
Legend (album), 408
Lenin, V. I., 312
Lennon, John, 274, 330
Leslie, Colin, 315–16
    as BM's business manager, 368–69
    on BM's generosity, 318–19, 321, 399–400
    on BM's relationship with Blackwell, 323–24
"Let Him Go" (song), 59, 73
"Letter, The" (song), 104
Levy, Morris, 213
Lewis, Alva "Reggie," 117, 119, 127
Lewis, Jim, 290, 291–93, *291*, 294, 295, 296–99
Library of Congress, 408
Life, Tek, 220, 233
"Life of Boby Marley" (multimedia program), xvi, xxiii, 324
Life of Contradiction (album), 150
Lindo, Earl "Wya," 127, 159, 204, 352, 374, 380, 403, 404–6
Lingard, Marlene, 136
Lips (Marley's bodyguard), 312, *313*
"Liquidator" (song), 151
"Little Boy Blue," 74
Little D, 233, 239
"Little Did You Know" (song), 33, 50
"Lively Up Yourself" (song), 137
"Living On The Front Line" (song), 350–51
Livingston, Neville O'Reilly, *see* Wailer, Bunny
Livingston, Pearl, 8, 364
Livingston, Thaddeus "Toddy," 5, 7, 8, 9, 10, 11, 88
London, 139, 145, 146, 147, 149, 157, 158, 163, 198, 204, 279, 280, 282, 286, 347, 403, 405

BM's post-shooting stay in, 201,
264–72, 274–75
Wailers in, 137–38, 140
London School of Economics, 221
London School of Technique, 152
"Lonesome Feeling" (song), 33, 43, 46, 53
"(Lord, I Gotta) Keep On Moving" (song),
74, 142, 143, 382, 383
Los Angeles, Calif., xx, xxii, 3, 10, 128, 186,
227, 235, 274, 299, 309, 311, 327, 328,
336, 372, 392, 403
Lotus (club), 48
"Love" (song), 98
"Love and Affection" (song), 69, 143
Lucea, Jamaica, xx
Lymon, Frankie, 25
Lyn, Robbie, 170, 203

Mackie, Bongo, 165
Madden, Dave, 224, 334–35
Madison Square Garden, 349, 371, 372, 373,
374, 375–78, 382
Mafia, 373, 374
"Maga Dog" (song), 43
Mairs, Jim, xxiv
Malachi, Prince, 312, 313
Malcolm X, 127
Manhattan Transfer Show, The (TV
show), 207, 226
Manley, Michael, xiii, xx, 132, 176, 179,
231, 232, 233, 243, 256, 258, 259, 265–
66, 288, 293
BM assassination attempt and, 231, 256, 258
in One Love Peace Concert meeting with
Seaga, 290–91, 295, 301
Rastafarian support for, 129
Smile Jamaica concert and, 216–17, 220,
221, 250, 251
Wailers' 1971–72 tour in support of, 128,
129, 130–31
Manticore Records, 270
Maple Leaf Garden, 333
Marcenine (Cedella Booker's cousin), 4
Marguerite (dancer-singer), 115
marijuana:
BM and, 72–73, 185, 361
in Rastafarian culture, 71, 75
Marley, Bob:
adolescence of, 8, 28–29
on African liberation, 303
alternative cancer treatments sought
for, 390–93
assassination attempt on, xxv, 215, 216,
219, 222–26, 255–62

Beeston Street recordings of, 18
birth of, 1
Cedella's rejection of, 11
chemotherapy of, 389, 390
childhood of, 2–4, 5–7
copyrights hidden by, 177–78
daily routine of, 364–65
diet and exercise habits of, 192–93
donkey of, 2, 89, 90, 92
estate of, 407
as father, 401–2
father's rejection of, 7
first recordings of, 16–17
foot injury of, 89
funeral and burial of, 398
generosity and charitable works of, 318–
22, 399–400
as good listener, 21
guitar learned by, 43
Hope Road headquarters of, see Hope
Road, as Tuff Gong headquarters
humility of, 399–400
intensive rehearsing by, 38, 64, 90, 169,
194, 195, 196–97
international success of, xxvi,
268, 277–78
intuitive powers of, xxvii, 4
lasting influence of, 407–8
loneliness of, 400–401
marijuana smoking by, 72–73, 185, 361
Marley family's rejection of, 2, 205
melanoma of, xxii, xxv, 5, 284–87, 331,
371, 379–85, 386–98
in move back to Nine Mile, 85–86
musical piracy and, 108, 139–40
1976 tour of, 221
in 1978 return to Jamaica, 288–304
on One Love Peace Concert, 300–302
Order of Merit awarded to, xv, 397
perfectionism of, 272–73, 329
political education of, 179–80,
220, 346–47
as Rastafarian, xv, 72–73, 77, 109, 172,
206, 215, 262, 303, 305–6, 321, 392
record shops of, 82, 83, 174–75
Rock and Roll Hall of Fame induc-
tion of, 407
seizure of, 379
self-confidence of, 54–55
singing style of, 43
singlemindedness about music of, 64–65,
101–2, 135, 169, 272
soccer playing by, 190–91, 194, 282, 285–
86, 338, 364–65, 371, 387

Marley, Bob (*continued*)
  songwriting methods of, 122,
    365–66, 405
  spirituality and charisma of, 56, 103–4,
    105, 252–53, 273, 333–34, 406
  stage shows of, 68–70
  stress and frustration of, 84–85,
    111, 144, 328
  toe amputation rejected by, 285
  toe injury of, 282–84, 286
  U.N. peace award given to, 305
  welding trade learned by, 16
  writer's block of, 87–88, 90
  see also Bob Marley and the Wail-
    ers; Wailers
Marley, Cedella, 401–3
Marley, Christopher, 1–2, 287
Marley, Damian "Junior Gong," xvii,
  198, 371, 397
Marley, Norval Sinclair, 1–2, 4–5, 7, 108,
  205, 266, 380
Marley, Rita Anderson, xvi, xxvi, 29, 60, 69,
  72, 73, 74, 75, 85, 91, 101, 106, 107–8,
  110, 155, 177, 189, 191, 208, 222, 223, 241,
  246, 253, 298, 333, 350, 395, 397, 401
  and BM's affairs, 83, 162, 388
  BM's cancer and, 384, 388–90, 392
  BM's estate and, 386, 407
  BM's marriage to, 64, 67–68, 81–84
  BM's relationship with, 59–60, 66
  on Haile Selassie's visit, 76–77
  JAD contract of, 95, 97, 98
  Kelso's break with, 84
  at Nine Mile, 87, 88, 89, 92–93
  off-the-books record sales of, 125–26
  shooting of, 224, 231, 236, 240, 244
  as singer, 59, 60–61, 60, 62–63, 96, 98,
    105, 183–84, 204, 317, 363
  in Smile Jamaica concert, 244–45, 247
  Tosh and, 63–66
  Wailers and, 61–64
  in Zimbabwe, 352, 355, 358, 359
Marley, Robert, Jr., 83
Marley, Sharon, 59, 66
Marley, Stephanie, 224
Marley, Stephen, 352, 355, 357, 397
Marley, Ziggy, 289, 352, 355, 357, 397,
  401, 402, 403
Marley (film), 401
Marley family, 2, 108–9, 205, 287
Marley Museum (Kingston), 305
Marsh, Tony, 293
Marshall, Austin "Bucky," 288,
  296–97, 298

Marvin, Junior, 268–69, 269, 280, 282,
  283, 284, 310, 352, 356, 363, 376, 377,
  403, 404, 405
  background of, 269–70
  on BM's 1978 return to Jamaica, 289–90
  on BM's melanoma, 285
  BM's relationship with, 272–73
  on BM's songwriting method, 271
  on BM's spirituality, 273, 406
  on cohesiveness of Wailers Band, 306–7
  on final show in Pittsburgh, 382–83
  on Jamaican peace movement, 299
  on One Love Peace Concert, 294–95
  Wailers Band joined by, 270–73
  on Zimbabwe independence con-
    cert, 357–58
Marx, Karl, 312
Marxism, 312, 347
"Mary's Boy Child" (song), 143
Masekela, Hugh, 99
Masouri, John, xxv, 117–18, 167
"Masquerade Dance" (song), 136
Massop, Claudie, 124, 288, 296–97
Matrix (San Francisco nightclub), 173
Matthews, Winston "Pipe," 8–9
Mayer, Roger, 271
Mayer, Tom, xxiv
Mayfield, Curtis, 42, 58, 61, 104
Maypen Cemetery, 132
Mazobere, Reverend, 350
McCalla, Nate, 213
McCook, Tommy, 44
McGarrity, Gayle, 153–55, 154, 173, 179–80,
  204–6, 220–21, 265–66
  on BM's loneliness, 400–401
  and BM's political education,
    220, 346–47
McGregor, Freddie, 317, 369
McIntosh, Donna, 352
McQueen, Steve, 390, 391
Meditations, 293
Melchizedek the High Priest, *see* Smith,
  Earl "Chinna"
"Mellow Mood" (song), 100, 101, 120, 137
Melody Makers, 402
Menelik II, Emperor of Ethiopia, 312
Merritone, 48
Meters, 119
Miami, Fla., 284, 286, 323–24, 364, 366,
  371, 384, 385, 386, 387, 389, 397
Michael, Ras, 17–19, 18, 293–94
Mico Teachers College, 28
Midem convention, 277
Midnight Ravers (radio show), 26, 27

"Midnight Ravers" (song), 195
Mighty Diamonds, 293
Milan, 367–68
Miller, Glenn, 61
Miller, Jacob, 235, 293, 372
Mills, Denise, 284, 352, 354
Mills, Ruel, xix
Mimms, Garnett, 32
Ministry of Culture, Jamaica, 217
Miss World pageant, 198, 199, 201, 203, 221, 264, 265–66, 267
"Misty Morning" (song), 87
Mitchell, Billy, 292, 298
Mittoo, Jackie, 44, 99, 212
Mix Dat Studio, 230
Mona Heights Community Center, Kingston, xxvii
Montreal Gazette, 293
Moore, "Dizzy Johnny," 44
Mother's Story, A (Booker), xxiv–xxv
Motown Records, 315, 369
Mount Sinai Hospital, 379
Mount Wilson, Los Angeles, 3
Mowatt, Judy, 129, 130, 183–85, 183, 204, 223, 242, 244, 252, 316–18, 331, 333, 352, 355, 356
    on Gabon trip, 338–39
    on 1980 tour, 367–68
    on Survival album, 326–27
    on Zimbabwe tour, 358–59, 361–62
"Mr. Talkative" (song), 177
Mugabe, Robert, 347, 350, 351, 352
Munich, 392
music business, Jamaican, exploitation of artists by, 111–12, 121, 176–77
"My Boy Lollipop" (song), 100, 113
"My Dream Island" (song), 48

Nairobi, 312
NARAS (National Academy of Recording Arts and Sciences), xxiii
Nash, Johnny, xvi, xxv, xxvi, 90, 94, 95, 96, 97, 98, 99, 100, 101, 102, 103, 104, 105, 108, 113, 133–35, 136, 137, 138, 140–41, 143–44, 145, 148, 150, 190, 207
    BM and, 107
    BM's relationship with, 133–34
    BM's touring with, 141
    Wailers' relationship with, 141–42
Nassau, Bahamas, 264, 327
National Heroes Park, Kingston, 216, 220, 221, 246
National Stadium, 68–70, 174, 203, 204–5, 292, 300

National Video Festival, xxiii
Natty Dread (album), xiv, 179, 184, 185–87, 194, 322, 367
"Natty Dread" (song), 405
"Natural Mystic" (song), 357
Nazarene, 88
Nazi Party, 393
Neita, Churchill, 84
Nelson, Ricky, 2
New Orleans, La., 119, 239
New York, N.Y., 84, 100, 103, 105, 119, 133, 160, 186, 221, 228, 275, 298, 305, 330, 349, 371, 373, 374–75, 378, 385, 386, 388, 392
New York Times, 165–66, 376, 407
New Zealand, 361, 403
"Nice Time" (song), 88, 90, 91, 100, 142
Nigeria, 1
Nighthawk (record label), xxii
Nimble (donkey), 2, 89, 90, 92
Nine Mile, Jamaica, 87–90, 109, 128, 324, 398, 401
    BM's childhood in, 1, 2, 4, 5, 7
    BM's return to, 85–86, 87, 92–93
Nixon, Richard, 328
Nixon administration, 132
Nkomo, Joshua, 350
Nkrumah, 303
Nockeby, Sweden, 134, 135–36, 137
"No More Trouble" (song), 195
No Nuclear War (album), xxii
Norman, Jimmy, 101–3, 102, 104, 105
"Nothing From Nothing Leaves Nothing" (song), 203
No Woman, No Cry (R. Marley), 59
"No Woman No Cry" (song), 75, 155, 185, 359, 367
NPR, xx
Nuggets for the Needy show, 51
Nyabinghi drum festival, 289–90, 321
"Nyabinghi men," 71

OAU (Organisation of African Unity), 326
"Oh Lord I Got To Get There" (song), 141
Old Grey Whistle Test, The (TV show), 156
Omariah (Marley's grandfather), 2, 4
Omega Conference, 391
"One Cup of Coffee" (song), 16, 164
"One Foundation" (song), 164–65
One Love: Life with Bob Marley and the Wailers (Jaffe and Steffens), 162, 186
"One Love" (song), 17, 69, 143, 296, 299, 408
One Love at Studio One (album), 213

One Love Peace Concert, xxi, xxv, 17, 90,
    259, 272, 285, 288, 290, 291, 292–96,
    299–301, 302, 304, 305, 315
  film of, *see Heartland Reggae*
One World Music Festival, 60
"Opportunity" (song), 62
Order of Merit award, xv, 397
Oromia region, 312
Osibisa, 142

Pablo, Augusta, 127
Palace Theatre, 49, 50–51, 52, 53
Pareles, Jon, 165–66
Paris, 273, 277, 278
  BM in, 282, 283
Parkins, Eddie, 54
"Pass It On" (song), 16, 164, 182
Patterson, Alvin "Seeco," 25, 30, 32, 46, 47,
    251, 271, 272, 290, 352, 365, 376, 377,
    378, 403, 405
  on Wailers' first recording session, 29–31
Paul, Stefan, 394–95
Pavilion, Pauley, 327
Peace Council, 293, 298
Pendergrass, Teddy, 333
People Funny Boy (Katz), 125
People's National Party (PNP), 35, 40, 73,
    119, 128, 130, 131, 216–17, 219–20, 242,
    258, 288, 293
Performing Rights Society (PRS), 177
Perry, Lee "Scratch," xxv, 107, 108, 115, 119,
    123–26, 128, 132, 164, 180, 207, 218
  in songwriting credit disputes, 120–21
  Wailers' break with, 126
  Wailers' recordings for, 117, 120–21,
    122–23, 139
  Wailers' verbal contract with, 120, 123–24
Pever, Mary, 296
Philadelphia, Pa., 214, 330, 349
Phillips, Vivian, 376
Philp, Geoffrey, xxvii
*Photos of the Century, The: 100 Historic
    Moments* (Robin), 307
Pierson, Leroy Jodie, xxii, xxiii
"Pimper's Paradise" (song), 366–67
piracy, musical, 108, 139–40, 145
Pitterson, Karl, 151, 166, 266–68,
    267, 335–36
Pitts, Ibis, 4, 399
Pittsburgh, Pa., 119, 380, 381, 382, 387, 405
Planno, Mortimo, 88, 91, 92, 113, 114, 177
  as BM's manager, 96, 97–98, 108
  duplicity of, 109–10
  as Rastafarian guru, xvii, 14, 74, 75, 75

Platt, Tony, 159
"Play Play Play" (song), 94
PNP Musical Bandwagon, 128, 129–31
Poitier, Sidney, 160
Polygram, 369, 387
"Positive Vibration" (song), 355
Pottinger, Mr., 316
Pottinger, Sonia, 119, 145, 322
"Pound Get A Blow" (song), 94
Presley, Elvis, 2, 108, 110
Preston, Billy, 203
Price, Lloyd, 104
Prickly Pole, Jamaica, 92, 93
Purdie, Bernard, 99, 103
"Put It On" (song), 57, 69, 142

Queen, 381, 382
Queen Mary, 57, 183
Queen's Theatre, 10, 176

Race Course, Kingston, 113
Race Today, xv
racism, 7, 220
Radio Jamaica, 24
Rainbow Theatre, 280, 408
Rainey, Chuck, 99
Randy's Studio, 120, 170, 207, 316
Ranglin, Ernest, 25, 31, 212
Rasta and Resistance (Campbell), 354
Rastafarian faith, Rastas, 17, 38, 40, 44, 61,
    90, 95, 110, 121, 134, 138, 180, 183, 184,
    185, 187, 191, 202, 210, 211, 239, 245,
    260, 281, 286, 289, 290, 292, 301, 312,
    314, 338, 343, 351, 353, 355
  bad reputation of, 71–72, 96–97, 203–4
  BM as, xv, 72–73, 77, 109, 172, 206, 215,
    262, 303, 305–6, 321, 392
  government repression of, 97, 179
  "isms" rejected by, xv, 109, 165,
    182, 346–47
  language of, 72
  Manley supported by, 129
  marijuana and, 71, 75
  Planno as guru of, xvii, 14, 74, 75, 75
  Twelve Tribes and, 196, 214, 219, 223,
    230, 233, 235, 240, 300, 313, 317, 319,
    354, 388–89, 400
  Wailers as, 21, 72, 75, 77–78, 158, 166
"Rasta Man Chant" (song), 157, 165
Rastaman Vibration (album), 206, 208–9,
    210, 212, 214, 221, 317, 326
"Rastaman Vibration" (song), 276
"Rasta Shook Them Up" (song), 72
Real Mona, 111

"Real Situation" (song), 363, 366, 367
"Rebel Music (3 O'Clock Roadblock)"
    (song), 186
Rebel Music (Simon), xxv, 307
Recher Theater, 269
"Redder Than Red" (song), 137
"Redemption Song" (song), 363,
    364, 366, 381
Red Hills, 201
Rediffusion Network, 24
Regal Theatre, 51
reggae, 119, 136, 158, 291
    American exposure to, 100, 172
    commercialization of, 172, 176
Reggae Archives, 4, 15, 17, 55, 57, 120,
    154, 161, 196, 211, 219, 227, 324,
    342, 402, 403
Reggae Beat (radio show), xx–xxi, xxii, 54,
    128, 181, 217, 255, 299, 327
Reggae Got Soul (album), 270
"Reggae On Broadway" (song), 100,
    140, 141, 143
Reggae Sun Ska Festival, 216
Reggae Sunsplash Festival, xxii, 30, 183,
    349, 394, 395
Reid, Duke, 23, 24, 25, 27, 48, 56, 119,
    121, 145, 322
"Reincarnated Souls" (song), 158
"Remember Me" (song), 184
"Rescue Me" (song), 78
"Return of Django" (song), 117, 119
"Revolution" (song), 186
Rhodesia, *see* Zimbabwe
Richards, Mikey "Boo," 115
Richards, Pete and Calvin, 34
Richards, Sylvia, 46
Richie, Lionel, 376, 377
Richmond, Jamaica, 94
"Ringo" (song), 142
Rittenhouse, Dr., 391
RJR Rediffusion, 24, 37, 90
Robbie and Sly, 170, 203
Robbins, Marty, 161
Rock and Roll Hall of Fame and
    Museum, 148, 407
"Rock It Baby" (song), 100
rocksteady, 54, 100, 105, 119
"Rock Steady" (song), 103
"Rock Sweet Rock" (song), 59
Rod of Correction, 129
Roderick's (sound system), 24
Rodriguez, Rico, 268
Rolling Stone, xix
Rolling Stones, 113, 309, 311

Romeo, Max, 119
"Roots" (song), 404
Roots Rasta, 390
"Roots Rock Reggae" (song), 355
Ross, Diana, 184, 311
Rossin, Lars, 135–36
Rothman, Dr., 379–80
Rothman, Milton (lawyer), 380
Rottach-Egern, Germany, 392, 395
Roulette Records, 213
Roxbury, Mass., 350
Roxy (Los Angeles), xxi, 328–29
Roy, Binghi, 233, 239
Royal College of Surgeons, 284
Royal House of Judah, 279
"Rude Boy" (song), 41, 57, 69, 142
Rufaro Stadium, 352, 354–59
"Running Away" (song), 271
Russell, Greg and Compton, 242, 248, 251
Russell Heights, Kingston, 96, 98, 370, 371
Russia, 303, 393

Sadkin, Alex, 208, 323, 363
Saigon, 227, 261
St. Andrew's High School, 121, 315
Saint Ann, Jamaica, 1, 315
St. George's school, 177
St. Mark's Church, 350
St. Peter's Square, 267
St. Thomas, 5
Salewicz, Chris, xxv
San Clemente, Calif., 328
San Diego, Calif., 300, 306, 327
San Diego Sports Arena, 156, 300, 300, 328
San Francisco, Calif., xix, 173, 202
San Siro Stadium, 367–68
Santa Barbara, Calif., 309
Santa Cruz, Calif., 309–10, 310, 311
Sausalito, Calif., 173
Scandinavia, 134, 306
Schaffer, Jan, 135
Schollin, Christina, 134
Scott, Ricardo "Ras Cardo," 12–13
"Screw Face" (song), 137
Seaga, Edward, xv, 35, 129, 131, 132, 232, 233,
    259, 293, 397, 407
    linked to assassination attempt, 255, 256,
    257, 258, 398
    in One Love Peace Concert meeting with
    Manley, 290–91, 295, 301
Seaton, B. B., 56
Seawind Hotel, 183
See't Yah (TV show), 90, 92
Seka, Mohmmadu "Johnny," 305

"Selassie Is The Chapel" (song), 110
Senegal, 305
Shakat Music, 213
Shakespeare, William, 366
Shashamane, Ethiopia, 257, 312, 313–14, *313*
Shearer, Hugh, 102
Sheraton, 199, 203, 225, 307
"She Used To Call Me Da Da" (song), 324
Shower Posse (Blake), 373
Shower Posse gang, 373
Sibbles, Leroy, 56
"Simmer Down" (song), xxvi, 22, 29, 31–32,
    33–34, 36–38, 40, 47, 51, 57, 69, 119
Simms, Arthur, 326
Simon, Kate, xxv, 307–8, *307*
Simone, Nina, 202
Simpson, Louis, 231
Simpson, Mrs., 5
Sims, Danny, xvi, xxv, 94–97, 102, *102*, 103,
    104, 105–6, 108–9, 113, 132, 139, 140–
    42, 150, *175*, 208, 384, 389, 390
  on BM's cancer, 286–87,
    379–80, 386–88
  BM's contracts with, 97–98, 101, 107–8,
    133–34, 136–37, 147, 177
  BM's first meeting with, 95–96
  on BM's relationship with Nash, 141
  on BM's seizure, 379
  and BM's Sony contract, 140, 144–45,
    146–48, 177
  on BM's stay at Issels's clinic, 394
  Bunny Wailer's relationship with, 98
  on last show in Pittsburgh, 387
  Madison Square Garden security
    arranged by, 373–74
  on Madison Square Garden
    shows, 375–77
  and 1980 tour, 371–80
  on Peter Tosh, 105
  on recording Jamaican musi-
    cians, 99–100
  rehired as BM's manager, 317
  Tosh's relationship with, 98
  tour and new contract negotiations can-
    celed by, 387
Sims, Donnice, 342–45
Sims, Eddie, 339–40, 342
Sinatra, Frank, 274
ska, 100, 152
Skatalites, 22, 32, 37, 44, 73–74, 88, 114–
    15, 142, 152
Sky Rocket (sound system), 24
Sledger (Marley's cousin), 2
"Slipping Into Darkness" (song), 142

Sloan Kettering hospital, 379–80, 386, 387,
    388, 389, 390, 391, 392
Sly and the Family Stone, 172–73
Small, Millie, 100, 145, 165
"Small Axe" (song), 120–21, 142, 164
"Smile Jamaica" (song), 218–19, 223
Smile Jamaica concert, xxi, 216–18, 219, 223,
    225, 226, 227, 229, 230, 235, 239, 240,
    241–53, 255, 256, 258, 261, 288, 403
Smith, CC, xxiii, *69*
Smith, Dessie, 319–20, *320*, 346, 378, 379
  on BM as father, 401
  on BM's cancer, 384
  on BM's daily routine, 364–65
  on BM's songwriting method, 365–66
  in collaboration with BM, 366–67
  on final show in Pittsburgh, 381
Smith, Earl "Chinna," 210
Smith, Matthew, 302
Smith, Slim, xix, 50
Smykle, Paul, 308
S.O.B.'s, *102*
"So Jah Seh" (song), 252
Solomonic Production, 181
Sombrero (club), 53, 123
Some Girls (album), 309
"So Much Things To Say" (song), 404
Songs of Freedom (Salewicz), xxv
Sons of Negus, xix, 251, 294
Sony Records, 132, 141, 212, 213, 379, 387
  BM's contract with, 140, 144–45,
    146–48, 177
Sony Studios, 141, 146
"Soon Come" (song), 104
Soul Almighty (album), *300*
"Soul Almighty" (song), 120
"Soul Captives" (song), 113, 114
Soulettes, 59, *60*, 61, 63, 66, 73, 74, 81, 116
"Soul Rebel" (song), 104
Soul Rebels (album), 122
Soul Revolution (album), 122
"Soul Shakedown Party" (song), 113
Soul Syndicate, 210
sound systems (mobile devices), 47, 50
  contests between, 24–25
South Africa, 1, 265, 266, 303, 347
Southern Rhodesia, *see* Zimbabwe
Soviet Union, 301
Spain, 205
Spanish Town, Jamaica, 23
Spaulding, Tony, 176, 242, 244, 245, 247
Speakeasy, 159
Spencer Davis Group, 146
Sporty, King, 56, 208, 331, *332*, 333

SS (Schutzstaffel), 393
Stanford University, 180
Star, 289
Starlight Bowl, 311
Steblecki, Joe, 347, 354
Steckles, Garry, 293
Steffens, Mary, xx, 20, 309
"Stepping Razor" (song), 177
Stevens, Cat, 103
Stewart, Tinga, 130
"Stir It Up" (song), 100, 142, 170
Stitt, King, 331
Stockholm, Sweden, 136, 137, 140
Stone, Sly, 172–73
"Straight and Narrow Way" (song), 33, 37
Strawberry Hill, Jamaica, as BM's post-
    shooting hideout, 231, 234, 237, 238–
    40, 242, 244, 253, 261
Streisand, Barbra, 147
Studio One, xvi, xxv, 22, 25, 32, 37,
    44, 47, 54, 56, 57–59, 63, 81, 107,
    119, 195, 219
Studio 17, 96
Success Club, 50
Sugar Ray Robinson Foundation, 328
"Sunday Morning" (song), 59
"Sun Is Shining" (song), 87
Sunset Marquis Hotel, 20
Supremes, 74
Survival (album), xxi, xxiii, 306, 314, 315,
    322–27, 330, 350–51, 363, 366
Survival tour, 331–36
Sutton, Pepe, 371, 372
Sutton-Smith, John, 291
Swaby, John, 293
Sweden, BM in, 107, 133, 134–37, 140
Swing, xx

Taitt, Lynn, 99
Take a Giant Step (film), 134
Talamon, Bruce, 328, 337, 338
Talkin' Blues (album), 182, 194
"Talkin' Blues" (song), 177, 178
Tanamo, Lord, 47
Taubman, Lowell, 287
Taylor, April, 340
Taylor, Don, 139, 145, 175, 177, 207–8, 221,
    222, 259, 285, 292–93, 298, 315, 330,
    331, 345, 386, 389
    on Blackwell's relationship with
        BM, 277–78
    BM's dismissal of, 340–42, 371
    as BM's manager, 175–76, 327–28
    gambling habit of, 255

as possible primary assassination
    target, 255, 257
shooting of, 224–25, 231, 236,
    240, 255, 257
Techniques, xix, 33, 50
Technology, University of, 75
Tee, Richard, 99
"Teenager in Love" (song), 47
Temptations, 74
"Ten To One" (song), 58
"Terror" (song), 16
"Them Belly Full (But We Hungry)" (song),
    17, 186, 355
Theocratic Government, 321
"There's A Reward" (song), 46
"There She Goes" (song), 43
Third World, xvii, 51, 121, 129, 170, 171, 231,
    235, 242, 243, 248, 251, 315
Thomas, Michael, xix
Thompson, Dennis, 47–48, 119–20, 170,
    195, 352, 362
    as BM's recording engineer, 207
    on final show in Pittsburgh, 381–82, 383
    on Zimbabwe independence con-
        cert, 356–57
Thompson, Errol, 295
Time, xiii, 267, 270, 408
"Time Will Tell" (song), 254
Tivoli Gardens, Jamaica, 132, 220, 258, 290
Tompkins, Dera, 348–57, 349, 359–61
Toots and the Maytals, 12, 38, 39, 41, 54, 203
Tom the Great Sebastian (sound system), 24
Torno, Randy, 293
Toronto, Ont., 99, 296, 333
Tosh, Peter, xiv, xxi, xxii, 12, 17, 18, 20, 25,
    26, 28, 29, 31, 36, 37, 40–44, 46, 49,
    50, 56, 58, 59, 60, 62, 67, 72, 73, 75, 77,
    78, 80, 85, 88, 89–90, 93, 97, 98–99,
    101, 104, 121, 124–25, 126, 127, 139,
    140, 145, 152–53, 155, 158, 159, 160, 164,
    166, 171, 173, 184, 187, 189, 190, 193,
    202, 274, 295, 301, 403
    background of, 19
    BM's strained relationship with, 167–68,
        169, 174, 180–81
    in Burbank reunion with BM, 311–12
    in departure from Wailers, 168, 174, 179,
        181, 182–83
    first guitar of, 19–20
    guitar playing by, 74
    humor of, 21
    on Jamaican peace movement, 301, 304
    journalists and, 275–76
    in One Love Peace Concert, 17, 294

Tosh, Peter (*continued*)
    Rita Marley and, 63–66
    seriousness of, 21
    Sims and, 95, 96, 98, 105
    solo career of, 182, 186
    on Wailers' first stage shows, 51–52
    Wailers joined by, 19
Traffic, 146, 308
Treasure Isle, 322, 323
Trench Town, 8–10, 12, 13–14, 20, 25, 26, 27,
    28, 29, 34, 36, 37–38, 59, 60, 61, 62,
    74, 77, 83, 86, 88, 92, 95, 96, 97, 108,
    110, 111, 113, 154, 155, 162, 163, 176, 177,
    193, 201, 207, 220, 259, 266, 317, 400
Trench Town Records, xix
"Trench Town Rock" (song), 171
Trench Town School, 27
Trench Town Sports Complex, 175, 176
Trinidad, 24, 160, 325
Trinity, 293
Trojan Records, 122, 139–40, 145–46, 213
"Trouble On The Road Again" (song), 90
Tubby, King, 322
Tuff Gong (record label), xv, 107, 116, 121,
    137, 315–17, 324, 369
    headquarters of, *see* Hope Road, as Tuff
      Gong headquarters
    see also Wail'n Soul'm
Tuff Gong (studio), 163, 315, 316–17, 322–23
"Turn Your Lights Down Low"
    (song), 200, 266
Twelve Tribes Foundation, 321
Twelve Tribes of Israel, *196*, 223, 230, 300,
    313, 354, 388–89, 400
    in aftermath of BM assassination attempt,
      233–34, 240
    BM and, 214, 219, 235, 317–18, 319
Twelve Tribes Sound System, 324

U2, 277
United Nations, 305
Universal Amphitheater (Los Angeles), 30
Uprising (album), 362, 363–67, 368, 405
Uprising tour, 387
Upsetter Records, 121, 164
Upsetters (band), 115, 117, 119

Valentine, Ricky, 130
Vaughan, Stevie Ray, 274
Venneri, Joe, 100, *102*
    on BM's spirituality, 103–4
Video Lab, 228
Vietnam War, 227
Vikings (band), 52

Vikings (gang), 109–10
Village Gate, 229
Vill Sa Garna Tro (*Want So Much to Believe*)
    (film), 134–35, 136, 137
Vineyard Town theatre, 10
VIP (club), 47–48
Virgin Islands, 207
Virgona, Marco, 393
V-Rocket (sound system), 24

Wailer, Bunny, xiv, xvi, xxvi, *6*, 9, 10, 11, 12,
    16, 17, 25, 26, 28, 36, 37, 39, 41, 42,
    43–44, 46, 56, 58, 61, 62, 64, 65, 66,
    68–70, 73, 74, 75, 83, 85, 95, 101, 112,
    113, 114–16, 121–26, 130, 139, 140, 142–
    44, 145, 150, 151–53, 156–57, 158–59,
    160, 161, 163–64, 165, 171, 172, 174,
    180, 181, 183, 184, 186, 189, 190, 193,
    202, 207, 307, 356, 385
    on "Best of Wailers" as album title, 115
    on Blackwell's royalties payments
      to Dodd, 149
    on BM's childhood, 5, 6
    on BM's first recordings, 16
    on BM's marriage to Rita, 67–68
    on BM's songwriting methods, 122
    on Cole as Wailers' promoter, 137–38
    in departure from Wailers, 166–
      68, 169, 179
    on Haile Selassie's visit, 77–78
    in JAD recording sessions, 104–5
    on Nash's relationship with Wailers, 141
    1967 arrest and imprisonment of,
      93, 94, 97
    on Nine Mile sojourn, 87–90
    on Perry's reneging on contract, 123–24
    on Planno's duplicity, 109–10
    in release from prison, 104
    Sim's relationship with, 98
    solo career of, 182
    as songwriter, 48–49
    on songwriting credit disputes, 120
    on Tosh, 20–21
    unpublished memoir of, xxii–xxiii
    on Wailers' break with Dodd, 80–82
    on Wailers' first recording session, 31
    on Wailers' first stage shows, 50–51
    on Wailers' name, 13–14
Wailers (original lineup), xiv, xvi–xvii, xix,
    xx, xxi, xxii, xxiii, xxvi, 5, *11*, 17–18,
    20, 22–23, 25, 26, 27, 28–34, *32*, 34,
    35–39, 40–58, 59, 60, *60*, 66, 67, 72,
    73–74, *78*, 93, 94, 100–106, 107–9,
    111–12, *118*, 119–32, 133, 139, 143–45,

146–48, 149–56, 159–66, 170, 175, 177,
    178, 180–82, 183, 184, 189, 190, 191,
    195, 203, 315
Barrett brothers as rhythm section
    for, 117, 128
BM as leader of, 45
Braithwaite's departure from, 42
in break with Dodd, 80–82
in break with Perry, 126
Bunny's departure from, 166–
    68, 169, 179
Cole's promotion of, 112, 137–39
collaborative writing by, 48–49
Dodd's alleged mistreatment of, 46
in England, 142–43, 156–57, 158–59
first recording session of, 29–30
first stage shows by, 49–50
founding of, 12, 21
guitar playing by, 43
Higgs's mentoring of, 15–16, 22, 25, 28
Island recordings of, 149–50
JAD recordings of, 101, 107, 110
Kelso's departure from, 82, 83–84
Kong and, 112–16
last stage shows of, 187–88, 194, 204–5
in London, 137–38, 140
naming of, 13–14, 41
Nash's relationship with, 141–42
1973 breakup of, xxv
1973 U.S. tour of, 171–74
at Nine Mile, 85–90
Perry and, 117, 120–21, 122–24, 139
in PNP campaign tour, 128, 129–31
Rita Marley and, 61–64
Sims and, 97–98
simultaneous Top Ten hits of, 56–57
stage shows of, 68–70
Studio One recordings of, 22, 29, 44–45,
    81–82, 149–50
Tosh's departure from, 168, 174, 179,
    181, 182–83
Tosh's joining of, 19
Tuff Gong recordings of, 121
Tuff Gong releases of, 137
U.S. tour planned by, 166–67
see also Bob Marley and the Wailers
Wailers Band, xxiii, 179, 195, 210, 222,
    268, 269, 276
favorite songs of, 403–6
as songwriting collaborators, 405
see also Bob Marley and the Wail-
    ers; Wailers
Wailing Blues: The Story of Bob Marley's
    Wailers (Masouri), xxv, 117–18

Wailing Souls, 9
Wailing Wailers, 81
    see also Wailers (orginial lineup)
Wail'n Soul'm (record label), 46, 81,
    105, 107, 116
    see also Tuff Gong (record label)
Wail'n Soul'm Time (radio program), 94
"Waiting In Vain" (song), 200, 266,
    276, 310, 405
"Wake Up And Live" (song), 324–25
Waldorf-Astoria (New York), 305
Walker, Constantine "Vision," 60–61, 60,
    63, 66, 73–74, 75, 78, 85, 87, 88
    as fill-in for BM in Wailers, 59–60
    on Haile Selassie's visit, 77
Walker, Jeff, xxi, 217, 225–26, 232, 233, 239–
    40, 241–43, 261, 327
    aftermath of assassination attempt filmed
    by, 235–37
    on BM assassination attempt, 230–31
    on BM's decision to do Smile Jamaica
    concert, 241–42, 244–45, 246–47
    on BM's flight to Bahamas, 253
    on BM's Smile Jamaica performance,
    250–51, 252
    on motive for assassination
    attempt, 256, 257
    on Smile Jamaica filming, 248–49
"Walk the Proud Land" (song), 170
Walton, Tom, 213
Want So Much to Believe (Vill Sa Garna Tro)
    (film), 134–35, 136, 137
"War" (song), 356, 381, 404
Ward Theatre, 49, 50, 51–52
Warm December (film), 160
Watt, Jean, 88
WBAI (radio station), 8, 26, 27
WBLS (radio station), 371, 372
"We And Dem" (song), 363, 366
"We Getting The Fight" (song), 367
Wesley, Segree, 8–9, 9, 11–12, 21, 42–43,
    48–49, 72, 83, 85–86, 87, 172, 185,
    208, 380–81
    on BM's marriage to Rita, 67
    on BM's singing style, 43
    on BM's singlemindedness, 64–65
    on Madison Square Garden
    shows, 377–78
    on Rita Marley, 64–65
    on "Simmer Down" release, 38
    on Wailers' first stage shows, 51
West Germany, 392
West Indies, University of the, 40, 72, 74,
    179, 180, 302

"What Goes Around Comes Around"
    (song), 175
What's Goin' On (album), 198
"What's New Pussycat?" (song), 33, 47
"What's Your Name" (song), 61
"Where Is The Love?" (song), 103
White, Bob, 146–47
Who Feels It (album), 363
"Who Is Mr. Brown" (song), 122
Williams, Errol, 10, 13
Williams, Noel, *see* Sporty, King
Willoughby, Neville, 90–93, *91*, 94, 95–96,
    97–99, 101, 104, 108, 134, 169–70
    BM filmed by, 92
    BM interviewed by, 93, 288–89
    on BM's singlemindedness about
        music, 169
    on One Love Peace Concert, 294, 295–96
Wilmington, Del, 68, 80
Wilson, Cecelia, 316
Wilson, Delroy, 10, 39, 66
Wilson, Dion, 4, 399
Wilson, Jackie, 202
Wilson, Roy, 25–26, 39, 41, 46
Winkler, Tony, xxiv–xxv
Wint, Elaine, 250
Winwood, Stevie, 146, 270
"Wisdom" (song), 90
Witter, Michael, 173, 179

Wonder, Stevie, 187, 194, 205, 216, 271,
    305, 372, 378
"Work" (song), 363, 383, 405
Wright, Betty, 287, 331–34, 336–37,
    338, 340–42
    on BM's spirituality and charisma, 333–34
Wright, Winston, 115, 204

Ya Ya (Marley's great-grandmother), 7
Year of the Rasta Child concert, 327
Yesehaq, Archbishop Abuna, 391, 392
"You Got Soul" (song), 101
"Young, Gifted And Black" (song), 151

ZANU (Zimbabwe African National
    Union), 351, 361
ZANU Patriotic Front (freedom fighters),
    352, 353, 355, 358
Zema, 395–97
Zimbabwe, xxv, 286, 303, 314, 326, 347–62,
    349, 363, 367, 387, 403, 404
    BM's tour of, 346, 347–48, 351–62
    freedom fighters in, 352, 353, 355, 358
    Independence Day celebration in, 354–59
    Tompkins in, 350–57, 359–61
"Zimbabwe" (song), 301, 313–14, 347–48,
    356, 357, 359, 360
Zion, 72, 77, 363, 398
"Zion Train" (song), 363, 364, 366